COLLECTED WHEEL PUBLICATIONS

VOLUME 5

NUMBERS 61 – 75

BPE

BPS Pariyatti Editions

BPS Pariyatti Editions
An imprint of Pariyatti Publishing
www.pariyatti.org

Although this is an American edition, we have left any British spelling of words unchanged.

First BPS Pariyatti Edition, 2020
ISBN: 978-1-68172-140-8 (Print)
ISBN: 978-1-68172-141-5 (PDF)
ISBN: 978-1-68172-142-2 (ePub)
ISBN: 978-1-68172-143-9 (Mobi)
LCCN: 2018940050

Contents

WH 61 The Simile of the Cloth
Nyanaponika Thera ... 1

WH 62 The Discourse on Effacement
Nyanaponika Thera ... 17

WH 63 & 64 Aids to the Abhidhamma Philosophy
Dr. C. B. Dharmasena ... 41

WH 65 & 66 The Way of Wisdom
Edward Conze ... 75

WH 67 to 69 Last Days of the Buddha
Sister Vajirā, Francis Story ... 115

WH 70 to 72 Anāgārika Dharmapāla
Bhikkhu Sangharakshita ... 195

WH 73 The Blessings of Piṇḍapāta
Bhikkhu Khantipālo ... 269

WH 74 & 75 German Buddhist Writers ... 291

Key to Abbreviations

A	Aṅguttara Nikāya	Paṭis	Paṭisambhidamagga
Ap	Apadāna	Peṭ	Peṭakopadesa
Bv	Buddhavaṃsa	S	Saṃyutta Nikāya
Cp	Cariyāpiṭaka	Sn	Suttanipāta
D	Dīgha Nikāya	Th	Theragātha
Dhp	Dhammapada	Thī	Therigātha
Dhs	Dhammasaṅgaṇī	Ud	Udāna
It	Itivuttaka	Vibh	Vibhaṅga
Ja	Jātaka verses and commentary	Vin	Vinaya-piṭaka
Khp	Khuddakapāṭha	Vism	Visuddhimagga
M	Majjhima Nikāya	Vism-mhṭ	Visuddhimagga Sub-commentary
Mil	Milindapañha	Vv	Vimānavatthu
Nett	Nettipakaraṇa	Nidd	Niddesa

The above is the abbreviation scheme of the Pali Text Society (PTS) as given in the *Dictionary of Pali* by Margaret Cone.

The commentaries, *aṭṭhakathā*, are abbreviated by using a hyphen and an "a" ("-a") following the abbreviation of the text, e.g., *Dīgha Nikāya Aṭṭhakathā* = D-a. Likewise the sub-commentaries are abbreviated by a "ṭ" ("-ṭ") following the abbreviation of the text.

The sutta reference abbreviation system for the four Nikāyas, as is used in Bhikkhu Bodhi's translations is:

AN	Aṅguttara Nikāya	DN	Dīgha Nikāya
MN	Majjhima Nikāya	Sn	Saṃyutta Nikāya
J	Jātaka story	Mv	Mahāvagga (Vinaya Piṭaka)
Cv	Cullavagga (Vinaya Piṭaka)	SVibh	Suttavibhaṅga (Vinaya Piṭaka)

The Simile of the Cloth

Two Discourses of the Buddha

Edited with Introduction and Notes by

Nyanaponika Thera

WHEEL PUBLICATION NO. 61

Introduction

This discourse of the Buddha—the seventh in the Collection of Middle Length Texts (Majjhima Nikāya)—deals first with a set of sixteen defilements of the human mind; and in its second part, with the disciple's progress to the highest goal of Arahatship, which can be achieved if—and only if—these impurities are gradually reduced and finally eliminated. While there are also defilements of insight which must be removed for the attainment of the goal, the sixteen defilements dealt with here are all of an ethical nature and are concerned with man's social behavior. Only the last of these sixteen, negligence, may also refer to purely personal concerns as well as to one's relations with others.

A glance through the list (see Note 2) will show that all these sixteen defilements derive from greediness and selfishness, from aversion, self-assertion and conceit, or their combinations. If we take, for instance, contempt, being a weaker nuance of (5) denigration, we see that aversion and conceit contribute to it; (7) envy is fed by greediness and aversion. The pairs of contributive factors here exemplified do not, of course, occur at the same moment of consciousness; but their repeated, separate presence favors the arising of such derivatives as contempt and envy. On the other hand, if those secondary defilements such as contempt and envy (and all the others) appear frequently, they will bring about a close serial association of their "feeders," as for instance hate motivated by conceit, or hate motivated by greed; and these may easily become habitual sequences, automatic chain reactions in our impulsive life.

Interlocked in such a manner, the negative forces in our mind—the defilements, roots of evil, and fetters—will become more powerful and much more difficult to dislodge. They will form "closed systems" hard to penetrate, covering ever larger areas of our mind. What may first have been isolated occurrences of unwholesome thoughts and acts, will grow into hardened traits of character productive of an unhappy destiny in future lives (see Discourse, Section 2). And in all these grave consequences, the secondary or derivative defilements have a great share. Hence it is of vital importance that we do not fall victim to the last in the list of those defilements—negligence—and are not negligent in watchfulness and self-control.

"Out of regard for your own good, it is proper to strive with heedfulness; out of regard for others' good, it is proper to strive with heedfulness; out of regard for your own and others' good, it is proper to strive with heedfulness." (SN 12:22)

As to "others' good," how much more pleasant and harmonious will be human relations, individual and communal, if there is less pettiness and peevishness, fewer vanities and jealousies, and less self-assertiveness in words and deeds! As already remarked: if these minor blemishes are reduced, the larger and more serious defilements will have fewer opportunities. How often do deadly conflicts and deep involvement in guilt arise from petty but unresolved resentments!

The composition of our list of defilements alone makes it clear that the Buddha was well aware of the social impact of these impurities; and the structure of the discourse shows that he regarded the removal of these defilements as an integral part of the mental training aiming at deliverance. Hence we may summarize this part of the discourse by saying that our social conduct strongly affects the chances of our spiritual progress.

The nature of that influence is illustrated by the simile of the cloth. If the texture of our mind is tarnished by blemishes in our social behavior, "the new coloring" of higher mentality (*adhicitta*) and higher wisdom (*adhipaññā*) cannot penetrate. The stains that soil the single strands of thought will show through the superficial coloring; and besides, the impure matter will reduce the porosity of the tissue, i.e., the receptivity of our mind, and thus prevent full absorption of any results gained in meditation or understanding. Through the accumulating "waste products" of uninhibited defilements, a mental atmosphere is created that resists any depth penetration of spiritual forces and values.

First, in accordance with the method of *satipaṭṭhāna*, right mindfulness, the presence of the defilements in one's behavior has to be clearly noticed and honestly acknowledged, without attempts at evasion, at minimizing or self-justification, for instance, by giving them more "respectable" names. This is what is implied in the words of the discourse: "Knowing (the respective blemish) to be a defilement of the mind..." Such knowledge by itself may often discourage the recurrence of the defilements or weaken the strength of their manifestations. According to the Buddhist Teachers of Old (see Note 4, para. 1), this knowledge should be extended to the nature of the defilements, the causes and circumstances of their arising, their cessation, and the means of effecting their cessation. This is an example of how to apply to an actual situation the formula of the Four Noble Truths as embodied in the contemplation of mind-objects (*dhammānupassanā*) of the Satipaṭṭhāna Sutta. Another example is the application of the four truths to higher states of mind, the Divine Abidings, for the purpose of developing insight (Section 13 and notes 13, 14).

When the Noble Disciple, on attaining to one of the higher paths, sees himself freed from the defilements, deep joy will arise in him, enthusiasm for the goal and the way, and an unshakable confidence in the Triple Gem. So says our text (Section 6–10). But a foretaste of all these fruits and blessings can already be gained by him who has succeeded in noticeably weakening and reducing the defilements. Such enthusiasm and strengthened confidence, being derived from his personal experience, will be of great value to him, adding wings to his further progress. To the extent of his experience, he will have verified for himself the virtues of the Dhamma:

"Well proclaimed by the Blessed One is the Dhamma, realizable here and now, possessed of immediate result, bidding you to come and see, accessible, and knowable individually by the wise."

For rendering this discourse, use has been made chiefly of the translation by the Venerable Ñāṇamoli Thera (from an unpublished manuscript), and also of the translations by the Venerable Soma Thera and I. B. Horner. Grateful acknowledgement is offered to these able translators. For some key passages, however, the Editor decided to use his own version, partly for the reason of conformity with the commentarial explanations. The Notes have been supplied by the Editor. In these Notes, it was thought desirable to furnish the commentarial references supporting the renderings chosen, and in these cases the inclusion of Pali words was unavoidable. But an effort has been made to make these notes intelligible and helpful to readers who are not familiar with the Pali language as well.

The Simile of the Cloth

Vatthūpama Sutta

1. Thus have I heard. Once the Blessed One was staying at Sāvatthī, in Jeta's Grove, Anāthapiṇḍika's monastery. There he addressed the monks thus: "Monks."—"Venerable sir," they replied. The Blessed One said this:

2. "Monks, suppose a cloth were stained and dirty, and a dyer dipped it in some dye or other, whether blue or yellow or red or pink, it would take the dye badly and be impure in color. And why is that? Because the cloth was not clean. So too, monks, when the mind is defiled[1] an unhappy destination [in a future existence] may be expected.

"Monks, suppose a cloth were clean and bright, and a dyer dipped it in some dye or other, whether blue or yellow or red or pink, it would take the dye well and be pure in color. And why is that? Because the cloth was clean. So too, monks, when the mind is undefiled, a happy destination [in a future existence] may be expected.

3. "And what, monks, are the defilements of the mind?[2] (1) Covetousness and unrighteous greed are a defilement of the mind; (2) ill will is a defilement of the mind; (3) anger is a defilement of the mind; (4) hostility... (5) denigration... (6) domineering... (7) envy... (8) jealousy... (9) hypocrisy... (10) fraud... (11) obstinacy... (12) presumption... (13) conceit... (14) arrogance... (15) vanity... (16) negligence is a defilement of the mind.[3]

4. "Knowing, monks, covetousness and unrighteous greed to be a defilement of the mind, the monk abandons them.[4] Knowing ill will to be a defilement of the mind, he abandons it. Knowing anger to be a defilement of the mind, he abandons it. Knowing hostility to be a defilement of the mind, he abandons it. Knowing denigration to be a defilement of the mind, he abandons it. Knowing domineering to be a defilement of the mind, he abandons it. Knowing envy to be a defilement of the mind, he abandons it. Knowing jealousy to be a defilement of the mind, he abandons it. Knowing hypocrisy to be a defilement of the mind, he abandons it. Knowing fraud to be a defilement of the mind, he abandons it. Knowing obstinacy to be a

defilement of the mind, he abandons it. Knowing presumption to be a defilement of the mind, he abandons it. Knowing conceit to be a defilement of the mind, he abandons it. Knowing arrogance to be a defilement of the mind, he abandons it. Knowing vanity to be a defilement of the mind, he abandons it. Knowing negligence to be a defilement of the mind, he abandons it.

5. "When in the monk who thus knows that covetousness and unrighteous greed are a defilement of the mind, this covetousness and unrighteous greed have been abandoned; when in him who thus knows that ill will is a defilement of the mind, this ill will has been abandoned; ... when in him who thus knows that negligence is a defilement of the mind, this negligence has been abandoned.[5]

6. He thereupon gains unwavering confidence in the Buddha[6] thus: 'Thus indeed is the Blessed One; he is accomplished, fully enlightened, endowed with [clear] vision and [virtuous] conduct, sublime, knower of the worlds, the incomparable guide of men who are tractable, the teacher of gods and men, enlightened and blessed.'

7. He gains unwavering confidence in the Dhamma thus: 'Well proclaimed by the Blessed One is the Dhamma, realizable here and now, possessed of immediate result, bidding you come and see, accessible and knowable individually by the wise.

8. He gains unwavering confidence in the Sangha thus: 'The Sangha of the Blessed One's disciples has entered on the good way, has entered on the straight way, has entered on the true way, has entered on the proper way; that is to say, the four pairs of men, the eight types of persons; this Sangha of the Blessed One's disciples is worthy of gifts, worthy of hospitality, worthy of offerings, worthy of reverential salutation, the incomparable field of merit for the world.'

9. "When he has given up, renounced, let go, abandoned and relinquished [the defilements] in part,[7] he knows: 'I am endowed with unwavering confidence in the Buddha... in the Dhamma... in the Sangha; and he gains enthusiasm for the goal, gains enthusiasm for the Dhamma,[8] gains gladness connected with the Dhamma. When he is gladdened, joy is born in him; being joyous in mind, his body becomes tranquil; his body being tranquil, he feels happiness; and the mind of him who is happy becomes concentrated.[9]

10. "He knows: 'I have given up, renounced, let go, abandoned and relinquished [the defilements] in part'; and he gains enthusiasm

for the goal, gains enthusiasm for the Dhamma, gains gladness connected with the Dhamma. When he is gladdened, joy is born in him; being joyous in mind, his body becomes tranquil; when his body is tranquil, he feels happiness; and the mind of him who is happy becomes concentrated.

11. "If, monks, a monk of such virtue, such concentration and such wisdom[10] eats almsfood consisting of choice hill-rice together with various sauces and curries, even that will be no obstacle for him.[11]

"Just as cloth that is stained and dirty becomes clean and bright with the help of pure water, or just as gold becomes clean and bright with the help of a furnace, so too, if a monk of such virtue, such concentration and such wisdom eats almsfood consisting of choice hill-rice together with various sauces and curries, even that will be no obstacle for him.

12. "He abides, having suffused with a mind of loving-kindness[12] one direction of the world, likewise the second, likewise the third, likewise the fourth, and so above, below, around and everywhere, and to all as to himself; he abides suffusing the entire universe with loving-kindness, with a mind grown great, lofty, boundless and free from enmity and ill will.

"He abides, having suffused with a mind of compassion... of sympathetic joy... of equanimity one direction of the world, likewise the second, likewise the third, likewise the fourth, and so above, below, around and everywhere, and to all as to himself; he abides suffusing the entire universe with equanimity, with a mind grown great, lofty, boundless and free from enmity and ill will.

13. "He understands what exists, what is low, what is excellent,[13] and what escape there is from this [whole] field of perception.[14]

14. "When he knows and sees[15] in this way, his mind becomes liberated from the canker of sensual desire, liberated from the canker of becoming, liberated from the canker of ignorance.[16] When liberated, there is knowledge: 'It is liberated'; and he knows: 'Birth is exhausted, the life of purity has been lived, the task is done, there is no more of this to come.' Such a monk is called 'one bathed with the inner bathing'."[17]

15. Now at that time the brahmin Sundarika Bhāradvāja[18] was seated not far from the Blessed One, and he spoke to the Blessed One thus: "But does Master Gotama go to the Bahukā River to bathe?"

"What good, brahmin, is the Bahukā River? What can the Bahukā River do?"

"Truly, Master Gotama, many people believe that the Bahukā River gives purification, many people believe that the Bahukā River gives merit. For in the Bahukā River many people wash away the evil deeds they have done."

16. Then the Blessed One addressed the brahmin Sundarika Bhāradvāja in these stanzas:[19]

Bahukā and Adhikakkā,[20]
Gayā and Sundarikā,
Payagā and Sarassati,
And the stream Bahumati—
A fool may there forever bathe,
Yet will not purify his black deeds.

What can Sundarikā bring to pass?
What can the Payagā and the Bahukā?
They cannot purify an evildoer,
A man performing brutal and cruel acts.

One pure in heart has evermore
The Feast of Cleansing[21] and the Holy Day;[22]
One pure in heart who does good deeds
Has his observances perfect for all times.

It is here, O brahmin, that you should bathe[23]
To make yourself a safe refuge for all beings.
And if you speak no untruth,
Nor work any harm for breathing things,

Nor take what is not offered,
With faith and with no avarice,
To Gayā gone, what would it do for you?
Let any well your Gayā be!

17. When this was said, the brahmin Sundarika Bhāradvāja spoke thus:

"Magnificent, Master Gotama! Magnificent, Master Gotama! The Dhamma has been made clear in many ways by Master Gotama, as though he were righting the overthrown, revealing the hidden, showing the way to one who is lost, or holding up a lamp in the dark for those with eyesight to see forms.

18. "I go to Master Gotama for refuge, and to the Dhamma, and to the Sangha. May I receive the [first ordination of] going forth under Master Gotama, may I receive the full admission!

19. And the brahmin Sundarika Bhāradvāja received the [first ordination of] going forth under the Blessed One, and he received the full admission. And not long after his full admission, dwelling alone, secluded, diligent, ardent and resolute, the venerable Bhāradvāja by his own realization understood and attained in this very life that supreme goal of the pure life, for which men of good family go forth from home life into homelessness. And he had direct knowledge thus: "Birth is exhausted; the pure life has been lived; the task is done; there is no more of this to come."

And the venerable Bhāradvāja became one of the Arahats.

Notes

1. "So too, monks, if the mind is defiled..." Comy: "It may be asked why the Buddha had given this simile of the soiled cloth. He did so to show that effort brings great results. A cloth soiled by dirt that is adventitious (i.e., comes from outside; *āgantukehi malehi*), if it is washed can again become clean because of the cloth's natural purity. But in the case of what is naturally black, as for instance (black) goat's fur, any effort (of washing it) will be in vain. Similarly, the mind too is soiled by adventitious defilements (*āgantukehi kilesehi*). But originally, at the phases of rebirth(consciousness) and the (sub-conscious) life-continuum, it is pure throughout (*pakatiyā pana sakale pi paṭisandhi-bhavaṅga-vare paṇḍaraṃ eva*). As it was said (by the Enlightened One): 'This mind, monks, is luminous, but it becomes soiled by adventitious defilements' (A I 49). But by cleansing it one can make it more luminous, and effort therein is not in vain."

2. "Defilements of the mind" (*cittassa upakkilesā*). Comy.: "When explaining the mental defilements, why did the Blessed One mention greed first? Because it arises first. For with all beings wherever they arise, up to the level of the (Brahmā heaven of the) Pure Abodes, it is first greed that arises by way of lust for existence (*bhava-nikanti*). Then the other defilements will appear, being produced according to circumstances. The defilements of mind, however, are not limited to the sixteen mentioned in this discourse. But one should understand that, by indicating here the method, all defilements are included." Sub.Comy. mentions the following additional defilements: fear, cowardice, shamelessness and lack of scruples, insatiability, evil ambitions, etc.

3. The Sixteen Defilements of Mind:

    1. *abhijjhā-visama-lobha*, covetousness and unrighteous greed
    2. *byāpāda*, ill will
    3. *kodha*, anger
    4. *upanāha*, hostility or malice
    5. *makkha*, denigration or detraction; contempt
    6. *paḷāsa*, domineering or presumption
    7. *issā*, envy
    8. *macchariya*, jealousy, or avarice; selfishness
    9. *māyā*, hypocrisy or deceit
    10. *sāṭheyya*, fraud
    11. *thambha*, obstinacy, obduracy
    12. *sārambha*, presumption or rivalry; impetuosity
    13. *māna*, conceit

14. *atimāna*, arrogance, haughtiness
15. *mada*, vanity or pride
16. *pamāda*, negligence or heedlessness; in social behavior, this leads to lack of consideration.

The defilements (3) to (16) appear frequently as a group in the discourses, e.g., in MN 3; while in MN 8 (reproduced in this publication) No. 15 is omitted. A list of seventeen defilements appears regularly in each last discourse of Books 3 to 11 of the Aṅguttara Nikāya, which carry the title *Rāgapeyyāla*, the Repetitive Text on Greed (etc.). In these texts of the Aṅguttara Nikāya, the first two defilements in the above list are called greed (*lobha*) and hate (*dosa*), to which delusion (*moha*) is added; all the fourteen other defilements are identical with the above list.

4. "Knowing covetousness and unrighteous greed to be a defilement of the mind, the monk abandons them."

Knowing (*viditvā*). Sub.Comy.: "Having known it either through the incipient wisdom (*pubbabhāga-pañña* of the worldling, i.e., before attaining to stream-entry) or through the wisdom of the two lower paths (stream-entry and once-returning). He knows the defilements as to their nature, cause, cessation and means of effecting cessation." This application of the formula of the Four Noble Truths to the defilements deserves close attention.

Abandons them (*pajahati*). Comy.: "He abandons the respective defilement through (his attainment of) the noble path where there is 'abandoning by eradication' (*samucchedapahāna-vasena ariya-maggena*)," which according to Sub.Comy. is the "final abandoning" (*accantapahāna*). Before the attainment of the noble paths, all "abandoning" of defilements is of a temporary nature. See Nyanatiloka Thera, *Buddhist Dictionary*, s.v. *pahāna*.

According to the Comy., the sixteen defilements are finally abandoned by the noble paths (or stages of sanctity) in the following order:

"By the path of stream-entry (*sotāpatti-magga*) are abandoned: (5) denigration, (6) domineering, (7) envy, (8) jealousy, (9) hypocrisy, (10) fraud.

"By the path of nonreturning (*anāgāmi-magga*): (2) ill will, (3) anger, (4) malice, (16) negligence.

"By the path of Arahatship (*arahatta-magga*): (1) covetousness and unrighteous greed, (11) obstinacy, (12) presumption, (13) conceit, (14) arrogance, (15) vanity."

If, in the last group of terms, covetousness is taken in a restricted sense as referring only to the craving for the five sense objects, it is finally abandoned by the path of nonreturning; and this is according to Comy. the meaning intended here. All greed, however, including the hankering after fine material and immaterial existence, is eradicated only on the path of Arahatship; hence the classification under the latter in the list above.

Comy. repeatedly stresses that wherever in our text "abandoning" is mentioned, reference is to the nonreturner (*anāgāmi*); for also in the case of defilements overcome on stream-entry (see above), the states of mind which produce those defilements are eliminated only by the path of nonreturning.

5. Comy. emphasizes the connection of this paragraph with the following, saying that the statements on each of the sixteen defilements should be connected with the next paragraphs, e.g., "when in him... ill will has been abandoned, he thereupon gains unwavering confidence..." Hence the grammatical construction of the original Pali passage—though rather awkward in English—has been retained in this translation.

The disciple's direct experience of being freed of this or that defilement becomes for him a living test of his former still imperfectly proven trust in the Buddha, Dhamma and Sangha. Now this trust has become a firm conviction, an unshakable confidence, based on experience.

6. "Unwavering confidence" (*aveccappasāda*). Comy.: "unshakable and immutable trust." Confidence of that nature is not attained before stream-entry because only at that stage is the fetter of sceptical doubt (*vicikicchā-saṃyojana*) finally eliminated. Unwavering confidence in the Buddha, Dhamma and Sangha are three of four characteristic qualities of a stream-winner (*sotāpannassa aṅgāni*); the fourth is unbroken morality, which may be taken to be implied in Section 9 of our discourse referring to the relinquishment of the defilements.

7. "When he has given up...(the defilements) in part" (*yatodhi*): that is, to the extent to which the respective defilements are eliminated by the paths of sanctitude (see Note 4). *Odhi*: limit, limitation. *yatodhi* = *yato odhi*; another reading: *yathodhi* = *yathā-odhi*.

Bhikkhu Ñāṇamoli translates this paragraph thus: "And whatever (from among those imperfections) has, according to the limitation (set by whichever of the first three paths he has attained), been given up, has been (forever) dropped, let go, abandoned, relinquished."

In the Vibhaṅga of the Abhidhamma Piṭaka, we read in the chapter Jhāna-vibhaṅga: "He is a bhikkhu because he has abandoned defilements limitedly; or because he has abandoned defilements without limitation" (*odhiso kilesānaṃ pahānā bhikkhu*; *anodhiso kilesānaṃ pahānā bhikkhu*).

8. "Gains enthusiasm for the goal, gains enthusiasm for the Dhamma" (*labhati Atthavedaṃ labhati dhammavedaṃ*).

Comy.: "When reviewing (*paccavekkhato*)* the abandonment of the defilements and his unwavering confidence, strong joy arises in the nonreturner in the thought: 'Such and such defilements are now abandoned by me.' It is like the joy of a king who learns that a rebellion in the frontier region has been quelled."

* ["Reviewing" (*paccavekkhana*) is a commentarial term, but is derived, apart from actual meditative experience, from close scrutiny of sutta passages like our present one. "Reviewing" may occur immediately after attainment of the jhānas or the paths and fruitions (e.g., the last sentence of Section 14), or as a reviewing of the defilements abandoned (as in Section 10) or those remaining. See *Visuddhimagga*, transl. by Ñāṇamoli, p. 789.]

Enthusiasm (*veda*). According to Comy., the word *veda* occurs in the Pali texts with three connotations: 1. (Vedic) scripture (*gantha*), 2. joy (*somanassa*), 3. knowledge (*ñāṇa*). "Here it signifies joy and the knowledge connected with that joy."

Attha (rendered here as "goal") and *dhamma* are a frequently occurring pair of terms obviously intended to supplement each other. Often they mean letter (*dhamma*) and spirit (or meaning: *attha*) of the doctrine; but this hardly fits here. These two terms occur also among the four kinds of analytic knowledge (*paṭisambhidā-ñāṇa*; or knowledge of doctrinal discrimination). *Attha-paṭisambhidā* is explained as the discriminative knowledge of "the result of a cause"; while *dhamma-paṭisambhidā* is concerned with the cause or condition.

The Comy. applies now the same interpretation to our present textual passage, saying: "*attha-veda* is the enthusiasm arisen in him who reviews his unwavering confidence; *dhamma-veda* is the enthusiasm arisen in him who reviews 'the abandonment of the defilement in part,' which is the cause of that unwavering confidence..." Hence the two terms refer to "the joy that has as its object the unwavering confidence in the Buddha, and so forth; and the joy inherent in the knowledge (of the abandonment; *somanassa-mayā ñāṇa*)."

Our rendering of *Attha* (Skt.: *artha*) b; "goal" is supported by Comy.: "The unwavering confidence is called *Attha* because it has to be reached (*araṇiyato*), i.e., to be approached (*upagantabbato*)," in the sense of a limited goal, or resultant blessing.

Cf. AN 5:10: *tasmiṃ dhamme attha-paṭisaṃvedī ca hoti dhammapaṭisaṃvedī ca; tassa Atthapaṭisaṃvedino dhammapaṭisaṃvedino pāmojjaṃ jayati...* This text continues, as our present discourse does, with the arising of joy (or rapture; *pīti*) from gladness (*pāmojja*). *Attha* and *dhamma* refer here to the meaning and text of the Buddha word.

9. The Pali equivalents for this series of terms* are: 1. *pāmojja* (gladness), 2. *pīti* (joy or rapture), 3. *passaddhi* (tranquility), 4. *sukha* (happiness), 5. *samādhi* (concentration). Nos. 2, 3, 5 are factors of enlightenment (*bojjhaṅga*). The function of tranquility is here the calming of any slight bodily and mental unrest resulting from rapturous joy, and so transforming the latter into serene happiness followed by meditative absorption. This frequently occurring passage illustrates the importance given in the Buddha's Teaching

to happiness as a necessary condition for the attainment of concentration and of spiritual progress in general.

* [Here the noun forms are given, while the original has, in some cases, the verbal forms.]

10. "Of such virtue, such concentration, such wisdom" (*evaṃ-silo evaṃ-dhammo evaṃ-pañño*). Comy.: "This refers to the (three) parts (of the Noble Eightfold Path), namely, virtue, concentration and wisdom (*sīla, samādhi, paññā-kkhandha*), associated (here) with the path of nonreturning." Comy. merely refers *dhammo* to the path-category of concentration (*sāmadhi-kkhandha*). Sub.Comy. quotes a parallel passage "*evaṃ-dhammā ti Bhagavanto ahesuṃ,*" found in the Mahāpadāna Sutta (Dīgha 14), the Acchariya-abbhūtadhamma Sutta (MN 123), and the Nālandā Sutta of the Satipaṭṭhāna Saṃyutta. The Dīgha Comy. explains *samādhi-pakkha-dhammā* as "mental states belonging to concentration."

11. "No obstacle," i.e., for the attainment of the path and fruition (of Arahatship), says Comy. For a nonreturner who has eliminated the fetter of sense-desire, there is no attachment to tasty food.

12. "With a mind of Loving-kindness" (*mettā-sahagatena cetasā*). This, and the following, refer to the four Divine Abidings (*brahma-vihārā*). On these see Wheel Nos. 6 and 7.

13. "He understands what exists, what is low, what is excellent" (*so 'atthi idaṃ atthi hinaṃ atthi paṇitaṃ...' pajānāti*).

Comy.: "Having shown the nonreturner's meditation on the Divine Abidings, the Blessed One now shows his practice of insight (*vipassanā*), aiming at Arahatship; and he indicates his attainment of it by the words: 'He understands what exists,' etc. This nonreturner, having arisen from the meditation on any of the four Divine Abidings, defines as 'mind' (*nāma*) those very states of the Divine Abidings and the mental factors associated with them. He then defines as 'matter' (*rūpa*) the heart base (*hadaya-vatthu*) being the physical support (of mind) and the four elements which, on their part, are the support of the heart base. In that way he defines as 'matter' the elements and corporeal phenomena derived from them (*bhūtupādāyadhammā*). When defining 'mind and matter' in this manner, 'he understands what exists' (*atthi idan'ti*; lit. 'There is this'). Hereby a definition of the truth of suffering has been given."

"Then, in comprehending the origin of that suffering, he understands 'what is low.' Thereby the truth of the origin of suffering has been defined. Further, by investigating the means of giving it up, he understands 'what is excellent. Hereby the truth of the path has been defined."

14. "... and what escape there is from this (whole) field of perception" (*atthi uttari imassa saññāgatassa nissaraṇaṃ*). Comy.: "He knows: 'There is

Nibbāna as an escape beyond that perception of the Divine Abidings attained by me.' Hereby the truth of cessation has been defined."

15. Comy.: "When, by insight-wisdom (*vipassanā*), he thus knows the Four Noble Truths in these four ways (i.e., 'what exists,' etc.); and when he thus sees them by path-wisdom (*magga-paññа*).

16. *Kāmāsavā bhavāsavā avijjāsavā.* The mention of liberation from the cankers (*āsavā*) indicates the monk's attainment of Arahatship which is also called "exhaustion of the cankers" (*āsavakkhaya*).

17. "Bathed with the inner bathing" (*sināto antarena sinānena*). According to the Comy., the Buddha used this phrase to rouse the attention of the brahmin Sundarika Bhāradvāja, who was in the assembly and who believed in purification by ritual bathing. The Buddha foresaw that if he were to speak in praise of "purification by bathing," the brahmin would feel inspired to take ordination under him and finally attain to Arahatship.

18. Bhāradvāja was the clan name of the brahmin. Sundarika was the name of the river to which that brahmin ascribed purifying power. See also the Sundarika-Bhāradvāja Sutta in the Suttanipāta.

19. Based on Bhikkhu Ñāṇamoli's version, with a few alterations.

20. Three are fords; the other four are rivers.

21. The text has Phaggu which is a day of brahmanic purification in the month of Phagguṇa (February-March). Ñāṇamoli translates it as "Feast of Spring."

22. Uposatha.

23. "It is here, O brahmin, that you should bathe." Comy.: i.e., in the Buddha's Dispensation, in the waters of the Noble Eightfold Path.

In the Therīgāthā, the nun Puṇṇikā speaks to a brahmin as follows:

Who indeed told you this, ignorant to the ignorant,
"Truly he is released from his evil action by ablution in water?"
Now (if this is so), all frogs and turtles will go to heaven,
And alligators and crocodiles and the other water-dwellers.

Sheep-butchers, pork-butchers, fishermen, animal-trappers,
Thieves and executioners, and other evildoers,
Even they will be released from their evil action by ablution in water.

If these streams carried away
For you the evil previously done,
They would carry away your merit too;
Thereby you would be devoid of both.

Transl. by K. R. Norman,
Elders' Verses II, P.T.S., 1971.

The Discourse on Effacement

Two Discourses of the Buddha

Edited with Introduction and Notes by
Nyanaponika Thera

WHEEL PUBLICATION NO. 62

Introduction

The Buddha's Discourse on Effacement (Sallekha Sutta; quoted as MN 8) is the eighth of the Collection of Middle Length Texts (Majjhima Nikāya). Its subject matter is closely connected with that of preceding text, The Simile of the Cloth (MN 7); these two discourses supplement each other in several ways.

The Simile of the Cloth speaks of sixteen defilements of social conduct as impeding the progress on higher stages of the path to deliverance. The present Discourse on Effacement widens the range to forty-four detrimental qualities of mind which must be effaced. These include thirteen of the sixteen defilements in MN 7 (items 1–11, 14 and 16 of list in Section 3 of MN 7), but they go beyond the realm of social ethics, extending also to the hindrances, the path factors, etc.; and special attention is given to the effacement of wrong views (Section 12, No. 44). This discourse supplements MN 7 also by dealing with the practical methods of effacement, from the very beginning with thought-arising (Section 13), on to avoidance (Section 14), etc.; and these methods apply as well to the purification from the sixteen defilements given in MN 7. On the other hand, the 7th discourse gives more details about the higher stages of progress that follow after the initial and partial purification.

(Section 12) "Effacement" means the radical removal of detrimental qualities of mind. The forty-four Modes of Effacement (as we may call them) are enumerated in this discourse no less than five times, and the first formulation (in Section 12) is very significant: "Others will be harmful, we shall not be harmful here," and so forth through all the other items. This bespeaks of the Buddha's realistic outlook as befitting a world that cannot be improved by mere wishing nor by "preaching at it." There is no use nor hope in waiting for our neighbour to change his ways. "Cleanup campaigns" should start at our own door, and then the neighbours may well be more responsive to our own example than to our preaching. Besides, if the aim is the radical effacement of mental defilements, we cannot afford to waste time and be deviated from our task by sidelong glances at the behavior of others. Here lurks, in addition, the danger of pride. Hence the

Suttanipāta (v. 918) warns that "though possessing many a virtue one should not compare oneself with others by deeming oneself better or equal or inferior." It is a "virtue that squints" (Chungtze) that will deprive the progress on the path of the element of self-forgetting joyous spontaneity.

There is yet another reason for the injunction not to look to others' behavior or misbehavior, and this applies particularly to the defilements of social conduct mentioned in the Simile of the Cloth. It is quite human to feel disappointed if one's selflessness, kindliness, modesty, and so on, do not find much response in the behavior of others. Such disappointment may well discourage a person not only from continuing to live according to his moral standard, but also from advancing further on the road to selflessness towards higher states of mental development. Such a person, after an initial disappointment, may easily be led to retire into the role of the "disgruntled moralist" as a respectable cloak for an egocentric life. Here we meet the limitations and risks of a morality solely motivated by the social response to it. To avoid such a blind alley on one's road of progress, it is important to make from the very beginning that "declaration of moral independence," which we may summarize thus: "Others may act, speak and think wrongly, but we shall act, speak and think rightly—thus effacement can be done."

(Section 13) But the Buddha, as a knower of the human heart, was well aware that such a single or even repeated resolve will not always be strong enough to stir people into action. Hence, as an encouragement to those who may feel disheartened by their failures, he speaks now of the importance of the "arising of thoughts" aiming at carrying out those acts of effacement. But again, these thoughts will not be effective unless they are regularly and systematically cultivated and are not allowed to lapse into oblivion. Then gradually they will be absorbed by our mind and heart, and we shall fully identify ourselves with those values. In that way these thoughts and aspirations will grow stronger and will be able to overcome the resistance of inertia and antagonistic forces, from within and without. The Master said, "To whatsoever one frequently gives attention and repeatedly reflects on, to that the mind will turn" (MN 19). The great German mystic of the Middle Ages, Meister Eckhart, goes even a step further by saying: "If you do not have the longing, have at least a longing for the longing."

(Section 14) Next to cultivating "the heart's resolve," the first direct step towards effacing the defilements is to know them, that is, the clear and honest confrontation with them in one's own mind, as we pointed out when considering the Simile of the Cloth (see the Introduction to it, p. 3). This will surely help in preventing their re-arising. But for strengthening and extending that effect, it is necessary to cultivate also the positive counterparts of those forty-four negative qualities, as taught in the instruction on avoidance. The Buddha's formulation in this section conveys the encouraging word that there actually exists such a road for avoiding or circumventing the wrong path. The Buddha said: "If it were not possible to give up what is evil, I would not tell you to give it up; if it were not possible to develop what is good, I would not tell you to develop it" (AN 2:2).

In the field of insight (*vipassanā*), this method is called "abandoning by the opposite" (*tadaṅgapahāna*), but by extension we may apply this term also to the wider range of our present context.

(Section 15) Apart from its highest purpose, the cultivation of positive qualities of mind is, on any level, a road of progress, a "way that leads upwards." It brings results here and now, and leads to a favorable and happy rebirth. It will preserve and unfold what is best in us and prevent it from deterioration. Considering the fearful possibilities in man's own nature and in the realms of existence, this is no mean benefit of training the mind for the final effacement of defilements, even if the results remain modest for a long time.

(Section 16) For him who has advanced so far, there is now the warning in the text that he should not set himself up as a saviour of others while "there is still more to do" for him. At this stage, the disciple may have effected some partial effacement, but still the fires of greed, hatred and delusion are not quenched in him; or, to express it with the other metaphor here used, he is still immersed in the mire. Though his chances for freeing himself from that bog of *saṃsāra* have improved, any wrong step, or just his negligence and lack of persevering effort, may cause a setback. Hence a determined effort should now be made for the final "quenching," for radical effacement.

(Sections 1–11) This warning against an overestimation of one's position links up with the first sections of our text which we have still to consider. They likewise deal with the overrating of one's achievements, here in the fields of insight and meditative absorptions. Even initial steps in these fields may result in experiences having such a strong impact on the mind that it is psychologically understandable if they lead to overestimation. This does not necessarily mean overrating oneself through pride, but overrating the position of one's achievements on the path of progress. One may believe them to be complete in their field while they are only partial or to be final while they are only temporary suppressions.

(Section 3) If confronted with "wrong views on self and world," one will, at first sight, be inclined to believe that any trace of them in oneself can be eliminated by intellectual refutation, that is, by proving to one's own satisfaction that they are untenable. And if one has a firm conviction in the truth of the Dhamma, it will be easy to assume that one has discarded wrong views for good. In that overestimation one may even go as far as to believe that one has entirely overcome the first of the ten fetters, personality-belief, and hence is on the way to stream-entry, or has even reached it. But this can never be achieved on the intellectual level alone, nor even on the first stages of insight-meditation, which in themselves are no mean achievement.

Misconceptions of self and world, which may be quite instinctive and unphilosophical, are deeply anchored in man's nature. They are rooted not only in his intellectual opinions (*diṭṭhi*), but also in his cravings (*taṇhā*) and in his pride and self-assertion (*māna*). All these three roots of wrong attitudes identify the alleged self or ego with the five aggregates (*khandha*) comprising personality-and-environment. These wrong attitudes towards self and world may manifest themselves on various levels: as casual thought-arisings, as a habitual bias, and in words and deeds (see Note 8). Only if the self-identification with the actual "objects of wrong views," i.e., the five aggregates, is radically dissolved on the stage of stream-entry, can it be said that wrong views of self and world have been totally eliminated, together with the bias towards them. As also craving and pride are involved in the formation of wrong views, efforts for their effacement have to be undertaken also on the level of ethical behavior. Hence the ethical part of the forty-four Modes of Effacement has validity also for the removal of wrong views.

(Sections 4–11) The eight meditative attainments lift the human consciousness to sublime heights of refinement; yet, in the case of each, the Buddha emphatically says that they are not states of effacement, as he understands them. They can effect only temporary subsidence of defilements, and if unsupported by mature virtue and insight, they cannot penetrate deep enough into the recesses of the mind for a radical removal of moral and intellectual defilements. It comes as a kind of anticlimax that after mentioning those sublime meditative attainments, the Buddha now speaks (in Section 12) of such quite "ordinary and earth-bound" ethical qualities as harmlessness, and ascribes to them, and not to the meditative absorptions, the capacity of leading to effacement. This juxtaposition implies, indeed, a very strong emphasis on the necessity of a sound ethical foundation for any spiritual progress. Often we find that mystic thought, in India and elsewhere, evolving a monastic system from wrongly interpreted unificatory meditative experience, has either ignored ethics or found it difficult to give it a convincing place and motivation in its system. The exultation of mystic experience also often leads the meditator to a premature feeling of having gone "beyond good and evil." Such developments illustrate the wisdom of the Buddha in insisting on a sound ethical basis instead of an exclusive reliance on mystic experience.

* * *

When examining closely the structure of this discourse, we find in it a repeated balancing of contrasting attitudes of mind and of complementary qualities required for progress on the path. Just now we have observed that meditative achievements have to be balanced with deeply rooted ethical virtues, which will also provide a link between the "lone meditator" and "common humanity." With the last of the forty-four Modes of Effacement the effacing of wrong views is taken up again, linking up with the beginning of the discourse and balancing the stress on ethical values in most of the other modes. In the phrasing of that last mode we note the stress laid on the overcoming of opinionatedness and tenacity. This points to the fact that, for the initial "loosening up" and final overcoming of wrong views, the following ethical modes are of decisive importance: amenability (34) and an increasing freedom from a domineering attitude (27), obstinacy (32) and arrogance (33).

The entire discourse seems to be designed to meet, in a very thorough manner, two opposite psychological obstacles on the path: discouragement in the face of its difficulties, and overrating of partial results. The first part of the discourse (Secs. 1–11) deals with the latter extreme, by stressing the limitations of initial and partial progress. But for meeting any discouragement caused by these warnings, the Compassionate Master speaks of the value of seemingly simple ethical virtues and stresses the importance of the heart's earnest resolve (Section 13) as the first step which anyone can take who is serious about treading the path of actual effacement.

These features of the discourse, without being stated explicitly, are inherent in its very structure. They will reveal themselves by a close scrutiny as here attempted, and particularly by the actual practice of the teachings concerned. The Buddha appears here as the great Teacher of the Middle Path and the incomparable guide of men's hearts, deeply concerned that those who tread the path may avoid the pitfalls of extreme emotional reactions and of one-sided emphasis on any single aspect of the threefold totality of training: in virtue, concentration and insight.

As in the preceding discourse, the rendering of the present one also has been chiefly based on Ñāṇamoli Thera's manuscript translation. To a lesser extent use has been made of phrasings by Soma Thera and I. B. Horner; and for some passages the Editor's own version has been included.

The Discourse on Effacement

Sallekha Sutta

1. Thus have I heard. Once the Blessed One was staying at Sāvatthī, in Jeta's Grove, Anāthapiṇḍika's monastery.

2. Then one evening the venerable Mahā-Cunda[1] rose from meditative seclusion and went to the Blessed One. Having paid homage to him, he sat down at one side and spoke thus to the Blessed One:

3. "Venerable sir, there are these various views that arise in the world concerning self-doctrines or world-doctrines.[2] Does the abandoning and discarding of such views come about in a monk who is only at the beginning of his [meditative] reflections?"[3]

"Cunda, as to those several views that arise in the world concerning self-doctrines and world-doctrines, if [the object] in which[4] these views arise, in which they underlie and become active,[5] is seen with right wisdom[6] as it actually is,[7] thus: 'This is not mine,[8] this I am not,[9] this is not my self'[10] then the abandoning of these views, their discarding,[11] takes place in him [who thus sees].

The Eight Attainments

4. "It may be, Cunda, that some monk, detached from sense-objects, detached from unsalutary ideas, enters into the first absorption that is born of detachment, accompanied by thought-conception and discursive thinking, and filled with rapture and joy, and he then might think: 'I am abiding in effacement.' But in the Noble One's discipline it is not these [attainments] that are called 'effacement'; in the Noble One's discipline they are called 'abidings in ease here and now.'[12]

5. "It may be that after the stilling of thought conception and discursive thinking, he gains the inner tranquillity and harmony of the second absorption that is free of thought-conception and discursive thinking, born of concentration and filled with rapture and joy; and he then might think: 'I am abiding in effacement.' But in the Noble One's discipline it is not these [attainments] that are called 'effacement'; in the Noble One's discipline they are called 'abidings in ease here and now.'

6. "It may be that after the fading away of rapture, the monk dwells in equanimity, mindful and clearly aware, and he experiences a happiness in his body of which the Noble Ones say: 'Happily lives he who dwells in equanimity and is mindful!'—that third absorption he wins; and he then might think: 'I am abiding in effacement.' But in the Noble One's discipline it is not these [attainments] that are called 'effacement'; in the Noble One's discipline they are called 'abidings in ease here and now.'

7. "It may be that with the abandoning of pleasure and pain, and with the previous disappearance of joy and grief, he enters upon and abides in the fourth absorption, which is beyond pleasure and pain and has purity of mindfulness due to equanimity; and he then might think: 'I am abiding in effacement.' But in the Noble One's discipline it is not these [attainments] that are called 'effacement'; in the Noble One's discipline they are called 'abidings in ease here and now.'

8. "It may be that, with the entire transcending of perceptions of corporeality,[13] with the disappearance of perceptions of sense-response,'[14] with non-attention to perceptions of variety,[15] thinking 'Space is infinite,' some monk enters upon and abides in the sphere of infinite space; and he then might think: 'I am abiding in effacement.' But in the Noble One's discipline it is not these [attainments] that are called 'effacement'; in the Noble One's discipline they are called 'peaceful abidings.'

9. "It may be that by entirely transcending the sphere of infinite space, thinking 'Consciousness is infinite,' some monk enters and abides in the sphere of infinite consciousness; and he then might think: 'I am abiding in effacement.' But in the Noble One's discipline it is not these [attainments] that are called 'effacement'; in the Noble One's discipline they are called 'peaceful abidings.'

10. "It may be that by entirely transcending the sphere of infinite consciousness, some monk enters and abides in the sphere of nothingness; and he then might think: 'I am abiding in effacement.' But in the Noble One's discipline it is not these [attainments] that are called 'effacement'; in the Noble One's discipline they are called 'peaceful abidings.'

11. "It may be that, by entirely transcending the sphere of nothingness, some monk enters and abides in the sphere of neither-perception-nor-nonperception; and he then might think:

'I am abiding in effacement.' But in the Noble One's discipline it is not these [attainments] that are called 'effacement'; in the Noble one's discipline they are called 'peaceful abidings.'

Effacement

12. "But herein, Cunda, effacement should be practiced by you:[16]

(1) Others will be harmful; we shall not be harmful here—thus effacement can be done.[17]
(2) Others will kill living beings; we shall abstain from killing living beings here—thus effacement can be done.
(3) Others will take what is not given; we shall abstain from taking what is not given here—thus effacement can be done.
(4) Others will be unchaste; we shall be chaste here—thus effacement can be done.
(5) Others will speak falsehood; we shall abstain from false speech here—thus effacement can be done.
(6) Others will speak maliciously; we shall abstain from malicious speech here—thus effacement can be done.
(7) Others will speak harshly; we shall abstain from harsh speech here—thus effacement can be done.
(8) Others will gossip; we shall abstain from gossip here—thus effacement can be done.
(9) Others will be covetous; we shall not be covetous here—thus effacement can be done.
(10) Others will have thoughts of ill will; we shall not have thoughts of ill will here—thus effacement can be done.
(11) Others will have wrong views; we shall have right view here—thus effacement can be done.
(12) Others will have wrong intention; we shall have right intention here—thus effacement can be done.
(13) Others will use wrong speech; we shall use right speech here—thus effacement can be done.
(14) Others will commit wrong actions; we shall do right actions here—thus effacement can be done.
(15) Others will have wrong livelihood; we shall have right livelihood here—thus effacement can be done.
(16) Others will make wrong effort; we shall make right effort here—thus effacement can be done.

(17) Others will have wrong mindfulness; we shall have right mindfulness here—thus effacement can be done.
(18) Others will have wrong concentration; we shall have right concentration here—thus effacement can be done.
(19) Others will have wrong knowledge; we shall have right knowledge here—thus effacement can be done.
(20) Others will have wrong deliverance; we shall have right deliverance here—thus effacement can be done.
(21) Others will be overcome by sloth and torpor; we shall be free from sloth and torpor here—thus effacement can be done.
(22) Others will be agitated; we shall be unagitated here—thus effacement can be done.
(23) Others will be doubting; we shall be free from doubt here—thus effacement can be done.
(24) Others will be angry; we shall not be angry here—thus effacement can be done.
(25) Others will be hostile; we shall not be hostile here—thus effacement can be done.
(26) Others will denigrate; we shall not denigrate here—thus effacement can be done.
(27) Others will be domineering; we shall not be domineering here—thus effacement can be done.
(28) Others will be envious; we shall not be envious here—thus effacement can be done.
(29) Others will be jealous; we shall not be jealous here—thus effacement can be done.
(30) Others will be fraudulent; we shall not be fraudulent here—thus effacement can be done.
(31) Others will be hypocrites; we shall not be hypocrites here—thus effacement can be done.
(32) Others will be obstinate; we shall not be obstinate here—thus effacement can be done.
(33) Others will be arrogant; we shall not be arrogant here—thus effacement can be done.
(34) Others will be difficult to admonish; we shall be easy to admonish here—thus effacement can be done.
(35) Others will have bad friends; we shall have noble friends here—thus effacement can be done.

(36) Others will be negligent; we shall be heedful here—thus effacement can be done.
(37) Others will be faithless; we shall be faithful here—thus effacement can be done.
(38) Others will be shameless; we shall be shameful here—thus effacement can be done.
(39) Others will be without conscience; we shall have conscience here—thus effacement can be done.
(40) Others will have no learning; we shall be learned here—thus effacement can be done.
(41) Others will be idle; we shall be energetic here—thus effacement can be done.
(42) Others will be lacking in mindfulness; we shall be established in mindfulness here—thus effacement can be done.
(43) Others will be without wisdom; we shall be endowed with wisdom—thus effacement can be done.
(44) Others will misapprehend according to their individual views, hold on to them tenaciously and not easily discard them;[18] we shall not misapprehend according to individual views nor hold on to them tenaciously, but shall discard them with ease—thus effacement can be done.

The Arising of Thought

13. "Cunda, I say that even the arising of a thought concerned with salutary things [and ideas][19] is of great importance, not to speak of bodily acts and words conforming [to such thought].[20] Therefore, Cunda:

(1) The thought should be produced: 'Others will be harmful; we shall not be harmful here.'
(2) The thought should be produced: 'Others will kill living beings; we shall abstain from killing living beings here.'
(3)–(43)...
(44) The thought should be produced: 'Others will misapprehend according to their individual views, hold on to them tenaciously and not easily discard them; we shall not misapprehend according to individual views nor hold on to them tenaciously, but shall discard them with ease.'

Avoidance

14. "Suppose, Cunda, there were an uneven road and another even road by which to avoid it; and suppose there were an uneven ford and another even ford by which to avoid it.[21] So too:

(1) A person given to harmfulness has non-harming by which to avoid it.
(2) A person given to killing living beings has abstention from killing by which to avoid it.
(3) A person given to taking what is not given has abstention from taking what is not given by which to avoid it.
(4) A person given to unchastity has chastity by which to avoid it.
(5) A person given to false speech has abstention from false speech by which to avoid it.
(6) A person given to malicious speech has abstention from malicious speech by which to avoid it.
(7) A person given to harsh speech has abstention from harsh speech by which to avoid it.
(8) A person given to gossip has abstention from gossip by which to avoid it.
(9) A person given to covetousness has non-covetousness by which to avoid it.
(10) A person given to thoughts of ill will has non-ill will by which to avoid it.
(11) A person given to wrong view has right view by which to avoid it.
(12) A person given to wrong intention has right intention by which to avoid it.
(13) A person given to wrong speech has right speech by which to avoid it.
(14) A person given to wrong action has right action by which to avoid it.
(15) A person given to wrong livelihood has right livelihood by which to avoid it.
(16) A person given to wrong effort has right effort by which to avoid it.
(17) A person given to wrong mindfulness has right mindfulness by which to avoid it.

(18) A person given to wrong concentration has right concentration by which to avoid it.
(19) A person given to wrong knowledge has right knowledge by which to avoid it.
(20) A person given to wrong deliverance has right deliverance by which to avoid it.
(21) A person overcome by sloth and torpor has freedom from sloth and torpor by which to avoid it.
(22) A person given to agitation has non-agitation by which to avoid it.
(23) A person given to doubting has freedom from doubt by which to avoid it.
(24) A person given to anger has freedom from anger by which to avoid it.
(25) A person given to hostility has freedom from hostility by which to avoid it.
(26) A person given to denigrating has non-denigrating by which to avoid it.
(27) A person given to domineering has non-domineering by which to avoid it.
(28) A person given to envy has non-envy by which to avoid it.
(29) A person given to jealousy has non-jealousy by which to avoid it.
(30) A person given to fraud has non-fraud by which to avoid it.
(31) A person given to hypocrisy has non-hypocrisy by which to avoid it.
(32) A person given to obstinacy has non-obstinacy by which to avoid it.
(33) A person given to arrogance has non-arrogance by which to avoid it.
(34) A person difficult to admonish has amenability by which to avoid it.
(35) A person given to making bad friends has making good friends by which to avoid it.
(36) A person given to negligence has heedfulness by which to avoid it.
(37) A person given to faithlessness has faith by which to avoid it.
(38) A person given to shamelessness has shame by which to avoid it.

(39) A person without conscience has conscience by which to avoid it.
(40) A person without learning has acquisition of great learning by which to avoid it.
(41) A person given to idleness has energetic endeavor by which to avoid it.
(42) A person without mindfulness has the establishment of mindfulness by which to avoid it.
(43) A person without wisdom has wisdom by which to avoid it.
(44) A person given to misapprehending according to his individual views, to holding on to them tenaciously and not discarding them easily, has non-misapprehension of individual views, non-holding on tenaciously and ease in discarding by which to avoid it.

The Way Upward

15. "Cunda, as all unsalutary states lead downward and all salutary states lead upward, even so, Cunda:

(1) A person given to harmfulness has harmlessness to lead him upward.[22]
(2) A person given to killing living beings has abstention from killing to lead him upwards.
(3)–(43)...
(44) A person given to misapprehending according to his individual views, to holding on to them tenaciously and not discarding them easily, has non-misapprehension of individual views, non-holding on tenaciously and ease in discarding to lead him upward.

Quenching

16. "Cunda, it is impossible that one who is himself sunk in the mire[23] should pull out another who is sunk in the mire. But it is possible, Cunda, that one not sunk in the mire himself should pull out another who is sunk in the mire.

"It is not possible, Cunda, that one who is himself not restrained, not disciplined and not quenched [as to his passions],[24] should make others restrained and disciplined, should make them attain to the full quenching [of passions].[25] But it is possible, Cunda, that one who is himself restrained, disciplined and fully quenched [as to his passions] should make others restrained and disciplined, should make them attain to the full quenching [of passions]. Even so, Cunda:[26]

(1) A person given to harmfulness has harmlessness by which to attain to the full quenching [of it].
(2) A person given to killing living beings has abstention from killing by which to attain to the full quenching [of it].
(3)–(43)...
(44) A person given to misapprehending according to his individual views, to holding on to them tenaciously and not discarding them easily, has non-misapprehension of individual views, non-holding on tenaciously and ease in discarding by which to attain the quenching [of them].

Conclusion

17. "Thus, Cunda, I have shown to you the instruction on effacement, I have shown to you the instruction on thought's arising, I have shown to you the instruction on avoidance, I have shown to you the instruction on the way upward, I have shown to you the instruction on quenching.

18. "What can be done for his disciples by a Master who seeks their welfare and has compassion and pity on them, that I have done for you, Cunda.[27] There are these roots of trees, there are empty places. Meditate, Cunda, do not delay, lest you later regret it. This is my message to you."

Thus spoke the Blessed One. Satisfied, the venerable Cunda rejoiced in the Blessed One's words.

[The concluding verse added by the Theras of the First Council:]

Deep like the ocean is this Suttanta on Effacement,
Dealing with forty-four items,
showing them in five sections.

Notes

1. Māha-Cunda Thera was the brother of the venerable Sāriputta Thera.

2. Self-doctrines or world-doctrines (*attavāda, lokavāda*). According to Comy., this refers: (a) to the twenty types of personality-belief (*sakkāya-diṭṭhi*), i.e., four for each of the five aggregates (*khandha*); (b) to eight wrong views about self and world, as being eternal, not eternal, both eternal and not eternal, neither eternal nor not eternal, and the same four alternatives concerning finite and infinite.

3. In a monk who is only at the beginning of his (meditative) reflections (*ādim-eva manasikaroto*). Comy.: "This refers to one who is at the beginning of his insight-meditation (*vipassanā-bhāvanā*) and has not yet attained to stream-entry," when the fetter of personality-belief is finally eliminated. The beginner's insight-practice extends from the "discernment of mentality and corporeality" (*nāmarūpa-pariccheda*) up to the "knowledge of rise and fall" (*udayabbaya-ñāṇa*), on which see *Path of Purification* (*Visuddhimagga*), Chs. XVIII, XX, XXI.

According to the Comy., the Thera's question concerns those who overrate the degree of their achievement, i.e., those who believe that, in their meditative practice, they have achieved this or that result while actually they have not. Overestimation (*abhimāna*), in that sense, "does not arise in ignorant common people (*bāla-puthujjana*) who are entirely engrossed in worldly life, nor does it arise in Noble Disciples (*ariya-sāvaka*); because in a stream-winner the overestimation does not arise that he is a once-returner, etc. Self-overestimation can occur only in one who actually practices (meditation) and has temporarily subdued the defilements by way of tranquillity or insight. Māha-Cunda Thera, being an arahant, was no self-overrater himself, but in formulating his question, he put himself in the place of one who is; or, as others say, there may have been such "self-overraters" among his pupils, and for conveying to them the Buddha's reply, he put his question.

4. (The object) in which (*yattha*). Comy.: *yattha* (where) = *yasmiṃ ārammaṇe*. The object, or basis, the five aggregates, because all false views on self and world can refer only to the five aggregates or to one of them. See *Discourse on the Snake Simile* (Wheel No. 47/48), p. 8, and *Anattā and Nibbāna*, by Nyanaponika Thera (Wheel No. 11), p. 18 (quotation).

5. In which these views arise (*yāttha uppajjanti*), i.e., arise for the first time, without having occurred earlier (Comy.).

Underlie (*anusenti*), i.e., habitually occur (cf. *anusaya*, "tendency," which may be latent or active). Comy.: "This refers to views which, having been indulged in repeatedly, have become strong and have not been removed." Sub.Comy.: "By ultimate elimination (*samuccheda-vinaya-vasena*)."

Become active (*samudācaranti*). Comy.: "Wrong views have arrived at the (action) doors of body and speech," i.e., which have found expression in words and deeds.

6. With right wisdom (*sammappaññāya*). Comy.: "With insight-wisdom, ending with the knowledge pertaining to the path of stream-entry."

7. As it actually is (*yathā-bhūtaṃ*). Comy.: "Because the five aggregates exist only in that manner (i.e., as something 'that is not mine,' etc.). But if conceived in the way 'It is mine,' etc., it simply does not exist (*n'ev'atthi*)."

8. This is not mine: hereby craving (*taṇhā*) is rejected.

9. This I am not: this refers to the rejection of conceit (*māna*).

10. This is not my self: this refers to the rejection of false views (*diṭṭhi*).

11. Abandoning... discarding (*pahānaṃ... paṭinissaggo*). Comy.: "Both terms are synonymous with the ultimate eradication of wrong views, taking place at stream-entry when the fetter of personality belief is destroyed."

12. Now the Buddha speaks, on his own, of another type of "self-overrater," i.e., of those who have realized any of the eight meditative attainments (*samāpatti*) and believe that this signifies true "effacement" (sallekha).

The common meaning of *sallekha** is austere practice or asceticism; but in the Buddha's usage it is the radical "effacing" or removal of the defilements.

*[*Sallekha* (= *saṃ-lekha*) is derived from the verbal root *likh*, to scratch; hence *likhati* (a) to scratch in, to write; (b) to scratch off, to remove: *sallikhati*, "to remove fully." An interesting parallel is "ascesis," derived from the Greek *askeuein*, to scratch. The rendering "effacement" is Ñāṇamoli Thera's; Soma Thera has "cancelling"; I. B. Horner, "expunging."]

The eight stages of meditation given here in the discourse, consist of the four fine-material absorptions (*rūpajjhāna*) and the four immaterial absorptions (*arūpajjhāna*). Comy. says that these meditative attainments "are in common with the ascetics outside (the Buddha's Dispensation)."

Comy.: "The overrater's meditative absorption is neither 'effacement' nor is it the 'path of practice for effacement' (*sallekha-paṭipadā*). And why not? Because that jhāna is not used by him as a basis for insight; that is, after rising from jhāna he does not scrutinize the (physical and mental) formations" (see *Visuddhimagga* transl. by Ñāṇamoli, Ch. XVIII, 3). His jhāna produces only one-pointedness of mind, and is, as our text says, an "abiding in ease here and now."

13. "By 'perceptions of corporeality' (*rūpasaññā*) are meant the absorptions of the fine-material sphere (*rūpajjhāna*) as well as those things that are their objects" (*Visuddhimagga*).

14. Perceptions of sense-response (lit. resistance, *paṭighasaññā*) are perceptions arisen through the impact of the physical sense bases (eye, etc.) and their objects.

15. Perceptions of variety (*nānattā-saññā*) are perceptions that arise in a variety of fields, or various perceptions in various fields. This refers to all perceptions belonging to the sense sphere (*kāmāvacara*).

16. Comy.: "Now, the Blessed One shows in forty-four ways where effacement should be practiced. But why are harmlessness and the other states regarded as effacement, unlike the eight meditative attainments? Because they are a basis for the supramundane (*lokuttara-pādaka*); while, for outsiders, the eight attainments are merely a basis for (continuing) the round of existence (*vaṭṭa-padaka*), (because by non-Buddhists they are practiced for the sake of rebirth in higher worlds). But in the Buddha's Dispensation, even the Going for Refuge is a basis for the supramundane.

Sub.Comy.: "If one, wishing to overcome the suffering of *saṃsāra*, goes with joyful confidence for refuge to the Triple Gem, then this Refuge will be for him a supporting condition for higher virtue, etc. (i.e., higher mentality and higher wisdom), and it may gradually lead him to the attainment of the path of understanding (*dassana-magga*; i.e., stream-entry)."

The Forty-four Ways of Effacement

(1) Harmful and harmless are not attached to a group of standard doctrinal categories as most of the other qualities are. On "harmlessness" see Note 17.

(2)–(11) are the courses of action (*kammapatha*), unsalutary (*akusala*) and salutary (*kusala*), referring to body (2–4), speech (5–8) and mind (9–11).

(12)–(18) are the last seven factors of the eightfold path (wrong and right), also called the eight states of wrongness or rightness (*micchatta, sammatta*). The first path factor, right (or wrong) view, is not separately mentioned, being identical with (11).

(19)–(20) are often added to the eightfold path.

(21)–(23) are the last three of the five hindrances (*nivaraṇa*); the first two are identical with (9) and (10), and therefore not repeated here.

(24)–(33) are ten of the sixteen defilements (*upakkilesa*) mentioned in MN 7 (Simile of the Cloth).

(34)–(36) are called in the Commentary the miscellaneous factors (*pakinnakā*).

(37)–(43) are the seven "good qualities" (*saddhāmma*), mentioned in MN 53 Comy.: "In this connection they are mentioned as forming the complete equipment required for insight (*vipassanā-sambhāro paripūro*)."

(44) is unattached to any group of terms. (See Note 18).

17. Comy.: "Harmlessness is called 'effacement,' because it effaces harmfulness, i.e., it cuts it off (*chindati*). This method of explanation applies to all other terms."

Sub.Comy.: "But why is harmlessness (or nonviolence, *ahiṃsā*) mentioned at the very beginning? Because it is the root of all virtues; harmlessness, namely, is a synonym of compassion. Especially, it is the root-cause of morality because it makes one refrain from immorality which has as its characteristic mark the harming of others. Just as the killing of living beings has the harming of others as its mark, so also the taking away of others' property; for 'robbing a man's wealth is worse than stabbing him.'* Similarly, chastity removes the cause for the pains of child bearing, etc., and there is hardly a need to mention the harm done by adultery.

* [This is given in Pali as direct speech or quote; perhaps it was a common adage.]

"Obvious is also the harm done to others by deception, by causing dissension and by backbiting. The mark of harming others is also attached to gossip because it takes away what is beneficial and causes to arise what is not beneficial; to covetousness, as it causes one to take what is not given; to ill will, as it causes killing, etc.; to wrong views, as they are the cause of all that is unbeneficial. One who holds wrong views may, in the conviction of acting righteously, kill living beings and incite others to do likewise. There is nothing to say about other and lesser immoral acts induced by false views.

"Harmlessness (i.e., the principle of non-violence) has the characteristic mark of making one refrain from immorality which, on its part, has the mark of harming. Hence harmlessness is an especially strong productive cause of morality; and morality, again, is the basis for concentration of mind, while concentration is the basis for wisdom. In that way harmlessness (non-violence) is the root of all virtues.

"Furthermore, in the case of the highest type of men (*uttamapurisa*) who have noble aspirations, who act considerately and wisely, also their mental concentration and their wisdom, just as their morality, is conducive to the weal and happiness of others. In that way, too, compassion is the root of all virtues, and therefore it has been mentioned at the beginning.

"Now (after harmlessness) the salutary courses of action (*kusala-kammapatha*; 2–11) are to show that these states are produced by harmlessness. Then follow the eight states of rightness (11–18) to show that they must be brought about by basing them on morality, which is the root of these virtues. Now the separation from the hindrances (21–23, and 16, 17) is included to indicate that this is the primary task for one intent on purifying (his practice of) the eightfold path. Then follows the cleansing from the defilements (24–33) to indicate that effacement is accomplished by giving up anger (24), etc.

And the cleansing from the defilements will be successful when aided by amenability to advice, noble friendship and heedful diligence (34–36).

"Now the seven noble qualities (37–43) are included to show that they will come to perfection in him who is endowed with amenability and the other (two factors); and that they, on their part, after having strengthened insight, will lead to the paths of sanctitude. (See end of Note 16.)

"Finally, the passage on 'misapprehending according to one's individual views,' etc. (44) is meant to indicate that for such a one (i.e., for one bent on effacement) that wrong attitude is an obstacle to the attainment of the supramundane virtues and is, therefore, to be avoided totally. This passage on misapprehending (about which see Note 18) is also meant to show that one who, by the right conduct here described, is in the process of attaining one of the paths of sanctitude, will be led to the acme of effacement (by this last-mentioned threefold way of effacement).

"In this manner should be understood the purpose of stating these forty-four modes of effacement as well as the order in which they appear in the discourse."

18. Comy.: "A single wrong view (or wrong attitude), which is an obstacle for the supramundane qualities and hence does not lead to emancipation, is here described in three aspects:

(a) Others will misapprehend according to their individual views (*sandiṭṭhi-parāmāsi*). Sub.Comy.: *sa(ṃ)* = *attano*, one's own. *Parāmāsi* means setting aside the actual nature of a thing, one conceives it differently (*sabhāvaṃ atikkamitvā parato āmasana*).

(b) Hold on tenaciously (*ādhānaggāhī*). Sub. Comy.: *ādhāna* = *daḷha*, tight, firm.

(c) Discards not easily. Comy.: "There are those who can discard their views on seeing a convincing reason. But others, even if shown many reasons, cannot give up their views; and of them it is said that they 'do not discard easily.' It refers to those who cling firmly to a subjective view that has occurred to them, believing 'only this is the truth.' Even if the Buddhas or others show them reasons, they do not relinquish their views. Such people, whatever idea they conceive, be it in accordance with Dhamma or not, will say: 'So it has been told by our teacher. So we have learned it'; and they will withdraw into themselves like a turtle drawing its limbs into its shell. They hold on to their views with the tight grip of a crocodile and do not let go."

19. Salutary: *kusala*, also translated by wholesome, profitable, skillful. These salutary things, says Sub. Comy., are the modes of effacement mentioned.

20. Sub.Comy.: "For those who cannot take up, by actual application, the

practice of effacement, even the arising of a thought (*cittuppādo*), i.e., an inclination for it, is of great importance.

Comy. says that a salutary thought is of great importance as it leads entirely to weal and happiness, and as it is the cause for the subsequent actions conforming to it. Examples are given beginning with the intention to give almsfood to monks, up to the aspiration for Buddhahood. The Sub.Comy., however, says that in some cases the importance is not in the thought itself but only in the actual execution of it. This certainly applies to the intention to give alms, etc. But in the efforts for effacing the defilements, the formation of a mental attitude directed towards it, in other words, the heart's resolve, is certainly an important factor.

This section of the discourse has been condensed in the present translation. But he who has chosen the path of effacement as his way of practice (*paṭipadā*) is well advised to repeat all forty-four items, linking them with his heart's earnest resolve. Also, the last two sections of the discourse have been condensed.

21. Comy.: "*Parikkamana* (lit. going around, circumventing) has the meaning of 'avoiding' (*parivajjana*). For the avoiding of harmfulness there is the ready road of harmlessness, walking on which one may easily experience felicity among humans or deities, or one may cross over (by that ford) from this world (to the other shore, Nibbāna). The same method of explanation applies to the other sentences."

22. Comy.: "The meaning is this: Any unsalutary states of mind, whether they produce rebirth or not, and whether, in a given rebirth, they produce kamma results or not—all, because of their type, i.e., by being unsalutary, lead downwards (to lower worlds). They are just like that because, on the occasion of their yielding a kamma result, that result will be undesirable and unpleasant.

"Any salutary states of mind, whether they produce rebirth or not, and whether, in a given rebirth, they produce kamma results or not—all, because of their type, lead upwards. They are just like that because, on the occasion of their yielding a kamma result, that result will be desirable and pleasant.

"The connection (in the discourse, between the general principle stated first, and its specific application to the forty-four cases) is as follows: just as unsalutary states lead downwards, so it is with that one state of harmfulness for him who is harmful. Just as all salutary states lead upwards, so it is with that one state of harmlessness for him who is harmless."

23. Comy.: "In the Noble One's discipline, the 'mire' is a name for the five sense desires."

24. Not fully quenched (*aparinibbuta*). Comy.: "with defilements not extinguished (*anibbuta-kilesa*)."

25. Comy.: "There may be those who object that this is not correct because some come to penetration of the Dhamma (*dhammābhisamaya*, i.e., stream-entry) after listening to an exposition of the Teaching by monks or nuns, male or female lay followers, who are still worldlings (*puthujjana*; i.e., have not attained to any of the paths of sanctitude). Hence one who is still in the mire can pull out others. (Reply:) This should not be understood in that way. It is the Blessed One who here does the pulling out.

"Suppose there is a king who sends a letter to the border region, and the people there, unable to read it by themselves, have the letter read to them by another able to do it. Having learned of the contents, they respond with respect, knowing it as the king's order. But they do not think that it is the letter reader's order; he will receive praise only for his smooth and fluent reading of the letter. Similarly, even if preachers of the ability of Sāriputta Thera expound the Dhamma, still they are just like readers of a letter written by another. Their sermon should truly be attributed to the Blessed One, like the decree to the king. The preachers, however, receive their limited praise, just because they expound the Dhamma with a smooth and fluent diction. Hence that statement in the discourse is correct."

26. For the connection between the modes of effacement and the preceding simile, Comy. gives two alterative explanations:

(a) Just as one who is not sunk in the mire himself can pull others out of it, similarly he who is harmless himself can quench another's harmful volition.

(b) Just as only he who has quenched his own passions can help one who has not quenched them, similarly only a volition of harmlessness can quench a harmful volition.

27. Comy.: "So far goes a compassionate teacher's task namely, the correct exposition of his teaching; that, namely, the practice (according to the teaching; *paṭipatti*), is the task of the disciples."

Aids to the Abhidhamma Philosophy

Three Charts for the study of Consciousness and Matter

With and explanatory essay

by

Dr. C. B. Dharmasena

M.B.B.S. (London)

WHEEL PUBLICATION NO. 63/64

Consciousness and Matter

An analytical explanation of three charts by
Dr. C. B. Dharmasena M.B.B.S. (London)

Introduction

No enthusiastic follower of the Buddha, nor earnest seeker after the truth, and no student of psychology or philosophy, be he a follower of the Buddha or not, can afford to do without a knowledge of the Abhidhamma philosophy, which has been handed down to us by one who not only attained perfection himself but pointed out to us the path by which we ourselves may obtain permanent release from all suffering. The Buddha has passed on to us not only the knowledge of his philosophy, but also the practical manner by which each one of us may convert that knowledge into understanding, through meditative development along the lines of the "One and only way, the Way of the Fourfold Setting up of Mindfulness";[1] therefore the oftrepeated criticism that Buddhism is only a philosophy and not a religion, is without

1. i. *The Mahā Satipaṭṭhāna Sutta.* No. 22 of the *Dīgha Nikāya.*

ii. *The Way of Mindfulness* by Bhikkhu Soma (3rd ed., Buddhist Publication Society, Kandy).

iii. *The Heart of Buddhist Meditation* by the Venerable Nyanaponika Mahā Thera, published by Rider & Co., London. This book was read by chance to such good purpose by Rear Admiral E. H. Shattock that he did a special journey to Rangoon in Burma by air, in order that he might do a course in meditation at the same meditation centre at which its author had his training in meditation. Thereafter he wrote a book *An Experiment in Mindfulness* (Rider & Co., London) wherein he states, "Meditation therefore, is a really practical occupation, it is in no sense necessarily a religious one, though it is usually thought of as such. It is itself basically academic, practical and profitable. It is, I think, necessary to emphasize this point, because some only associate meditation with holy people, and regard it as an advanced form of the pious life ... This is not a tale of a conversion, but of an attempt to test the reaction of a well-tried Eastern system on a typical Western mind."

any foundation whatsoever. This is further illustrated by the well-known parable of the raft,[2] where the Buddha says, "The doctrine taught by me is for crossing over, and not for retaining, even as the raft that was once used to cross over a stretch of water is now of no more use and should be cast away, and not placed on the head and carried, just because the raft had been once useful for crossing over."

It is our good fortune that the subject matter of the Abhidhamma philosophy, which runs into seven books, two of which are quite large, has been compressed into a brief compendium, the *Abhidhammatthasaṅgaha,* written by Anuruddha Thera in the Pāli language. This compendium has served for several centuries, and still continues to serve, as the best introduction to the study of the Abhidhamma throughout Ceylon (now Sri Lanka) and Burma (now Myanmar). This book is referred to by the late Venerable Ñāṇatiloka in the following terms: "A very succinct resume of all the essential doctrines of the Abhidhamma is given in that ingenious little vade mecum called the *Abhidhammatthasaṅgaha* written by Anuruddha. In Burma, of one who wishes to study the Abhidhamma, it is expected that one first thoroughly learns by heart and masters this short epitome; once he has mastered it, he will have grasped the whole substance of the Abhidhamma." Those of us who are not conversant with the Pāli language have an excellent translation of this book into English by the Venerable Anuruddha Mahā Thera. It is named *A Manual of Abhidhamma.*[3]

The Abhidhamma is not a speculative but a descriptive philosophy, where the description is complete, and is based on scientific method. The description of a thing or phenomenon is made not only by its minute analysis but also by its synthesis, followed by a combination of analysis and synthesis; and finally the description is completed in accordance with the axiom that "nothing arises from a single cause," with a statement of its relations to other things or phenomena. The atom, at one

2. *Alagaddūpama Sutta, Majjhima Nikāya* No. 22; P.T.S. Translation Series (*The Middle Length Sayings*), Vol. 7, p. 135; also in The Wheel Nos. 48/49, Buddhist Publication Society, Kandy).

3. *A Manual of Abhidhamma* by Nārada Mahā Thera (Buddhist Publication Society). See bibliography at the end of this book.

time thought to be indivisible, is in recent times known to be a complex structure composed of still smaller and more fundamental units, the proton, the neutron, and the electron; and even as these fundamental units within the atom, instead of being compact and static as was thought at one time, are now known to be separated from one another by distances enormous by comparison with the minuteness of the size of these "particles," and moving at incredible speeds; and even as the differences in the various qualities displayed by different objects of matter are not as previously imagined properties of the mass possessed by atoms, but of the forces between the minute units that go to compose the atom. Likewise, in the Abhidhamma philosophy, taught by the Buddha over two thousand five hundred years ago, he has told us that the so-called living being can be analysed ultimately into three fundamental or *paramattha dhamma*, i.e. *citta* (mind or consciousness), *cetasikā* (mental concomitants), and *rūpa* (corporeality or body); the first two together comprise *nāma* in the *nāma-rūpa* combination, *rūpa*, the third of the *paramatthas,* is described by the Buddha as being mainly made up of four primary "qualities," and of the space element, along with *upādāya-rūpa* (conditioned or derived corporeality).

The difference in the appearance of objects is due to the vastly different proportions in which the primary elements or qualities, and conditioned corporeality, blend.[4] Time and again the Buddha emphasized the lack of anything permanent in this ever changing body. With reference to the first two *paramatthas*, i.e. *citta* and *cetasika*, which together, as already mentioned, make up the term *nāma* in the *nāma-rūpa* combination that constitutes the so-called living being, the Buddha emphasizes this fact even further, when he states[5] "It were better, bhikkhus, if the ignorant, unconverted man regard the body which is composed of the four elements as an ego, rather than the mind. And why do I say so? Because it

4. Majjhima Nikāya or *The Middle Length Sayings*, I.B. Horner's translation: 140. Dhātuvibhaṅga Sutta; 28. Mahāhatthipadopama Sutta; 62. Mahā Rāhulovāda Sutta. *Path of Purification* (*Visuddhimagga*), Bhikkhu Ñāṇamoli's translation XI, (31-38), (81-92) and (109).

5. H. C. Warren, *Buddhism in Translation*, section 18, from *Saṃyutta Nikāya* (XII 62)

is evident, Bhikkhus, that this body, which is composed of the four elements, lasts one year, lasts two years ... fifty years, lasts a hundred years and even more. But that which is called the mind, intellect, consciousness, keeps up an incessant round by day and by night of perishing as one thing, and springing up as another."

Explanation of the Charts

The scope of this article is limited and precise. As an aid to the study of the Abhidhamma philosophy three charts are presented and how they may be used with maximum benefit is explained. The first is a modification of the excellent chart published in *The Buddhist Dictionary*, and in *The Guide to the Abhidhamma*, both by the Ven. Ñāṇatiloka, to whom I owe a great deal for my first introduction to the Buddha Dhamma. This chart analyses *citta* or consciousness, which is the first of the three fundamentals or *paramattha* that constitutes the so-called being. The analysis is made in a graphic and concise way, and in a readily assimilated and easily remembered form under groups and sub-groups of all the eighty-nine types into which *citta* or consciousness is divided in the Abhidhamma philosophy. The second chart sets out the individual functions of each of these 89 types of *citta*, also in a graphic and easily assimilated form, and it is arranged along the same lines, and with the identical numbers as in the first chart, so that these two charts may be readily and frequently compared. The third chart deals with the arising and grouping of material qualities.

It is important to realize at the very outset that all these charts are meant to be used along with the study of *The Manual of Abhidhamma*, already mentioned; and all I propose to do in this article is to state as briefly as possible how these charts may be used with maximum profit in such a study. In doing so I propose to commence with the abbreviations used, to state what they stand for, and in some instances give their meaning or the corresponding Pāli term.

Chart I—Consciousness

In Chart I Nos. (1–8),

joy:	stands for joyful, which in Pāli is *somanassa*;
ind:	for indifferent (*upekkhā*);
know:	for knowledge (*ñāṇa*); Nos. (22–33)
w.view:	stands for wrong view (*diṭṭhi*);
ple:	for pleasant (*sukha*);
up:	for *upekkhā* (indifferent);
so:	for *somanassa* (joyful);
pain:	for painful (*dukkha*).

Let us now study the chart together in a general way, and see what information we can get out of it. Looking at the end of the chart we see that there are 89 types of *citta* or consciousness. These are divided into four vertical columns or classes; and again the same 89 are divided into 4 horizontal layers called spheres, planes, or in Pāli *bhūmi.* The caption in the small cage at the top of the vertical column reads "moral (*kusala*) 21," that is to say that the first vertical column contains all the morally wholesome states of consciousness or *kusala citta,* and of these there are 21. Looking down the left-hand margin of this column we see by way of confirmation that the serial numbers read 1–21. Similarly reading the caption in the small cages at the top of each of the three remaining vertical columns simultaneously with the serial numbers on the left-hand margin of the same column, we see that the second column contains immoral types of consciousness, or *akusala citta,* of which there are 12 (22–33); the third column deals with resultant consciousnesses or *vipāka citta* which add up to 36 (34–69); and the last or fourth column is reserved for the remaining 20 (70–80) which are named inoperative or *kriyā*, since they are neither moral nor immoral nor the resultants of these two.

Now, if we turn our attention to the last line on the first horizontal layer reserved for *citta* of the sensuous sphere, and look at the right-hand margin of each of the four vertical columns into which this layer is divided, we see that in this sphere there are 8 moral, 12 immoral, 23 resultant and 11 inoperative *citta*, which add up to a total of 54. Further, if we run our eye down the second vertical column we realize that immoral or *akusala citta* are found only in the sensuous sphere. A closer study of the sensuous sphere reveals the existence of divisions except in the first vertical column, which deals with moral *citta*. There are three divisions in the second column, i.e. eight immoral *citta* rooted in greed (22–29), two rooted in hate (30–31) and two rooted in delusion (32–33); another three in the third column i.e. eight kinds of moral resultant consciousness without roots (34–41), eight moral resultants with roots (42–49);[6]and seven immoral resultants without roots (50–56); making a total of 23 resultant *citta* belonging to the sensuous sphere. We note that there are no immoral resultants with roots. In the fourth column, reserved for inoperative or *kriyā citta*, there are only two divisions, i.e. three without roots (70–72); and eight with roots (73–80), making a total of 11.

We shall now make a very important observation, which will simplify considerably and consolidate our study of *citta* or consciousness not only of the sensuous sphere but, as we shall see later, of the remaining three spheres as well. We note that the Pāli term for the eight types of *citta* (1–8), in the first column is *mahā* (great) *kusala citta*; we also note that there are two other sets of eight bearing a similar name in the third and fourth columns, *mahā vipāka citta* (42–49), and *mahā kriyā citta* (73–80); and each of these is analogous to *citta* (1–8), indicating clearly that there is a very close similarity between the three sets of eight. The similarity is so close that with a detailed study of the first set we shall know the other two sets equally well. We shall therefore make such a study of the first set (1–8), with the chart in front of us. We note that one moral *citta* becomes divided into eight by way of three qualities printed just below the top of the first column at right angles to the rest of the chart. The first division is made by way of feeling (*vedanā*), which may be either joyful (*somanassa*), or indifferent (*upekkhā*) so that at the first division we have:

A. One moral consciousness with joyful feeling and
B. One moral consciousness with indifferent feeling.

---

6. The term root, or in Pāli *hetu* (lit. cause), is applied to the six roots: three immoral (*akusala*), i.e. attachment (*lobha*), hatred (*dosa*), and ignorance (*moha*); and three moral (*kusala*), i.e. non-attachment (*alobha*), goodwill (*adosa*), and wisdom (*amoha*).

We see that the next division is made by way of the *citta* being accompanied (*sampayutta*) by knowledge (*ñāṇa*), or not being accompanied (*vippayutta*) by knowledge. A and B are thus each divided into two, which gives us four types of *citta*:

A. c. One moral consciousness, with joyful feeling, and accompanied by knowledge;
A. d. One moral consciousness, with joyful feeling, and not accompanied by knowledge;
B. c. One moral consciousness, with indifferent feeling, and accompanied by knowledge;
B. d. One moral consciousness, with indifferent feeling, and not accompanied by knowledge.

Finally, the above four types of *citta* are divided into two each, (1) by way of the *citta* arising spontaneously within oneself, without inducement by others, and the thought being put into effect without hesitation or wavering (this is given the expressive term *asaṅkhārika* in Pāli), and (2) by way either of the *citta* arising only after inducement, or even if it had arisen without another's influence, of being put into effect only after much hesitation, being disturbed with such thoughts as "Will I be put to too much inconvenience were I to undertake this? Will the cost be excessive? Should I be antagonizing someone who is useful to me, were I to do this good deed?" This type is called *sasaṅkhārika* in Pāli.

This third division will finally give us the following eight moral (*kusala*) *citta*:

A. c. i. One consciousness, with joyful feeling, accompanied by knowledge; and spontaneous;
A. c. ii. One consciousness, with joyful feeling, accompanied by knowledge; and induced or with hesitation;
A. d. i. One consciousness, with joyful feeling, not accompanied by knowledge; and spontaneous;
A. d. ii. One consciousness, with joyful feeling, not accompanied by knowledge; and induced or with hesitation;
B. c. i. One consciousness, with indifferent feeling, accompanied by knowledge; and spontaneous;
B. c. ii. One consciousness, with indifferent feeling,

accompanied by knowledge; and induced or with hesitation;

B. d. i. One consciousness, with indifferent feeling, not accompanied by knowledge; and spontaneous;

B. d. ii. One consciousness, with indifferent feeling, not accompanied by knowledge; and induced or with hesitation.

These eight types of consciousness derived by us in the above manner, we shall now profitably read off from the chart from the first column, both for the sake of gaining familiarity in the use of the chart, and for the sake of confirming in our own minds that the two sets are exactly the same, with the difference that the numbers in the latter are in serial order from 1 to 8. The corresponding Pāli name within brackets is also given underneath to help us to familiarize ourselves gradually with original Pāli nomenclature. We shall then have:

1. Consciousness with joyful feeling, accompanied by knowledge; and spontaneous (*somanassa-sahagata ñāṇasampayutta; asaṅkhārika citta*).
2. Consciousness with joyful feeling, accompanied by knowledge; and induced or with hesitation (*somanassa-sahagata; ñāṇasampayutta; sasaṅkhārika citta*).
3. Consciousness with joyful feeling; not accompanied by knowledge and spontaneous (*somanassa-sahagata; ñāṇavippayutta; asaṅkhārika citta*).
4. Consciousness with joyful feeling, not accompanied by knowledge; and induced or with hesitation (*somanassa-sahagata; ñāṇavippayutta; sasaṅkhārika citta*).
5. Consciousness with indifferent feeling; accompanied by knowledge; and spontaneous (*upekkhā-sahagata; ñāṇasampayutta; asaṅkhārika citta*).
6. Consciousness with indifferent feeling; accompanied by knowledge; and induced or with hesitation. (*upekkhā-sahagata ñāṇasampayutta; sasaṅkhārika citta*).
7. Consciousness with indifferent feeling, not accompanied by knowledge and spontaneous (*upekkhā-sahagata; ñāṇavippayutta; asaṅkhārika citta*).

8. Consciousness with indifferent feeling; not accompanied by knowledge; and induced or with hesitation. (*upekkhā-sahagata; ñāṇavippayutta; sasaṅkhārika citta*).

Practical examples by way of illustrating these eight moral *citta* will further help us to fix them in our mind:

1. One gives something to a beggar, spontaneously without hesitation, with understanding, and experiencing joy.
2. One gives something to a beggar, with understanding, and experiencing joy, but does so after deliberation, and hesitation, or only on being induced to do so by another.
3. A child sees a monk and remembering that its parents salute monks on meeting them, does so himself, spontaneously, experiencing joy, but without understanding why he does so; or a person automatically recites a holy text experiencing joy, without understanding the meaning of the text.
4. A child sees a monk and at the request of his mother salutes him, without understanding why he does so, but experiences joy in the act.

The remaining four types (5–8) should be understood in the same way, substituting indifference for joy.

If we now turn our attention to the allied sets of eight types of *citta* (42– 49), *mahā vipāka citta* in column three, and to (73–80) *mahā kriyā citta* in column four, and simultaneously look up the *Manual of Abhidhamma*, we shall see that the nomenclature is exactly the same as we have described above for *mahā kusala citta* (1– 8) in column one, but of course the functions are different in the three sets of eight, and this we shall see at a glance when we come to Chart II. We shall now turn our attention to the eight types of *citta* (22–29), in column two. Here too the division is exactly the same as in the three sets of eight already discussed, with the one difference that we substitute wrong view (*diṭṭhi*) for knowledge (*ñāṇa*). To illustrate this let us now read off from the chart in column two, the first line (22), the third line (24), and the eighth line (29):

22. One immoral *citta* rooted in greed; with joyful feeling; accompanied by wrong view; and spontaneous. (*somanassa-sahagata; diṭṭhi-sampayutta; asaṅkhārika citta*).

24. One immoral *citta* rooted in greed; with joyful feeling; not accompanied by wrong view; and spontaneous. (*somanassa-sahagata; diṭṭhi-vippayutta; asaṅkhārika citta*).
29. One immoral *citta* rooted in greed; with indifferent feeling; not accompanied by wrong view; and induced or with hesitation. (*upekkhā-sahagata; diṭṭhi-vippayutta; sasaṅkhārika citta*).

Lastly, immoral *citta* (30–31) rooted in hate (*dosa*), and immoral *citta* (32– 33) rooted in delusion (*moha*), are also named in exactly the same manner. Thus we have:

30. One immoral *citta* rooted in hate; with sad feeling; accompanied by rage; and spontaneous. (*domanassa-sahagata; paṭigha-sampayutta; asaṅkhārika citta*).
31. One immoral *citta* rooted in hate; with sad feeling; accompanied by rage; and *induced* or with hesitation. (*domanassa-sahagata; paṭigha-sampayutta; sasaṅkhārika citta*).
32. One immoral *citta* rooted in delusion; with indifferent feeling; and accompanied by *doubt*. (*upekkhā-sahagata; vicikicchā-sampayutta citta*).
33. One immoral *citta* rooted in delusion; with indifferent feeling; and accompanied by restlessness. (*upekkhā-sahagata; uddhacca-sampayutta citta*).

With the help of Chart I we have thus at one sitting, cursorily though it be, but methodically, disposed of four sets of eight, or 32 types of *citta*, along with four additional types of *citta* (30– 33), which add up to 36 out of a total of 54 types of *citta* belonging to the sensuous sphere. When we shall have gone over the same ground in the *Manual of Abhidhamma* in much greater detail two or three times, with constant reference to the chart, we shall have not isolated groups of *citta* recalled to mind with difficulty, but a clear and lasting mental picture of these 36 types of *citta* well co-ordinated and arranged in easily remembered form, and in a form capable of being recalled to mind rapidly and with ease. We shall then be able to assign in our own mind instantaneously and with precision the correct place in the chart to any scattered group or individual *citta* picked up at random.

We are now left with three gaps in the sensuous sphere in Chart I, in columns three and four, for the remaining 18 types of *citta*, all of which belong to the types of *citta* without roots (*ahetuka*). The gap in the upper one third of column three is taken up by the 8 moral resultants (34– 41), and that in the lower third of the same column by the 7 moral resultants (50–56), while the third gap in the upper half of column four is reserved for the 3 inoperative (*kriyā*) *citta* (70–72). Further it should be noted that all the 12 immoral (*akusala*) *citta* (22–33) in column two have as their resultants the 7 types of *citta* (50–56) in column three, while the 8 moral (*kusala*) *citta* (1–8) in column one have two sets of 8, or 16 *citta*, as their resultants in column three, i.e. 8 without roots (34–41), and 8 with roots (42–49) already described. Since these 18 types of *citta* have varied functions, unlike the 36 described earlier, we shall study them later more conveniently along with Chart II, which deals with functions.

It has to be noted that in the *Manual of Abhidhamma* the different groups of sense sphere consciousness are treated in quite a different order as follows: The 12 immoral *citta* (22–33), the 7 immoral resultants without roots (50–56), followed by the 8 moral resultants without roots (34–41), the 3 inoperative without roots (70–72), and finally the three sets of 8 each, Great (mahā) moral, resultant and inoperative (1–8, 42–49, and 73–80), the last set of eight applying only to Arahants. However, when Chart I is used along with the *Manual of Abhidhamma*, it will be found more useful at least at the second and subsequent readings to follow the order described in this article.

We shall now turn our attention to the types of consciousness in the second horizontal layer comprising form-sphere consciousness (*rūpāvacara citta*). These have three sets of five *citta* each, i.e.

(a) Form-sphere moral *citta* or ecstasies or *kusala rūpa jhānas* (9–13), which may be attained only by those who practise intent and regular meditation with the object of gaining one-pointedness and tranquillity of the mind (*samatha bhāvanā*);

(b) Form-sphere inoperative *citta* or *kriyā rūpa jhānas* (81–85), in column four which may be attained only by Arahants who practise the above meditation [both (a) and (b) are attained in this life]; and

(c) Form-sphere resultant consciousness (*rūpāvacara vipāka citta*) (57–61), which are experienced in the *rūpa* planes of existence or *brahma lokas*, after their death by those who attain form-sphere moral *jhānas* (9–13) above mentioned.

It is not feasible in this short article to describe these *jhānas*, which are explained in brief in pages 40–52 of the *Manual of Abhidhamma*, and in more detail in volume II, chapter 9 of the same Manual; and in the *Visuddhimagga* translated into English under the title *The Path of Purification*, by Bhikkhu Ñāṇamoli, chapter 4, paragraphs 74–202 (pages 142–176); chapter 11, paragraphs 120–126 (pages 406–408), and chapter 12, paragraphs 46 to the end of the chapter (pages 420–445). The whole of chapter 13, and also the last chapter of the *Manual of Abhidhamma*, give a detailed description of the various kinds of supernormal powers, which are attained with the fifth *jhāna* used as the basis.

Amongst these supernormal powers a few may be mentioned: "Having been one he becomes many, he appears and vanishes, he goes unhindered through walls and enclosures, he goes on water as though on earth, he travels in space like a winged bird, he gains the divine eye that penetrates into the minds of others, gives the knowledge of one's past lives, and of the passing away and reappearance of beings." The above chapters will be found to be of absorbing interest, and should be read by anyone interested in *yoga*-meditation, in parapsychological phenomena or in the power of the mind and in miracles. They are by no means peculiar to Buddhism, and they provide a workable hypothesis for explaining some of these phenomena.

The subject matter of the second, third, and fourth horizontal layers devoted to the form-sphere, formless-sphere, and supramundane consciousness respectively is so vast that any attempt to describe these types of consciousness is well beyond the scope of a short article of this nature. Hence I propose to confine myself almost exclusively to the extraction of whatever information we can derive from a mere perusal of the captions given in Chart I itself, and later from Chart II. We shall start with the second horizontal layer. The abbreviations used in the first vertical column of this layer containing *citta* 9–13, stand for the names of the five *jhāna* factors (*aṅga*) of the form-sphere consciousness.

Vit stands for *vitakka* (*initial application* of the mind towards the object);

vic for *vicāra* (*sustained application* of the mind with a close examination of the object);

pi for *pīti* (creating a *pleasurable interest* in the object);
su for *sukha* (bliss or *happiness* caused by enjoyment of the desired object). "Like the sight of an oasis in a desert to a weary traveler is *pīti*, like drinking the water and bathing therein is *sukha*";
ek for *ekaggatā* (one-pointedness of the mind, or *concentration*);
up for *upekkhā* (*indifference*, of a very special type).

The cage containing form-sphere moral consciousness (9–13) is reproduced below in English for the sake of simplicity:

9. Initial application-sustained application: interest, happiness, concentration.
10. Sustained application: interest, happiness, concentration.
11. Interest, happiness, concentration.
12. Happiness, concentration.
13. Indifference, concentration.

We see from the above that the first or most elementary *jhāna* contains all the five *jhāna* factors. In the subsequent *jhānas*, which are progressively more and more refined as the fourth *jhāna* is reached, one by one of the coarser *jhāna* factors are eliminated (*aṅgasamatikkamana*, transcending of the factors), until in the fourth *jhāna* we are left with only two factors, happiness and concentration; while in the fifth *jhāna* even the factor of Happiness is transcended as not being sufficiently refined and it is replaced by indifference, which is not the ordinary indifferent feeling of the sensuous-sphere consciousness already discussed; the *jhāna* indifference which is really a more refined type of *sukha* or happiness, has been developed by a strong will-power, and in the *rūpa jhānas* is present only in the fifth or highest of the *rūpa jhānas*. As we have already noticed, this elimination of the coarser factors in successive stages one by one is graphically represented in the chart in column one (9–13). Exactly the same diagramatic representation should appear in columns three and four along this horizontal layer, but for the sake of convenience and clarity these cages are merely marked as being analogous to (9–13), as was done in cages containing *citta* (42–49), and (73–80), in the sensuous-sphere.

We shall now turn our attention for a moment to the third horizontal layer This represents the Formless-sphere consisting of the four moral (14–17), and four inoperative (86–84) *jhānas* attained in this life by non-Arahants and Arahants respectively who practise these meditations; and of the four *arūpa lokas* (62–65), where worldlings (those who have not attained any of the supramundane states of consciousness), who die while they are experiencing *arūpāvacara kusala jhānas* are reborn. The nomenclature used is English in column one, Pāli in column three, while column four has been marked for the sake of clarity as merely allied to (14–17).

The fourth horizontal layer is reserved for supramundane consciousness, moral, and resultant *phala* is the term used instead of *vipāka*, as the results that follow are immediate (*akālika*). The nomenclature again is English in column one and Pāli in column three, which enables one to gain a gradual acquaintance with the Pāli terms. We also note that there are no *kriyā citta* in the supramundane types of consciousness. The subject matter of this article so far is described in chapter one of the *Manual of Abhidhamma*.

Chart II—Functions of Consciousness

We shall now turn our attention to Chart II, which deals with the *functions* of the 89 types of *citta* we have already discussed in Chart I. It will be noticed that they are arranged and numbered in exactly the same manner as in Chart I, into four vertical columns, which stands for moral, immoral, resultant, and inoperative classes in that sequence; and into four horizontal layers which signify sensuous-sphere, form-sphere, formless-sphere, and supramundane consciousness. The first thing that strikes the eye forcibly is the presence of a varied number of colours in the chart. Each colour represents a different function. There are eight colours in all, but two of the colours represent more than one function, for instance

Yellow represents three allied functions of *pat*, which stands for *paṭisandhi* or rebirth-consciousness. *Bha* stands for *bhavaṅga*, which will be explained later, and *cuti* for death-consciousness.

Purple represents five allied functions: *pañca-viññāṇa* (sense-sphere consciousness), i.e. seeing, hearing, smelling, tasting, and touching or contacting.

The remaining six colours represent one function each, making a total of 14 functions:

Light pink for *javana* (not to be confused with the word *jhāna* already described),

Emerald green for receiving (*sampaṭicchana*),

Olive green for investigating (*santīraṇa*),

Orange for registering (*tadālambana* or *tadārammaṇa*),

Light blue for adverting either at the sense-doors (*pañcadvārā-vajjana*), or at the mind-door (*mano-dvārāvajjana*), and lastly

Dark blue for determining (*votthapana*).

Although we have counted 14 functions, if the five allied and paralleled functions of seeing, hearing, smelling, tasting, and contacting are counted as one, since each occupies the same stage in the process of cognition (*pañca-dvāra-vīthi*) we are left with 10 functions represented by 8 colours, the yellow representing three functions as stated earlier.

If we turn our attention once again to the different colours, we see that several types of *citta* have only one function i.e. light pink represents *javana* only, emerald green is for receiving only, light blue represents adverting only, while on the contrary some types of *citta* have more than one function. Hence these are represented by more than one colour (except the yellow, which it should be remembered represents three functions), and these have in addition the actual number of functions they represent printed in numerals by the right hand margin of the name of the lowermost function printed on that particular cage. For instance,

No. 40 has two functions, olive green for investigation, and orange for registering (II).

No. 41 and 56 each has five functions, olive green for investigating, orange for registering, and yellow for rebirth-*bhavaṅga*-death (V).

No. 42–49 each has four functions, orange for registering, and yellow for rebirth-*bhavaṅga*-death (IV).

No. 57–61 and 62–65 each has three functions, yellow for rebirth-*bhavaṅga*-death (III).

No. 71 has two functions, light blue for adverting, and dark blue for determining (II).

No. 34–38 and 50–54 have a special marking (I) of V, since, as explained above, there is in reality only one function although apparently there are five.

This chart gives us more information if we study it further. It tells us the total number of *citta* that perform each different function, and their exact identity; for instance *javana* (light pink)—which is a much stronger thought than the others, and psychologically the most important stage in the process of cognition, for it is at this stage (except in the case of Arahants), that an action is judged to be moral or immoral—is represented by 21 moral *citta* (1–21), 12 immoral (22–23), 4 *phala* (supramundane resultants, 66–69) and 18 inoperative (72–89), adding up to a total of as many as 55 out of a total of 89 *citta*. *Pat* (*paṭisandhi*), *bha* (*bhavaṅga*), *cuti* (rebirth-*bhavaṅga*-death) (yellow) are represented by *citta* No. 41, 42–49 (8), 56 and 57–65 (9), or a total of 19 types of *citta*; receiving (emerald green) by No. 39 and 55, a total of 2; registering (orange) by No. 40, 41, 42–49 (8) and 56, making a total of 11; Investigating (olive green) by No. 40, 41, and 56 or a total of 3; adverting (light blue) by No. 70 and 71, a total of 2; determining by one single *citta*, No. 71, coloured in a darker shade of the same blue to indicate a close relationship which exists between the function of adverting at the mind-door and determining (*vottha-pana*) and sense-door consciousness (purple) by No. 34–38 (5), and 50–54 (5), a total of 10, or 2 if the five similar functions of seeing, hearing, smelling, tasting, and contacting, which together form *pañca-viññāṇa* or five-sense-door-consciousness are counted as one.

A helpful analogy for remembering the various functions described above is to consider *citta* and its functions as an engineering workshop, in which 89 workers of 4 different grades (representing the four different spheres or planes) do 14 different jobs at 10 different positions in the workshop, closely allied types of work being done at one position. Most of the workers do only one job, for instance the one function of *javana* is done by as many as 55 workers, while some workers do more than one job, up to a maximum of five, but of course only one job is done by such a worker at any one time. Still further information may be gained in a form which may be easily remembered if pages 168–172 of the *Manual of Abhidhamma* are read along with Chart II.

We now come to a most interesting and very important subject, the process of cognition or *citta-vīthi* described in chapter 4 of the *Manual of Abhidhamma*. It will be rather difficult to follow the subject unless one has read through chapters 2 and 3 of the Manual. But if these two chapters have been studied, Chart II will be found to be of great value in the study of chapter 4, and of the Chart on page 30 and the text in the two pages that follow, which form an introduction to chapter 4. For instance in a five-sense-door thought-process the various thought-moments which vary from resultant (*bhavaṅga*), No. 41, or one of 42–49, or 56 to inoperative (adverting at sense-door, No. 70), from inoperative back to resultant (*pañca-viññāṇa*, receiving and investigating), one of No. 34–38, 39, and 41, or one of Nos. 50–56, 55 and 56; and once more from resultant to inoperative (determining, No. 71), and then to kamma (moral or immoral *javana*, i.e. one of No. 1–8, or 22–33), and finally from *javana* back to resultant (registering and *bhavaṅga*) may be followed with a clarity scarcely possible in any other way. We may now profitably investigate the three horizontal arrows marked in Chart II in the sensuous sphere, connecting either column I or column II, kamma (moral or immoral) to column III (resultant).[7] We see from the lowest arrow that 11 out of the 12 immoral *citta* in column 2 (22–32) produce rebirth (*paṭisandhi*) into states of woe through one single *citta* No. 56 (*akusala santīraṇa upekkhā*).

Before we begin to study the next two arrows we should bear in mind with reference to moral *citta* 1–8 the four of them—vide Chart I—i.e. 3, 4, 7, 8 which are not accompanied by knowledge (*ñāṇavippayutta*) have only the two roots non-attachment (*alobha*) and goodwill (*adosa*); while the remaining four, i.e. 1, 2, 5, 6 which are accompanied by knowledge (*ñāṇasampayutta*), have a third root, wisdom, (*amoha*), in addition. Both types of *citta*, those accompanied by knowledge (1, 2, 5, 6) and those not accompanied by knowledge (3, 4, 7, 8) have two classes each, i.e. a lofty (*ukkaṭṭha*) and a lower (*omaka*). From the highest horizontal arrow we see that the lower class of the four *citta*, with roots (*dvihetuka omaka*), 3, 4, 7, 8, produces rebirth through one *citta* No. 41 (*kusala santīraṇa upekkhā*) to those unfortunate humans who are born deaf, dumb, blind, or with other defects, mental, bodily, or endocrinal. This observation emphasises the importance of knowledge and understanding accompanying the performance of good deeds if we wish as all of us do, to be born with all our faculties intact. The

7. *Manual of Abhidhamma*, pages 241, 242, 245, 252 and 253.

middle arrow shows us that the four *citta* with three roots, 1, 2. 5, 6, and the lofty class of *citta* with two roots, 3, 4, 7, 8, produce rebirth through one or the other of *citta* 42–49. Greater detail with reference to this interesting subject of rebirth is not depicted graphically in the chart for fear of confusing the chart with too many details.

But a brief summary of these details as given in page 242 of the *Manual of Abhidhamma* is as follows:- That moral kamma of the lofty class with three roots (*tihetuka ukkaṭṭha*) produces rebirth similarly accompanied by three rows (*tihetuka paṭisandhi*) through one or the other of the corresponding resultant *citta*, 42, 43, 46, 47. That moral kamma with three roots of a lower class (*tihetuka omaka*), and moral kamma with two roots of a lofty class (*dvihetuka paṭisandhi*), through one or the other of *citta*, 44, 45, 48, 49.

One may be excused if one fails to follow what I have just been trying to convey in the absence of the basic knowledge of this subject given in chapters 2, 3, and 4 of the *Manual of Abhidhamma*. I would therefore stress what I have already stated previously that neither the three charts nor this short article are meant to be used except as a help in the study of the *Manual of Abhidhamma*; it is by no means an epitome of the manual itself, which is already "a very succinct resume of the Abhidhamma philosophy."

Before I conclude the subject of *citta* or consciousness I wish to make an observation on the subject of *bhavaṅga-citta*. Unfortunate attempts have been made to find a suitable word and a definition in terms of Western psychology for the *bhavaṅga-citta*, but such attempts have only led to confusion. In the circumstances it is best that the original term *bhavaṅga* be used without a misleading translation.

Paṭisandhi-bhavaṅga-cuti (rebirth-*bhavaṅga*-death) are allied functions performed at different moments of time. Rebirth and death are each performed only once in one's lifetime. The function of *paṭisandhi* has already been performed by us at conception, and the same consciousness has been taken over as *bhavaṅga-citta* which will continue for the rest of our lives until *cuti* consciousness replaces it at death. Between (re)birth, and death in this existence there continues during all hours of deep sleep an unbroken stream of *bhavaṅga* consciousness. During the rest of the time every moment an activity is performed either by thought, word, or deed it is a *citta-vīthi* or thought-process that functions.

Each thought-process is made up of 17 thought-moments. The extremely short duration of a full thought-process may be gauged by an illustration. For instance when one sees a tray full of mixed flowers for the short duration of a second or two, during which time one gets an idea of their different colours, and shapes, of their varying states of preservation, of the different odours they emanate and of their different names and associations in the light of previous experience, one does not appreciate all these facts in the course of one thought-process. On the contrary an innumerable number of thought-processes, each consisting of 17 thought-moments are necessary to enable one to recognise each varying appreciation which springs in one's mind simultaneously with the momentary glimpse of the flowers on that tray. This is possible because "in the twinkling of an eye, billions of thought-processes may arise and perish" (*Manual of Abhidhamma*, page 291).

Each thought-process is divided into 17 thought-moments which perform varying functions, which include at the commencement and often at the end several thought-moments of *bhavaṅga* consciousness. In a five-sense-door thought-process (*pañca-dvāra Citta-vīthi*) out of a total of 17 thought-moments either 3 or 5 or 10 thought-moments are made up of *bhavaṅga* consciousness depending on whether the process is 'very great,' or 'great' or 'slight' respectively; and in a very 'slight' thought-process there is merely a vibration in the *bhavaṅga* consciousness, with no other function taking place. Again in a mind-door thought-process (*mano-dvāra citta-vīthi*) out of the total of 17 thought-moments either 7 or 9 thought-moments are made up of *bhavaṅga* consciousness, depending on whether the object is 'clear' or 'obscure.' Thus we see that *bhavaṅga* consciousness exists for extremely minute intervals at the beginning, and often at the end of each thought-process during about half the period of our waking hours and continues in an unbroken stream during the hours we are asleep. These observations are sufficient for one to realise the important role of *bhavaṅga* consciousness in our existence. *Bhava* means existence or life, and *aṅga* means the (chief) factor i.e. the chief factor which clings to one's existence, and maintains life, for as soon as *bhavaṅga* ceases to function in the absence of any other function performed in the course of a thought-process, the function of *cuti*-consciousness makes its appearance, and life in this existence ceases.

The function of *paṭisandhi* has already been performed by us at conception as the first function of a thought-process; since then the function of *bhavaṅga* is being performed by us both during sleep, and when we are awake. Eleven of the twelve remaining functions are also being performed during each second we are awake, there only remains the fourteenth or last function to be performed, which is *cuti-citta*; or death-consciousness. In the light of this analysis, along with meditation of mindfulness of death we are in a position to face death with equanimity, and a calmness that certainly no emotion can ever hope to achieve, nor even faith not founded on knowledge and reason. The ability to face a crisis with facility and a stoic indifference can be best ensured by a correct appreciation of things as they truly are (*yathābhūta-ñāṇa*).

One not infrequently hears Buddhists with an education of a kind which makes them say that all religions teach one to be good, hence it is not very material as to which religion one follows. A life of 'goodness' that they have in view, in such a glib statement, connotes rebirth in a heaven (celestial realm, or *deva loka*), where happiness is of a much lower grade than that in the *rūpa* and *arūpa lokas* attained through the *jhānas*, which cannot be gained by good conduct alone, but require in addition to *sīla* a high degree of concentration (*samādhi*) through intense and prolonged meditation with the object of obtaining tranquillity and one-pointedness of the mind (*samatha-bhāvanā*). It ought to interest such Buddhists to learn what the Buddha has to say even of these exquisite states of happiness[8]: "Having reached any one of these high states (*rūpa* and *arūpa jhānas*) the bhikkhu by reflection comprehends that the happiness of each one of these states, however excellent, however exquisite it may be, is effected, is thought out, is impermanent, and is liable to stopping. Firm in this conviction the bhikkhu attains the matchless security not yet attained, from the bonds (Nibbāna)."

The appreciation that all conditioned existence and whatever happiness is found therein, however exquisite it may be, is temporary and liable to change and is therefore unsatisfactory, and the knowledge that there is a permanent escape from this unsatisfactory state, by a secure and sure path, built on knowledge,

8. *Majjhima Nikāya* No. 52 (*Aṭṭhakanāgara Sutta*).

leading to understanding, makes Buddhism the most practical of all religions, and not merely an abstract philosophy as has already been stressed at the very beginning of this article. It needs constant stressing that it is correct knowledge that acts as the most powerful incentive to *saddhā* (faith), which enables us to keep on treading the secure and sure path already referred to, and to the development of a habit of meditation which alone can convert that knowledge we have acquired into understanding and realisation.

Chart III—Material Qualities

We now come to the last of the three charts, the headlines of which indicate that it deals with the arising (*samuṭṭhāna*), and the grouping (*kalāpa*) of material qualities (*rūpa*). Before the chart can be understood it is necessary to study the enumeration (*samuddesa*) of material qualities, which is given in tabular form in the *Manual of Abhidhamma,* or in any of the other translations already mentioned. Only a very brief summary of the eleven types into which the 28 material qualities are divided need be stated here:

Type i. The four great essentials.
Type ii. The five 'sensitive' material qualities (*pasāda-rūpa*) of eye, ear, nose, tongue, and body.
Type iii. The five 'sense fields' (*gocara-rūpa*), colours and shape (*vaṇṇa*), sound, smell, taste (and touch).
Type iv. The two material qualities of sex (*bhava-rūpa*), female and male.
Type v. The heart base, or the 'seat of consciousness' (*hadaya-rūpa*).
Type vi. The vital principle or (physical) life faculty (*jīvita-rūpa*).
Type vii. Physical nutriment (*āhāra-rūpa*), or nutrient essence (*ojā*).
Type viii. Limiting material qualities (*pariccheda-rūpa*), or element of space (*ākāsa-dhātu*).
Type ix. The two material qualities of expression or intimation (*viññatti-rūpa*): vocal intimation (*vacī-viññatti*) and body intimation (*kāya-viññatti*).
Type x. The three 'mutable' material qualities of lightness, pliancy and adaptability,
Type xi. The four characteristics of material qualities (*lakkhaṇa-*

rūpa): the first arising, continuity, decay and death (impermanence).

Two important terms used in the chart need clarification. The eight *inseparable* material qualities (*avinibbhoga-rūpa*) marked A.1. in the chart, are made up of the four great essentials (type i) i.e. of extension (*paṭhavī*), cohesion (*āpo*), heat (*tejo*), and motion (*vāyo*); of three of the five sense fields (*gocara-rūpa*) in type iii, i.e. visible form (*vaṇṇa*), smell (*gandha*), and taste (*rasa*) and of type vii, nutrient essence (*oja*). The eight *controlling* material faculties mentioned in the first vertical column and marked F consist of the five sensitive material qualities (type iii); of the two material qualities of sex (type iv) and of the vital principle (*jīvita-rūpa*, type vi). The material heart base (type v) is marked E in the chart.

It needs emphasising once again that these charts are only meant to be used along with the study of the appropriate chapter in any one of the translations of the *Abhidhammatthasaṅgaha* already mentioned—chapter vi with reference to Chart III. A methodical scrutiny of the chart reveals that it deals with the arising (*samuṭṭhāna*), and the grouping (*kalāpa*) of material qualities. We note four pairs of vertical columns marked action (*kamma*), mind (*citta*), seasonal conditions (*utu*), and food (*āhāra*). These are the four ways in which material phenomena arise, represented by the left hand side of each pair of vertical columns, and are grouped as depicted on the right hand side of each pair of columns

In the *arising* of material phenomena we see that '*action-derived*' material qualities (*kammaja rūpa*) are composed of the eight inseparables and the element of space, the eight controlling material faculties and the heart base, making a total of 18 material qualities as denoted in the chart.

'*Mind-derived*' material qualities (*cittaja rūpa*) depicted in the second pair of vertical columns are made up of the eight inseparables and the element of space, of the three material qualities of lightness etc., of the two related qualities of articulate sound and vocal intimation; and of body intimation, making a total of 15.

'*Seasonal-derived*' material qualities (*utuja-rūpa*) are composed of the eight inseparables and the element of space, the three qualities of lightness etc. and of inarticulate sound, making a total of 13. Lastly,

'*Food-derived*' material qualities (*āhāra rūpa*) made up of the eight inseparables and the element of space; and the three qualities of lightness etc., making a total of 12.

We may also read off from the chart another set of observations. The eight inseparables and the element of space marked A, arise in *all four ways*. The three qualities of lightness, softness, and adaptability marked B arise in *three ways*, from mind, seasonal conditions and food. Sound marked C in *two ways*, articulate sound from mind, and inarticulate sound from seasonal conditions such as wind. And the following arise from one *single* cause: vocal and bodily intimation marked D are 'mind-derived'; the heart base marked E and each of the eight controlling faculties marked f are 'kamma-derived'; the four characteristics (*lakkhaṇa rūpa*) type xi do not arise from any cause; hence these are not depicted in the chart.

Lastly, with reference to the *grouping* of material qualities (*rūpa kalāpa*), we see from the chart clearly, and in a way which may be easily remembered, how they are made up. It will be noticed that the element of space is not reckoned with in the grouping (*kalāpa*); although it is counted in the arising of material qualities.

'*Action-derived*' (*kammaja*) material qualities arrange themselves into *nine* different groups. 1. The eight inseparables and the vital principle from the vital-nonad (*jīvita navaka*). 2–9. The vital-nonad plus *one at time* of the remaining seven controlling faculties of eye, ear, nose, tongue, body, female-decad, male-decad, and the basis-decad.

'*Mind-derived*' (*cittaja*) qualities arrange themselves into *six* different groups: 1. The eight Inseparables form the 'pure octad'.

2. This along with body intimation forms the 'body intimation-nonad'.

3. The 'pure octad,' along with articulate sound and vocal intimation, which are depicted in the chart as closely related form the 'vocal intimation-decad.'

4. The 'pure octad' along with the three qualities of lightness etc. form the 'un-decad of lightness.'

5. The 'pure octad' along with the three qualities of lightness etc. and body intimation form the 'do-decad of lightness and body intimation,' and lastly

6. The 'pure octad,' along with the three qualities etc., and related articulate sound and vocal intimation form the 'tri-decad of lightness and vocal intimation.'

'*Seasonal-derived*' (*utuja*) qualities form four different groups:

1. The 'pure octad.'
2. This, along with inarticulate sound, forms the 'sound-nonad'.
3. The 'pure octad' along with the three qualities of lightness etc. form the 'un-decad of lightness,' and
4. The 'pure octad' along with the three qualities of lightness etc. and sound form the 'do-decad of sound.'

'*Food-derived*' (*āhāraja*) qualities have only *two* groups, the 'pure octad' and the 'un-decad of lightness.'

Thus we have 18, 15, 13, and 12 qualities going to form material qualities derived respectively from kamma, mind, seasonal conditions, and food; and 9, 6, 4, and 2 groupings (*kalāpa*) respectively from the same causes, and all these are depicted, and are easily read off from the chart.

Although one must admit that the Abhidhamma philosophy is a difficult subject, the appreciation of its basic principles is not so difficult as it is generally made out to be; and with the excellent translations now available, a knowledge of Pāli though desirable is not essential. A systematic study of the bare essentials of the subject as outlined in one of the translations of the *Abhidhammatthasaṅgaha* will give one an inkling of the way in which corporeal phenomena arise, and of the way consciousness arises by the coming together of such corporeal phenomena-sensitive material qualities (*pasāda-rūpa*) and the various sense fields (*gocara-rūpa*). Thinking over these vital problems of life frequently, and discussing them from time to time one gets an appreciation of these most interesting problems. The next and most difficult step is the conversion of this knowledge into understanding and insight, which is a very different thing from knowledge. This *can only be done* by meditative development (*bhāvanā*), regularly practised for gradually increasing periods each day for years on end, for a whole lifetime, or in the case of a very vast majority of us for several lifetimes. This is the only method which enables one to get rid of the notion of an ego so deeply ingrained in each and every one of us, and which is the cause of this endless round of rebirths. This purification of one's view and the shedding of the notion of an ego is the first step on the path to Nibbāna.

'And when full vision comes,
three outlooks pass away:-
doubt, personality, and ritual.'

Of the Abhidhamma the Venerable Kassapa says[9] "Slowly the *puthujjana,* the worldling, is introduced to Truth and the value of the higher life that alone opens the Path to Deliverance ... He feels that his seeing falls far below the intuitive insight of *paṭisambhidā,* the exact individual analysis of the Noble Disciple who has tasted the fruition of the Paths. He longs for some view, however dim of that true vision ... Here he feels that he at last enjoys a picture of the Truth. It is not seeing truth face to face, it is a picture; but it is a true picture, a glimpse however faint, of the Truth that the Noble Ones have attained."

9. Foreword to the *Guide to the Abhidhamma,* Ven. Nyanatiloka 2nd Edition, Page xiii.

Chart 1

CONSCIOUSNESS (CITTA)

TYPES (89): CLASSES (4): PLANES (SPHERES) (4)

SENSUOUS PHERE (KĀMĀVACARA CITTA)

MORAL (Kusala) 21					IMMORAL (Akusala) 12				
MORAL CONSCIOUSNESS (*Mahā Kusala Citta*) 8					CONSCIOUSNESS ROOTED IN GREED (*Lobha Mūla Citta*) 8				
Feeling	accompanied by- (sampayutta)	not accompanied by- (vippayutta)	spontaneous and unhesitating (asaṅkhārika)	instigated or hesitating. (sasaṅkhārika)	Feeling	accompanied by- (sampayutta)	not accompanied by- (vippayutta)	spontaneous and unhesitating (asaṅkhārika)	instigate or hesitating. (sasaṅkhārika)
1. joy :	know :		+		22. joy :	w. view :		+	
2. joy :	know :			+	23. joy :	w. view :			+
3. joy :		know :	+		24. joy :		w. view :	+	
4. joy :		know :		+	25. joy :		w. view :		+
5. ind :	know :		+		26. ind :	w. view :		+	
6. ind :	know :			+	27. ind :	w. view :			+
7. ind :		know :	+		28. ind :		w. view :	+	
8. ind :		know : (ñāṇa)		+	29. ind :		w. view :		+
					Con: rooted in hate, ... 2 (Dosa Mūla C:)				
					30. sad	rage.		+	
					31. sad	rage.			+
					Con: rooted in delusion, ... 2 (Moha Mūla C:)				
					32. ind :	doubt		+	
					33. ind :	restlessness		+	
				8					12

FORM-SPHERE MORAL CON:
(Arūpāvacara Kusala C:) *Jhāna* 5

9. vit-vic-pi-su-ek : I.
10. vic-pi-su-ek : II.
11. pi-su-ek : III.
12. su-ek : IV.
13. *up-ek* : V.

FORMLESS-SPHERE MORAL CON:
(Arūpāvacara Kusala C:) 4
Jhana Con : (*up-ek*:) dwelling on :-

14. "infinity of SPACE" VI.
15. "Infinity of CONSCIOUSNESS" VII.
16. "NOTHINGNESS" VIII.
17. "PERCEPTION neither is, nor is not" IX.

MORAL SUPRAMUNDANE CON: 4
(Lokuttara Magga). Path of :-

18. "Stream Entrance"
19. "Once-returning"
20. "Non-returning"
21. "Arahatship". 21

Chart 1 Continued ....

<table>
<tr><th colspan="2">Morally Indeterminate (avyākata)</th></tr>
<tr><th>RESULTANT (Vipāka) 36</th><th>INOPERATIVE (Kriya) 20</th></tr>
<tr><td>MORAL RESULTANT CONSCIOUSNESS
without ROOTS 8
(Ahetuka Kusala Vipāka C.)
34. ind: Eye-Con:
35. ind: Ear-C:
36. ind: Nose-C:
37. ind: Tongue-C:
38. ple: Body-C:
} SENSE-CONSC-IOUSNESS (Pañca-viññāṇa)
39. ind: RECEIVING-C: (Sampaṭicchana; Manodhātu; Mind-element).
40. joy: INVESTIGATING C: (Somanassa Santīrana).
41. ind: INVESTIGATING C: (Upekkhā Santīrana)</td><td>INOPERATIVE C: without ROOTS (Ahetuka kriya) 3

70. ind: FIVE-SENSE-DOOR ADVERTING C: (Pañcadvārāvajjana; Mano-dhātu; Mind-element)

71. ind: MIND-DOOR-ADVERT C: (Manodvārāvajjana); Mano-viññāṇa-dhātu; Mind-conscious:- el:)

72. joy: The SMILE of the ARAHAT' (so: Hasituppāda; Mano-viññāṇa-dhātu; Mind-con: el:).</td></tr>
<tr><td>42–49 = (1–8). 8
MORAL RESULT: CON: with ROOTS.
(Sahetuka kusala vipāka C:,
Mahā Vipāka C:)</td><td rowspan="2">73–80 = (1–8). 8
INOPERATIVE C: with ROOTS
(Sahetuka kāmāvacara kriya C:,
Mahā Kriya Citta)

11</td></tr>
<tr><td>IMMORAL RESULTANT CONSC:
without ROOTS. 7
(Ahetuka Kusala Vipāka C.)
50. ind: Eye-Con:
51. ind: Ear-C:
52. ind: Nose-C:
53. ind: Tongue-C:
54. pain: Body-C:
} SENSE-CONSC-IOUSNESS (Pañca-viññāṇa)
55. ind: RECEIVING-C: (Sampaṭicchana; Manodhātu; Mind-element).
56. ind: INVESTIGATING C:
(Upekkhā Santīrana). 23</td></tr>
<tr><td>FORM-SPHERE RESULTANT C: 5
(Rūpāvacara Vipāka C:
57. I.
58. II.
59. = (9–13) III.
60. IV.
61. V.</td><td>FORM-SPHERE INOPERATIVE
(Rūpāvacara Kriya C: 5
81.
82.
83. = (9–13)
84.
85.</td></tr>
<tr><td>FORMLESS-SPH: RESULTANT C:
(Arūpāvacara Vipāka C: 4
(up-ek:) VI-IX
62. (14). Ākāsañāñc-āyatana. VI.
63. (15). Viññāṇañc-āyatana. VII.
64. = (16). Akiñcaññ-āyatana. VIII.
65. (17). Nevasaññānāsaññ-āyatana. IX.</td><td>FORM-SPH: INOPERATIVE
(Rūpāvacara Kriya C: 4
81.
82.
83. = (9–13)
84.
85. 20</td></tr>
<tr><td>RESULT: SUPRAMUNDANE C: 4
(Lokuttara Phala C:
(up-ek:) VI-IX
66. = (18). Sotāpatti Phala
67. = (15). Sakadāgāmi Phala
68. = (20). Anāgāmi Phala
69. = (21). Arahatta Phala 36</td><td></td></tr>
</table>

Chart 2

FUNCTIONS OF CONSCIOUSNESS (Viññāṇa kicca)

	MORAL (Kusala) 21	IMMORAL (Akusala) 12	RESULTANT (Vipāka) 36	INOPERATIVE (Kriya) 20
SENSUOUS SPHERE (KĀMĀVACARA CITTA)			Result of good kamma, *without* roots (Ahetuka kusala vipāka citta.) (34–41) 8	Inoperative citta, *without* roots. (Ahetuka kriya citta). (70–72) 3
			34-38. Pañca-viññāṇa. EYE-CONSCIOUSNESS (or any one of the other four). $\frac{(I)}{V}$ 5	70. Pañcadvārāvajjana. ADVERTING (at sense door). 1
			39. Sampaṭicchana upekkhā. RECEIVING 1	71. Mano-dvārāvajjana. ADVERTING (at mind door). 1
			40. Santīraṇa somanassa. INVESTIGATING 1 ↓ REGISTERING (Tadālambana). (II)	↓ DETERMINING (Voṭṭhapana) (II)
	→	Lower class of 3, 4, 7 & 8, →	41. Santīraṇa uppekkhā INVESTIGATING $\frac{1}{8}$ ↓ REGISTERING (Tadālambana). PAT:- BHA:- CUTI. (V)	72. 'The Smile of the Arahat (Somanassa Hasituppāda C.) $\frac{1}{3}$ JAVANA
	Sensuous-sphere Moral Consciousness, *Mahā Kusala Citta* (1–8). 8 →	1, 2, 5 & 6 and lofty class of, 3, 4, 7 & 8 →	42 - 49. Result of good kamma, *with* roots (Sahetuka kusala vipāka); *Mahā Vipāka*. C. 8 ↓ REGISTERING (Tadālambana). PAT:- BHA:- CUTI- (IV) =(1–8).	Inoperative consciousness *with* roots, *Mahā Kriya Citta*, (Sahetuka kāmāvacara kriya citta) (73–80). 8

Chart 2 Continue ....

1. 2. 3. 4. 5. 6. J A V A N A 7. 8.	Immoral consciousness. (22–33). 12 Rooted in : 22–29. Greed (Lobha) 8 30–31. Hate (Dosa) 2 32–33. Delusion (Moha) 2 12 JAVANA 22–32 (11) →	Result of bad kamma, *without* roots (Ahetuka akusala vipāka citta). (50-56). 7 50-54 Pañca-viññāṇa. 5 EYE-CONSCIOUSNESS (or any one of the other four). $\frac{1}{V}$ 55. Sampaṭicchana upekkhā. 1 RECEIVING 56. Santīraṇa upekkhā $\frac{1}{7}$ INVESTIGATING REGISTERING (Tadālambana). → PAT:- BHA:- CUTI. (V)	73. 74. 75. 76. 77. 78. 79. JAVANA 80. = (1–8).
9. Form-sphere moral C. 5 10. (Rūpāvacara kusala C.) 11. 12. J A V A N A 13.		57. Form-sphere result: C 5 58. (Rūpāvacara vipāka C.) 59. PAT:- BHA:- CUTI. (III) 60. 61. = (9–13).	81. Form-sp: Inoperative C. 5 82. (Rūpāvacara kriya C.) 83. JAVANA 84. 85. = (9–13).
14. Formless-sphere 15. moral C. (Arūpāvacara 16. kusala citta) 4 17. JAVANA		62. Formless-sp: resultant C. 4 63. (Arūpāvacara vipāka C.) 64. PAT:- BHA:- CUTI. (III) 65. =(14–17).	86. Formless-sp: Inoperative C. 4 87. (Arūpāvacara kriya C.) 88. JAVANA 89. =(14–17). 20
18. Moral Supramundane C. 4 4 19. (Lokuttara Magga C.) 20. 21. J A V A N A 21		66. Resultant Supramundane C. 4 4 67. (Lokuttara Phala Javana). 68. JAVANA 69. =(18–21). 36 36	

Chart 3
MATERIAL QUALITIES - Their ARISING & GROUPING
(Rūpa-Samuṭṭhāna & Kalāpa)

1. ACTION (Kamma)

ARISING (samuṭṭhana)	ARISING (samuṭṭhāna)	GROUPING (kalāpa): vital-nonad	eye-decad	ear-dec:	nose-dec:	tongue-dec:	body-dec:	female-dec:	male-dec:	basis-dec:
A 1. INSEPARABLE MATERIAL QUALITIES	8	8	8	8	8	8	8	8	8	8
2. (element of space)	(1)									
______ B.										
______ C.										
______ D.										
E Heart Base	1									I
F. CONTROLLING MATERIAL FACULTIES.	8									
1. Eye (Sensitive material Qualities)			I							
2. Ear (Sensitive material Qualities)				I						
3. Nose (Sensitive material Qualities)					I					
4. Tongue (Sensitive material Qualities)						I				
5. Body (Sensitive material Qualities)							I			
6. Feminity (Sex)								I		
7. Masculinity (Sex)									I	
8. *VITAL PRINCIPLE*		1	1	1	1	1	1	1	1	1
	<u>18</u>	1. 9.	2. 10.	3. 10.	4. 10.	5. 10.	6. 10.	7. 10.	8. 10.	9. 10.

Chart 3 Continue ....

Chart 3
MATERIAL QUALITIES - Their ARISING & GROUPING
(Rūpa-Samuṭṭhāna & Kalāpa)

2. MIND (Citta)							
ARISING	GROUPING						
	ARISING (samuṭṭhāna)	pure octad	body intimation nonad.	vocal intimation decd.	un-decad, of Buoyancy etc.	do-decad of body int: Buo: etc.	tridecad of vocal intimation, sound, Buoyancy etc.
INSEPARABLE MATERIAL QUALITIES (element of space) B. Material qualities of Buoyancy, Pliancy and Adaptability	8 (1)	8	8	8	8	8	8
C. Sound (articulate) 1	3				3	3	3
D. intimation Vocal. 1	2			2			2
Body.	1		1			1	
	15	1. 8.	2. 9.	3. 10	4. 11.	5. 12.	6. 13.

Bibliography

For those who wish to make a more extensive study of Abhidhamma the following works are available:

A Manual of Abhidhamma. Nārada Mahāthera (Buddhist Publication Society, Kandy)

Abhidhamma for the Beginner. Egerton C. Baptist (M. D. Gunasena & Co. Ltd., 217, Olcott Mawatha, Colombo)

Compendium of Philosophy. Shwe Zan Aung (Pali Text Society, London)

The Psychology and Philosophy of Buddhism. Dr. W. F. Jayasuriya. (M.D. Gunasena & Co., Colombo)

Guide through the Abhidhamma Piṭaka. Nyanatiloka Mahāthera (Buddhist Publication Society, Kandy)

Abhidhamma Studies. Nyanaponika Mahāthera (Buddhist Publication Society)

By the same author:

"The Peerless Physician," in *Buddha the Healer.* (The Wheel No. 22)

"Purification of Mind" in The Wheel Nos. 39/40

The Way of Wisdom

The Five Spiritual Faculties

by

Edward Conze

WHEEL PUBLICATION NO. 65/66

Part I
The Five Spiritual Faculties

Spiritual progress depends on the emergence of five cardinal virtues—faith, vigour, mindfulness, concentration and wisdom. The conduct of the ordinary worldling is governed by his sense-based instincts and impulses. As we progress, new spiritual forces gradually take over, until in the end the five cardinal virtues dominate and shape everything we do feel and think. These virtues are called, in Sanskrit and Pāli, *indriya,* variously translated by faculties, controlling faculties, or spiritual faculties.[1] The same five virtues are called powers (*bala*) if emphasis is on the fact that they are "unshakable by their opposites."

1. Faith

Faith is called "the seed," and without it the plant of spiritual life cannot start at all. Without faith one can, as a matter of fact, do nothing worthwhile at all. This is true not only of Buddhism, but of all religions, and even the pseudo-religions of modern times, such as Communism. And this faith is much more than the mere acceptance of beliefs. It requires the combination of four factors—intellectual, volitional, emotional and social.

1. *Intellectually,* faith is an assent to doctrines which are not substantiated by immediately available direct factual evidence. To be a matter of faith, a belief must go beyond the available evidence and the believer must be willing and ready to fill up the gaps in the evidence with an attitude of patient and trusting acceptance. Faith, taken in this sense, has two opposites, i.e., a dull unawareness of the things which are worth believing in, and doubt or perplexity. In any kind of religion some assumptions are taken on trust and accepted on the authority of scriptures or teachers.

Generally speaking, faith is, however, regarded as only a preliminary step, as a merely provisional state. In due course

---

1. The word *indriya* is derived from the Vedic god Indra, the ruler of the gods in the ancient pantheon. Hence the word suggests the idea of dominance or control.

direct spiritual awareness will know that which faith took on trust, and longed to know: "Now we see through a glass darkly, but then face to face." Much time must usually elapse before the virtue of wisdom has become strong enough to support a vigorous insight into the true nature of reality. Until then quite a number of doctrinal points must be taken on faith.

What then in Buddhism are the objects of faith? They are essentially four: (1) the belief in karma and rebirth; (2) the acceptance of the basic teachings about the nature of reality, such as conditioned co-production, emptiness, etc.; (3) confidence in the "Three Refuges," the Buddha, the Dharma and the Order; and (4) a belief in the efficacy of the prescribed practices, and in Nirvāṇa as the final way out of our difficulties. I shall say more about them when I have dealt with the other aspects of faith.

2. In this sceptical age we, anyway, dwell far too much on the intellectual side of faith. *śraddhā* (Pāli: *saddhā*) the word we render as "faith," is etymologically akin to Latin *cor,* "the heart," and faith is far more a matter of the heart than of the intellect. It is, as Prof. Radhakrishnan incisively puts it, the "striving after self-realization by concentrating the powers of the mind on a given idea." *Volitionally,* faith implies a resolute and courageous act of will. It combines the steadfast resolution that one *will* do a thing with the self-confidence that one *can* do it. Suppose that people living on the one side of a river are doomed to perish from many enemies, diseases and famine. Safety lies on the other shore. The man of faith is then likened to the person who swims across the river, braving its dangers, saving himself and inspiring others by his example. Those without faith will go on dithering along the hither bank. The opposites to this aspect of faith are timidity, cowardice, fear, wavering, and a shabby, mean and calculating mentality.

3. *Emotionally,* faith is an attitude of serenity and lucidity. Its opposite here is worry, the state of being troubled by many things. It is said that someone who has faith loses the "five terrors," i.e., he ceases to worry about the necessities of life, about loss of reputation, death, unhappy rebirth and the impression he may make on an audience. It is fairly obvious that the burden of life must be greatly lightened by belief in karma, emptiness, or not-self. Even an unpleasant fate can be accepted more easily

when it is understood as a dispensation of justice, when vexations are explained as an inevitable retribution, when law seems to rule instead of blind chance, when even apparent loss is bound to turn into true gain. And if there is no self, what and whom do we worry about? If there is only one vast emptiness, what is there to disturb our radiance?

4. *Socially*, and that is more difficult to understand, faith involves trust and confidence in the Buddha and the Sangha. Its opposite here is the state of being submerged in cares about one's sensory social environment, cares which spring from either social pressure or social isolation. The break with the normal social environment is, of course, complete only in the case of the monk who, as the formula goes, "in faith forsakes his home." To a lesser extent it must be carried out by every practitioner of the Dharma, who must "live apart" from his society, in spirit if not in fact. The company of others and the help we expect from them are usually a mainstay of our sense of security. By going for refuge to the Buddha and the Sangha one turns from the visible and tangible to the invisible and elusive. By placing one's reliance on spiritual forces one gains the strength to disregard public opinion and social discouragement. Some measure of defiant contempt for the world and its ways is inseparable from a spiritual life. The spiritual man does not "belong" to his visible environment, in which he is bound to feel rather a stranger. He belongs to the community of the saints, to the family of the Buddha. Buddhism substitutes a spiritual for the natural environment, with the Buddha for the father, the *Prajñāpāramitā* for the mother, the fellow-seekers for brothers and sisters, relatives and friends. It is with these more invisible forces that one must learn to establish satisfactory social relations. In carrying out this task, faith requires a considerable capacity for renunciation.

This concludes our survey of the four factors which go into the making of faith. Like other spiritual qualities, faith is somewhat paradoxical in that in one sense it is a *gift* which one cannot obtain by merely wanting to, and in another sense it is a *virtue* that can be cultivated. The capacity for faith varies with the constitution of the individual and his social circumstances. It is usual to classify types of personality according to whether they are dominated by greed, hatred or confusion. Those who walk in greed are said to be more susceptible to faith than the other two, because of the kinship which exists between faith and greed. To quote Buddhaghosa (Vism III.75): "As on the unwholesome plane greed clings and takes no offence, so faith on the wholesome plane. As greed searches for objects of sense-desire, so faith for the qualities of morality, etc. As greed does not let go that which is harmful, so faith does not let go that which is beneficial."

As regards social conditions, there are ages of faith and ages of unbelief. The present age rather fosters unbelief. It puts a premium on intellectual smartness, so that faith is easily held to indicate nothing but a weak head or a lack of intellectual integrity. It multiplies the distractions from the sensory world to such an extent that the calm of the invisible world is harder to reach than ever. It exposes the citizen to so great a variety of conflicting viewpoints that he finds it hard to make a choice. The prestige of science, the concern with a high standard of living, and the disappearance of all institutions of uncontested authority are the chief foes of faith in our present-day society. It is largely a matter of temperament whether we believe that matters will improve in the near future.

As a virtue, faith is strengthened and built up by self-discipline, and not by discussing opinions. Intellectual difficulties are by no means the most powerful among the obstacles to faith. Doubts are inevitable, but how one deals with them depends on one's character. The first of our four "articles of faith" well illustrates this situation. There are many sound reasons for accepting the rebirth doctrine. This is not the place to expound them, and I must be content to refer the reader to the very impressive *East-West Anthology* on reincarnation which J. Head and S. L. Cranston have published in 1961 (New York, The Julian Press Inc.). Yet, although belief in rebirth is perfectly rational and does not conflict with any known fact, the range of the average person's vision is so limited that he has no access to the decisive evidence, which is direct and immediate experience.

The rebirth doctrine assumes at least two things: (1) that behind the natural causality which links together events in the world of sense there are other, invisible chains of a moral causality, which assures that all good acts are rewarded, all bad actions punished; and (2) that this chain of moral sequences is not interrupted by death, but continues from rebirth to rebirth. To the average person these two assumptions cannot be proved absolutely, conclusively and beyond the possibility of a doubt. However plausible they may seem on rational grounds, Buddhism teaches that they become a matter of direct experience only after the "superknowledges" (*abhijñā, abhiññā*) have been developed. The fourth "superknowledge" is the recollection of one's own previous rebirths, and the fifth the knowledge of the rebirths of other people, by which one "sees that whatever happens to them happens in accordance with their deeds." There are many well-authenticated cases of persons spontaneously remembering certain details of one or the other of their own previous lives, and these people obviously have an additional reason for belief in rebirth which is lacking in those who cannot recall ever having lived before. Full certitude on the issue is, however, given to those only who can, on the basis of the fourth *jhāna* and by taking definite prescribed and disciplined steps on emerging from that *jhāna*, "recall their manifold former lives," according to the well-known formula: "There I was, that was my name, that was my family, that was my caste, such was my food, this was the happiness, this the suffering which I experienced, this was the duration of my life-span. Deceased there I was born elsewhere and there had this name, etc." When a monk has practiced properly and successfully, "these things become as clear to him as if lit up by a lamp" (Vism XIII, 23).

Until that time comes, we cannot claim that we *fully know* the doctrine of karma and rebirth to be true. We take it partly on faith. And this faith of ours is maintained less by our dialectical skill as by the virtues of patience and courage. For we must be willing to wait patiently until we are spiritually ripe for the emergence of the super-knowledges, however far off that might seem to be. And secondly, we must be willing to take risks. Life nowhere offers a one hundred per cent security, and for our convictions least of all. Employed in gaining wealth a merchant must risk his property. Employed in taking life, a soldier must risk his own life. Employed in saving his soul, the spiritual man must risk his own soul. The stake automatically increases with the prospect of gain. Of course, we may be mistaken. I sometimes wonder what I would think if, on dying, I would not, as I now fondly imagine, wake up on the *Bardo* plane, but find myself confronted with Acheron and the three-headed Cerberus, or, worse still, were ill-treated with fire and brimstone in a Christian hell. The experience would, I admit, be rather disconcerting. All that I can say in the face of such uncertainty is that I am willing to take the consequences, and that I hope that my fund of boldness, audacity and good humour will not run out.

One has the choice to magnify intellectual doubts, or to minimize them. It seems not unreasonable that one should blame the difficulties of the teaching on one's own distance from the truth, one's own intellectual and moral imperfections. How can one expect to remember one's past lives, if at present one cannot even recall hour by hour what one did during one single day a mere month ago? If one hesitates to accept, as not immediately obvious, the doctrine that this world is the result of ignorance and of the craving of non-existent individuals for non-existent objects—is this not perhaps due to the very denseness of one's own ignorance, for which one can collect plenty of proofs all day long? Doubts are effectively overcome when one purifies one's own life, so as to become more worthy of knowledge. It is a condition of all learning that one accepts a great deal on trust, that one gives the teacher the benefit of the doubt. Otherwise one can learn nothing at all, and remains shut out from all truth. To have faith means to take a deep breath, to tear oneself away from the daily cares and concerns, and to turn resolutely to a wider and more abiding reality. At first we are, by ourselves, too stupid and inexperienced to see the tracks which lead to salvation. So we must put our trust in the Sages of the past, and listen intently to their words, dimmed by distance and the noise of the present day, but still just audible.

One last word about tolerance, without which faith remains raw and unsure of itself. It is a perpetual trial to our faith that we should constantly meet with people who believe differently. We are easily tempted to wish this irritant removed, to coerce others, if only by argument, and to annihilate them, if only by dubbing them fools. Intolerance for people of other faiths, though often mistaken for ardour, betrays nothing so much as doubts within oneself. We can, of course, always console ourselves by assuming that the others, in their own way, believe what we do, and that in the end it all comes to the same thing. But that does not always sound very convincing, and what we must, I am afraid, learn to do is to bear with their presence.

2. Vigour

Next to faith, vigour (Skt: *virya;* Pāli: *viriya*). Little need be said about the need for being energetic if one wants to achieve something. Without vigour, without strenuous effort, without perseverance, one obviously cannot make much progress. Everybody knows what "vigour" is, although a generation which made the fortune of the discoverers of "night-starvation" might wish that it had more of it.

The fact that faith and vigour are virtues does not, however, imply that they are good all through, and that, regardless of the consequences, they should be strengthened at all times. Excess is to be deprecated, even in virtues. All the five virtues must be regarded as one whole. Their balance and harmony is almost as important as the virtues themselves.[2] They support each other to some extent, but they also stand in each other's way. The one must sometimes be used to correct the excess of the other. In this way, concentration must come to the rescue of the latent faults of vigour. When vigour and energy have it all their own way, tranquillity is in danger. We all know people with a large dash of adrenalin in their blood, who are always busy, perhaps even "madly efficient," but not particularly restful. Vigour by itself leads to excitement, and has to be controlled by a development of concentrated calm.

Similarly, faith alone, without wisdom, can easily become mere credulity. Wisdom alone can teach what is worth believing. This can be illustrated by Don Quixote, who in literature is perhaps the purest embodiment of faith, and whose actions demonstrate that too much faith, by itself, is not necessarily a good thing. Cervantes' novel gives a fine and detailed description of all the chief attributes of faith. Don Quixote vigourously, fearlessly, without complaining, and even serenely endures all tribulations because he wants to help others, all of them equally, according to their needs. When he dashes into the middle of the boiling lake, he

2. See Selected Texts below, Section 5.

reaches the very height of self-abandonment of which faith as such is capable. "And just when he does not know what will happen to him, he finds himself among flowery fields beautiful beyond those of Elysium." His faith has conquered the senses, it transmutes the data of common-sense experience, and the barber's basin becomes Mambrino's helmet.[3] And yet, when we consider the intellectual basis of his faith, we find that it consists in nothing more than a belief in the truth and veracity of the Romances which describe the fictitious and not particularly edifying doings of the knight-errants of the past. This is the reason why his adventures form a sorry sight, why he is a caricature even of a knight of the Middle Ages, why, shorn of all common-sense, faith in this case becomes slightly pathological.

Mr. Blyth claims that "the Don Quixote of the First Part is Zen incarnate,"[4] that "the man who surpasses Hakuin, Rinzai, Eno, Daruma and Shakyamuni himself is Don Quixote de la Mancha, Knight Errant."[5] Zen, it seems, like all good things, can be abused. It is not very probable that, when the cloak of "Zen" is thrown over them, all donkeys do become tigers, all absurdities profundities. Irrationalism is not without its attractions, but can be overdone. To suggest that one scripture, one conviction, one faith is as good as another, smacks rather more of the spiritual nihilism of our present age, than of the wisdom of Seng-t'san. I admit that I have always liked Don Quixote for saying that the "perfection" of madness does not consist in going "mad for some actual reason or other" but "in running mad without the least constraint or necessity." But still I cannot help feeling that there is some difference, intangible perhaps, but nevertheless real, between the perfection of madness and the perfection of wisdom.

3. Don Quixote fights "commending himself to God and his mistress" and he feels himself as an instrument of Dulcinea who infuses valour into his arms. "She fights in me, she is victorious in me and I live and breathe in her, receive life and being itself from her." He thus belongs to the large band of those who sustain their faith by the love of a feminine being and his Dulcinea corresponds to the Virgin Mary of the Catholics and to the Tāra and Prajñāpāramitā of Mahāyāna Buddhism.

4. *Zen in English Literature,* 1948, p.199.

5. Ibid., p.201.

Don Quixote's faith was a rather puerile one, because he had no judgment, and his vision was defective. Blyth himself admits in the end that Don Quixote "lacks the Confucian virtue of Prudence, the balance of the powers of the mind" (p.210). I am not so sure about prudence, but the "balance of the powers of the mind" is certainly not only a Confucian, but also a Buddhist virtue, and a very essential one. Buddhaghosa, whom I am expounding here, leaves us in no doubt on this matter.[6] What distinguishes a bhikkhu from a knight-errant is that he is essentially sober and calm, that his view of the world is sweetly rational, that he avoids violence in the pursuit of his aims, and that his estimate of his own role in the world does not greatly exceed his actual size in relation to the universe.

3. Mindfulness

A Buddhist owes his soberness to the cultivation of the third virtue of *mindfulness* (Skt: *smṛti*, Pāli: *sati*). Whereas faith and vigour, when driven to excess, must be restrained by their counterparts, i.e., wisdom and tranquil concentration, the virtue of mindfulness does not share this disability. "Mindfulness should be strong everywhere. For it protects the mind from excitedness, into which it might fall since faith, vigour and wisdom may excite us;[7] and from indolence, into which it might fall since concentration favours indolence. Therefore, mindfulness is desirable everywhere, like a seasoning of salt in all sauces, like the prime minister in all state functions. Hence it is said: 'The Lord has declared mindfulness to be useful everywhere, for the mind finds refuge in mindfulness and mindfulness is its protector. Without mindfulness there can be no exertion or restraint of the mind.'"[8]

Although traces of it are not altogether absent in other religious and philosophical disciplines, in Buddhism alone mindfulness occupies a central position. If one were asked what distinguishes Buddhism from all other systems of thought, one

6. See Vism IV. 45–49.

7. Faith lends itself to emotional excitement; vigour to the excitement of doing things and wanting to do more; wisdom to the excitement of discovery.

8. Vism IV. 49.

would have to answer that it is the *dharma*-theory and the stress laid on mindfulness. Mindfulness is not only the seventh of the steps of the holy eightfold path, the third of the five virtues, and the first of the seven limbs of enlightenment. On occasions it is almost equated with Buddhism itself. So we read at the beginning of the Satipaṭṭhāna Sutta[9] that "the four applications of mindfulness are the one and only way (*ekāyano maggo*) that leads beings to purity, to the transcending of sorrow and lamentation, to the appeasement of pain and sadness, to entrance upon the right method and to the realization of Nirvāṇa." [10]

What then is "mindfulness"? The Abhidharma, guided by the etymology of the Sanskrit term (*smṛti* from the root √*smṝ*, "to remember"), defines it as an act of remembering which prevents ideas from "floating away," and which fights forgetfulness, carelessness and distraction. This definition by itself, though correct, does not really make the function of this virtue very clear to us today. The theoretical assumptions which underlie the various practices summed up in the word "mindfulness" are too much taken for granted. What one assumes is that the mind consists of two disparate parts—a depth which is calm and quiet, and a surface which is disturbed. The surface layer is in perpetual agitation and turmoil. The centre, at the bottom of the mind, beyond both the conscious and the unconscious mind as modern psychologists understand it, is quite still. The depth is, however, usually overlaid to such an extent that people remain incredulous when told of a submerged spot of stillness in their inmost hearts. In most cases the surface is so turbulent that the calm of the depth can be realized only in rare intervals.

Mindfulness and concentration are the two virtues which are concerned with the development of inward calm. The principal enemies of spiritual quietude are: (1) the senses; (2) the movements of the body; (3) the passions, wants and desires; and (4) discursive thinking. They have the power to be enemies when: (1) they are not subjected to any discipline; and (2) when the ego identifies itself with what takes place on the surface of the mind, participating

9. MN 10/M 157.

10. The commentary to this passage should be consulted. It has been translated in Bhikkhu Soma, *The Way of Mindfulness*, 1949, pp.18-31.

heartily in it, and the illusion arises that these activities are "my" doings, "my" concerns and the sphere in which "I" live and have my being. When thus busy with worldly things, we have neither strength nor freedom. In order to conquer these enemies of spiritual quietude we must: (1) withdraw the senses from their objects, as the tortoise draws in its limbs; (2) keep watch on our muscular movements; (3) cease wanting anything, and dissociate all wants from the ego; and (4) cut off discursive thinking.

By an effort of the imagination one must try to see oneself at rest, floating freely, with no force exerted on one's spiritual self. The practice of mindfulness then is a series of efforts which aim at maintaining this isolation. Mindfulness is the name given to the measures which we take to protect the patch of inner calm, which may at first not seem very large. One, as it were, draws a line round this domain and at its boundaries keeps watch on trespassers. The expectation is that conscious attention will disintegrate the power of the enemies, diminish their number, and dissociate them from the ego. However diverse in nature the numerous exercises which come under the heading of mindfulness may seem to be, they all have in common this one purpose, that of guarding the incipient and growing calm in one's heart.

1. First, as regards the *sensory stimuli,* there is the "restraint of the senses," also called the "guarding of the doors of the senses." For two reasons sense stimulation may disturb inner calm: (1) because it gives an occasion for undesirable states, like greed, hate, etc., to invade and flood the mind; (2) because attention to the sensory world, however necessary and apparently innocuous, distracts from the object of wisdom, which is the emptiness of *dharmas.* One cannot grasp what is meant by "restraint of the sense dominants," if one regards it as quite a natural thing that the mind should dwell on sense-linked objects. This is, indeed, most unnatural. In its natural purity thought abides in the calm contemplation of emptiness. The mind which sees, hears, etc., is a fallen mind.

The capacity of sense-experience to compel the mind to act in a certain way is greatly diminished if each sensory stimulus is examined at the point where it passes the threshold of consciousness. Attention, normally passive, involuntary and compulsive, is subjected to voluntary control. In the process of imposing some control on the senses one will be surprised to find how keen they are to function, how eager to find suitable objects with which to feed one's impulses and instincts, one's hopes and fears, one's interests and appetites, satisfactions and grievances. It is not so bad that one should see things, hear sounds, etc., but it is a threat to spiritual health when one gets interested and entranced, when one takes up what is seen and heard and seizes on it as a sign of what matters.

The practice of mindfulness is not confined to taking note of what enters the mind by way of the sense-organs. One also tries to determine what is allowed to enter, and to generally reduce the number of sensory impacts by restraining the use of the physical organ, for instance, when one walks with eyes directed only a few feet or yards ahead. In addition, by an effort of the will one refuses to co-operate with one's habitual impulses in building up a mere casual observation into a thing of moment to which one returns again and again. Finally the intruder is weakened and worn down by appropriate reflections. He is kept out of the heart and devalued—as trivial, as already passed, as nothing in particular, and by thinking that "this does not concern me at all, this means nothing to me, it is only a waste when salvation and Nirvāṇa are considered."

2. Secondly, as regards the *muscular movements of the body*—an unquiet body is a concomitant of a disturbed mind, both its cause and symptom. It is important to mindfulness that one should consciously notice the position and movement of the body when walking, eating, speaking, etc., and suppress and correct those movements which are uncontrolled, hasty and uncoordinated. This practice can, it is true, not be carried out at all times. In London traffic, for instance, the unhurried and unflurried demeanour of the mindful has little survival value. Where, however, it can be applied, we come to cherish this exercise which pulls us together, sometimes to an amazing extent in an amazingly short time. Insignificant as it may seem, compared with the splendours of Buddhist art and metaphysics, this training is their indispensable foundation stone. It is by his dignified and self-possessed deportment that the bhikkhu is recognized. And, of course, we should not forget that the mindful attention to muscular movements includes the breathing practices, which are a most fruitful source of insight.

3. Where we have to face the disturbance of the passions and of *stray thoughts* in general, the defence of our inward calm becomes more difficult. Mindfulness itself turns into incipient concentration.

At this point one may ask whether the practice of the five cardinal virtues, from faith to wisdom, is at all likely to be furthered by writing articles about them. It is, of course, not an entirely useless undertaking to guard the traditional teaching from current misunderstandings, quite apart from the pleasure of putting fleas into peoples' ears, and fomenting discussions about the importance of faith, or the value of erudition. But what about the virtues themselves? Thomas à Kempis once said that he would rather feel compunction than know the definition of it. What matters to a Buddhist is that he should be strong in faith, vigour, mindfulness, concentration and wisdom, and what use to him is the knowledge of how they are defined? Detailed advice on how these virtues should be practiced, it is true, can never be given in articles written for the general reader. Such advice must always be addressed to one person at a time, must take their individual constitution into account, and can, therefore, be given only by word of mouth.

On the other hand, if mindfulness is a virtue, then the ability to recollect one's own virtues is also a feature of the Buddhist life. And how can one attend to the presence or absence of mental states in oneself if one is unable to recognize them for what they are? The Satipaṭṭhāna Sutta recommends systematic meditation on the wholesome and unwholesome mental states which arise in the mind. To quote the Sutta, one knows, for instance: (1) when there is vigour that there is vigour; (2) when there is no vigour that there is no vigour; (3) how the vigour which did not exist came to be produced; and (4) how and under what conditions it will grow to greater perfection. Psychology is so vital to Buddhist instruction because one cannot know anything definite about the furniture of one's mind unless one is acquainted with the categories into which mental conditions can be analyzed. A mindful man is well informed about his own mental condition. His capacity for introspection is highly developed. And his interest in his own mind will not really make him self-centred as long as he remembers that he has to deal with the rise and fall of impersonal processes.

In addition, in the case of the higher mental states, rational clarity is imperative if constant self-deception and wasteful groping in the dark are to be avoided. In a new country a map is helpful so that one may know where one is. The manuals of mystical theology written by the practicing contemplatives of the Catholic Church are also rich in descriptions of the sublimer virtues.

But this is not all. Where the Buddhist virtues are described for a lay audience one must not omit to mention the all-important fact that the upper ranges of these virtues demand a reformation of the conduct of life which is greater than almost any layman is willing to undertake. The higher mindfulness, and nearly the whole range of concentration and wisdom, presuppose a degree of withdrawal from the world which is incompatible with the life of an ordinary citizen. Those who are unwilling to achieve a radical seclusion from the world can practice these virtues only in a very rudimentary form. It is quite idle to pretend that they do not involve a complete break with the established habits of life and thought. Unless we make the sacrifices involved in withdrawing from the world, we are bound to remain strangers to the fullness of mindfulness, concentration and wisdom.

But if the monastic life is a necessary condition for these virtues, why talk about them at all? Partly because it is salutary, though painful, that we should see their absence in us, and partly because they constitute the subjective counterpart of the scriptures which we read. The Suttas describe the world as it appears on a spiritual level on which concentration and wisdom have come to maturity. The understanding of the scriptures is furthered by an understanding of the subjective attitude which corresponds to them. And so, although we are forced to go beyond the range of our immediate experience, and although the description tends to become more intangible as it rises to loftier heights, we will now, leaving aside the higher ranges of mindfulness, try to explain the traditional definitions of concentration and wisdom, as they are handed down to us.

4. Concentration

Concentration (*samādhi*) continues the work of mindfulness. It deepens our capacity to regain the peaceful calm of our inner nature. But here we are at once faced with the difficulty that in

Buddhist psychology "concentration" occurs twice: (1) as a factor essential to all thought; and (2) as a special, and rather rare, virtue.

1. In its simplest form, concentration is the narrowing of the field of attention in a manner and for a time determined by the will. The mind is made one-pointed, does not waver, does not scatter itself, and it becomes steady like the flame of a lamp in the absence of wind. Without a certain degree of one-pointedness no mental activity at all can take place. Each mental act lasts, strictly speaking, for one moment only, and is at once followed by another. The function of concentration is to provide some stability in this perpetual flux, by enabling the mind to stand in, or on, the same object, without distraction, for more than one moment. In addition it is a synthetic quality (*samādhi* = synthesis), that binds together a number of mental states which arise at the same time, "as water binds the lather of soap."

Buddhaghosa stresses the fact that intellectual concentration is also found in unwholesome thoughts. The mind must be undistracted so that the murderer's knife does not miss, the theft does not miscarry. A mind of single intent is capable of doing what it does more effectively, be it good or bad. The higher degrees of this kind of concentration owe much to the presence of the "hunting instinct," and can best be observed in a stoat following a rabbit. Intellectual concentration is a quality which is ethically and spiritually neutral. Many scientific workers have an unusually high capacity for concentrated thought. Anyone acquainted with the "scientific humanists" who inhabit our big cities will, however, agree that their intellectual achievements are not conducive to either peace of mind or spiritual progress. When Sir Isaac Newton boiled his watch instead of the egg his landlady had given him, he thereby showed the intensity with which he focussed his mind on his intellectual task. But the result of his intellectual labours has been to cast a dark shadow over the spiritual radiance of the universe, and ever since, the celestial harmonies have become nearly inaudible. As H. W. Longfellow, in his poem "The Arsenal at Springfield," has put it:

> Is it, O man, with such discordant noises,
> With such accursed instruments as these,
> Thou drownest Nature's sweet and kindly voices,
> And jarrest the celestial harmonies?

2. How then does concentration as a spiritual virtue differ from concentration as a condition of the intellect? Spiritual or transic concentration results less from intellectual effort than from a rebirth of the whole personality, including the body, the emotions, and the will. It cannot possibly be achieved without some discipline over the body, since we must be able to endure the prescribed posture, practice the prescribed breathing exercises, and so on. It is further built on a change of outlook which we can well describe as "ethical." Tradition is quite unambiguous on this point. Before spiritual concentration can be even approached, we must have stilled or suppressed five vices, which are known as the "five hindrances": sense desire, ill will, sloth and torpor, excitedness and sense of guilt, and doubt. Where these hindrances are present, where concentrated thought is fused with greed, the desire to excel, to get a good job, etc., there concentration as a spiritual virtue is not found.

In this sense physical ease and self-purification are the first two distinctive features of spiritual concentration. The third is the shift in attention from the sensory world to another subtler realm. The methods by which this shift is effected are traditionally known as the four trances (*jhāna*) and the four formless attainments. They are essentially a training in increasing introversion, achieved by progressively diminishing the impact of the outer stimuli. As a result of their successful withdrawal and renunciation the spiritually concentrated release the inward calm which dwells in their hearts. This concentration cannot be won, however, unless no attention is given to sensory data, and everything sensory is viewed as equally unimportant. Subjectively it is marked by a soft, tranquil and pacified passivity, objectively by the abstraction into an unearthly world of experience which lifts one above the world, and bestows a certainty greater than anything the senses may teach. The experience is so satisfying that it burns up the world, and only its cold ashes are found when one returns to it.

5. Wisdom

And so we come to wisdom (Skt: *prajñā;* Pāli: *paññā*), the highest virtue of all.

"Wisdom is based on concentration, because of the saying: 'One who is concentrated knows, sees what really is.'"[11] Is concentration then an indispensable pre-condition of wisdom? The answer lies in distinguishing three stages of wisdom, according to whether it operates on the level of: (1) *learning* about what tradition has to say concerning the psychological and ontological categories which form the subject-matter of wisdom; (2) *discursive reflection* on the basic facts of life; and (3) *meditation development.*[12] The third alone requires the aid of transic concentration,[13] whereas without it there can be proficiency in the first two. And the wisdom which consists of learning and reflection should not be despised.

The main stream of Buddhist tradition has always greatly esteemed *learning.* Our attitude to the apple of knowledge differs from that of many Christians. On the whole, we regard it as rather more nourishing than baneful. The wisdom, which is the fifth and crowning virtue, is not the wisdom that can be found in the untutored child of nature, the corny sage of the backwoods, or the self-made philosopher of the suburbs. It can operate only after a great deal of traditional information has been absorbed, a great deal of sound learning acquired. The required skill in metaphysical and psychological analysis would be impossible without a good knowledge of the material on which this skill ought to be exercised. From this point of view learning is perhaps less to be regretted than its absence.

The second stage, after learning, is *reflection,* which is an operation of the intellect. Even the relative beginner can greatly increase his wisdom by discursive meditations on the basic facts of life. Finally, it is on the level of *mental development* (*bhāvanā*) that this meditation technique reaches its maturity, and then it does, indeed, require the aid of mindfulness and concentration.

"Wisdom" is, of course, only a very approximate equivalent of *prajñā.* To the average person nowadays "wisdom" seems to

11. S III 13; Vism XIV.7.
12. E.g., *Abhidharmakoṣa*, VI, pp.142-144.
13. *Triṃśikā* by Vasubandhu, ed. S. Levi, 1925–26.

denote a compound made up of such qualities as sagacity, prudence, a well-developed sense of values, serenity, and sovereignty over the world won by the understanding of the mode of its operation. The Buddhist conception of "wisdom" is not unlike this, but more precise. It is best clarified by first giving its connotations, and then its actual definition.

As for the connotations, we read in the *Dhammasaṅgaṇi*:[14] "On that occasion the dominant[15] of wisdom is wisdom, understanding,[16] search, research, search for *dhamma*;[17] discernment, discrimination, differentiation, erudition, expert skill, subtlety, clarity,[18] reflection, investigation,[19] amplitude,[20] sagacity,[21] a guide (to true welfare and to the marks as they truly are), insight, comprehension, a goad (which urges the mind to move back on the right track); wisdom, wisdom as virtue, wisdom as strength (because ignorance cannot dislodge it), the sword of wisdom (which cuts through the defilements), the lofty (and overtowering) height of wisdom, the light,[22] lustre and splendour of wisdom, the treasure[23] of wisdom, absence of delusion, search for *dharmas*, right view." From mere

---

14. Sec. 16; commentary in *Atthasālinī*, PTS, 1897 (=Asl), pp.147-49.

15. *Indriya*. As 122: "Through overwhelming ignorance it is a 'dominant' in the sense of 'dominant influence'; or it is a 'dominant' because by exercising discernment (*dassana*) it dominates (associated *dharmas*)."

16. As 123: "As a clever surgeon knows which foods are suitable and which are not, so wisdom, when it arises, understands *dharmas* as wholesome or unwholesome, serviceable or unserviceable, low or exalted, dark or bright, similar or dissimilar." Similarly *Abhidharmakoṣa*, I,3; II,154.

17. Dhamma: the four holy Truths (Asl).

18. *Vebhabyā; aniccādinaṃ vibhāvanā-bhāva-vasena*. Or "a critical attitude"?

19. Or "examination."

20. Or "breadth." Wisdom is rich and abundant, or massive.

21. *Medha;* also "mental power." "As lightning destroys even stone-pillars, so wisdom smashes the defilements; alternatively, it is able to grasp and bear in mind."

22. *Milindapañhā*, I 61: "It is like a lamp which a man would take into a dark house. It would dispel the darkness, would illuminate, shed light, and make the forms in the house stand out clearly."

23. Because it gives delight, is worthy of respect (or "variegated"), hard to get and hard to manifest, incomparable and a source of enjoyment to illustrious beings.

cleverness wisdom is distinguished by its spiritual purpose, and we are told expressly[24] that it is designed "to cut off the defilements."

Now to the actual definition: "Wisdom penetrates[25] into *dharmas* as they are in themselves. It disperses the darkness of delusion, which covers up the own-being of *dharmas*."[26]

What then does wisdom meditate about? Wisdom may be held to concern itself with three possible topics: (1) true reality; (2) the meaning of life; (3) the conduct of life. Buddhist tradition assumes that the second and third depend on the first. In its essence wisdom is the strength of mind which permits contact with the true reality, which is also called the realm of *dharmas*. Delusion, folly, confusion, ignorance and self-deception are the opposites of wisdom. It is because ignorance, and not sin, is the root evil that wisdom is regarded as the highest virtue. A holiness which is devoid of wisdom is not considered impossible, but it cannot be gained by the path of knowledge, to which alone these descriptions apply. The paths of faith, of love, of works, etc., have each their own several laws.

As the unfaltering penetration into the true nature of objects, wisdom is the capacity to meditate in certain ways about the dharmic constituents of the universe. The rules of that meditation have been laid down in the scriptures, particularly in the Abhidharma, and a superb description can be found in the latter part of Buddhaghosa's *Path of Purification.* Mindfulness and concentration were, as we saw, based on the assumption of a duality in the mind—between its calm depth and its excited surface. Wisdom similarly assumes a duality between the surface and depth of all things. Objects are not what they appear to be. Their true reality, in which they stand out as *dharmas,* is opposed to their appearance to commonsense, and much strength of wisdom is required to go beyond the deceptive appearance and to penetrate to the reality of *dharmas* themselves.

24. *Milindapañhā,* as translated in my *Buddhist Scriptures,* 151–52 (see Appendix, Ia).

25. As 123: "This penetration is unfaltering (*akkhalita*), like the penetration of an arrow shot by a skilled archer."

26. Vism XIV.7. *Dhammasabhāva-paṭivedhalakkhaṇā paññā; dhammānaṃ sabhāvapaṭicchādaka-mohandhakāra-viddhaṃsanarasā.*

Part II
Selected Texts

1. The Five Faculties

(a) From the Milindapañhā

The king said: "Is it through wise attention that people become exempt from further rebirth?"—"Yes, that is due to wise attention, and also to wisdom, and the other wholesome *dharmas.*"—"But is not wise attention the same as wisdom?"—"No, Your Majesty. Attention is one thing, and wisdom another. Sheep and goats, oxen and buffaloes, camels and asses have attention, but wisdom they have not."—"Well put, Venerable Nāgasena."

The king said: "What is the mark of attention, and what is the mark of wisdom?"—"Consideration is the mark of attention, cutting off that of wisdom."—"How is that? Give me a simile."—"You know barley-reapers, I suppose?"—"Yes, I do."—"How then do they reap the barley?"—"With the left hand they seize a bunch of barley, in the right hand they hold a sickle, and they cut the barley off with that sickle."—"Just so, Your Majesty, the yogin seizes his mental processes with his attention, and by his wisdom he cuts off the defilements."—"Well put, Venerable Nāgasena."

The king said: "When you just spoke of 'the other wholesome *dharmas*,' which ones did you mean?"—"I meant morality, faith, vigour, mindfulness and concentration."—"And what is the mark of morality?"—"Morality has the mark of providing a basis for all wholesome *dharmas*, whatever they may be. When based on morality, all the wholesome *dharmas* will not dwindle away."—"Give me an illustration."—"As all plants and animals which increase, grow, and prosper, do so with the earth as their support, with the earth as their basis, just so the yogin, with morality as his support, with morality as his basis, develops the five cardinal virtues, i.e., the cardinal virtues of faith, vigour, mindfulness, concentration, and wisdom."

"Give me a further illustration."

"As the builder of a city when constructing a town first of all clears the site, removes all stumps and thorns, and levels it; and only after that he lays out and marks off the roads and cross-roads, and so builds the city, even so the yogin develops the five cardinal virtues with morality as his support, with morality as his basis."

The king said: "What is the mark of *faith?*"—"Faith makes serene, and it leaps forward."—"And how does faith make serene?"—"When faith arises it arrests the five hindrances, and the heart becomes free from them, clear, serene and undisturbed."—"Give me an illustration."—"A universal monarch might on his way, together with his fourfold army, cross over a small stream. Stirred up by the elephants and horses, by the chariots and infantry, the water would become disturbed, agitated and muddy. Having crossed over, the universal monarch would order his men to bring some water for him to drink. But the king would possess a miraculous water-clearing gem, and his men, in obedience to his command, would throw it into the stream. Then at once all fragments of vegetation would float away, the mud would settle at the bottom, the stream would become clear, serene and undisturbed, and fit to be drunk by the universal monarch. Here the stream corresponds to the heart, the monarch's men to the yogin, the fragments of vegetation and the mud to the defilements, and the miraculous water-clearing gem to faith."

"And how does faith leap forward?"—"When the yogin sees that the hearts of others have been set free, he leaps forward, by way of aspiration, to the various fruits of the holy life, and he makes efforts to attain the yet unattained, to find the yet unfound, to realize the yet unrealized."—"Give me an illustration."—"Suppose that a great cloud were to burst over a hill-slope. The water then would flow down the slope, would first fill all the hill's clefts, fissures, and gullies, and would then run into the river below, making its banks overflow on both sides. Now, suppose further that a great crowd of people had come along, and unable to size up either the width or the depth of the river, should stand frightened and hesitating on the bank. But then some man would come along, who, conscious of his own strength and power, would firmly tie on his own loin-cloth and jump across the river. And the great crowd of people, seeing him on the other side, would cross likewise. Even so the yogin, when he has seen that the hearts of others have been set free, leaps forward, by aspiration, to the various fruits of the holy life, and he makes efforts to attain the yet unattained, to find the yet unfound, to realize the yet unrealized. And this is what the Lord has said in the Saṃyutta Nikāya:

By faith the flood is crossed,
By wakefulness the sea;
By vigour ill is passed;
By wisdom cleansed is he."

"Well put, Nāgasena!"

The king asked: "And what is the mark of *vigour?*"—"Vigour props up, and, when propped up by vigour, all the wholesome *dharmas* do not dwindle away."—"Give me a simile."—"If a man's house were falling down, he would prop it up with a new piece of wood, and, so supported, that house would not collapse."

The king asked: "And what is the mark of *mindfulness?*"—"Calling to mind and taking up."

"How is calling to mind a mark of mindfulness?"—"When mindfulness arises, one calls to mind the *dharmas* which participate in what is wholesome and unwholesome, blameable and blameless, inferior and sublime, dark and light, i.e., these are the four applications of mindfulness, these the four right efforts, these the four roads to psychic power, these the five cardinal virtues, these the five powers, these the seven limbs of enlightenment, this is the holy eightfold path; this is calm, this insight, this knowledge and this emancipation. Thereafter the yogin tends those *dharmas* which should be tended, and he does not tend those which should not be tended; he partakes of those *dharmas* which should be followed, and he does not partake of those which should not be followed. It is in this sense that calling to mind is a mark of mindfulness."—"Give me a simile."—"It is like the treasurer of a universal monarch, who each morning and evening reminds his royal master of his magnificent assets: 'So many elephants you have, so many horses, so many chariots, so much infantry, so many gold coins, so much bullion, so much property; may Your Majesty bear this in mind.' In this way he calls to mind his master's wealth."

"And how does mindfulness take up?"—"When mindfulness arises, the outcome of beneficial and harmful *dharmas* is examined in this way: 'These *dharmas* are beneficial, these harmful; these *dharmas* are helpful, these unhelpful.' Thereafter the yogin removes the harmful *dharmas,* and takes up the beneficial ones; he removes the unhelpful *dharmas,* and takes up the helpful ones. It is in this sense that mindfulness takes up."—"Give me a comparison."—"It is like the invaluable adviser of a universal monarch who knows what is beneficial and what is harmful to his royal master, what is helpful and what is unhelpful. Thereafter what is harmful and unhelpful can be removed, what is beneficial and helpful can be taken up."

The king asked: "And what is the mark of *concentration?*"—"It stands at the head. Whatever wholesome *dharmas* there may be, they all are headed by concentration, they bend towards concentration, lead to concentration, incline to concentration."—"Give me a comparison."—"It is as with a building with a pointed roof: whatever rafters there are, they all converge on the top, bend towards the top, meet at the top, and the top occupies the most prominent place. So with concentration in relation to the other wholesome *dharmas.*"—"Give me a further comparison."—"If a king were to enter battle with his fourfold army, then all his troops—the elephants, cavalry, chariots and infantry—would be headed by him, and would be ranged around him. Such is the position of concentration in relation to the other wholesome *dharmas.*"

The king then asked: "What then is the mark of *wisdom?*"—"Cutting off is, as I said before, one mark of wisdom. In addition it illuminates."—"And how does wisdom illuminate?"—"When wisdom arises, it dispels the darkness of ignorance, generates the illumination of knowledge, sheds the light of cognition, and makes the holy truths stand out clearly. Thereafter the yogin, with his correct wisdom, can see impermanence, ill, and not-self."—"Give me a comparison."—"It is like a lamp which a man would take into a dark house. It would dispel the darkness, would illuminate, shed light, and make the forms in the house stands out clearly."—"Well put, Venerable Nāgasena."

Milindapañhā, pp. 51–62; translated by Edward Conze.

(b) From the Akṣayamati Sūtra

The five faculties are faith, vigour, mindfulness, concentration, and wisdom. Here what is *faith?* By this faith one has faith in four *dharmas.* Which four? He accepts the right view which assumes renewed becoming in the world of birth-and-death; he puts his trust in the ripening of karma, and knows that he will experience the fruit of any karma, that he may have done; even to save his life he does not do any evil deed. He has faith in the mode of life of a Bodhisattva, and, having taken up this discipline, he does not long for any other vehicle. He believes when he hears all the doctrines which are characterized by the true, clear, and profound knowledge of conditioned co-production, by such terms as lack of self, absence of a being, absence of a soul, absence of a person; and by emptiness, the signless and the wishless. He follows none of the false doctrines, and believes in all the qualities (*dharmas*) of a Buddha, his powers, grounds of self-confidence, and all the rest; and when in his faith he has left behind all doubts, he brings about in himself those qualities of a Buddha. This is known as the virtue of faith. His *vigour* consists of his bringing about (in himself) the *dharmas* in which he has faith. His *mindfulness* consists in his preventing the qualities which he brings about by vigour from being destroyed by forgetfulness. His *concentration* consists in his fixing his one-pointed attention on these very same qualities. With the faculty of *wisdom* he contemplates those *dharmas* on which he has fixed his one-pointed attention, and penetrates to their reality. The cognition of those *dharmas* which arises in himself and which has no outside condition is called the virtue of wisdom. Thus these five virtues, together, are sufficient to bring forth all the qualities of a Buddha.

Akṣayamati Sūtra (quoted in *Śikṣāsamuccaya*); translated by Edward Conze.

2. The Restraint of the Senses

(a) From Aśvaghoṣa's Saundaranandakāvya

By taking your stand on mindfulness you must hold back from the sense-objects your senses, unsteady by nature. Fire, snakes, and lightning are less inimical to us than our own senses, so much more dangerous. For they assail us all the time. Even the most vicious enemies can attack only some people at some times, and not at others, but everybody is always and everywhere weighed down by his senses. And people do not go to hell because some enemy has knocked them down and cast them into it; it is because they have been knocked down by their unsteady senses that they are helplessly dragged there. Those attacked by external enemies may, or may not, suffer injury to their souls; but those who are weighed down by the senses suffer in body and soul alike. For the five senses are rather like arrows which have been smeared with the poison of fancies, have cares for their feathers, and happiness for their points, and fly about in the space provided by the range of the sense-objects; shot off by *Kāma,* the God of Love, they hit men in their very hearts as a hunter hits a deer, and if men do not know how to ward off these arrows, they will be their undoing; when they come near us we should stand firm in self-control, be agile and steadfast, and ward them off with the great armour of mindfulness. As a man who has subdued his enemies can everywhere live and sleep at ease and free from care, so can he who has pacified his senses. For the senses constantly ask for more by way of worldly objects, and normally behave like voracious dogs who can never have enough. This disorderly mob of the senses can never reach satiety, not by any amount of sense-objects; they are rather like the sea, which one can go on indefinitely replenishing with water.

In this world the senses cannot be prevented from being active, each in its own sphere. But they should not be allowed to grasp either the general features of an object, or its particularities. When you have beheld a sight-object with your eyes, you must merely determine the basic element (which it represents, e.g., it is a sight-object), and should not under any circumstances fancy it as, say, a "woman" or a "man." But if now and then you have inadvertently grasped something as a "woman" or a "man," you should not follow that up by determining the hairs, teeth, etc., as lovely. Nothing should be subtracted from the datum, nothing added to it; it should be seen as it really is, as what it is like in real truth.

If you thus try to look continually for the true reality in that which the senses present to you, covetousness and aversion will soon be left without a foothold. Coveting ruins those living beings who are bent on sensuous enjoyment by means of pleasing forms, like an enemy with a friendly face who speaks loving words, but plans dark deeds. But what is called "aversion" is a kind of anger directed towards certain objects, and anyone who is deluded enough to pursue it is bound to suffer for it either in this or a future life. Afflicted by their likes and dislikes, as by excessive heat or cold, men will never find either happiness or the highest good as long as they put their trust in the unsteady senses.

Saundaranandakāvya, XIII, 30–56; translated by Edward Conze.

(b) From the Prajñāpāramitā

The Lord: When he practices the perfection of meditation for the sake of other beings his mind becomes undistracted. For he reflects that "even worldly meditation is hard to accomplish with distracted thoughts, how much more so is full enlightenment. Therefore, I must remain undistracted until I have won full enlightenment."...

Moreover, Subhūti, a Bodhisattva, beginning with the first thought of enlightenment, practices the perfection of meditation. His mental activities are associated with the knowledge of all modes when he enters into meditation. When he has seen forms with his eye, he does not seize upon them as signs of realities which concern him, nor is he interested in the accessory details. He sets himself to restrain that which, if he does not restrain his organ of sight, might give him occasion for covetousness, sadness or other evil and unwholesome *dharmas* to reach his heart. He watches over the organ of sight. And the same with the other five sense-organs—ear, nose, tongue, body and mind.

Whether he walks or stands, sits or lies down, talks or remains silent, his concentration does not leave him. He does not fidget with his hands or feet, or twitch his face; he is not incoherent in his speech, confused in his senses, exalted or uplifted, fickle or idle, agitated in body or mind. Calm is his body, calm is his voice, calm is his mind. His demeanour shows contentment, both in private and public... He is frugal, easy to feed, easy to serve, of good life and habits; though in a crowd he dwells apart; even and unchanged, in gain and loss; not elated, not cast down.

Thus in happiness and suffering, in praise and blame, in fame and disrepute, in life or death, he is the same unchanged, neither elated nor cast down. And so with foe or friend, with what is pleasant or unpleasant, with holy or unholy men, with noises or music, with forms that are dear or undear, he remains the same, unchanged, neither elated nor cast down, neither gratified nor thwarted. And why? Because he sees all *dharmas* as empty of marks of their own, without true reality, incomplete and uncreated.

Prajñāpāramitā, ch. 68; translated by Edward Conze.

(c) From the Visuddhimagga

This is the morality which consists in the restraint of the senses: "Here someone: (1) having seen a form with his eye, does not seize on its general appearance, or the (accessory) details of it. That which might, so long as he dwells unrestrained as to the (controlling) force of the eye, give occasion for covetous, sad, evil and unwholesome *dharmas* to flood him, that he sets himself to restrain; he guards the controlling force of the eye, and brings about its restraint. And likewise (2) when he has heard sounds with the ear, (3) smelled smells with the nose, (4) tasted tastes with the tongue, (5) touched touchables with the body, (6) cognized mind-objects (*dharmas*) with the mind." (M I 180).

Having seen a form with his eye: when he has seen a form with the visual consciousness which is capable of seeing forms, and which in normal language is usually called the "eye," though it actually is its tool. For the Ancients have said: "The eye cannot see forms because it is without thought; thought cannot see forms because it is without eye. When the object knocks against the door (of sight) one sees with the thought which has eye-sensibility for its basis." In the expression "one sees with the eye," only accessory equipment is indicated, just as one may say, "one shoots with a bow" (and not "with an arrow"). Therefore, the meaning here is: "having seen form with visual consciousness."

He does not seize on its general appearance (lit. "the sign"): he does not seize on its appearance as man or woman, or its appearance as attractive, etc., which makes it into a basis for the defiling passions. But he stops at what is actually seen. *He does not seize on the details of it:* he does not seize on the variety of its accessory features, like the hands or feet, the smile, the laughter, the talk, the looking here, the looking away, etc., which are in common parlance called "details" (*anubyañjana*) because they manifest the defiling passions, by again and again (*anu anu*) tainting with them (*byañjanato*). But he seizes only on that which is really there, i.e., the impurity of the 32 parts of the body) like Mahātissa, the Elder, who lived on Mount Cetiya. Once that Elder went from Mount Cetiya to Anuradhapura, to gather alms. In a certain family the daughter-in-law had quarrelled with her husband, and adorned and beautified like a heavenly maiden, she left Anuradhapura early in the morning, and went away to stay with some relatives. On the way she saw the Elder, and, as her mind was perverted, she gave a loud laugh. The Elder looked to see what was the matter; he acquired, at the sight of her teeth (bones), the notion of repulsiveness (impurity), and thereby reached Arahatship... The husband who ran after her on same road, saw the Elder, and asked him whether he had by any chance seen a woman. The Elder replied:

> "Whether what went along here
> Was a man or a woman, I do not know.
> But a collection of bones is moving
> Now along this main road."

[*That which might,* etc.: that which might be the reason, or that non-restraint of the faculty of the eye which might be the cause, why in this person, when he *dwells* without having restrained the faculty of the eye with the gate of mindfulness, i.e., when he has left the door of the eye open, such *dharmas* as covetousness, etc., *flood* him, i.e., pursue and submerge him.

That he sets himself to restrain:] he sets himself to close this faculty of the eye with the gate of mindfulness. And one who sets himself to do that, of him it is said that he *guards the controlling force of the eye,* and *brings about its restraint.*

But it is not with reference to the faculty of the eye itself that there is restraint or non-restraint (i.e., it does not apply to the initial stage of the impact of stimulus on the eye), and it is not concerning the eye considered as a sensitive organ that mindfulness arises, or the lack of it. But it is at (the stage of the apperception of the object, with such and such a meaning and significance, and the volitional reaction to it, which is technically known as) the "impulsive moment," that there is lack of restraint, if and when immorality arises then, or lack of mindfulness, or lack of cognition, lack of patience or laziness. Nevertheless one speaks of the non-restraint of the sense of sight. And why? Because when the mind is in that condition, also the door (of the eye) is unguarded. The situation can be compared with that of a city: when its four gates are unguarded, then, although in the interior of the city the doors of the houses, the storerooms and private rooms are well guarded, nevertheless all the property in the city is actually unguarded and unprotected, and robbers can, once they have entered through the city gates, do whatever they like. In the same sense also the door (of the eye) is unguarded when, in consequence of the arising of immorality, etc., there is lack of restraint at the "impulsive moment."

But when morality, etc., arise at that moment, then the door (of sight) also is guarded. Just again as with the city: When the city-gates are well guarded, then, although in the interior the doors of the houses, etc., are unguarded, nevertheless all the property in the city is actually well guarded and well protected; for the city-gates being closed, robbers cannot enter. Just so also the door (of the eye) is guarded when morality, etc., arise at the "impulsive moment." The same explanation applies to: when he has heard sounds with the ear, etc. The restraint of the senses thus consists, in short, in the avoiding of the seizing of the general appearance, etc., of sight-objects, etc., which lead to one's being pursued by the defiling passions.

And it should be achieved through mindfulness. For it is effected by mindfulness, in so far as the sense-organs when they are governed by mindfulness, can no longer be influenced by convetousness, etc. Therefore, we should remember the "Fire Sermon" (S IV 168) which says: "It were better, monks, if the eye were stroked with a heated iron bar, afire, ablaze, aflame, than that one should seize on either the general appearance or the details of the forms of which the eye is aware." The disciple should achieve a thorough restraint of the senses, in that, by unimpaired mindfulness, he prevents that seizing on the general appearance, etc., which makes the consciousness which proceeds through the door of the eye, etc., with forms, etc., for its range (province), liable to be flooded (influenced) by covetousness, etc.

And one should become like Cittagutta, the Elder, who lived in the great Kurandaka Cave. In that cave there was a delightful painting which showed the seven Buddhas leaving for the homeless life. One day numerous monks were wandering about in the cave, going from lodging to lodging. They noticed the painting and said: "What a delightful painting, Venerable Bhikkhu!" The Elder replied: "For more than sixty years, brethren, I have lived in this cave, and I have never known whether there is a painting here or whether there is not. Today only I have learned it from you people, who use your eyes." For all that time during which the Elder had lived there, he had never lifted up his eyes and looked more closely at the cave. At the entrance to the cave there was a large ironwood tree. To that also the Elder had never looked up; but he knew that it was in flower when each year he saw the filaments which had fallen down on the ground.

All the sons of good family who have their own welfare at heart should, therefore, remember:

"Let not the eye wander like forest ape,
Or trembling wood deer, or affrighted child.
The eyes should be cast downwards; they should look
The distance of a yoke; he shall not serve
His thought's dominion, like a restless ape."

Vism I.42, 53–59, 100, 104–5, 109; transl. by Edward Conze.

3. The Control of the Mind

The Sutta on the Composition of Ideas:[27]

[If, whilst attending to a certain sign, there arise, with reference to it, in the disciple evil and unwholesome ideas, connected with greed, hate or delusion, then the disciple:]

I. should, by means of this sign (= cause, occasion) attend to another sign which is more wholesome;

II. or he should investigate the peril of these ideas: "Unwholesome

27. A full translation of this text has been published, as Wheel No. 21, *The Removal of Distracting Thoughts* (*Vitakkasanthāna Sutta*). Translated by Soma Thera. Kandy.

truly are these ideas! Blameworthy are these ideas! Of painful result are these ideas!";

III. or he should pay no attention to these ideas;

IV. or he should attend to the composition of the factors which effect these ideas;

V. or, with teeth clenched and tongue pressed against the gums, he should by means of sheer mental effort hold back, crush and burn out the (offending) thought.

In doing so, these evil and unwholesome ideas, bound up with greed, hate or delusion, will be forsaken and disappear; from their forsaking thought will become inwardly settled and calm, composed and concentrated. This is called the effort to overcome.

The Commentary says:

I. Unwholesome ideas may arise with reference to beings—be they desirable, undesirable, or unconsidered—or to things, such as one's possessions, or things which annoy, like stumps or thorns. The wholesome counter-ideas which drive them out arise from the following practices, which are directly opposed to them:

Greed about beings: Meditation about the repulsiveness of the body.

Greed about things: Attention to their impermanence.

Hate for beings: The development of friendliness.

Hate for things: Attention to the elements: which of the physical elements composing the thing am I angry with?

Delusion about beings and things:

(1) When he has, in his general bewilderment, neglected his duties to a teacher, he wakes himself up by doing some tiresome work, such as carrying water.
(2) When he has been hazy in attending to the teacher's explanation of the doctrine, he wakes himself up by doing some tiresome work.
(3) He removes his doubts by questioning authorities.
(4) At the right time he listens respectfully to the Dharma.
(5) He acquires the skill in distinguishing between correct and faulty conclusions, and knows that "this is the reason for that, this is not the reason."

These are the direct and correct antidotes to the faulty ideas.

II. He investigates them with the power of wisdom, and rejects them like a snake's carcass.

III. He should not remember those ideas, not attend to them, but become one who is otherwise engaged. He should be like someone who, not wanting to see a certain sight-object, just closes his eyes; when these ideas arise in his mind, he should take hold of his basic subject of meditation, and become engaged in that. It may help him to break the spell of intruding thoughts and to occupy his mind otherwise, if he recites with great faith a passage from the Scriptures, or reads out a passage in praise of the Buddha or Dharma; or he may sort out his belongings, and enumerate them one by one: "these are the scissors," "this is the needle," etc.; or he should do some sewing; or he should do some good work for a given period of time. And after that he should return to his basic subject of meditation.

IV. He should analyze the conditions for these ideas and ask himself: "What is their cause, what their condition, what the reason for their having arisen?"

V. He should put forth great vigour, and with a wholesome thought he should hold back an unwholesome one.

Majjhima Nikāya, No. 20, and *Papañcasūdani* (summary); translated by Edward Conze

4. The Buddha's Sayings on the Faculties from the Saṃyutta Nikāya (Indriya Saṃyutta)

(a) At their Best

There are these five faculties, monks: the faculty of faith, the faculty of vigour, the faculty of mindfulness, the faculty of concentration and the faculty of wisdom.

Where can the faculty of faith be seen (at its best)? In the four characteristic qualities of a stream-winner.[28]

Where can the faculty of vigour be seen (at its best)? In the four right efforts.[29]

---

28. *Sotāpattiyaṅgāni:* The four are: unshakable faith in the Buddha, Dhamma and Sangha; and perfect morality.

29. *Sammappadhāna:* the effort of avoiding or overcoming evil and unsalutary states, and of developing and maintaining good and salutary states.

Where can the faculty of mindfulness be seen (at its best)? In the four foundations of mindfulness.[30]

Where can the faculty of concentration be seen (at its best)? In the four meditative absorptions.[31]

Where can the faculty of wisdom be seen (at its best)? In the Four Noble Truths.[32]

Sutta 8 (PTS, S IV 196); translated by Nyanaponika Mahāthera

(b) The Measure of Achievement

By accomplishment and perfection in the five faculties one is an arahant. If the faculties are weaker, one is a nonreturner; if they are still weaker, one is a once-returner, or a stream-winner, or a Dhamma-devotee (*dhammānusārin*), or a faith-devotee (*saddhānusārin*).

Thus, monks, through the difference of faculties, there is difference of result; and the difference of results makes for the difference of individuals.

Sutta 13; translated by Nyanaponika Mahāthera

Thus, monks, he who practices the five faculties to their perfection, wins to perfection (of arahantship). He who practices them partially, wins a partial result. Not barren (of results), I say, are the five faculties.

Sutta 14; translated by Nyanaponika Mahāthera

But he who is entirely, in any degree and respect, without these five faculties, stands outside, in the class of ordinary men (*puthujjana*).

Sutta 18 (S IV 200-202); translated by Nyanaponika Mahāthera

30. *Satipaṭṭhāna:* mindfulness as to body, feelings, state of mind and mind-objects.

31. *Jhāna*.

32. The truths of suffering, its origin, its cessation and the way to its cessation. The Commentary says that, in the field ascribed here to each faculty, the respective faculty is dominant at the height of its particular function, while the other four are concomitant and are supporting the dominant function. But the faculty of wisdom is the highest in rank among the five.

(c) Rooted in Experience

Thus I have heard. On one occasion when the Exalted One lived in the Eastern Cottage at Sāvatthī, he addressed the Venerable Sāriputta as follows:

"Do you believe, Sāriputta, that the faculty of faith, if cultivated and regularly practiced, leads to the Deathless, is bound for the Deathless, ends in the Deathless; that the faculty of vigour... the faculty of mindfulness... the faculty of concentration... the faculty of wisdom, if cultivated and regularly practiced, leads to the Deathless, is bound for the Deathless, ends in the Deathless?"

"Herein, O Lord, I do not follow the Exalted One out of faith. Those by whom this is unknown, unseen, uncognized, unrealized and unexperienced by wisdom, they will herein follow others out of faith. But those by whom this is known, seen, cognized, realized and experienced by wisdom, they have no uncertainty, no doubt about it that these five faculties, if cultivated and regularly practiced, lead to the Deathless, are bound for the Deathless, end in the Deathless. By me, O Lord, it has been known, seen, cognized, realized and experienced by wisdom and I have no uncertainty, no doubt about it that the faculty of faith... the faculty of vigour... the faculty of mindfulness... the faculty of concentration... the faculty of wisdom, if cultivated and regularly practiced, leads to the Deathless, is bound for the Deathless, ends in the Deathless."

"Well said, Sāriputta, well said," spoke the Lord (and he repeated in approval the words of the Venerable Sāriputta).

Sutta 44 (S IV 220); translated by Nyanaponika Mahāthera

(d) Wisdom, the Crowning Virtue—1

It is through cultivating and regularly practicing one faculty that a canker-free bhikkhu makes known his knowledge (of final attainment):[33] "Ceased has rebirth, fulfilled is the holy life, the task is done, nothing further remains after this." Which is the one faculty? The faculty of wisdom.

In a noble disciple endowed with wisdom, faith that goes along with it, is firmly established; vigour that goes along with it, is firmly established; mindfulness that goes along with it, is firmly

33. That is, of his having attained arahantship.

established; concentration that goes along with it, is firmly established. This, monks, is the one faculty through the cultivating and regularly practicing of which, a canker-free bhikkhu makes known his knowledge (of final attainment): "Ceased has rebirth, fulfilled is the holy life, the task is done, nothing further remains after this."

Sutta 45 (S IV 222); translated by Nyanaponika Mahāthera

(e) Wisdom, the Crowning Virtue—II

Just as among all heartwood fragrances that of the red sandalwood is deemed best, so, monks, among states that partake of enlightenment the faculty of wisdom is deemed best, namely, for the purpose of enlightenment.

Which, monks, are the states partaking of enlightenment? The faculty of faith is a state partaking of enlightenment and it leads to enlightenment. The faculty of vigour... the faculty of mindfulness... the faculty of concentration... the faculty of wisdom is a state partaking of enlightenment and it leads to enlightenment.

And among them, the faculty of wisdom is deemed best, namely, for the purpose of enlightenment.

Sutta 55 (S IV 231); translated by Nyanaponika Mahāthera

(f) The Acme of Faith

Thus I have heard. On one occasion, the Exalted One dwelt among the Anga people, at Āpana, a town of the Angas. There the Exalted One addressed the Venerable Sāriputta as follows:

"A noble disciple, Sāriputta, who has single-minded confidence in the Perfect One, can he have uncertainty or doubt concerning the Perfect One's dispensation?"

"A noble disciple, Lord, who has single-minded confidence in the Perfect One, cannot have uncertainty or doubt concerning the Perfect One's dispensation.

"Of a noble disciple endowed with faith it can be expected, Lord, that he will live employing his vigour to the overcoming of unsalutary states and the acquisition of salutary states, energetic, with strenuous exertion, unremittingly applying himself to things salutary. This vigour of his, O Lord, is his faculty of vigour.

"Of a noble disciple who is endowed with faith and employs his vigour, it can be expected, Lord, that he will be mindful, equipped with the highest mindfulness and circumspection, and that he remembers well and keeps in mind what has been done and said long ago. This mindfulness of his, Lord, is his faculty of mindfulness.

"Of a noble disciple who is endowed with faith, employing his vigour, keeping his mindfulness alert, it can be expected, Lord, that making the highest relinquishment (Nibbāna) his object, he will obtain concentration, will obtain unification of mind. This concentration of his, Lord, is his faculty of concentration.

"Of a noble disciple endowed with faith, vigour and mindfulness, and whose mind is concentrated, it can be expected, Lord, that he will know this: 'Without a conceivable beginning and end is this round of existence; no first beginning can be perceived of beings hastening and hurrying on (through this round of rebirths), enveloped in ignorance and ensnared by craving. The entire fading away and cessation of this very ignorance which is a mass of darkness, this is the state of peace, this is the state sublime, namely, the quiescence of all formations, the relinquishment of all substrata of existence, the extinction of craving, dispassion, cessation, Nibbāna.' This wisdom of his, Lord, is the faculty of wisdom.

"The noble disciple who has faith, after thus striving again and again, after thus applying mindfulness again and again, after thus concentrating his mind again and again, is now fully convinced: 'These teachings which before I had only heard, I now dwell in their personal experience, and having penetrated them with wisdom, I now see them (myself).' This faith of his, Lord, is his faculty of faith."

"Well said, Sāriputta, well said," spoke the Exalted One (and he repeated in approval the words of the Venerable Sāriputta).

Sutta 50 (S IV 225ff.); translated by Nyanaponika Mahāthera

5. The Balance of the Faculties

[According to the *Visuddhimagga,* the balance of the faculties (*indriya-samatta*) is one of the ten kinds of skill in absorption (*appanā-kosalla*), and it is one of the seven things that lead to the arising of the enlightenment factor "investigation of (material and mental) phenomena" (*dhammavicaya-sambojjhaṅga*).]

Imparting balance to the faculties is the equalizing of the controlling faculties of faith, vigour, mindfulness, concentration and wisdom. For if the faith faculty is strong and the others weak, then the vigour faculty cannot perform its function of exerting, the mindfulness faculty its function of attending to the object, the concentration faculty its function of excluding distraction, the wisdom faculty its function of seeing. So the (excessive) strength of the faith faculty should be reduced by reflecting on the phenomenal nature (of faith and its objects), and by not paying attention to what has caused the excessive strength of the faith faculty. Then if the *vigour faculty* is too strong, the faith faculty cannot perform its function of convincing, nor can the rest of the faculties perform their several functions. So in that case the excessive strength of the vigour faculty should be reduced by cultivating (the enlightenment factors of) tranquillity, concentration and equanimity. So, too, with the other factors, for it should be understood that when any one of them is too strong the others cannot perform their several functions.

However, what is particularly recommended is the balancing of faith with wisdom, and concentration with vigour. For one who is strong in faith and weak in wisdom places his confidence foolishly in an unworthy object. One strong in wisdom and weak in faith errs on the side of cunning and is as hard to cure as a sickness caused by medicine. But with the balancing of the two, faith and wisdom, a man has confidence only in a deserving object.

If there is too much of concentration and too little of vigour, the mind will be overpowered by indolence to which concentration inclines. But if vigour is too strong and concentration too weak, the mind will be overpowered by agitation to which vigour inclines. But concentration coupled with vigour cannot lapse into indolence, and vigour coupled with concentration cannot lapse into agitation. So these two should be balanced; for absorption comes with the balancing of the two.

Again (concentration and faith should be balanced). One working on concentration needs strong faith, since it is with such faith and confidence that he reaches absorption.

As to (the balancing of) concentration and wisdom, one working on concentration (i.e., who practices tranquillity; *samatha*) needs strong one-pointedness of mind, since that is how he reaches full absorption; and one working on insight (*vipassanā*) needs strong wisdom, since that is how he reaches penetration of (the phenomena's) characteristics; but with the balancing of the two he reaches full absorption as well.

Strong mindfulness, however, is needed in all instances; for mindfulness protects the mind from lapsing into agitation through faith, vigour and wisdom, which tend to agitation, and from lapsing into indolence through concentration, which tends to indolence. So it is as desirable in all instances as a seasoning of salt in all curries, as a prime minister in all the king's business. Hence it is said (in the commentaries): "It was declared by the Exalted One that 'mindfulness, indeed, is of universal use.' Why? Because the mind has mindfulness as its refuge, and mindfulness is manifested as protection, and there is no exertion and restraint of the mind without mindfulness."

Vism IV.45–49. Adapted from Bhikkhu Ñāṇamoli's translation: The Path of Purification.

Acknowledgments

With our thanks to translator and publishers for permission to reprint, we acknowledge as follows the sources of the translations included in the Appendix:

Text 1 (a) and 2 (a):
Buddhist Scriptures. Translated by Edward Conze. Harmondsworth: Penguin Books, 1960, pp. 151–155, 103–104.

Text 1 (b) and 2 (b):
Buddhist Text through the Ages. Edited by Edward Conze. Oxford: Bruno Cassirer, 1954, pp. 185–186, 138–139.

Texts 2 (c) and 3:
Buddhist Meditation, by Edward Conze. London: George Allen & Unwin, 1956, pp. 78–82, 83–85.

Text 5:
The Path of Purification (*Visuddhimagga*). Translated by Bhikkhu Ñāṇamoli. Kandy: Buddhist Publication Society, 1975.

Last Days of the Buddha

The Mahāparinibbāna Sutta

Translated from the Pāli by

Sister Vajirā & Francis Story

Revised Edition

WHEEL PUBLICATION NO. 67/68/69

Foreword

The translation of the Mahāparinibbāna Sutta which is offered here is a work of collaboration, but is based upon a text prepared by Sister Vajirā of Germany, to whom credit for the initial work must be given. The final revision of the text was done by Mr Francis Story. The notes and references which, it is hoped, will help in the understanding of the text have been contributed by the Venerable Nyanaponika Mahāthera, much of the material for them being taken from the Pāli Commentary.

Every effort has been made to give a faithful rendering of the original Pāli. The greater part of the sutta is straightforward narrative, but it also includes references to profound aspects of the Dhamma, which have to be understood in their precise meaning if the full import of the Buddha's last exhortations is to be conveyed. In the choice which inevitably arises between terminological exactitude and literary form, the translators have endeavoured to preserve the former with as little sacrifice as possible of the latter. Those who understand the difficulties of Pāli translation will appreciate that this is no easy task, and will readily overlook the absence of those literary graces which only a freer rendering would have permitted.

As in previous translations, some repetitions have been omitted and some repetitive passages condensed.

Buddhist Publication Society

Foreword to the Revised Edition

In this revised edition of *Last Days of the Buddha*, a number of stylistic changes have been made, aimed at improved readability. The word *Bhagavā*, untranslated in the original edition, has been replaced by "the Blessed One"; several archaic expressions, which gave a slightly Biblical flavour to the diction, have been replaced by their modern counterparts; awkward sentences have been reformulated; and greater consistency was aimed at in the rendering of certain terms and expressions. The notes have also been revised in certain respects. The titles of the chapters and sections have been supplied by the translator and editors, though the division of the work into six recitation units dates back to the period when the Canon was transmitted orally from one generation to the next.

Introduction

Of the thirty-four discourses (suttas) that make up the Dīgha Nikāya (Collection of Long Discourses), ours, the sixteenth, is the longest, and so altogether maintains the first place where length is concerned.

It preserves the principal feature of the Buddhist sutta, insofar as it is, like others, a rehearsal of events as they have been witnessed. On account of its unique composition, however, it is, more than other suttas, capable not only of winning the affection of the pious Buddhist, as it naturally does, but also of attracting the general reader, since it is indeed a fine specimen of sacred universal literature.

It gives a good general idea of the Buddha's Teaching, too, even though it hardly offers anything that is not found—and often more extensively dealt with—in other suttas.

At the end of his life, after almost half a century's ministry, the Master had long since taught all that was necessary for attaining the ideal. During the last period his primary concern, therefore, was to impress on his followers the necessity of unflinchingly putting into practice those very same teachings: an appeal that could, of course, hardly fail in stirring their hearts more than ever before.

The Sangha came, indeed, to witness the greatest event in its history, and was keenly aware of it, especially since the Master had announced his Parinibbāna three months ahead. The impression on the bhikkhus who flocked to him in large numbers as he was pressing northward was tremendous, and could not fail to be reflected vividly in the oral account. (The Buddhist canon was originally, as is well known, altogether oral.) Because of its particular import and abundance, this material was soon formed into one body; and so our sutta came to be.

In this connection, it is hardly possible not to remember gratefully the Venerable Ānanda. His share in the preservation of the Master's word is paramount to any other bhikkhu's, and his figure is inseparable from our texts. This was to become manifest for all time in the Mahāparinibbāna Sutta, which is plainly unimaginable without him. For it is Ānanda, and again

Ānanda, whom the Master addresses, having tested for twenty-five years his sure grasp and brilliant memory and also his indefatigable personal devotion. But Ānanda too, here more than elsewhere, by his constant queries, worries, and amazements, becomes without intending it a central figure beside the Master himself, which undoubtedly increases the attractiveness of the text. Thus, then, Ānanda, gentle and pleasant as his name, and yet almost throughout his career incurring the reproach of the brethren, was immortalized along with his beloved Master, and—as we may add—along with his strange position between praise and blame, assuming mystic character in the third chapter.

The third chapter, almost exclusively, is devoted to depicting the circumstances connected with the Master's relinquishment of life, which is the dramatic culmination of events. It overwhelmingly drives home the purely metaphysical significance of the Parinibbāna, or at least ought to do so. For the Buddha neither succumbed to his fatal illness nor did he give way to the appeal of Māra (which is identical with the non-appeal of Ānanda), but sovereignly let go of existence at a timely hour, just as forty-five years earlier, on becoming fully enlightened, he had duly taken upon himself the wearisome task of teaching men. This fact is most thought-provoking, and consistently leads to the conclusion that by his Parinibbāna, indeed, the Buddha bore the last and highest possible testimony to his Teaching, which permits of no lingering inclination to self-preservation and continuance, but on the contrary reaches the highest exultation ending it all. The Master's Parinibbāna is, therefore, the one sorrowful event in the history of Buddhism that turns out, in its true meaning, to be really the most blissful.

Sister Vajirā
Ceylon
May 1961

The Mahāparinibbāna Sutta

Suppose, Ānanda, the river Ganges had become full to the brim, ford and all, drinkable for crows, and a weak man approached, thinking: "By the strength of my arms, I shall cut across and reach safely beyond!"—but he would not be able to do so. Even so, Ānanda, he who rejoices not when the dissolution of personality is being proclaimed, who is not pleased with it, who does not settle down in it and feels not released, such a one is comparable to that weak man.

Majjhima Nikāya No. 64

Homage to the Blessed One, the Holy One,
the Fully Enlightened One

Part One
In Magadha

1. Thus have I heard. Once the Blessed One[1] dwelt at Rājagaha, on the hill called Vultures' Peak. At that time the king of Magadha, Ajātasattu, son of the Videhi queen,[2] desired to wage war against the Vajjis. He spoke in this fashion: "These Vajjis, powerful and glorious as they are, I shall annihilate them, I shall make them perish, I shall utterly destroy them."

2. And Ajātasattu, the king of Magadha, addressed his chief minister, the brahmin Vassakāra, saying: "Come, brahmin, go to the Blessed One, pay homage in my name at his feet, wish him good health, strength, ease, vigour, and comfort, and speak thus:

1. *Bhagavā*: also rendered "the Auspicious One" or "the Exalted One"; the most frequent appellation of the Buddha, though not restricted to Buddhist usage.
2. *Ajātasattu Vedehiputta*. Comy. says that Ajātasattu's mother was a Kosala princess and not the daughter of the Vedehi king. Hence Comy. explains *vedehiputta* as "son of a wise mother." Ajātasattu became king of the powerful state of Magadha after murdering his father, King Bimbisāra (see DN 2).

'O Lord, Ajātasattu, the king of Magadha, desires to wage war against the Vajjis. He has spoken in this fashion: "These Vajjis, powerful and glorious as they are, I shall annihilate them, I shall make them perish, I shall utterly destroy them." ' And whatever the Blessed One should answer you, keep it well in mind and inform me; for Tathāgatas[3] do not speak falsely."

3. "Very well, sire," said the brahmin Vassakāra in assent to Ajātasattu, king of Magadha. And he ordered a large number of magnificent carriages to be made ready, mounted one himself, and accompanied by the rest, drove out to Rājagaha towards Vultures' Peak. He went by carriage as far as the carriage could go, then dismounting, he approached the Blessed One on foot. After exchanging courteous greetings with the Blessed One, together with many pleasant words, he sat down at one side and addressed the Blessed One thus: "Venerable Gotama, Ajātasattu, the king of Magadha, pays homage at the feet of the Venerable Gotama and wishes him good health, strength, ease, vigour, and comfort. He desires to wage war against the Vajjis, and he has spoken in this fashion: 'These Vajjis, powerful and glorious as they are, I shall annihilate them, I shall make them perish, I shall utterly destroy them.' "

Conditions of a Nation's Welfare

4. At that time the Venerable Ānanda[4] was standing behind the Blessed One, fanning him, and the Blessed One addressed the Venerable Ānanda thus: "What have you heard, Ānanda: do the Vajjis have frequent gatherings, and are their meetings well attended?"

"I have heard, Lord, that this is so."

"So long, Ānanda, as this is the case, the growth of the Vajjis is to be expected, not their decline.

"What have you heard, Ānanda: do the Vajjis assemble and disperse peacefully and attend to their affairs in concord?"

"I have heard, Lord, that they do."

---

3. *Tathāgata*: lit. "Thus-gone" or "Thus-come"; likewise an appellation of the Buddha, which he generally used when speaking of himself.

4. Ānanda was a cousin of the Buddha and his personal attendant for twenty-four years. He attained arahatship after the passing away of the Buddha, just before the commencement of the First Council, at which he was the reciter of the Dīgha Nikāya and the authority for the Sutta Piṭaka.

"So long, Ānanda, as this is the case, the growth of the Vajjis is to be expected, not their decline.

"What have you heard, Ānanda: do the Vajjis neither enact new decrees nor abolish existing ones, but proceed in accordance with their ancient constitutions?"

"I have heard, Lord, that they do."

"So long, Ānanda, as this is the case, the growth of the Vajjis is to be expected, not their decline.

"What have you heard, Ānanda: do the Vajjis show respect, honour, esteem, and veneration towards their elders and think it worthwhile to listen to them?"

"I have heard, Lord, that they do."

"So long, Ānanda, as this is the case, the growth of the Vajjis is to be expected, not their decline.

"What have you heard, Ānanda: do the Vajjis refrain from abducting women and maidens of good families and from detaining them?"

"I have heard, Lord, that they refrain from doing so."

"So long, Ānanda, as this is the case, the growth of the Vajjis is to be expected, not their decline.

"What have you heard, Ānanda: do the Vajjis show respect, honour, esteem, and veneration towards their shrines, both those within the city and those outside it, and do not deprive them of the due offerings as given and made to them formerly?"

"I have heard, Lord, that they do venerate their shrines, and that they do not deprive them of their offerings."

"So long, Ānanda, as this is the case, the growth of the Vajjis is to be expected, not their decline.

"What have you heard, Ānanda: do the Vajjis duly protect and guard the arahats, so that those who have not come to the realm yet might do so, and those who have already come might live there in peace?"

"I have heard, Lord, that they do."

"So long, Ānanda, as this is the case, the growth of the Vajjis is to be expected, not their decline."

5. And the Blessed One addressed the brahmin Vassakāra in these words: "Once, brahmin, I dwelt at Vesālī, at the Sarandada shrine, and there it was that I taught the Vajjis these seven

conditions leading to (a nation's) welfare.[5] So long, brahmin, as these endure among the Vajjis, and the Vajjis are known for it, their growth is to be expected, not their decline."

Thereupon the brahmin Vassakāra spoke thus to the Blessed One: "If the Vajjis, Venerable Gotama, were endowed with only one or another of these conditions leading to welfare, their growth would have to be expected, not their decline. What then of all the seven? No harm, indeed, can be done to the Vajjis in battle by Magadha's king, Ajātasattu, except through treachery or discord. Well, then, Venerable Gotama, we will take our leave, for we have much to perform, much work to do."

"Do as now seems fit to you, brahmin." And the brahmin Vassakāra, the chief minister of Magadha, approving of the Blessed One's words and delighted by them, rose from his seat and departed.

Welfare of the Bhikkhus

6. Then, soon after Vassakāra's departure, the Blessed One addressed the Venerable Ānanda thus: "Go now, Ānanda, and assemble in the hall of audience as many bhikkhus as live around Rājagaha."

"Very well, Lord." And the Venerable Ānanda did as he was requested and informed the Blessed One: "The community of bhikkhus is assembled, Lord. Now let the Blessed One do as he wishes."

Thereupon the Blessed One rose from his seat, went up to the hall of audience, took his appointed seat there, and addressed the bhikkhus thus: "Seven conditions leading to welfare I shall set forth, bhikkhus. Listen and pay attention to what I shall say."

"So be it, Lord."

"The growth of the bhikkhus is to be expected, not their decline, bhikkhus, so long as they assemble frequently and in large numbers; meet and disperse peacefully and attend to the affairs of the Sangha in concord; so long as they appoint no new rules, and do not abolish the existing ones, but proceed in accordance with the code of training (Vinaya) laid down; so long as they show respect, honour, esteem, and veneration towards the elder bhikkhus, those of long standing, long gone forth, the fathers

5. The discourse referred to here is AN 7:19.

and leaders of the Sangha, and think it worthwhile to listen to them; so long as they do not come under the power of the craving that leads to fresh becoming; so long as they cherish the forest depths for their dwellings; so long as they establish themselves in mindfulness, so that virtuous brethren of the Order who have not come yet might do so, and those already come might live in peace; so long, bhikkhus, as these seven conditions leading to welfare endure among the bhikkhus and the bhikkhus are known for it, their growth is to be expected, not their decline.

7. "Seven further conditions leading to welfare I shall set forth, bhikkhus. Listen and pay attention to what I shall say."

"So be it, Lord."

"The growth of the bhikkhus is to be expected, not their decline, bhikkhus, so long as they do not delight in, are not pleased with, and are not fond of activities, talk, sleep, and company; so long as they do not harbour, do not come under the spell of evil desires; have no bad friends, associates, or companions; and so long as they do not stop halfway on account of some trifling achievement. So long, bhikkhus, as these seven conditions leading to welfare endure among the bhikkhus and the bhikkhus are known for it, their growth is to be expected, not their decline.

Seven Good Qualities[6]

8. "Seven further conditions leading to welfare I shall set forth, bhikkhus. Listen and pay attention to what I shall say."

"So be it, Lord."

"The growth of the bhikkhus is to be expected, not their decline, bhikkhus, so long as they shall have faith, so long as they have moral shame and fear of misconduct, are proficient in learning, resolute, mindful, and wise. So long, bhikkhus, as these seven conditions leading to welfare endure among the bhikkhus, and the bhikkhus are known for it, their growth is to be expected, not their decline.

---

6. The group-names, which are not in the original, are supplied from other references to the qualities concerned; here *satta saddhammā*, about which see AN 7:63; MN 53. In the Comy. to MN 8 they are called "the complete equipment required for insight" (BPS Wheel No. 61/62, p.48).

Seven Factors of Enlightenment[7]

9. "Seven further conditions leading to welfare I shall set forth, bhikkhus. Listen and pay attention to what I shall say."

"So be it, Lord."

"The growth of the bhikkhus is to be expected, not their decline, bhikkhus, so long as they cultivate the seven factors of enlightenment, that is: mindfulness, investigation into phenomena, energy, bliss, tranquillity, concentration, and equanimity. So long, bhikkhus, as these seven conditions leading to welfare endure among the bhikkhus, and the bhikkhus are known for it, their growth is to be expected, not their decline.

Seven Perceptions

10. "Seven further conditions leading to welfare I shall set forth, bhikkhus. Listen and pay attention to what I shall say."

"So be it, Lord."

"The growth of the bhikkhus is to be expected, not their decline, bhikkhus, so long as they cultivate the perception of impermanence, of egolessness, of (the body's) impurity, of (the body's) wretchedness, of relinquishment, of dispassion, and of cessation. So long, bhikkhus, as these seven conditions leading to welfare endure among the bhikkhus, and the bhikkhus are known for it, their growth is to be expected, not their decline.

Six Conditions to be Remembered[8]

11. "Six further conditions leading to welfare I shall set forth, bhikkhus. Listen and pay attention to what I shall say."

"So be it, Lord."

"The growth of the bhikkhus is to be expected, not their decline, bhikkhus, so long as they attend on each other with loving-kindness in deed, word, and thought, both openly and in private; so long as in respect of what they receive as due offerings, even the contents of their alms bowls, they do not make use

---

7. *Satta bojjhaṅgā.* See Piyadassi Thera, *The Seven Factors of Enlightenment* (BPS Wheel No. 1).

8. *Sārāṇiyā dhammā*: also at MN 48, AN 6:11, 12.

of them without sharing them with virtuous members of the community; so long as, in company with their brethren, they train themselves, openly and in private, in the rules of conduct, which are complete and perfect, spotless and pure, liberating, praised by the wise, uninfluenced (by mundane concerns), and favourable to concentration of mind; and in company with their brethren, preserve, openly and in private, the insight that is noble and liberating, and leads one who acts upon it to the utter destruction of suffering. So long, bhikkhus, as these six conditions leading to welfare endure among the bhikkhus, and the bhikkhus are known for it, their growth is to be expected, not their decline.

Counsel to the Bhikkhus

12. And the Blessed One, living at Rājagaha, at the hill called Vultures' Peak, often gave counsel to the bhikkhus thus:

"Such and such is virtue; such and such is concentration; and such and such is wisdom.[9] Great becomes the fruit, great is the gain of concentration when it is fully developed by virtuous conduct; great becomes the fruit, great is the gain of wisdom when it is fully developed by concentration; utterly freed from the taints[10] of lust, becoming, and ignorance is the mind that is fully developed in wisdom."

13. When the Blessed One had stayed at Rājagaha as long as he pleased, he addressed the Venerable Ānanda thus: "Come, Ānanda, let us go to Ambalaṭṭhikā."

"So be it, Lord."

And the Blessed One took up his abode at Ambalaṭṭhikā, together with a large community of bhikkhus.

14. At Ambalaṭṭhikā the Blessed One came to stay in the king's rest house; and there, too, the Blessed One often gave counsel to the bhikkhus thus:

9. Virtue (*sīla*), concentration (*samādhi*), and wisdom (*paññā*) are the three divisions of the Noble Eightfold Path. Our text stresses again and again the importance of a full development of all three for final liberation.

10. *Āsava*: those defiling factors—sensual desire, craving for existence, and ignorance—primarily responsible for maintaining bondage to the cycle of rebirths. Also translated as "cankers" or "corruptions." Later texts add a fourth, the taint of wrong views.

"Such and such is virtue; such and such is concentration; and such and such is wisdom. Great becomes the fruit, great is the gain of concentration when it is fully developed by virtuous conduct; great becomes the fruit, great is the gain of wisdom when it is fully developed by concentration; utterly freed from the taints of lust, becoming, and ignorance is the mind that is fully developed in wisdom."

15. When the Blessed One had stayed at Ambalaṭṭhikā as long as he pleased, he addressed the Venerable Ānanda thus: "Come, Ānanda, let us go to Nālandā."

"So be it, Lord."

And the Blessed One took up his abode at Nālandā together with a large community of bhikkhus, and came to stay in the mango grove of Pāvārika.

Sāriputta's Lion's Roar[11]

16. Then the Venerable Sāriputta went to the Blessed One, respectfully greeted him, sat down at one side, and spoke thus to him:

"This faith, Lord, I have in the Blessed One, that there has not been, there will not be, nor is there now, another recluse or brahmin more exalted in Enlightenment than the Blessed One."

"Lofty indeed is this speech of yours, Sāriputta, and lordly! A bold utterance, a veritable sounding of the lion's roar! But how is this, Sāriputta? Those Arahats, Fully Enlightened Ones of the past—do you have direct personal knowledge of all those Blessed Ones, as to their virtue, their meditation,[12] their wisdom, their abiding, and their emancipation?"[13]

"Not so, Lord."

"Then how is this, Sāriputta? Those Arahats, Fully Enlightened

11. Sāriputta was the chief disciple of the Buddha and the one who excelled in wisdom. For a full account of his life and works, see Nyanaponika Thera, *The Life of Sāriputta* (BPS Wheel No. 90/92).

12. *Evaṃ-dhammā*. Comy. & Sub. Comy.: This refers to concentration and to the mental qualities belonging to concentration (*samādhipakkhiyā dhammā*) such as energy, mindfulness, etc. Comy. explains "abiding" (*vihāra*) as abiding in the attainment of cessation (*nirodha-samāpatti*).

13. *Evaṃ-vimuttā*: their deliverance from defilements and from future rebirths.

Ones of the future—do you have direct personal knowledge of all those Blessed Ones, as to their virtue, their meditation, their wisdom, their abiding, and their emancipation?"

"Not so, Lord."

"Then how is this, Sāriputta? Of me, who am at present the Arahat, the Fully Enlightened One, do you have direct personal knowledge as to my virtue, my meditation, my wisdom, my abiding, and my emancipation?"

"Not so, Lord."

"Then it is clear, Sāriputta, that you have no such direct personal knowledge of the Arahats, the Fully Enlightened Ones of the past, the future, and the present. How then dare you set forth a speech so lofty and lordly, an utterance so bold, a veritable sounding of the lion's roar, saying: 'This faith, Lord, I have in the Blessed One, that there has not been, there will not be, nor is there now another recluse or brahmin more exalted in Enlightenment than the Blessed One'?"

17."No such direct personal knowledge, indeed, is mine, Lord, of the Arahats, the Fully Enlightened Ones of the past, the future, and the present; and yet I have come to know the lawfulness of the Dhamma. Suppose, Lord, a king's frontier fortress was strongly fortified, with strong ramparts and turrets, and it had a single gate, and there was a gatekeeper, intelligent, experienced, and prudent, who would keep out the stranger but allow the friend to enter. As he patrols the path that leads all around the fortress, he does not perceive a hole or fissure in the ramparts even big enough to allow a cat to slip through. So he comes to the conclusion: 'Whatever grosser living things are to enter or leave this city, they will all have to do so just by this gate.' In the same way, Lord, I have come to know the lawfulness of the Dhamma.

"For, Lord, all the Blessed Ones, Arahats, Fully Enlightened Ones of the past had abandoned the five hindrances,[14] the mental defilements that weaken wisdom; had well established their minds in the four foundations of mindfulness;[15] had duly cultivated the

14. On the five hindrances, see Nyanaponika Thera, *The Five Mental Hindrances* (BPS Wheel No. 26).

15. On the four foundations of mindfulness, see Chapter 2:14. The seven factors of enlightenment are enumerated in 1:9.

seven factors of enlightenment, and were fully enlightened in unsurpassed, supreme Enlightenment.

"And, Lord, all the Blessed Ones, Arahats, Fully Enlightened Ones of the future will abandon the five hindrances, the mental defilements that weaken wisdom; will well establish their minds in the four foundations of mindfulness; will duly cultivate the seven factors of enlightenment, and will be fully enlightened in unsurpassed, supreme Enlightenment.

"And the Blessed One too, Lord, being at present the Arahat, the Fully Enlightened One, has abandoned the five hindrances, the mental defilements that weaken wisdom; has well established his mind in the four foundations of mindfulness; has duly cultivated the seven factors of enlightenment, and is fully enlightened in unsurpassed, supreme Enlightenment."

18. And also in Nālandā, in the mango grove of Pāvārika, the Blessed One often gave counsel to the bhikkhus thus:

"Such and such is virtue; such and such is concentration; and such and such is wisdom. Great becomes the fruit, great is the gain of concentration when it is fully developed by virtuous conduct; great becomes the fruit, great is the gain of wisdom when it is fully developed by concentration; utterly freed from the taints of lust, becoming, and ignorance is the mind that is fully developed in wisdom."

19. When the Blessed One had stayed at Nālandā as long as he pleased, he addressed the Venerable Ānanda thus:

"Come, Ānanda, let us go to Pāṭaligāma."

"So be it, Lord."

And the Blessed One took up his abode at Pāṭaligāma together with a large community of bhikkhus.

20. Then the devotees of Pāṭaligāma came to know: "The Blessed One, they say, has arrived at Pāṭaligāma." And they approached the Blessed One, respectfully greeted him, sat down at one side, and addressed him thus: "May the Blessed One, Lord, kindly visit our council hall." And the Blessed One consented by his silence.

21. Knowing the Blessed One's consent, the devotees of Pāṭaligāma rose from their seats, respectfully saluted him, and keeping their right sides towards him, departed for the council hall. Then they prepared the council hall by covering the floor all over, arranging seats and water, and setting out an oil lamp.

Having done this, they returned to the Blessed One, respectfully greeted him, and standing at one side, announced: "Lord, the council hall is ready, with the floor covered all over, seats and water prepared, and an oil lamp has been set out. Let the Blessed One come, Lord, at his convenience.

22. And the Blessed One got ready, and taking his bowl and robe, went to the council hall together with the company of bhikkhus. After rinsing his feet, the Blessed One entered the council hall and took his seat close to the middle pillar, facing east. The community of bhikkhus, after rinsing their feet, also entered the council hall and took seats near the western wall, facing east, so that the Blessed One was before them. And the devotees of Pāṭaligāma, after rinsing their feet and entering the council hall, sat down near the eastern wall, facing west, so that the Blessed One was in front of them.

The Fruits of an Immoral and a Moral Life

23. Thereupon the Blessed One addressed the devotees of Pāṭaligāma thus: "The immoral man, householders, by falling away from virtue, encounters five perils: great loss of wealth through heedlessness; an evil reputation; a timid and troubled demeanour in every society, be it that of nobles, brahmins, householders, or ascetics; death in bewilderment; and, at the breaking up of the body after death, rebirth in a realm of misery, in an unhappy state, in the nether world, in hell.

24. "Five blessings, householders, accrue to the righteous man through his practice of virtue: great increase of wealth through his diligence; a favourable reputation; a confident deportment, without timidity, in every society, be it that of nobles, brahmins, householders, or ascetics; a serene death; and, at the breaking up of the body after death, rebirth in a happy state, in a heavenly world."

25. And the Blessed One spent much of the night instructing the devotees of Pāṭaligāma in the Dhamma, rousing, edifying, and gladdening them, after which he dismissed them, saying: "The night is far advanced, householders. You may go at your convenience."

"So be it, Lord." And the devotees of Pāṭaligāma rose from their seats, respectfully saluted the Blessed One, and keeping their right sides towards him, departed. And the Blessed One, soon after their departure, retired into privacy.

26. At that time Sunidha and Vassakāra, the chief ministers of Magadha, were building a fortress at Pāṭaligāma in defence against the Vajjis. And deities in large numbers, counted in thousands, had taken possession of sites at Pāṭaligāma. In the region where deities of great power prevailed, officials of great power were bent on constructing edifices; and where deities of medium power and lesser power prevailed, officials of medium and lesser power were bent on constructing edifices.

27. And the Blessed One saw with the heavenly eye, pure and transcending the faculty of men, the deities, counted in thousands, where they had taken possession of sites in Pāṭaligāma. And rising before the night was spent, towards dawn, the Blessed One addressed the Venerable Ānanda thus: "Who is it, Ānanda, that is erecting a city at Pāṭaligāma?"

"Sunidha and Vassakāra, Lord, the chief ministers of Magadha, are building a fortress at Pāṭaligāma, in defence against the Vajjis."

28. "It is, Ānanda, as if Sunidha and Vassakāra had taken counsel with the gods of the Thirty-three. For I beheld, Ānanda, with the heavenly eye, pure and transcending the faculty of men, a large number of deities, counted in thousands, that have taken possession of sites at Pāṭaligāma. In the region where deities of great power prevail, officials of great power are bent on constructing edifices; and where deities of medium and lesser power prevail, officials of medium and lesser power are bent on constructing edifices. Truly, Ānanda, as far as the Aryan race extends and trade routes spread, this will be the foremost city Pāṭaliputta, a trade-centre.[16] But Pāṭaliputta, Ānanda, will be assailed by three perils—fire, water, and dissension."

29. Then Sunidha and Vassakāra went to the Blessed One, and after courteous greeting to the Blessed One, and exchanging many pleasant words, they stood at one side and addressed him thus: "May the Venerable Gotama please accept our invitation for tomorrow's meal, together with the community of bhikkhus."

16. *Puṭa-bhedanaṃ*. Comy. explains as the breaking open, the unpacking, of boxes (*puṭa*) of merchandise for the purpose of distribution. But probably it refers to the bursting open of the seed-box of the *pāṭali* flower.

And the Blessed One consented by his silence.

30. Knowing the Blessed One's consent, Sunidha and Vassakāra departed for their own abodes, where they had choice food, hard and soft, prepared. And when it was time, they announced to the Blessed One: "It is time, Venerable Gotama; the meal is ready."

Thereupon the Blessed One got ready in the forenoon, and taking bowl and robe, he went together with the community of bhikkhus to the abode of Sunidha and Vassakāra, where he took the seat prepared for him. And Sunidha and Vassa-kāra themselves attended on the community of bhikkhus headed by the Buddha, and served them with choice food, hard and soft. When the Blessed One had finished his meal and had removed his hand from the bowl, they took low seats and sat down at one side.

31. And the Blessed One thanked them with these stanzas:

"Wherever he may dwell, the prudent man
Ministers to the chaste and virtuous;
And having to these worthy ones made gifts,
He shares his merits with the local devas.

And so revered, they honour him in turn,
Are gracious to him even as a mother
Is towards her own, her only son;
And he who thus enjoys the devas' grace,
And is by them beloved, good fortune sees."

After this, the Blessed One rose from his seat and departed.

Crossing the Ganges

32. Then Sunidha and Vassakāra followed behind the Blessed One, step by step, saying: "Through whichever gate the recluse Gotama will depart today, that we will name the Gotama-gate; and the ford by which he will cross the river Ganges shall be named the Gotama-ford." And so it came to pass, where the gate was concerned.

33. But when the Blessed One came to the river Ganges, it was full to the brim, so that crows could drink from it. And some people went in search of a boat or float, while others tied up a raft, because they desired to get across. But the Blessed One, as quickly as a strong man might stretch out his bent arm or draw in

his outstretched arm, vanished from this side of the river Ganges, and came to stand on the yonder side.

34. And the Blessed One saw the people who desired to cross searching for a boat or float, while others were binding rafts. And then the Blessed One, seeing them thus, gave forth the solemn utterance:

"They who have bridged the ocean vast,
Leaving the lowlands far behind,
While others still their frail rafts bind,
Are saved by wisdom unsurpassed."

Part Two
The Journey to Vesālī

The Four Noble Truths

1. Now the Blessed One spoke to the Venerable Ānanda, saying: "Come, Ānanda, let us go to Koṭigāma."

"So be it, Lord." And the Blessed One took up his abode at Koṭigāma together with a large community of bhikkhus.

2. And the Blessed One addressed the bhikkhus, saying: "Bhikkhus, it is through not realizing, through not penetrating the Four Noble Truths that this long course of birth and death has been passed through and undergone by me as well as by you. What are these four? They are the noble truth of suffering; the noble truth of the origin of suffering; the noble truth of the cessation of suffering; and the noble truth of the way to the cessation of suffering. But now, bhikkhus, that these have been realized and penetrated, cut off is the craving for existence, destroyed is that which leads to renewed becoming, and there is no fresh becoming."

3. Thus it was said by the Blessed One. And the Happy One, the Master, further said:

"Through not seeing the Four Noble Truths,
Long was the weary path from birth to birth.
When these are known, removed is rebirth's cause,
The root of sorrow plucked; then ends rebirth."

4. And also at Koṭigāma the Blessed One often gave counsel to the bhikkhus thus: "Such and such is virtue; such and such is concentration; and such and such is wisdom. Great becomes the fruit, great is the gain of concentration when it is fully developed by virtuous conduct; great becomes the fruit, great is the gain of wisdom when it is fully developed by concentration; utterly freed from the taints of lust, becoming, and ignorance is the mind that is fully developed in wisdom."

5. When the Blessed One had stayed at Koṭigāma as long as he pleased, he spoke to the Venerable Ānanda, saying: "Come, Ānanda, let us go to Nādikā."

"So be it, Lord." And the Blessed One took up his abode in Nādikā together with a large community of bhikkhus, staying in the Brick House.

The Four Specific Attainments

6. Then the Venerable Ānanda approached the Blessed One and, after greeting him respectfully, sat down at one side. And he said to the Blessed One: "Here in Nādikā, Lord, there have passed away the bhikkhu Sāḷha and the bhikkhunī Nandā. Likewise there have passed away the layman Sudatta and the laywoman Sujātā; likewise the layman Kakudha, Kāliṅga, Nikaṭa, Kaṭissabha, Tuṭṭha, Santuṭṭha, Bhadda, and Subhadda. What is their destiny, Lord? What is their future state?"

7. "The bhikkhu Sāḷha, Ānanda, through the destruction of the taints in this very lifetime has attained to the taint-free deliverance of mind and deliverance through wisdom, having directly known and realized it by himself.[17]

"The bhikkhunī Nandā, Ānanda, through the destruction of the five lower fetters (that bind beings to the world of the senses), has arisen spontaneously (among the Suddhāvāsa deities) and will come to final cessation in that very place, not liable to return from that world.

"The layman Sudatta, Ānanda, through the destruction of the three fetters (self-belief, doubt, and faith in the efficacy of rituals and observances), and the lessening of lust, hatred, and delusion, has become a once-returner and is bound to make an end of suffering after having returned but once more to this world.

"The laywoman Sujātā, Ānanda, through the destruction of the three fetters has become a stream-enterer, and is safe from falling into the states of misery, assured, and bound for Enlightenment.

"The layman Kakudha, Ānanda, through the destruction of the five lower fetters (that bind beings to the world of the senses), has arisen spontaneously (among the Suddhāvāsa deities), and will

17. The stage of arahatship, the last of the four stages of deliverance. The next three paragraphs refer to disciples on the three lower stages, respectively, the non-returner, once-returner, and stream-enterer (*anāgāmi, sakadāgāmi, sotāpanna*).

come to final cessation in that very place, not liable to return from that world.

"So it is with Kāliṅga, Nikaṭa, Kaṭissabha, Tuṭṭha, Santuṭṭha, Bhadda, and Subhadda, and with more than fifty laymen in Nādikā. More than ninety laymen who have passed away in Nādikā, Ānanda, through the destruction of the three fetters, and the lessening of lust, hatred, and delusion, have become once-returners and are bound to make an end of suffering after having returned but once more to this world.

"More than five hundred laymen who have passed away in Nādikā, Ānanda, through the complete destruction of the three fetters have become stream-enterers, and are safe from falling into the states of misery, assured, and bound for Enlightenment.

The Mirror of the Dhamma

8. "But truly, Ānanda, it is nothing strange that human beings should die. But if each time it happens you should come to the Tathāgata and ask about them in this manner, indeed it would be troublesome to him. Therefore, Ānanda, I will give you the teaching called the Mirror of the Dhamma, possessing which the noble disciple, should he so desire, can declare of himself: 'There is no more rebirth for me in hell, nor as an animal or ghost, nor in any realm of woe. A stream-enterer am I, safe from falling into the states of misery, assured am I and bound for Enlightenment.' "

9. "And what, Ānanda, is that teaching called the Mirror of Dhamma, possessing which the noble disciple may thus declare of himself?

"In this case, Ānanda, the noble disciple possesses unwavering faith in the Buddha thus: 'The Blessed One is an Arahat, the Fully Enlightened One, perfect in knowledge and conduct, the Happy One, the knower of the world, the paramount trainer of beings, the teacher of gods and men, the Enlightened One, the Blessed One.'

"He possesses unwavering faith in the Dhamma thus: 'Well propounded by the Blessed One is the Dhamma, evident, timeless,[18] inviting investigation, leading to emancipation, to be comprehended by the wise, each for himself.'

18. Or: "not delayed (in its results)."

"He possesses unwavering faith in the Blessed One's Order of Disciples thus: 'Well faring is the Blessed One's Order of Disciples, righteously, wisely, and dutifully: that is to say, the four pairs of men, the eight classes of persons. The Blessed One's Order of Disciples is worthy of honour, of hospitality, of offerings, of veneration—the supreme field for meritorious deeds in the world.'

"And he possesses virtues that are dear to the Noble Ones, complete and perfect, spotless and pure, which are liberating, praised by the wise, uninfluenced (by worldly concerns), and favourable to concentration of mind.

10. "This, Ānanda, is the teaching called the Mirror of the Dhamma, whereby the noble disciple may thus know of himself: 'There is no more rebirth for me in hell, nor as an animal or ghost, nor in any realm of woe. A stream-enterer am I, safe from falling into the states of misery, assured am I and bound for Enlightenment.'"

11. And also in Nādikā, in the Brick House, the Blessed One often gave counsel to the bhikkhus thus: "Such and such is virtue; such and such is concentration; and such and such is wisdom. Great becomes the fruit, great is the gain of concentration when it is fully developed by virtuous conduct; great becomes the fruit, great is the gain of wisdom when it is fully developed by concentration; utterly freed from the taints of lust, becoming, and ignorance is the mind that is fully developed in wisdom."

12. When the Blessed One had stayed in Nādikā as long as he pleased, he spoke to the Venerable Ānanda, saying: "Come, Ānanda, let us go to Vesālī."

"So be it, O Lord." And the Blessed One took up his abode in Vesālī together with a large community of bhikkhus, and stayed in Ambapālī's grove.

Mindfulness and Clear Comprehension

13. Then the Blessed One addressed the bhikkhus, saying: "Mindful should you dwell, bhikkhus, clearly comprehending; thus I exhort you.

14. "And how, bhikkhus, is a bhikkhu mindful? When he dwells contemplating the body in the body, earnestly, clearly comprehending, and mindfully, after having overcome desire and

sorrow in regard to the world; and when he dwells contemplating feelings in feelings, the mind in the mind, and mental objects in mental objects, earnestly, clearly comprehending, and mindfully, after having overcome desire and sorrow in regard to the world, then is he said to be mindful.

15. "And how, bhikkhus, does a bhikkhu have clear comprehension? When he remains fully aware of his coming and going, his looking forward and his looking away, his bending and stretching, his wearing of his robe and carrying of his bowl, his eating and drinking, masticating and savouring, his defecating and urinating, his walking, standing, sitting, lying down, going to sleep or keeping awake, his speaking or being silent, then is he said to have clear comprehension.

"Mindful should you dwell, bhikkhus, clearly comprehending; thus I exhort you."

Ambapālī and the Licchavis

16. Then Ambapālī the courtesan came to know: "The Blessed One, they say, has arrived at Vesālī and is now staying in my Mango Grove." And she ordered a large number of magnificient carriages to be made ready, mounted one of them herself, and accompanied by the rest, drove out from Vesālī towards her park. She went by carriage as far as the carriage could go, then alighted; and approaching the Blessed One on foot, she respectfully greeted him and sat down at one side. And the Blessed One instructed Ambapālī the courtesan in the Dhamma and roused, edified, and gladdened her.

17. Thereafter Ambapālī the courtesan spoke to the Blessed One, saying: "May the Blessed One, O Lord, please accept my invitation for tomorrow's meal, together with the community of bhikkhus." And by his silence the Blessed One consented.

Sure, then, of the Blessed One's consent, Ambapālī the courtesan rose from her seat, respectfully saluted him, and keeping her right side towards him, took her departure.

18. Then the Licchavis of Vesālī came to know: "The Blessed One, they say, has arrived at Vesālī and is now staying in Ambapālī's grove." And they ordered a large number of magnificient carriages to be made ready, each mounted one, and accompanied by the rest, drove out from Vesālī. Now, of these

Licchavis, some were in blue, with clothing and ornaments all of blue, while others were in yellow, red, and white.

19. And it so happened that Ambapālī the courtesan drove up against the young Licchavis, axle by axle, wheel by wheel, and yoke by yoke. Thereupon the Licchavis exclaimed: "Why do you drive up against us in this fashion, Ambapālī?"

"Thus it is, indeed, my princes, and not otherwise! For the Blessed One is invited by me for tomorrow's meal, together with the community of bhikkhus!"

"Give up the meal, Ambapālī, for a hundred thousand!"

But she replied: "Even if you were to give me Vesālī, sirs, together with its tributary lands, I would not give up a meal of such importance."

Then the Licchavis snapped their fingers in annoyance: "See, friends! We are defeated by this mango lass! We are utterly outdone by this mango lass!" But they continued on their way to Ambapālī's grove.

20. And the Blessed One beheld the Licchavis from afar, as they drove up. Then he spoke to the bhikkhus, saying: "Those of you, bhikkhus, who have not yet seen the Thirty-three gods, may behold the assembly of the Licchavis, and may gaze on them, for they are comparable to the assembly of the Thirty-three gods."

21. Then the Licchavis drove their carriages as far as the carriages could go, then alighted; and approaching the Blessed One on foot, they respectfully greeted him and sat down at one side. The Blessed One instructed the Licchavis in the Dhamma, and roused, edified, and gladdened them.

22. Thereafter the Licchavis spoke to the Blessed One, saying: "May the Blessed One, O Lord, please accept our invitation for tomorrow's meal, together with the community of bhikkhus."

"The invitation for tomorrow's meal, Licchavis, has been accepted by me from Ambapālī the courtesan."

Then the Licchavis snapped their fingers in annoyance: "See, friends! We are defeated by this mango lass! We are utterly outdone by this mango lass!" And then the Licchavis, approving of the Blessed One's words and delighted with them, rose from their seats, respectfully saluted him, and keeping their right sides towards him, took their departure.

23. Then, after the night had passed, Ambapālī the courtesan had choice food, hard and soft, prepared in her park, and announced it to the Blessed One: "It is time, O Lord; the meal is ready." Thereupon the Blessed One got ready in the forenoon, and taking bowl and robe, he went together with the community of bhikkhus to Ambapālī's dwelling, and there he took the seat prepared for him. And Ambapālī herself attended on the community of bhikkhus headed by the Buddha, and served them with choice food, hard and soft.

24. And when the Blessed One had finished his meal and had removed his hand from his bowl, Ambapālī the courtesan took a low seat, and placing herself at one side, spoke to the Blessed One, saying: "This park, O Lord, I offer to the community of bhikkhus headed by the Buddha." And the Blessed One accepted the park. He then instructed Ambapālī in the Dhamma, and having roused, edified, and gladdened her, he rose from his seat and departed.

25. And also at Vesālī, in Ambapālī's grove, the Blessed One often gave counsel to the bhikkhus thus: "Such and such is virtue; such and such is concentration; and such and such is wisdom. Great becomes the fruit, great is the gain of concentration when it is fully developed by virtuous conduct; great becomes the fruit, great is the gain of wisdom when it is fully developed by concentration; utterly freed from the taints of lust, becoming, and ignorance is the mind that is fully developed in wisdom."

26. When the Blessed One had stayed in Ambapālī's grove as long as he pleased, he spoke to the Venerable Ānanda, saying: "Come, Ānanda, let us go to the village of Beluva."

"So be it, Lord." And the Blessed One took up his abode in the village of Beluva together with a large community of bhikkhus.

The Blessed One's Deadly Sickness

27. At that time the Blessed One spoke to the bhikkhus, saying: "Go now, bhikkhus, and seek shelter anywhere in the neighbourhood of Vesālī where you are welcome, among acquaintances and friends, and there spend the rainy season. As for me, I shall spend the rainy season in this very place, in the village of Beluva."

"So be it, O Lord," the bhikkhus said.

28. But when the Blessed One had entered upon the rainy season, there arose in him a severe illness, and sharp and deadly pains came upon him. And the Blessed One endured them mindfully, clearly comprehending and unperturbed.

29. Then it occurred to the Blessed One: "It would not be fitting if I came to my final passing away without addressing those who attended on me, without taking leave of the community of bhikkhus. Then let me suppress this illness by strength of will, resolve to maintain the life process, and live on."

30. And the Blessed One suppressed the illness by strength of will, resolved to maintain the life process, and lived on. So it came about that the Blessed One's illness was allayed.

31. And the Blessed One recovered from that illness; and soon after his recovery he came out from his dwelling place and sat down in the shade of the building, on a seat prepared for him. Then the Venerable Ānanda approached the Blessed One, respectfully greeted him, and sitting down at one side, he spoke to the Blessed One, saying: "Fortunate it is for me, O Lord, to see the Blessed One at ease again! Fortunate it is for me, O Lord, to see the Blessed One recovered! For truly, Lord, when I saw the Blessed One's sickness it was as though my own body became weak as a creeper, everything around became dim to me, and my senses failed me. Yet, Lord, I still had some little comfort in the thought that the Blessed One would not come to his final passing away until he had given some last instructions respecting the community of bhikkhus."

32. Thus spoke the Venerable Ānanda, but the Blessed One answered him, saying: "What more does the community of bhikkhus expect from me, Ānanda? I have set forth the Dhamma without making any distinction of esoteric and exoteric doctrine; there is nothing, Ānanda, with regard to the teachings that the Tathāgata holds to the last with the closed fist of a teacher who keeps some things back. Whosoever may think that it is he who should lead the community of bhikkhus, or that the community depends upon him, it is such a one that would have to give last instructions respecting them. But, Ānanda, the Tathāgata has no such idea as that it is he who should lead the community of bhikkhus, or that the community depends upon him. So what instructions should he have to give respecting the community of bhikkhus?

"Now I am frail, Ānanda, old, aged, far gone in years. This is my eightieth year, and my life is spent. Even as an old cart, Ānanda, is held together with much difficulty, so the body of the Tathāgata is kept going only with supports. It is, Ānanda, only when the Tathāgata, disregarding external objects, with the cessation of certain feelings, attains to and abides in the signless concentration of mind,[19] that his body is more comfortable.

33. "Therefore, Ānanda, be islands unto yourselves, refuges unto yourselves, seeking no external refuge; with the Dhamma as your island, the Dhamma as your refuge, seeking no other refuge.

"And how, Ānanda, is a bhikkhu an island unto himself, a refuge unto himself, seeking no external refuge; with the Dhamma as his island, the Dhamma as his refuge, seeking no other refuge?

34. "When he dwells contemplating the body in the body, earnestly, clearly comprehending, and mindfully, after having overcome desire and sorrow in regard to the world; when he dwells contemplating feelings in feelings, the mind in the mind, and mental objects in mental objects, earnestly, clearly comprehending, and mindfully, after having overcome desire and sorrow in regard to the world, then, truly, he is an island unto himself, a refuge unto himself, seeking no external refuge; having the Dhamma as his island, the Dhamma as his refuge, seeking no other refuge.

35. "Those bhikkhus of mine, Ānanda, who now or after I am gone, abide as an island unto themselves, as a refuge unto themselves, seeking no other refuge; having the Dhamma as their island and refuge, seeking no other refuge: it is they who will become the highest,[20] if they have the desire to learn."

---

19. *Animitta cetosamādhi.* Comy. explains this term here as referring to the fruition-attainment of arahatship (*phalasamāpatti*), in which the Buddha becomes absorbed in the direct experience of Nibbāna and no longer attends to external objects or feels mundane feelings. In another context it can mean the concentration developed by intensive insight.

20. *Tamatagge*: a difficult word. Comy. takes it to stand for the superlative form, *aggatamā*, "highest," but alludes also to the Pāli word *tama*, "darkness." It is rather difficult to accept that a superlative suffix should be made to precede the word it qualifies. Tibetan and Chinese parallels (Waldschmidt, *Das Mahāparinirvāṇa-sūtra* Berlin, 1950–51, pp. 200 ff.) point to a meaning as "the highest." In the fragments of the Turfan Sanskrit version, these words

Part Three
Relinquishing the Will to Live

The Blessed One's Prompting

1. Then the Blessed One, getting ready in the forenoon, took bowl and robe and went into Vesālī for alms. After the alms round and meal, on his return, he spoke to the Venerable Ānanda, saying: "Take up a mat, Ānanda, and let us spend the day at the Cāpāla shrine."

"So be it, Lord." And the Venerable Ānanda took up a mat and followed behind the Blessed One, step by step.

2. And the Blessed One went to the Cāpāla shrine and sat down on the seat prepared for him. And when the Venerable Ānanda had seated himself at one side after he had respectfully saluted the Blessed One, the Lord said to him: "Pleasant, Ānanda, is Vesālī; pleasant are the shrines of Udena, Gotamaka, Sattambaka, Bahuputta, Sarandada, and Cāpāla."

3. And the Blessed One said: "Whosoever, Ānanda, has developed, practised, employed, strengthened, maintained, scrutinized, and brought to perfection the four constituents of psychic power could, if he so desired, remain throughout a world-period or until the end of it.[21] The Tathāgata, Ānanda, has

---

are not preserved. Comy. says: "*Tamatagge* = *tama-agge*; the '*t*' in the middle is inserted for euphonic reasons. The meaning is: these are the very highest, the most eminent (*ime aggatamā tamataggā*). Having cut every bondage of darkness (*tama-yoga*), those bhikkhus of mine will be on the very top, in the highest rank (*ativiya agge uttamabhāve*). Among them those will be on the very summit (*ati-agge*) who are desirous of training; and those whose resort is the four foundations of mindfulness will be at the very top of them."

21. *Kappaṃ vā tiṭṭheyya kappāvasesaṃ vā.* Comy. takes *kappa* not as "world-period" or "aeon," but as *āyu-kappa*, "life span," and explains *avasesa* (usually "remainder") by "in excess."

Comy.: "He may stay alive completing the life span pertaining to men at the given time. (Sub. Comy.: the maximum life span.) *Kappāvasesa*: 'in excess' (*atireka*), i.e. more or less above the hundred years said to be the normally highest life expectation."

done so. Therefore the Tathāgata could, if he so desired, remain throughout a world-period or until the end of it."

4. But the Venerable Ānanda was unable to grasp the plain suggestion, the significant prompting, given by the Blessed One. As though his mind was influenced by Māra,[22] he did not beseech the Blessed One: "May the Blessed One remain, O Lord! May the Happy One remain, O Lord, throughout the world-period, for the welfare and happiness of the multitude, out of compassion for the world, for the benefit, well being, and happiness of gods and men!"

5. And when for a second and a third time the Blessed One repeated his words, the Venerable Ānanda remained silent.

6. Then the Blessed One said to the Venerable Ānanda: "Go now, Ānanda, and do as seems fit to you."

"Even so, O Lord." And the Venerable Ānanda, rising from his seat, respectfully saluted the Blessed One, and keeping his right side towards him, took his seat under a tree some distance away.

Māra's Appeal

7. And when the Venerable Ānanda had gone away, Māra, the Evil One, approached the Blessed One. And standing at one side he spoke to the Blessed One, saying: "Now, O Lord, let the Blessed One come to his final passing away; let the Happy One utterly pass away! The time has come for the Parinibbāna of the Lord.

"For the Blessed One, O Lord, spoke these words to me: 'I shall not come to my final passing away, Evil One, until my bhikkhus and bhikkhunīs, laymen and laywomen, have come to be true disciples—wise, well disciplined, apt and learned, preservers of the Dhamma, living according to the Dhamma, abiding by the appropriate conduct, and having learned the Master's word, are

---

Among the numerous meanings of the word *kappa*, there is, in fact, that of time in general (*kāla*) and not only the duration of an aeon; but the meaning "life span" seems to have been ascribed to it only in this passage. Also, the meaning "in excess" for *avasesa* (usually "remainder") is unusual.

The four constituents of psychic power (*iddhipāda*) are concentration due to zeal, energy, purity of mind, and investigation.

22. According to Comy., Ānanda's mind had been influenced (*pariyuṭṭhitacitto*) by Māra's exhibiting a frightful sight which distracted his attention, preventing him from grasping the Buddha's suggestion.

able to expound it, preach it, proclaim it, establish it, reveal it, explain it in detail, and make it clear; until, when adverse opinions arise, they shall be able to refute them thoroughly and well, and to preach this convincing and liberating Dhamma.'[23]

8. "And now, O Lord, bhikkhus and bhikkhunīs, laymen and laywomen, have become the Blessed One's disciples in just this way. So, O Lord, let the Blessed One come to his final passing away! The time has come for the Parinibbāna of the Lord.

"For the Blessed One, O Lord, spoke these words to me: 'I shall not come to my final passing away, Evil One, until this holy life taught by me has become successful, prosperous, far-renowned, popular, and widespread, until it is well proclaimed among gods and men.' And this too has come to pass in just this way. So, O Lord, let the Blessed One come to his final passing away, let the Happy One utterly pass away! The time has come for the Parinibbāna of the Lord."

The Blessed One Relinquishes His Will to Live

9. When this was said, the Blessed One spoke to Māra, the Evil One, saying: "Do not trouble yourself, Evil One. Before long the Parinibbāna of the Tathāgata will come about. Three months hence the Tathāgata will utterly pass away."

10. And at the Cāpāla shrine the Blessed One thus mindfully and clearly comprehending renounced his will to live on. And upon the Lord's renouncing his will to live on, there came a tremendous earthquake, dreadful and astonishing, and thunder rolled across the heavens. And the Blessed One beheld it with understanding, and made this solemn utterance:

---

23. "Convincing and liberating." This stands for the one Pāli word *sappāṭihāriya*, an attempt to render the two connotations which the word has according to the commentaries and in the context of other occurrences in the Canon. The commentaries derive it from the verb *paṭiharati*, "to remove," and explain it as (1) the removal of what is adverse, e.g. opposition and objections (covered by "convincing"), and (2) the removal of inner obstructions, i.e. defilements such as greed, etc., effected by arahatship. It is probably to point to that latter meaning that the commentary to our present text paraphrases our passage as follows: "until they are able to preach the Teaching in its liberating (*niyyānika*) capacity."

"What causes life, unbounded or confined[24]—
His process of becoming[25]—this the Sage
Renounces. With inward calm and joy he breaks,
As though a coat of mail, his own life's cause."[26]

11. Then it came to the mind of the Venerable Ānanda: "Marvellous it is indeed, and most wonderful! The earth shakes mightily, tremendously! Dreadful and astonishing it is, how the thunders roll across the heavens! What could be the reason, what the cause, that so mighty an earthquake should arise?"

Eight Causes of Earthquakes

12. And the Venerable Ānanda approached the Blessed One, and respectfully greeting him, sat down at one side. Then he spoke to the Blessed One, saying: "Marvellous it is indeed, and most wonderful! The earth shakes mightily, tremendously! Dreadful and astonishing it is how the thunders roll across the heavens! What could be the reason, what the cause, that so mighty an earthquake should arise?"

13. Then the Blessed One said: "There are eight reasons, Ānanda, eight causes for a mighty earthquake to arise. What are those eight?

14. "This great earth, Ānanda, is established upon liquid, the liquid upon the atmosphere, and the atmosphere upon space. And when, Ānanda, mighty atmospheric disturbances take place, the liquid is agitated. And with the agitation of the liquid, tremors of the earth arise. This is the first reason, the first cause for the arising of mighty earthquakes.

---

24. *Tulaṃ atulañca sambhavaṃ*: lit. "the measurable and immeasurable productive cause (of life)," i.e. the volitional action causing rebirth in the confined, or limited sense-sphere, or in the unbounded fine-material and immaterial spheres.

25. *Bhavasaṅkhāra*: the formative force of becoming, in the sense of what forms existence.

26. *Kavacam iv'attasambhavaṃ*. Comy.: "He breaks through the entire net of defilements that envelops individual existence like a coat of mail; he breaks the defilements as a great warrior breaks his armour after a battle." The Sanskrit version has "like an egg shell" (*kosam iv' āṇḍa-sambhavaṃ*).

15. "Again, Ānanda, when an ascetic or holy man of great power, one who has gained mastery of his mind, or a deity who is mighty and potent, develops intense concentration on the delimited aspect of the earth element, and to a boundless degree on the liquid element, he, too, causes the earth to tremble, quiver, and shake. This is the second reason, the second cause for the arising of mighty earthquakes.

16–21. "Again, Ānanda, when the Bodhisatta departs from the Tusita realm and descends into his mother's womb, mindfully and clearly comprehending; and when the Bodhisatta comes out from his mother's womb, mindfully and clearly comprehending; and when the Tathāgata becomes fully enlightened in unsurpassed, supreme Enlightenment; when the Tathāgata sets rolling the excellent Wheel of the Dhamma; when the Tathāgata renounces his will to live on; and when the Tathāgata comes to pass away into the state of Nibbāna in which no element of clinging remains—then, too, Ānanda, this great earth trembles, quivers, and shakes.

"These, Ānanda, are the eight reasons, the eight causes for a great earthquake to arise.[27]

Eight Assemblies

22. "Now there are eight kinds of assemblies, Ānanda, that is to say, assemblies of nobles, brahmins, householders, ascetics, of the Four Great Kings, of the Thirty-three gods, of Māras, and of Brahmās.

23. "And I recall, Ānanda, how I have attended each of these eight kinds of assemblies, amounting to hundreds.[28] And before seating myself and starting the conversation or the discussion, I made my appearance resemble theirs, my voice resemble theirs. And so I taught them the Dhamma, and roused, edified, and gladdened them. Yet while I was speaking to them thus, they did

27. Comy.: "Even by this much the Venerable Ānanda was aware of the fact: 'Surely, today the Blessed One has renounced his will to live on.' Though the Blessed One knew that the Venerable Ānanda was aware of it, he did not give him another opportunity to ask him to stay on for the remainder of his life span, but he spoke to him about other eight-term groups beginning with the eight assemblies." Sub. Comy.: "Some say that the Buddha did so in order to divert the Venerable Ānanda and to prevent grief from arising in him."

28. See also the Mahāsīhanāda Sutta (MN 12).

not know me, and they would enquire of one another, asking: 'Who is he that speaks to us? Is it a man or a god?'

"Then having taught them the Dhamma, and roused, edified, and gladdened them, I would straightaway vanish. And when I had vanished, too, they did not know me, and they would enquire of one another, asking: 'Who is he that has vanished? Is it a man or a god?'

"And such, Ānanda, are the eight kinds of assemblies.

Eight Fields of Mastery

24. "Now there are eight fields of mastery,[29] Ānanda. What are those eight?

25. "When one, perceiving forms subjectively,[30] sees small forms, beautiful or ugly, external to himself,[31] and mastering them, is aware that he perceives and knows them as they are—this is the first field of mastery.

26. "When one, perceiving forms subjectively, sees large forms, beautiful or ugly, external to himself, and mastering them, is aware that he perceives and knows them as they are—this is the second field of mastery.

27. "When one, not perceiving forms subjectively,[32] sees small forms, beautiful or ugly, external to himself, and mastering them, is aware that he perceives and knows them as they are—this is the third field of mastery.

28. "When one, not perceiving forms subjectively, sees large forms, beautiful or ugly, external to himself, and mastering them, is aware that he perceives and knows them as they are—this is the fourth field of mastery.

29. "When one, not perceiving forms subjectively, sees forms external to himself that are blue, blue in colour, of a blue lustre like the blossoms of flax, or like fine Benares muslin which, burnished on both sides, is blue, blue in colour, of a blue lustre—when such

---

29. *Abhibhāyatana.*

30. That is: "perceiving forms on his own body." This refers to preliminary concentration.

31. This refers to the *kasiṇa-nimitta*, the after-image arising with full concentration.

32. He derives the "sign" from objects external to his body.

a one sees forms external to himself that are blue, and mastering them, is aware that he perceives and knows them as they are—this is the fifth field of mastery.

30. "When one, not perceiving forms subjectively, sees forms external to himself that are yellow, yellow in colour, of a yellow lustre like the Kanikāra blossom, or like fine Benares muslin which, burnished on both sides, is yellow, yellow in colour, of a yellow lustre—when such a one sees forms external to himself that are yellow, and mastering them, is aware that he perceives and knows them as they are—this is the sixth field of mastery.

31. "When one, not perceiving forms subjectively, sees forms external to himself that are red, red in colour, of a red lustre like the Bandhujīvaka blossom, or like fine Benares muslin which, burnished on both sides, is red, red in colour, of a red lustre—when such a one sees forms external to himself that are red, and mastering them, is aware that he perceives and knows them as they are—this is the seventh field of mastery.

32. "When one, not perceiving forms subjectively, sees forms external to himself that are white, white in colour, of a white lustre like the morning star, or like fine Benares muslin which, burnished on both sides, is white, white in colour, of a white lustre—when such a one sees forms external to himself that are white, and mastering them, is aware that he perceives and knows them as they are—this is the eighth field of mastery.

"These, Ānanda, are the eight fields of mastery.

Eight Liberations

33. "Now there are eight liberations, Ānanda. What are those eight?[33]

34. "Oneself having form,[34] one perceives forms; this is the first liberation.

35. "Being unaware of one's own form, one perceives forms external to oneself; this is the second liberation.

---

33. *Aṭṭha vimokkhā.*

34. *Rūpī.* This refers to form-sphere absorption (*rūpajjhāna*) obtained with form objects of one's own body.

36. "Experiencing loveliness, one is intent upon it;[35] this is the third liberation.

37. "By utterly transcending the perceptions of matter, by the disappearance of the perceptions of sense-reaction, and by giving no attention to diversity-perceptions, one becomes aware of, attains to, and abides in the sphere of infinite space; this is the fourth liberation.

38. "By utterly transcending the sphere of infinite space, one becomes aware of, attains to, and abides in the sphere of infinite consciousness; this is the fifth liberation.

39. "By utterly transcending the sphere of infinite consciousness, one becomes aware of, attains to, and abides in the sphere of nothingness; this is the sixth liberation.

40. "By utterly transcending the sphere of nothingness, one attains to and abides in the sphere of neither-perception-nor-non-perception; this is the seventh liberation.

41. "By utterly transcending the sphere of neither-perception-nor-non-perception, one attains to and abides in the cessation of perception and sensation; this is the eighth liberation.

"These, Ānanda, are the eight liberations.

Māra's Former Temptation

42. "There was a time, Ānanda, when I dwelt at Uruvelā, on the bank of the Nerañjarā River, at the foot of the goatherds' banyan-tree, soon after my supreme Enlightenment. And Māra, the Evil One, approached me, saying: 'Now, O Lord, let the Blessed One come to his final passing away! Let the Happy One utterly pass away! The time has come for the Parinibbāna of the Lord.'

43. "Then, Ānanda, I answered Māra, the Evil One, saying: 'I shall not come to my final passing away, Evil One, until my bhikkhus and bhikkhunīs, laymen and laywomen, have come to be true disciples—wise, well disciplined, apt and learned, preservers of the Dhamma, living according to the Dhamma, abiding by appropriate conduct and, having learned the Master's word, are able to expound it, preach it, proclaim it, establish it, reveal it,

35. *Subhan tveva adhimutto hoti.* Comy.: "Hereby, meditative absorption (*jhāna*), obtained through *blue-kasiṇas*, etc., of very pure colour is indicated."

explain it in detail, and make it clear; until, when adverse opinions arise, they shall be able to refute them thoroughly and well, and to preach this convincing and liberating Dhamma.

44. 'I shall not come to my final passing away, Evil One, until this holy life taught by me has become successful, prosperous, far-renowned, popular, and widespread, until it is well proclaimed among gods and men.'

45. "And again today, Ānanda, at the Cāpāla shrine, Māra, the Evil One, approached me, saying: 'Now, O Lord, bhikkhus and bhikkhunīs, laymen and laywomen, have come to be true disciples of the Blessed One—wise, well disciplined, apt and learned, preservers of the Dhamma, living according to the Dhamma, abiding in the appropriate conduct, and having learned the Master's word, are able to expound it, preach it, proclaim it, establish it, reveal it, explain it in detail, and make it clear; and when adverse opinions arise, they are now able to refute them thoroughly and well, and to preach this convincing and liberating Dhamma.

'And now, O Lord, this holy life taught by the Blessed One has become successful, prosperous, far-renowned, popular and widespread, and it is well proclaimed among gods and men. Therefore, O Lord, let the Blessed One come to his final passing away! Let the Happy One utterly pass away! The time has come for the Parinibbāna of the Lord.'

46. "And then, Ānanda, I answered Māra, the Evil One, saying: 'Do not trouble yourself, Evil One. Before long the Parinibbāna of the Tathāgata will come about. Three months hence the Tathāgata will utterly pass away.'

47. "And in this way, Ānanda, today at the Cāpāla shrine the Tathāgata has renounced his will to live on."

Ānanda's Appeal

48. At these words the Venerable Ānanda spoke to the Blessed One, saying: "May the Blessed One remain, O Lord! May the Happy One remain, O Lord, throughout the world-period, for the welfare and happiness of the multitude, out of compassion for the world, for the benefit, well being, and happiness of gods and men!"

49. And the Blessed One answered, saying: "Enough, Ānanda. Do not entreat the Tathāgata, for the time is past, Ānanda, for such an entreaty."

50–51. But for a second and a third time, the Venerable Ānanda said to the Blessed One: "May the Blessed One remain, O Lord! May the Happy One remain, O Lord, throughout the world-period, for the welfare and happiness of the multitude, out of compassion for the world, for the benefit, well being, and happiness of gods and men!"

52. Then the Blessed One said: "Do you have faith, Ānanda, in the Enlightenment of the Tathāgata?" And the Venerable Ānanda replied: "Yes, O Lord, I do."

"Then how, Ānanda, can you persist against the Tathāgata even up to the third time?"

53. Then the Venerable Ānanda said: "This, O Lord, I have heard and learned from the Blessed One himself when the Blessed One said to me: 'Whosoever, Ānanda, has developed, practised, employed, strengthened, maintained, scrutinized, and brought to perfection the four constituents of psychic power could, if he so desired, remain throughout a world-period or until the end of it. The Tathāgata, Ānanda, has done so. Therefore the Tathāgata could, if he so desired, remain throughout a world-period or until the end of it.' "

54. "And did you believe it, Ānanda?"

"Yes, O Lord, I did."

"Then, Ānanda, the fault is yours. Herein have you failed, inasmuch as you were unable to grasp the plain suggestion, the significant prompting given by the Tathāgata, and you did not then entreat the Tathāgata to remain. For if you had done so, Ānanda, twice the Tathāgata might have declined, but the third time he would have consented. Therefore, Ānanda, the fault is yours; herein have you failed.

55. "At Rājagaha, Ānanda, when dwelling at Vultures' Peak, I spoke to you, saying: 'Pleasant, Ānanda, is Rājagaha; pleasant is Vultures' Peak. Whosoever, Ānanda, has developed ... Therefore the Tathāgata could, if he so desired, remain throughout a world-period or until the end of it.'

56. "So also at the Banyan Grove, at Robbers' Cliff, at the Sattapaṇṇi Cave on the Vebhāra Mountain, at the Black Rock of Isigili, at the Serpents' Pool in the Cool Forest, at the Tapoda Grove, at the Bamboo Grove in the Squirrels' Feeding-ground, at Jīvaka's Mango Grove, and at Small Nook in the Deer Park

I spoke to you in the same words, saying: 'Pleasant, Ānanda, is Rājagaha, pleasant are these places. Whosoever, Ānanda, has developed ... Therefore the Tathāgata could, if he so desired, remain throughout a world-period or until the end of it.'

"But you, Ānanda, were unable to grasp the plain suggestion, the significant prompting given you by the Tathāgata, and you did not entreat the Tathāgata to remain. For if you had done so, Ānanda, twice the Tathāgata might have declined, but the third time he would have consented. Therefore, Ānanda, the fault is yours; herein you have failed.

57. "So also at Vesālī, Ānanda, at different times the Tathāgata has spoken to you, saying: 'Pleasant, Ānanda, is Vesāli; pleasant are the shrines of Udena, Gotamaka, Sattambaka, Bahuputta, Sarandada, and Cāpāla. Whosoever, Ānanda, has developed ... Therefore the Tathāgata could, if he so desired, remain throughout a world-period or until the end of it.'

"But you, Ānanda, were unable to grasp the plain suggestion, the significant prompting, given you by the Tathāgata, and you did not entreat the Tathāgata to remain. For if you had done so, Ānanda, twice the Tathāgata might have declined, but the third time he would have consented. Therefore, Ānanda, the fault is yours; herein you have failed.

58. "Yet, Ānanda, have I not taught from the very beginning that with all that is dear and beloved there must be change, separation, and severance? Of that which is born, come into being, is compounded and subject to decay, how can one say: 'May it not come to dissolution!' There can be no such state of things. And of that, Ānanda, which the Tathāgata has finished with, that which he has relinquished, given up, abandoned, and rejected—his will to live on—the Tathāgata's word has been spoken once for all: 'Before long the Parinibbāna of the Tathāgata will come about. Three months hence the Tathāgata will utterly pass away.' And that the Tathāgata should withdraw his words for the sake of living on—this is an impossibility.

The Last Admonition

59. "So, then, Ānanda, let us go to the hall of the Gabled House, in the Great Forest." And the Venerable Ānanda replied: "So be it, Lord."

60. Then the Blessed One, with the Venerable Ānanda, went to the hall of the Gabled House, in the Great Forest. And there he spoke to the Venerable Ānanda, saying: "Go now, Ānanda, and assemble in the hall of audience all the bhikkhus who dwell in the neighbourhood of Vesālī."

"So be it, Lord." And the Venerable Ānanda gathered all the bhikkhus who dwelt in the neighbourhood of Vesālī, and assembled them in the hall of audience. And then, respectfully saluting the Blessed One, and standing at one side, he said: "The community of bhikkhus is assembled, Lord. Now let the Blessed One do as he wishes."

61. Thereupon the Blessed One entered the hall of audience, and taking the seat prepared for him, he exhorted the bhikkhus, saying: "Now, O bhikkhus, I say to you that these teachings of which I have direct knowledge and which I have made known to you—these you should thoroughly learn, cultivate, develop, and frequently practise, that the life of purity may be established and may long endure, for the welfare and happiness of the multitude, out of compassion for the world, for the benefit, well being, and happiness of gods and men.

62. "And what, bhikkhus, are these teachings? They are the four foundations of mindfulness, the four right efforts, the four constituents of psychic power, the five faculties, the five powers, the seven factors of enlightenment, and the Noble Eightfold Path. These, bhikkhus, are the teachings of which I have direct knowledge, which I have made known to you, and which you should thoroughly learn, cultivate, develop, and frequently practise, that the life of purity may be established and may long endure, for the welfare and happiness of the multitude, out of compassion for the world, for the benefit, well being, and happiness of gods and men."

63. Then the Blessed One said to the bhikkhus: "So, bhikkhus, I exhort you: All compounded things are subject to vanish. Strive with earnestness. The time of the Tathāgata's Parinibbāna is near.

Three months hence the Tathāgata will utterly pass away."

64. And having spoken these words, the Happy One, the Master, spoke again, saying:

"My years are now full ripe, the life span left is short.
Departing, I go hence from you, relying on myself alone.
Be earnest, then, O bhikkhus, be mindful and of virtue pure!
With firm resolve, guard your own mind!
Whoso untiringly pursues the Dhamma and the Discipline
Shall go beyond the round of births and make an end of suffering."

Part Four
The Last Meal

The Elephant's Look

1. Then the Blessed One, getting ready in the forenoon, took bowl and robe and went into Vesālī for alms. After the alms round and meal, on his return, he looked upon Vesālī with the elephant's look,[36] and said to the Venerable Ānanda: "This, Ānanda, is the last time that the Tathāgata will look upon Vesālī. Come, Ānanda, let us go to Bhandagāma."

"So be it, O Lord." And the Blessed One took up his abode at Bhandagāma together with a large community of bhikkhus.

2. And the Blessed One addressed the bhikkhus, saying: "Bhikkhus, it is through not realizing, through not penetrating four principles that this long course of birth and death has been passed through and undergone by me as well as by you. What are those four? They are: noble virtue, noble concentration, noble wisdom, and noble emancipation. But now, bhikkhus, that these have been realized and penetrated, cut off is the craving for existence, destroyed is that which leads to renewed becoming, and there is no fresh becoming."

3. And having spoken these words, the Happy One, the Master, spoke again, saying:

> "Virtue, concentration, wisdom, and emancipation unsurpassed—
> These are the principles realized by Gotama the renowned;
> And, knowing them, he, the Buddha, to his monks has taught the Dhamma.
> He, the destroyer of suffering, the Master, the Seer, is at peace."

4. And also at Bhandagāma the Blessed One often gave counsel to the bhikkhus thus: "Such and such is virtue; such and such is

36. The Comy. says that the Buddhas, when looking back, turn the whole body round as an elephant does.

concentration; and such and such is wisdom. Great becomes the fruit, great is the gain of concentration when it is fully developed by virtuous conduct; great becomes the fruit, great is the gain of wisdom when it is fully developed by concentration; utterly freed from the taints of lust, becoming, and ignorance is the mind that is fully developed in wisdom."

5. When the Blessed One had stayed at Bhandagāma as long as he pleased, he spoke to the Venerable Ānanda: "Come, Ānanda, let us go to Hatthigāma."

"So be it, Lord." And the Blessed One took up his abode at Hatthigāma together with a large community of bhikkhus.

And when the Blessed One had stayed at Hatthigāma as long as he pleased, he took up his abode at Ambagāma, then at Jambugāma. And at each of these places the Blessed One often gave counsel to the bhikkhus thus: "Such and such is virtue; such and such is concentration; and such and such is wisdom. Great becomes the fruit, great is the gain of concentration when it is fully developed by virtuous conduct; great becomes the fruit, great is the gain of wisdom when it is fully developed by concentration; utterly freed from the taints of lust, becoming, and ignorance is the mind that is fully developed in wisdom."

6. And when the Blessed One had stayed at Jambugāma as long as he pleased, he spoke to the Venerable Ānanda: "Come, Ānanda, let us go to Bhoganagara."

"So be it, Lord." And the Blessed One took up his abode at Bhoganagara together with a large community of bhikkhus, and stayed in the Ānanda shrine.

The Four Great References

7. And there the Blessed One addressed the bhikkhus, saying: "Now, bhikkhus, I shall make known to you the four great references.[37] Listen and pay attention to my words." And those bhikkhus answered, saying:

37. In the earlier edition of this work, *mahāpadesa* was rendered as "great authorities." It is now known that the proper meaning of *apadesa* is not "authority," but "reference" or "source." Besides, from the passage it is clear that there are only two real "authorities"—the Discourses (Suttas) and the Discipline (Vinaya).

"So be it, Lord."

8–11. Then the Blessed One said: "In this fashion, bhikkhus, a bhikkhu might speak: 'Face to face with the Blessed One, brethren, I have heard and learned thus: This is the Dhamma and the Discipline, the Master's Dispensation'; or: 'In an abode of such and such a name lives a community with elders and a chief. Face to face with that community, I have heard and learned thus: This is the Dhamma and the Discipline, the Master's Dispensation'; or: 'In an abode of such and such a name live several bhikkhus who are elders, who are learned, who have accomplished their course, who are preservers of the Dhamma, the Discipline, and the Summaries. Face to face with those elders, I have heard and learned thus: This is the Dhamma and the Discipline, the Master's Dispensation'; or: 'In an abode of such and such a name lives a single bhikkhu who is an elder, who is learned, who has accomplished his course, who is a preserver of the Dhamma, the Discipline, and the Summaries. Face to face with that elder, I have heard and learned thus: This is the Dhamma and the Discipline, the Master's Dispensation.'

"In such a case, bhikkhus, the declaration of such a bhikkhu is neither to be received with approval nor with scorn. Without approval and without scorn, but carefully studying the sentences word by word, one should trace them in the Discourses and verify them by the Discipline. If they are neither traceable in the Discourses nor verifiable by the Discipline, one must conclude thus: 'Certainly, this is not the Blessed One's utterance; this has been misunderstood by that bhikkhu—or by that community, or by those elders, or by that elder.' In that way, bhikkhus, you should reject it. But if the sentences concerned are traceable in the Discourses and verifiable by the Discipline, then one must conclude thus: 'Certainly, this is the Blessed One's utterance; this has been well understood by that bhikkhu—or by that community, or by those elders, or by that elder.' And in that way, bhikkhus, you may accept it on the first, second, third, or fourth reference. These, bhikkhus, are the four great references for you to preserve."

12. And also at Bhoganagara, at the Ānanda shrine, the Blessed One often gave counsel to the bhikkhus thus: "Such and such is virtue; such and such is concentration; and such and such is wisdom. Great becomes the fruit, great is the gain of concentration when it is fully developed by virtuous conduct; great becomes the

fruit, great is the gain of wisdom when it is fully developed by concentration; utterly freed from the taints of lust, becoming, and ignorance is the mind that is fully developed in wisdom."

13. When the Blessed One had stayed at Bhoganagara as long as he pleased, he spoke to the Venerable Ānanda, saying: "Come, Ānanda, let us go to Pāvā."

"So be it, Lord." And the Blessed One took up his abode at Pāvā together with a great community of bhikkhus, and stayed in the Mango Grove of Cunda, who was by family a metalworker.

The Buddha's Last Meal

14. And Cunda the metalworker came to know: "The Blessed One, they say, has arrived at Pāvā, and is staying in my Mango Grove." And he went to the Blessed One, and having respectfully greeted him, sat down at one side. And the Blessed One instructed Cunda the metalworker in the Dhamma, and roused, edified, and gladdened him.

15. Then Cunda spoke to the Blessed One, saying: "May the Blessed One, O Lord, please accept my invitation for tomorrow's meal, together with the community of bhikkhus." And by his silence the Blessed One consented.

16. Sure, then, of the Blessed One's consent, Cunda the metalworker rose from his seat, respectfully saluted the Blessed One, and keeping his right side towards him, took his departure.

17. And Cunda the metalworker, after the night had passed, had choice food, hard and soft, prepared in his abode, together with a quantity of *sūkara-maddava*,[38] and announced it to the

---

38. *Sūkara-maddava*: a controversial term which has therefore been left untranslated. *Sūkara* = pig; *maddava* = soft, tender, delicate. Hence two alternative renderings of the compound are possible: (1) the tender parts *of* a pig or boar; (2) what is enjoyed *by* pigs and boars. In the latter meaning, the term has been thought to refer to a mushroom or truffle, or a yam or tuber. K.E. Neumann, in the preface to his German translation of the Majjhima Nikāya, quotes from an Indian compendium of medicinal plants, the *Rājanigaṇṭu*, several plants beginning with *sūkara*.

The commentary to our text gives three alternative explanations: (1) the flesh from a single first-born (wild) pig, neither too young nor too old, which had come to hand naturally, i.e. without intentional killing; (2)

Blessed One, saying: "It is time, O Lord, the meal is ready."

18. Thereupon the Blessed One, in the forenoon, having got ready, took bowl and robe and went with the community of bhikkhus to the house of Cunda, and there sat down on the seat prepared for him. And he spoke to Cunda, saying: "With the *sūkara-maddava* you have prepared, Cunda, you may serve me; with the other food, hard and soft, you may serve the community of bhikkhus."

"So be it, Lord." And with the *sūkara-maddava* prepared by him, he served the Blessed One; and with the other food, hard and soft, he served the community of bhikkhus.

19. Thereafter the Blessed One spoke to Cunda, saying: "Whatever, Cunda, is left over of the *sūkara-maddava*, bury that in a pit. For I do not see in all this world, with its gods, Māras, and Brahmās, among the host of ascetics and brahmins, gods and men, anyone who could eat it and entirely digest it except the Tathāgata alone."

And Cunda the metalworker answered the Blessed One saying: "So be it, O Lord." And what remained over of the *sūkara-maddava* he buried in a pit.

20. Then he returned to the Blessed One, respectfully greeted him, and sat down at one side. And the Blessed One instructed Cunda the metalworker in the Dhamma, and roused, edified, and gladdened him. After this he rose from his seat and departed.

21. And soon after the Blessed One had eaten the meal provided by Cunda the metalworker, a dire sickness fell upon him, even dysentery, and he suffered sharp and deadly pains. But the Blessed One endured them mindfully, clearly comprehending and unperturbed.

22. Then the Blessed One spoke to the Venerable Ānanda, saying: "Come, Ānanda, let us go to Kusinārā." And the Venerable Ānanda answered: "So be it, Lord."

23. *When he had eaten Cunda's food, I heard,*
With fortitude the deadly pains he bore.
From the sūkara-maddava a sore

---

a preparation of soft boiled rice cooked with the five cow-products; (3) a kind of alchemistic elixir (*rasāyanavidhi*). Dhammapāla, in his commentary to Udāna 8:5, gives, in addition, young bamboo shoots trampled by pigs (*sūkarehi maddita-vaṃsakalīro*).

And dreadful sickness came upon the Lord.
But nature's pangs he endured. "Come, let us go
To Kusinārā," was his dauntless word.[39]

The Clearing of the Waters

24. Now on the way the Blessed One went aside from the highway and stopped at the foot of a tree. And he said to the Venerable Ānanda: "Please fold my upper robe in four, Ānanda, and lay it down. I am weary and want to rest awhile."

"So be it, Lord." And the Venerable Ānanda folded the robe in four and laid it down.

25. And the Blessed One sat down on the seat prepared for him and said to the Venerable Ānanda: "Please bring me some water, Ānanda. I am thirsty and want to drink."

26. And the Venerable Ānanda answered the Blessed One: "But just now, Lord, a great number of carts, five hundred carts, have passed over, and the shallow water has been cut through by the wheels, so that it flows turbid and muddy. But the Kakutthā River, Lord, is quite close by, and its waters are clear, pleasant, cool, and translucent. It is easily approachable and delightfully placed. There the Blessed One can quench his thirst and refresh his limbs."

27–29. But a second time the Blessed One made his request, and the Venerable Ānanda answered him as before. And then for a third time the Blessed One said: "Please bring me some water, Ānanda. I am thirsty and want to drink."

30. Then the Venerable Ānanda answered, saying: "So be it, Lord." And he took the bowl and went to the stream. And the shallow water, which had been cut through by the wheels so that it flowed turbid and muddy, became clear and settled down, pure and pleasant as the Venerable Ānanda drew near.

31. Then the Venerable Ānanda thought: "Marvellous and most wonderful indeed is the power and glory of the Tathāgata!"

32. And he took up water in the bowl and carried it to the Blessed One, and said: "Marvellous and most wonderful indeed is the power and glory of the Tathāgata! For this shallow water,

39. Comy.: "These verses, and several to follow, were inserted by the elders who collected the Dhamma (texts at the First Council)."

which had been cut through by the wheels so that it flowed turbid and muddy, became clear and settled down, pure and pleasant as I drew near. Now let the Blessed One drink the water. Let the Happy One drink." And the Blessed One drank the water.

Pukkusa the Malla

33. Now it so happened that one Pukkusa of the Malla clan, who was a disciple of Āḷāra Kālāma, was passing by on his way from Kusinārā to Pāvā.[40]

34. And when he saw the Blessed One seated at the foot of a tree, he approached him, respectfully greeted him, and sat down at one side. And he spoke to the Blessed One, saying: "Marvellous it is, Lord, most wonderful it is, O Lord, the state of calmness wherein abide those who have gone forth from the world.

35. "For at one time, Lord, Āḷāra Kālāma was on a journey, and he went aside from the highway and sat down by the wayside at the foot of a tree to pass the heat of the day. And it came about, Lord, that a great number of carts, even five hundred carts, passed by him, one by one. And then, Lord, a certain man who was following behind that train of carts, approached and spoke to him, saying: 'Did you, sir, see a great number of carts that passed you by?' And Āḷāra Kālāma answered him: 'I did not see them, brother.' 'But the noise, sir, surely you heard?' 'I did not hear it, brother.' Then that man asked him: 'Then, sir, perhaps you slept?' 'No, brother, I was not sleeping.' 'Then, sir, were you conscious?' 'I was, brother.' Then that man said: 'Then, sir, while conscious and awake you still did not see the great number of carts, even five hundred carts, that passed you by one after another, nor heard the noise? Why, sir, your very robe is covered with their dust!' And Āḷāra Kālāma replied, saying: 'So it is, brother.'

36. "And to that man, O Lord, came the thought: 'Marvellous it is, most wonderful indeed it is, the state of calmness wherein abide those who have gone forth from the world!' And there arose in him great faith in Āḷāra Kālāma, and he went his way."

---

40. Āḷāra Kālāma was one of the Buddha's teachers before his Enlightenment. He taught the Bodhisatta how to attain the sphere of nothingness, but could not show him the path to Nibbāna.

37. "Now what do you think, Pukkusa? What is more difficult to do, more difficult to meet with—that a man, while conscious and awake, should not see a great number of carts, even five hundred carts, that passed him by one after another, nor hear the noise, or that one conscious and awake, in the midst of a heavy rain, with thunder rolling, lightning flashing, and thunderbolts crashing, should neither see it nor hear the noise?"

38. "What, O Lord, are five hundred carts—nay, six, seven, eight, nine hundred, or a thousand or even hundreds of thousands of carts—compared with this?"

39. "Now one time, Pukkusa, I was staying at Ātumā, and had my abode in a barn there. And at that time there was a heavy rain, with thunder rolling, lightning flashing, and thunderbolts crashing. And two farmers who were brothers were killed close to the barn, together with four oxen, and a great crowd came forth from Ātumā to the spot where they were killed.

40. "Now at that time, Pukkusa, I had come out of the barn and was walking up and down in thought before the door. And a certain man from the great crowd approached me, respectfully greeted me, and stood at one side.

41. "And I asked him: 'Why, brother, has this great crowd gathered together?' And he answered me: 'Just now, Lord, there was a heavy rain, with thunder rolling, lightning flashing, and thunderbolts crashing. And two farmers who were brothers were killed close by, together with four oxen. It is because of this that the great crowd has gathered. But where, Lord, were you?'

" 'I was here, brother.' 'Yet, Lord, did you not see it?' 'I did not see it, brother.' 'But the noise, Lord, you surely heard?' 'I did not hear it, brother.' Then that man asked me: 'Then, Lord, perhaps you slept?' 'No, brother, I was not sleeping.' 'Then, Lord, you were conscious?' 'I was, brother.' Then that man said: 'Then, Lord, while conscious and awake, in the midst of a heavy rain, with thunder rolling, lightning flashing, and thunderbolts crashing, you neither saw it nor heard the noise?' And I answered him, saying: 'I did not, brother.'

42. "And to that man, Pukkusa, came the thought: 'Marvellous it is, most wonderful indeed it is, the state of calmness wherein abide those who have gone forth from the world!' And there arose in him great faith in me, and he respectfully saluted me, and

keeping his right side towards me, he went his way."

43. When this had been said, Pukkusa of the Malla clan said to the Blessed One: "The faith, Lord, that I had in Āḷāra Kālāma I now scatter to the mighty wind, I let it be carried away as by a flowing stream! Excellent, O Lord, most excellent, O Lord! It is as if, Lord, one were to set upright what had been overthrown, or to reveal what had been hidden, or to show the path to one who had gone astray, or to light a lamp in the darkness so that those having eyes might see—even so has the Blessed One set forth the Dhamma in many ways. And so, O Lord, I take my refuge in the Blessed One, the Dhamma, and the Community of Bhikkhus. May the Blessed One accept me as his disciple, one who has taken refuge until the end of life."

44. Then Pukkusa of the Malla clan spoke to a certain man, saying: "Bring me at once, friend, two sets of golden-hued robes, burnished and ready for wear." And the man answered him: "So be it, sir."

45. And when the robes were brought, Pukkusa of the Malla clan offered them to the Blessed One, saying: "May the Blessed One, O Lord, out of compassion, accept this from me." And the Blessed One said: "Robe me, then in one, Pukkusa, and in the other robe Ānanda."

"So be it, Lord." And he thereupon robed the Blessed One in one, and in the other he robed the Venerable Ānanda.

46. And then the Blessed One instructed Pukkusa of the Malla clan in the Dhamma, and roused, edified, and gladdened him. And after that, Pukkusa rose from his seat, respectfully saluted the Blessed One, and keeping his right side towards him, went his way.

47. And soon after Pukkusa of the Malla clan had departed, the Venerable Ānanda arranged the set of golden-hued robes, burnished and ready for wear, about the body of the Blessed One. But when the set of robes was arranged upon the body of the Blessed One, it became as though faded, and its splendour dimmed.

48. And the Venerable Ānanda said to the Blessed One: "Marvellous it is, O Lord, most wonderful indeed it is, how clear and radiant the skin of the Tathāgata appears! This set of golden-hued robes, burnished and ready for wear, Lord, now that it is arranged upon the body of the Blessed One seems to have become faded, its splendour dimmed."

49. "It is so, Ānanda. There are two occasions, Ānanda, when the skin of the Tathāgata appears exceedingly clear and radiant. Which are these two? The night, Ānanda, when the Tathāgata becomes fully enlightened in unsurpassed, supreme Enlightenment, and the night when the Tathāgata comes to his final passing away into the state of Nibbāna in which no element of clinging remains. These, Ānanda, are the two occasions on which the skin of the Tathāgata appears exceedingly clear and radiant.

50. "And now today, in the last watch of this very night, Ānanda, in the Mallas' Sāla Grove, in the vicinity of Kusinārā, between two sāla trees, the Tathāgata will come to his Parinibbāna. So now, Ānanda, let us go to the Kakutthā River."

51. *Clad in Pukkusa's gift, the robes of gold,*
The Master's form was radiant to behold.

At the Kakutthā River

52. Then the Blessed One went to the Kakutthā River together with a great community of bhikkhus.

53. And he went down into the water and bathed and drank. And coming forth from the water again, he went to the Mango Grove, and there spoke to the Venerable Cundaka, saying: "Please fold my upper robe in four, Cundaka, and lay it down. I am weary and would rest awhile."

"So be it, Lord." And Cundaka folded the robe in four and laid it down.

54. And the Blessed One lay down on his right side, in the lion's posture, resting one foot upon the other, and so disposed himself, mindfully and clearly comprehending, with the time for rising held in mind. And the Venerable Cundaka sat down right in front of the Blessed One.

55. *The Buddha to Kakutthā's river came,*
Where cool and limpid flows the pleasant stream;
There washed in water clear his weary frame
The Buddha—he in all the world supreme!
And having bathed and drank, the Teacher straight
Crossed over, the bhikkhus thronging in his wake.

Discoursing holy truths, the Master great
Towards the Mango Grove his path did take.
There to the elder Cundaka he spoke:
"Lay down my robe, please, folded into four."
Then the elder, swift as lightning stroke,
Hastened the Teacher's bidding to obey.
Weary, the Lord then lay down on the mat,
And Cunda on the ground before him sat.

Relieving Cunda's Remorse

56. Then the Blessed One spoke to the Venerable Ānanda, saying: "It may come to pass, Ānanda, that someone will cause remorse to Cunda the metalworker, saying: 'It is no gain to you, friend Cunda, but a loss, that it was from you the Tathāgata took his last alms meal, and then came to his end.' Then, Ānanda, the remorse of Cunda should be dispelled after this manner: 'It is a gain to you, friend Cunda, a blessing that the Tathāgata took his last alms meal from you, and then came to his end. For, friend, face to face with the Blessed One I have heard and learned: "There are two offerings of food which are of equal fruition, of equal outcome, exceeding in grandeur the fruition and result of any other offerings of food. Which two? The one partaken of by the Tathāgata before becoming fully enlightened in unsurpassed, supreme Enlightenment; and the one partaken of by the Tathāgata before passing into the state of Nibbāna in which no element of clinging remains. By his deed the worthy Cunda has accumulated merit which makes for long life, beauty, well being, glory, heavenly rebirth, and sovereignty." ' Thus, Ānanda, the remorse of Cunda the metalworker should be dispelled."

57. Then the Blessed One, understanding that matter, breathed forth the solemn utterance:

Who gives, his virtues shall increase;
Who is self-curbed, no hatred bears;
Whoso is skilled in virtue, evil shuns,
And by the rooting out of lust and hate
And all delusion, comes to be at peace."

Part Five
At Kusinārā

Last Place of Rest

1. Then the Blessed One addressed the Venerable Ānanda, saying: "Come, Ānanda, let us cross to the farther bank of the Hiraññavatī, and go to the Mallas' Sāla Grove, in the vicinity of Kusinārā."

"So be it, Lord."

2. And the Blessed One, together with a large company of bhikkhus, went to the further bank of the river Hiraññavatī, to the Sāla Grove of the Mallas, in the vicinity of Kusinārā. And there he spoke to the Venerable Ānanda, saying:

3. "Please, Ānanda, prepare for me a couch between the twin sāla trees, with the head to the north. I am weary, Ānanda, and want to lie down."[41]

"So be it, Lord." And the Venerable Ānanda did as the Blessed One asked him to do.

Then the Blessed One lay down on his right side, in the lion's posture, resting one foot upon the other, and so disposed himself, mindfully and clearly comprehending.

4. At that time the twin sāla trees broke out in full bloom, though it was not the season of flowering. And the blossoms rained upon the body of the Tathāgata and dropped and scattered and were strewn upon it in worship of the Tathāgata. And celestial *mandārava* flowers and heavenly sandalwood powder from the sky rained down upon the body of the Tathāgata, and dropped and scattered and were strewn upon it in worship of the Tathāgata. And the sound of heavenly voices and heavenly instruments made music in the air out of reverence for the Tathāgata.

---

41. Comy.: "From the town of Pāvā it is three *gāvutas* (approx. five miles) to Kusinārā. Walking that distance with great effort and sitting down at twenty-five places on the way, the Blessed One reached the Sāla Grove at dusk when the sun had already set. Thus comes illness to man, crushing all his health. As if he wanted to point to this fact, the Blessed One spoke those words which deeply moved the whole world: 'I am weary, Ānanda, and want to lie down.' "

5. And the Blessed One spoke to the Venerable Ānanda, saying: "Ānanda, the twin sāla trees are in full bloom, though it is not the season of flowering. And the blossoms rain upon the body of the Tathāgata and drop and scatter and are strewn upon it in worship of the Tathāgata. And celestial coral flowers and heavenly sandalwood powder from the sky rain down upon the body of the Tathāgata, and drop and scatter and are strewn upon it in worship of the Tathāgata. And the sound of heavenly voices and heavenly instruments makes music in the air out of reverence for the Tathāgata.

6. "Yet it is not thus, Ānanda, that the Tathāgata is respected, venerated, esteemed, worshipped, and honoured in the highest degree. But, Ānanda, whatever bhikkhu or bhikkhunī, layman or laywoman, abides by the Dhamma, lives uprightly in the Dhamma, walks in the way of the Dhamma, it is by such a one that the Tathāgata is respected, venerated, esteemed, worshipped, and honoured in the highest degree. Therefore, Ānanda, thus should you train yourselves: 'We shall abide by the Dhamma, live uprightly in the Dhamma, walk in the way of the Dhamma.'"

The Grief of the Gods

7. At that time the Venerable Upavāṇa was standing before the Blessed One, fanning him. And the Blessed One rebuked him, saying: "Move aside, bhikkhu, do not stand in front of me."

8. And to the Venerable Ānanda came the thought: "This Venerable Upavāṇa has been in attendance on the Blessed One for a long time, closely associating with him and serving him. Yet now, right at the end, the Blessed One rebukes him. What now could be the reason, what the cause for the Blessed One to rebuke the Venerable Upavāṇa, saying: 'Move aside, bhikkhu, do not stand in front of me'?"

9–10. And the Venerable Ānanda told his thought to the Blessed One. The Blessed One said: "Throughout the tenfold world-system, Ānanda, there are hardly any of the deities that have not gathered together to look upon the Tathāgata. For a distance of twelve yojanas around the Sāla Grove of the Mallas in the vicinity of Kusinārā there is not a spot that could be pricked with the tip of a hair that is not filled with powerful deities. And these deities, Ānanda, are complaining: 'From afar have we come to look upon the Tathāgata. For rare in the world is the arising of Tathāgatas, Arahats, Fully Enlightened Ones. And this day, in the last watch of the night, the Tathāgata's Parinibbāna will come about. But this bhikkhu of great powers has placed himself right in front of the Blessed One, concealing him, so that now, at the very end, we are prevented from looking upon him.' Thus, Ānanda, the deities complain."

11. "Of what kind of deities, Lord, is the Blessed One aware?"

12–13. "There are deities, Ānanda, in space and on earth, who are earthly-minded; with dishevelled hair they weep, with uplifted arms they weep; flinging themselves on the ground, they roll from side to side, lamenting: 'Too soon has the Blessed One come to his Parinibbāna! Too soon has the Happy One come to his Parinibbāna! Too soon will the Eye of the World vanish from sight!'

14. "But those deities who are freed from passion, mindful and comprehending, reflect in this way: 'Impermanent are all compounded things. How could this be otherwise?' "

Ānanda's Concern

15. "Formerly, Lord, on leaving their quarters after the rains, the bhikkhus would set forth to see the Tathāgata, and to us there was the gain and benefit of receiving and associating with those very revered bhikkhus who came to have audience with the Blessed One and to wait upon him. But, Lord, after the Blessed One has gone, we shall no longer have that gain and benefit."

Four Places of Pilgrimage

16. "There are four places, Ānanda, that a pious person should visit and look upon with feelings of reverence.[42] What are the four?

17. " 'Here the Tathāgata was born!'[43] This, Ānanda, is a place that a pious person should visit and look upon with feelings of reverence.

---

42. See *The Four Sacred Shrines*, by Piyadassi Thera (BPS Bodhi Leaves No. 8).

43. At Lumbinī near Kapilavatthu, the ancestral seat of the Sakyans in the foothills of the Himalayas. An Asokan pillar marks the spot.

18. "'Here the Tathāgata became fully enlightened in unsurpassed, supreme Enlightenment!'[44] This, Ānanda, is a place that a pious person should visit and look upon with feelings of reverence.

19. "'Here the Tathāgata set rolling the unexcelled Wheel of the Dhamma!'[45] This, Ānanda, is a place that a pious person should visit and look upon with feelings of reverence.

20. "'Here the Tathāgata passed away into the state of Nibbāna in which no element of clinging remains!' This, Ānanda, is a place that a pious person should visit and look upon with feelings of reverence.

21. "These, Ānanda, are the four places that a pious person should visit and look upon with feelings of reverence. And truly there will come to these places, Ānanda, pious bhikkhus and bhikkhunīs, laymen and laywomen, reflecting: 'Here the Tathāgata was born! Here the Tathāgata became fully enlightened in unsurpassed, supreme Enlightenment! Here the Tathāgata set rolling the unexcelled Wheel of the Dhamma! Here the Tathāgata passed away into the state of Nibbāna in which no element of clinging remains!'

22. "And whoever, Ānanda, should die on such a pilgrimage with his heart established in faith, at the breaking up of the body, after death, will be reborn in a realm of heavenly happiness."

23. Then the Venerable Ānanda said to the Blessed One: "How, Lord, should we conduct ourselves towards women?"

"Do not see them, Ānanda."

"But, Lord, if we do see them?"

"Do not speak, Ānanda."

"But, Lord, if they should speak to us?"

"Then, Ānanda, you should establish mindfulness."

24. Then the Venerable Ānanda said: "How should we act, Lord, respecting the body of the Tathāgata?"

"Do not hinder yourselves, Ānanda, to honour the body of the Tathāgata. Rather you should strive, Ānanda, and be zealous on your own behalf,[46] for your own good. Unflinchingly, ardently, and resolutely you should apply yourselves to your own

44. At Buddha-Gayā, in Bihar.

45. At Isipatana near Benares (modern Sarnath).

46. *Sadatthe*. Comy.: "for the highest purpose, the goal of arahatship." There is a different reading, *sāratthe*, "for an essential purpose."

good. For there are, Ānanda, wise nobles, wise brahmins, and wise householders who are devoted to the Tathāgata, and it is they who will render the honour to the body of the Tathāgata."

25. Then the Venerable Ānanda said: "But how, Lord, should they act respecting the body of the Tathāgata?"

"After the same manner, Ānanda, as towards the body of a universal monarch."[47]

"But how, Lord, do they act respecting the body of a universal monarch?"

26. "The body of a universal monarch, Ānanda, is first wrapped round with new linen, and then with teased cotton wool, and so it is done up to five hundred layers of linen and five hundred of cotton wool. When that is done, the body of the universal monarch is placed in an iron[48] oil vessel, which is enclosed in another iron vessel, a funeral pyre is built of all kinds of perfumed woods, and so the body of the universal monarch is burned; and at a crossroads a stūpa is raised for the universal monarch. So it is done, Ānanda, with the body of a universal monarch. And even, Ānanda, as with the body of a universal monarch, so should it be done with the body of the Tathāgata; and at a crossroads also a stūpa should be raised for the Tathāgata. And whosoever shall bring to that place garlands or incense or sandalpaste, or pay reverence, and whose mind becomes calm there—it will be to his well being and happiness for a long time.

27. "There are four persons, Ānanda, who are worthy of a stūpa. Who are those four? A Tathāgata, an Arahat, a Fully Enlightened One is worthy of a stūpa; so also is a Paccekabuddha,[49] and a disciple of a Tathāgata, and a universal monarch.

---

47. *Cakkavatti-rājā*: the ideal king of righteousness according to Buddhist tradition.

48. *Āyasa*: generally "made of iron," has here according to Comy. the meaning "made of gold," for which there is also support in the Sanskrit usage of the word.

49. *Paccekabuddha* is one awakened or enlightened for himself alone. Such Paccekabuddhas arise at times when there is no Fully Enlightened One (*sammā-sambuddha*). Like the latter, they attain to Enlightenment by their own effort, but unlike them are not able to lead others to deliverance. See Ria Kloppenberg, *The Paccekabuddha: A Buddhist Ascetic* (BPS Wheel No. 305/307).

28–31. "And why, Ānanda, is a Tathāgata, an Arahat, a Fully Enlightened One worthy of a stūpa? Because, Ānanda, at the thought: 'This is the stūpa of that Blessed One, Arahat, Fully Enlightened One!' the hearts of many people will be calmed and made happy; and so calmed and with their minds established in faith therein, at the breaking up of the body, after death, they will be reborn in a realm of heavenly happiness. And so also at the thought: 'This is the stūpa of that Paccekabuddha!' or 'This is the stūpa of a disciple of that Tathāgata, Arahat, Fully Enlightened One!' or 'This is the stūpa of that righteous monarch who ruled according to Dhamma!'—the hearts of many people are calmed and made happy; and so calmed and with their minds established in faith therein, at the breaking up of the body, after death, they will be reborn in a realm of heavenly happiness. And it is because of this, Ānanda, that these four persons are worthy of a stūpa."

Ānanda's Grief

32. Then the Venerable Ānanda went into the vihāra[50] and leaned against the doorpost and wept: "I am still but a learner,[51] and still have to strive for my own perfection. But, alas, my Master, who was so compassionate towards me, is about to pass away!"

33. And the Blessed One spoke to the bhikkhus, saying: "Where, bhikkhus, is Ānanda?"

"The Venerable Ānanda, Lord, has gone into the vihāra and there stands leaning against the door post and weeping: 'I am still but a learner, and still have to strive for my own perfection. But, alas, my Master, who was so compassionate towards me, is about to pass away!' "

---

50. The word *vihāra*, given in the text, cannot refer here to a monastery or monks' living quarters. Comy. explains it as a pavilion (*maṇḍala-māla*). If the locality was used as a meeting place for the clan, as Comy. states, there may well have been a kind of shelter there. The couch in the open, which Ānanda was asked to prepare for the Master, was probably a seat for the chiefs of the Malla clan put up at that place.

51. *Sekha*. This signifies those at the three lower stages of emanicipation, before reaching arahatship. Ānanda, at that time, had reached the first of these stages, stream-entry.

34. Then the Blessed One asked a certain bhikkhu to bring the Venerable Ānanda to him, saying: "Go, bhikkhu, and say to Ānanda, 'Friend Ānanda, the Master calls you.' "

"So be it, Lord." And that bhikkhu went and spoke to the Venerable Ānanda as the Blessed One had asked him to. And the Venerable Ānanda went to the Blessed One, bowed down to him, and sat down on one side.

35. Then the Blessed One spoke to the Venerable Ānanda, saying: "Enough, Ānanda! Do not grieve, do not lament! For have I not taught from the very beginning that with all that is dear and beloved there must be change, separation, and severence? Of that which is born, come into being, compounded, and subject to decay, how can one say: 'May it not come to dissolution!'? There can be no such state of things. Now for a long time, Ānanda, you have served the Tathāgata with loving-kindness in deed, word, and thought, graciously, pleasantly, with a whole heart and beyond measure. Great good have you gathered, Ānanda! Now you should put forth energy, and soon you too will be free from the taints."[52]

Praise of Ānanda

36. Then the Blessed One addressed the bhikkhus, saying: "Bhikkhus, the Blessed Ones, Arahats, Fully Enlightened Ones of times past also had excellent and devoted attendant bhikkhus, such as I have in Ānanda. And so also, bhikkhus, will the Blessed Ones, Arahats, Fully Enlightened Ones of times to come.

37. "Capable and judicious is Ānanda, bhikkhus, for he knows the proper time for bhikkhus to have audience with the Tathāgata, and the time for bhikkhunīs, the time for laymen and for laywomen; the time for kings and for ministers of state; the time for teachers of other sects and for their followers.

38. "In Ānanda, bhikkhus, are to be found four rare and superlative qualities. What are the four? If, bhikkhus, a company of bhikkhus should go to see Ānanda, they become joyful on seeing him; and if he then speaks to them of the Dhamma, they are made joyful by his discourse; and when he becomes silent, they are disappointed. So it is also when bhikkhunīs, laymen, or

52. *Anāsavo*: that is, an arahat.

laywomen go to see Ānanda: they become joyful on seeing him; and if he then speaks to them of the Dhamma, they are made joyful by his discourse; and when he becomes silent, they are disappointed.

39. "In a universal monarch, bhikkhus, are to be found four rare and superlative qualities. What are those four? If, bhikkhus, a company of nobles should go to see the universal monarch, they become joyful on seeing him; and if he then speaks, they are made joyful by his talk; and when he becomes silent, they are disappointed. So it is also when a company of brahmins, of householders, or of ascetics goes to see a universal monarch.

40. "And in just the same way, bhikkhus, in Ānanda are to be found these four rare and superlative qualities."

The Past Glory of Kusinārā

41. When this had been said, the Venerable Ānanda spoke to the Blessed One, saying: "Let it not be, Lord, that the Blessed One should pass away in this mean place, this uncivilized township in the midst of the jungle, a mere outpost of the province. There are great cities, Lord, such as Campā, Rājagaha, Sāvatthī, Sāketa, Kosambī, and Benares—let the Blessed One have his final passing away in one of those. For in those cities dwell many wealthy nobles and brahmins and householders who are devotees of the Tathāgata, and they will render due honour to the remains of the Tathāgata."

42. "Do not say that, Ānanda! Do not say: 'This mean place, this uncivilized township in the midst of the jungle, a mere outpost of the province.' In times long past, Ānanda, there was a king by the name of Mahā Sudassana, who was a universal monarch, a king of righteousness, a conqueror of the four quarters of the earth, whose realm was established in security, and who was endowed with the seven jewels.[53] And that King Mahā Sudassana, Ānanda, had his royal residence here at Kusinārā, which was then called

53. The "seven jewels" of a universal monarch are: the magical wheel, emblem of his sovereignty, by which he conquers the earth without the use of force; his wonderful elephant; his horse; his beautiful wife; his precious gem; his treasurer; and his advisor. All are endowed with wondrous properties. For more on Mahā Sudassana, see the sutta which bears his name, DN 17.

Kusāvatī, and it extended twelve yojanas from east to west, and seven from north to south.

43. "And mighty, Ānanda, was Kusāvatī, the capital, prosperous and well populated, much frequented by people, and abundantly provided with food. Just as the royal residence of the deities, Āḷakamandā, is mighty, prosperous, and well populated, much frequented by deities and abundantly provided with food, so was the royal capital of Kusāvatī.

44. "Kusāvatī, Ānanda, resounded unceasingly day and night with ten sounds—the trumpeting of elephants, the neighing of horses, the rattling of chariots, the beating of drums and tabours, music and song, cheers, the clapping of hands, and cries of 'Eat, drink, and be merry!'

Lamentation of the Mallas

45. "Go now, Ānanda, to Kusinārā and announce to the Mallas: 'Today, Vāseṭṭhas, in the last watch of the night, the Tathāgata's Parinibbāna will take place. Approach, O Vāseṭṭhas, draw near! Do not be remorseful later at the thought: "In our township it was that the Tathāgata's Parinibbāna took place, but we failed to see him at the end! "'"

"So be it, Lord." And the Venerable Ānanda prepared himself, and taking bowl and robe, went with a companion to Kusinārā.

46. Now at that time the Mallas had gathered in the council hall for some public business. And the Venerable Ānanda approached them and announced: "Today, Vāseṭṭhas, in the last watch of the night, the Tathāgata's Parinibbāna will take place. Approach, Vāseṭṭhas, draw near! Do not be remorseful later at the thought: 'In our township it was that the Tathāgata's Parinibbāna took place, but we failed to see him at the end.' "

47. When they heard the Venerable Ānanda speak these words, the Mallas with their sons, their wives, and the wives of their sons, were sorely grieved, grieved at heart and afflicted; and some, with their hair all dishevelled, with arms uplifted in despair, wept; flinging themselves on the ground, they rolled from side to side, lamenting: "Too soon has the Blessed One come to his Parinibbāna! Too soon has the Happy One come to his Parinibbāna! Too soon will the Eye of the World vanish from sight!"

48. And thus afflicted and filled with grief, the Mallas, with their sons, their wives, and the wives of their sons, went to the Sāla Grove, the recreation park of the Mallas, to the place where the Venerable Ānanda was.

49. And the thought arose in the Venerable Ānanda: "If I were to allow the Mallas of Kusinārā to pay reverence to the Blessed One one by one, the night will have given place to dawn before they are all presented to him. Therefore let me divide them up according to clan, each family in a group, and so present them to the Blessed One thus: 'The Malla of such and such a name, Lord, with his wives and children, his attendants and his friends, pays homage at the feet of the Blessed One.' "

50. And the Venerable Ānanda divided the Mallas up according to clan, each family in a group, and presented them to the Blessed One. So it was that the Venerable Ānanda caused the Mallas of Kusinārā to be presented to the Blessed One by clans, each family in a group, even in the first watch of the night.

The Last Convert

51. Now at that time a wandering ascetic named Subhadda was dwelling at Kusinārā. And Subhadda the wandering ascetic heard it said: "Today in the third watch of the night, the Parinibbāna of the ascetic Gotama will take place."

52. And the thought arose in him: "I have heard it said by old and venerable wandering ascetics, teachers of teachers, that the arising of Tathāgatas, Arahats, Fully Enlightened Ones, is rare in the world. Yet this very day, in the last watch of the night, the Parinibbāna of the ascetic Gotama will take place. Now there is in me a doubt; but to this extent I have faith in the ascetic Gotama, that he could so teach me the Dhamma as to remove that doubt."

53. Then the wandering ascetic Subhadda went to the Sāla Grove, the recreation park of the Mallas, and drew near to the Venerable Ānanda, and told the Venerable Ānanda his thought. And he spoke to the Venerable Ānanda, saying: "Friend Ānanda, it would be good if I could be allowed into the presence of the ascetic Gotama."

54. But the Venerable Ānanda answered him, saying: "Enough, friend Subhadda! Do not trouble the Tathāgata. The Blessed One is weary."

55–56. Yet a second and a third time the wandering ascetic Subhadda made his request, and a second and a third time the Venerable Ānanda refused him.

57. And the Blessed One heard the talk between them, and he called the Venerable Ānanda and said: "Stop, Ānanda! Do not refuse Subhadda. Subhadda, Ānanda, may be allowed into the presence of the Tathāgata. For whatever he will ask me, he will ask for the sake of knowledge, and not as an offence. And the answer I give him, that he will readily understand."

58. Thereupon the Venerable Ānanda said to the wandering ascetic Subhadda: "Go then, friend Subhadda, the Blessed One gives you leave."

59. Then the wandering ascetic Subhadda approached the Blessed One and saluted him courteously. And having exchanged with him pleasant and civil greetings, the wandering ascetic Subhadda seated himself at one side and addressed the Blessed One, saying: "There are, Venerable Gotama, ascetics and brahmins who are heads of great companies of disciples, who have large retinues, who are leaders of schools, well known and renowned, and held in high esteem by the multitude, such teachers as Pūraṇa Kassapa, Makkhali Gosāla, Ajita Kesakambalī, Pakudha Kaccāyana, Sañjaya Belaṭṭhiputta, Nigaṇṭha Nātaputta. Have all of these attained realization, as each of them would have it believed, or has none of them, or is it that some have attained realization and others not?"

60. "Enough, Subhadda! Let it be as it may, whether all of them have attained realization, as each of them would have it believed, or whether none of them has, or whether some have attained realization and others not. I will teach you the Dhamma, Subhadda; listen and heed it well, and I will speak."

"So be it, Lord."

The Lion's Roar

61. And the Blessed One spoke, saying: "In whatsoever Dhamma and Discipline, Subhadda, there is not found the Noble Eightfold Path, neither is there found a true ascetic of the first, second, third, or fourth degree of saintliness. But in whatsoever Dhamma and Discipline there is found the Noble Eightfold Path, there is found a true ascetic of the first, second, third, and fourth degrees

of saintliness.[54] Now in this Dhamma and Discipline, Subhadda, is found the Noble Eightfold Path; and in it alone are also found true ascetics of the first, second, third, and fourth degrees of saintliness. Devoid of true ascetics are the systems of other teachers. But if, Subhadda, the bhikkhus live righteously, the world will not be destitute of arahats.

62. "*In age but twenty-nine was I, Subhadda,*
When I renounced the world to seek the Good;
Fifty-one years have passed since then, Subhadda,
And in all that time a wanderer have I been
In the domain of virtue and of truth,
And except therein, there is no saint (*of the first degree*).

"And there is none of the second degree, nor of the third degree, nor of the fourth degree of saintliness. Devoid of true ascetics are the systems of other teachers. But if, Subhadda, the bhikkhus live righteously, the world will not be destitute of arahats."

63. When this was said, the wandering ascetic Subhadda spoke to the Blessed One, saying: "Excellent, O Lord, most excellent, O Lord! It is as if, Lord, one were to set upright what had been overthrown, or to reveal what had been hidden, or to show the path to one who had gone astray, or to light a lamp in the darkness so that those with eyes might see—even so has the Blessed One set forth the Dhamma in many ways. And so, O Lord, I take my refuge in the Blessed One, the Dhamma, and the Community of Bhikkhus. May I receive from the Blessed One admission to the Order and also the higher ordination."

64. "Whoever, Subhadda, having been formerly a follower of another creed, wishes to receive admission and higher ordination in this Dhamma and Discipline, remains on probation for a period of four months. At the end of those four months, if the bhikkhus are satisfied with him, they grant him admission and higher ordination as a bhikkhu. Yet in this matter I recognize differences of personalities."

65. "If, O Lord, whoever, having been formerly a follower of another creed, wishes to receive admission and higher ordination

54. The four degrees of saintliness are the stream-enterer, the once-returner, the non-returner, and the arahat.

in this Dhamma and Discipline, remains on probation for a period of four months, and at the end of those four months, if the bhikkhus are satisfied with him, they grant him admission and higher ordination as a bhikkhu—then I will remain on probation for a period of four years. And at the end of those four years, if the bhikkhus are satisfied with me, let them grant me admission and higher ordination as a bhikkhu."

66. But the Blessed One called the Venerable Ānanda and said to him: "Ānanda, let Subhadda be given admission into the Order." And the Venerable Ānanda replied: "So be it, Lord."

67. Then the wandering ascetic Subhadda said to the Venerable Ānanda: "It is a gain to you, friend Ānanda, a blessing, that in the presence of the Master himself you have received the sprinkling of ordination as a disciple."

68. So it came about that the wandering ascetic Subhadda, in the presence of the Blessed One, received admission and higher ordination. And from the time of his ordination the Venerable Subhadda remained alone, secluded, heedful, ardent, and resolute. And before long he attained to the goal for which a worthy man goes forth rightly from home to homelessness, the supreme goal of the holy life; and having by himself realized it with higher knowledge, he dwelt therein. He knew: "Destroyed is birth; the higher life is fulfilled; nothing more is to be done, and beyond this life nothing more remains." And the Venerable Subhadda became yet another among the arahats, and he was the last disciple converted by the Blessed One himself.

Part Six
The Passing Away

The Blessed One's Final Exhortation

1. Now the Blessed One spoke to the Venerable Ānanda, saying: "It may be, Ānanda, that to some among you the thought will come: 'Ended is the word of the Master; we have a Master no longer.' But it should not, Ānanda, be so considered. For that which I have proclaimed and made known as the Dhamma and the Discipline, that shall be your Master when I am gone.

2. "And, Ānanda, whereas now the bhikkhus address one another as 'friend,' let it not be so when I am gone. The senior bhikkhus, Ānanda, may address the junior ones by their name, their family name, or as 'friend'; but the junior bhikkhus should address the senior ones as 'venerable sir' or 'your reverence.'[55]

3. "If it is desired, Ānanda, the Sangha may, when I am gone, abolish the lesser and minor rules.[56]

4. "Ānanda, when I am gone, let the higher penalty be imposed upon the bhikkhu Channa."[57]

"But what, Lord, is the higher penalty?"

"The bhikkhu Channa, Ānanda, may say what he will, but the bhikkhus should neither converse with him, nor exhort him, nor admonish him."

5. Then the Blessed One addressed the bhikkhus, saying: "It may be, bhikkhus, that one of you is in doubt or perplexity as to the Buddha, the Dhamma, or the Sangha, the path or the practice. Then question, bhikkhus! Do not be given to remorse later on

55. "Friend," in Pali is *āvuso*, "venerable sir" = *bhante*, "your reverence" = *āyasmā*.

56. Since Ānanda, at this point, did not ask what the minor rules were, the Sangha decided not to abolish any of the rules of the Vinaya.

57. Channa had been the Buddha's charioteer while the latter was still a prince living in the palace. Because of his prior connection with the Buddha, he was obdurate and refused to submit to discipline. This imposition of the "higher penalty" (*brahmadaṇḍa*) changed him into an obedient monk.

with the thought: 'The Master was with us face to face, yet face to face we failed to ask him.' "

6. But when this was said, the bhikkhus were silent. And yet a second and a third time the Blessed One said to them: "It may be, bhikkhus, that one of you is in doubt or perplexity as to the Buddha, the Dhamma, or the Sangha, the path or the practice. Then question, bhikkhus! Do not be given to remorse later on with the thought: 'The Master was with us face to face, yet face to face we failed to ask him.' "

And for a second and a third time the bhikkhus were silent. Then the Blessed One said to them: "It may be, bhikkhus, out of respect for the Master that you ask no questions. Then, bhikkhus, let friend communicate it to friend." Yet still the bhikkhus were silent.

7. And the Venerable Ānanda spoke to the Blessed One, saying: "Marvellous it is, O Lord, most wonderful it is! This faith I have in the community of bhikkhus, that not even one bhikkhu is in doubt or perplexity as to the Buddha, the Dhamma, or the Sangha, the path or the practice."

"Out of faith, Ānanda, you speak thus. But here, Ānanda, the Tathāgata knows for certain that among this community of bhikkhus there is not even one bhikkhu who is in doubt or perplexity as to the Buddha, the Dhamma, or the Sangha, the path or the practice. For, Ānanda, among these five hundred bhikkhus even the lowest is a stream-enterer, secure from downfall, assured, and bound for enlightenment."

8. And the Blessed One addressed the bhikkhus, saying: "Behold now, bhikkhus, I exhort you: All compounded things are subject to vanish. Strive with earnestness!"[58]

This was the last word of the Tathāgata.

58. *Handa dāni bhikkhave āmantayāmi vo: Vayadhammā saṅkhārā appamādena sampādetha.* Earnestness (*appamāda*) is explained as "presence of mindfulness." Comy.: "'You should accomplish all your duties without allowing mindfulness to lapse!' Thus did the Blessed One, while on the bed of his Parinibbāna, summarize in that one word on earnestness the advice he had given through forty-five years."

How the Blessed One Passed into Nibbāna

9. And the Blessed One entered the first jhāna. Rising from the first jhāna, he entered the second jhāna. Rising from the second jhāna, he entered the third jhāna. Rising from the third jhāna, he entered the fourth jhāna. And rising out of the fourth jhāna, he entered the sphere of infinite space. Rising from the attainment of the sphere of infinite space, he entered the sphere of infinite consciousness. Rising from the attainment of the sphere of infinite consciousness, he entered the sphere of nothingness. Rising from the attainment of the sphere of nothingness, he entered the sphere of neither-perception-nor-non-perception. And rising out of the attainment of the sphere of neither-perception-nor-non-perception, he attained to the cessation of perception and feeling.

10. And the Venerable Ānanda spoke to the Venerable Anuruddha, saying: "Venerable Anuruddha, the Blessed One has passed away."

"No, friend Ānanda, the Blessed One has not passed away. He has entered the state of the cessation of perception and feeling."[59]

11. Then the Blessed One, rising from the cessation of perception and feeling, entered the sphere of neither-perception-nor-non-perception. Rising from the attainment of the sphere of neither-perception-nor-non-perception, he entered the sphere of nothingness. Rising from the attainment of the sphere of nothingness, he entered the sphere of infinite consciousness. Rising from the attainment of the sphere of infinite consciousness, he entered the sphere of infinite space. Rising from the attainment of the sphere of infinite space, he entered the fourth jhāna. Rising from the fourth jhāna, he entered the third jhāna. Rising from the third jhāna, he entered the second jhāna. Rising from the second jhāna, he entered the first jhāna.

Rising from the first jhāna, he entered the second jhāna. Rising from the second jhāna, he entered the third jhāna. Rising from the third jhāna, he entered the fourth jhāna. And, rising from the fourth jhāna, the Blessed One immediately passed away.

59. Anuruddha, the elder brother of Ānanda, would have known this through the super-normal power of reading the minds of others, which he possessed.

The World's Echo

12. And when the Blessed One had passed away, simultaneously with his Parinibbāna there came a tremendous earthquake, dreadful and astounding, and the thunders rolled across the heavens.

13. And when the Blessed One had passed away, simultaneously with his Parinibbāna, Brahmā Sahampati[60] spoke this stanza:

"All must depart—all beings that have life
Must shed their compound forms. Yea, even one,
A Master such as he, a peerless being,
Powerful in wisdom, the Enlightened One, has passed away."

14. And when the Blessed One had passed away, simultaneously with his Parinibbāna, Sakka, king of the gods,[61] spoke this stanza:

"Transient are all compounded things,
Subject to arise and vanish;
Having come into existence they pass away;
Good is the peace when they forever cease."

15. And when the Blessed One had passed away, simultaneously with his Parinibbāna, the Venerable Anuruddha spoke this stanza:

"No movement of the breath, but with steadfast heart,
Free from desires and tranquil—so the sage
Comes to his end. By mortal pangs unshaken,
His mind, like a flame extinguished, finds release."

16. And when the Blessed One had passed away, simultaneously with his Parinibbāna, the Venerable Ānanda spoke this stanza:

"Then there was terror, and the hair stood up, when he,
The All-accomplished One, the Buddha, passed away."

17. Then, when the Blessed One had passed away, some bhikkhus, not yet freed from passion, lifted up their arms and

---

60. Brahmā Sahampati was a high divinity of the Brahma-world. It was he who originally requested the newly enlightened Buddha to teach the Dhamma to the world. See MN 26.

61. Sakka is the king of the gods in the Tāvatiṃsa heaven, and thus a lower figure in the cosmological hierarchy than Brahmā Sahampati.

wept; and some, flinging themselves on the ground, rolled from side to side and wept, lamenting: "Too soon has the Blessed One come to his Parinibbāna! Too soon has the Happy One come to his Parinibbāna! Too soon has the Eye of the World vanished from sight!"

But the bhikkhus who were freed from passion, mindful and clearly comprehending, reflected in this way: "Impermanent are all compounded things. How could this be otherwise?"

18. And the Venerable Anuruddha addressed the bhikkhus, saying: "Enough, friends! Do not grieve, do not lament! For has not the Blessed One declared that with all that is dear and beloved there must be change, separation, and severance? Of that which is born, come into being, compounded and subject to decay, how can one say: 'May it not come to dissolution!'? The deities, friends, are aggrieved."

"But, venerable sir, of what deities is the Venerable Anuruddha aware?"

"There are deities, friend Ānanda, in space and on the earth who are earthly-minded; with dishevelled hair they weep, with uplifted arms they weep; flinging themselves on the ground, they roll from side to side, lamenting: 'Too soon has the Blessed One come to his Parinibbāna! Too soon has the Happy One come to his Parinibbāna! Too soon has the Eye of the World vanished from sight!' But those deities who are freed from passion, mindful and clearly comprehending, reflect in this way: 'Impermanent are all compounded things. How could this be otherwise?' "

19. Now the Venerable Anuruddha and the Venerable Ānanda spent the rest of the night in talking on the Dhamma. Then the Venerable Anuruddha spoke to the Venerable Ānanda, saying: "Go now, friend Ānanda, to Kusinārā, and announce to the Mallas: 'The Blessed One, Vāseṭṭhas, has passed away. Do now as seems fitting to you.' "

"So be it, venerable sir." And the Venerable Ānanda prepared himself in the forenoon, and taking bowl and robe, went with a companion into Kusinārā.

20. At that time the Mallas of Kusinārā had gathered in the council hall to consider that very matter. And the Venerable Ānanda approached them and announced: "The Blessed One, Vāseṭṭhas, has passed away. Do now as seems fitting to you."

And when they heard the Venerable Ānanda speak these words, the Mallas with their sons, their wives, and the wives of their sons, were sorely grieved, grieved at heart and afflicted; and some, with their hair all dishevelled, with arms upraised in despair, wept; flinging themselves on the ground, they rolled from side to side, lamenting: "Too soon has the Blessed One come to his Parinibbāna! "Too soon has the Happy One come to his Parinibbāna! Too soon has the Eye of the World vanished from sight!"

Homage to the Remains

21. Then the Mallas of Kusinārā gave orders to their men, saying: "Gather now all the perfumes, flower-garlands, and musicians, even all that are in Kusinārā." And the Mallas, with the perfumes, the flower-garlands, and the musicians, and with five hundred sets of clothing, went to the Sāla Grove, the recreation park of the Mallas, and approached the body of the Blessed One. And having approached, they paid homage to the body of the Blessed One with dance, song, music, flower-garlands, and perfume, and erecting canopies and pavilions, they spent the day showing respect, honour, and veneration to the body of the Blessed One. And then the thought came to them: "Now the day is too far spent for us to cremate the body of the Blessed One. Tomorrow we will do it."

And for the second day, and a third, fourth, fifth, and sixth day, they paid homage to the body of the Blessed One with dance, song, music, flower-garlands, and perfume, and erecting canopies and pavilions, they spent the day showing respect, honour, and veneration to the body of the Blessed One.

But on the seventh day the thought came to them: "We have paid homage to the body of the Blessed One with dance, song, music, flower-garlands, and perfume, and have shown respect, honour, and veneration; let us now carry the body of the Blessed One southward to the southern part of the town and beyond, and let us there cremate the body of the Blessed One south of the town."

And eight Mallas of the foremost families, bathed from the crown of their heads and wearing new clothes, with the thought:

"We will lift up the body of the Blessed One," tried to do so but they could not.

22. Then the Mallas spoke to the Venerable Anuruddha, saying: "What is the cause, Venerable Anuruddha, what is the reason that these eight Mallas of the foremost families, bathed from the crown of their heads and wearing new clothes, with the thought: 'We will lift up the body of the Blessed One,' try to do so but cannot?"

"You, Vāseṭṭhas, have one purpose, the deities have another."

"Then what, venerable sir, is the purpose of the deities?"

"Your purpose, Vāseṭṭhas, is this: 'We have paid homage to the body of the Blessed One with dance, song, music, flower-garlands, and perfume, and have shown respect, honour, and veneration; let us now carry the body of the Blessed One southward to the southern part of the town and beyond, and let us there cremate the body of the Blessed One south of the town.' But the purpose of the deities, Vāseṭṭhas, is this: 'We have paid homage to the body of the Blessed One with heavenly dance, song, music, flower-garlands, and perfume, and have shown respect, honour, and veneration; let us now carry the body of the Blessed One northward to the northern part of the town; and having carried it through the northern gate, let us go through the centre of the town, and then eastward to the east of the town; and having passed through the east gate, let us carry it to the cetiya of the Mallas, Makuṭa-bandhana, and there let us cremate the body of the Blessed One.'"

"As the deities wish, venerable sir, so let it be."

23. Thereupon the whole of Kusinārā, even to the dust heaps and rubbish heaps, became covered knee-deep in *mandārava* flowers.[62] And homage was paid to the body of the Blessed One by the deities as well as the Mallas of Kusinārā. With dance, song, music, flower-garlands, and perfume, both divine and human, respect, honour, and veneration were shown. And they carried

62. A celestial flower which appears on earth only on special occasions, particularly in connection with the chief events in the life of the Buddha. Its appearance in the hands of the Ājīvaka ascetic signalled to the Venerable Mahā Kassapa that the Buddha's Parinibbāna had already taken place. (See Chapter 6, Section 26.)

the body of the Blessed One northward to the northern part of the town; and having carried it through the northern gate, they went through the centre of the town, and then eastward to the east of the town; and having passed through the east gate, they carried the body of the Blessed One to the cetiya of the Mallas, Makuṭa-bandhana, and there laid it down.

24. Then the Mallas of Kusinārā spoke to the Venerable Ānanda, saying: "How should we act, Venerable Ānanda, respecting the body of the Tathāgata?"

"After the same manner, Vāseṭṭhas, as towards the body of a universal monarch."

"But how, venerable Ānanda, do they act respecting the body of a universal monarch?"

"The body of a universal monarch, Vāseṭṭhas, is first wrapped round with new linen, and then with teased cotton wool. And again it is wrapped round with new linen, and again with teased cotton wool, and so it is done up to five hundred layers of linen and five hundred of cotton wool. When that is done, the body of the universal monarch is placed in an iron oil-vessel, which is enclosed in another iron vessel and a funeral pyre is built of all kinds of perfumed woods, and so the body of the universal monarch is burned. And at a crossroads a stūpa is raised for the universal monarch. So it is done, Vāseṭṭhas, with the body of a universal monarch.

"And even, Vāseṭṭhas, as with the body of a universal monarch, so should it be done with the body of the Tathāgata; and at a crossroads also a stūpa should be raised for the Tathāgata. And whoever shall bring to that place garlands or incense or sandalwood paste, or pay reverence, and whose mind becomes calm there—it will be to his well being and happiness for a long time."

25. Then the Mallas gave orders to their men, saying: "Gather now all the teased cotton wool of the Mallas!" And the Mallas of Kusinārā wrapped the body of the Blessed One round with new linen, and then with teased cotton wool. And again they wrapped it round with new linen, and again with teased cotton wool, and so it was done up to five hundred layers of linen and five hundred of cotton wool. When that was done, they placed the body of the Blessed One in an iron oil-vessel, which was enclosed in another iron vessel, and they built a funeral pyre of all kinds of perfumed

woods, and upon it they laid the body of the Blessed One.

26. Now at that time the Venerable Mahā Kassapa[63] was journeying from Pāvā to Kusinārā together with a large company of five hundred bhikkhus. And on the way, the Venerable Mahā Kassapa went aside from the highway and sat down at the foot of a tree.

And a certain Ājīvaka came by, on his way to Pāvā, and he had taken a *mandārava* flower from Kusinārā. And the Venerable Mahā Kassapa saw the Ājīvaka coming from a distance, and as he drew close he spoke to him, saying: "Do you know, friend, anything of our Master?"

"Yes, friend, I know. It is now seven days since the ascetic Gotama passed away. From there I have brought this *mandārava* flower."

27. Thereupon some bhikkhus, not yet freed from passion, lifted up their arms and wept; and some, flinging themselves on the ground, rolled from side to side and wept, lamenting: "Too soon has the Blessed One come to his Parinibbāna! Too soon has the Happy One come to his Parinibbāna! Too soon has the Eye of the World vanished from sight!"

28. Now at that time, one Subhadda, who had renounced only in his old age, was seated in the assembly.[64] And he addressed the bhikkhus, saying: "Enough, friends! Do not grieve, do not lament! We are well rid of that great ascetic. Too long, friends, have we been oppressed by his saying: 'This is fitting for you; that is not fitting for you.' Now we shall be able to do as we wish, and what we do not wish, that we shall not do."

But the Venerable Mahā Kassapa addressed the bhikkhus, saying: "Enough friends! Do not grieve, do not lament! For has not the Blessed One declared that with all that is dear and beloved there must be change, separation, and severance? Of that which is born, come into being, compounded, and subject to decay, how can one say: 'May it not come to dissolution!'?"

---

63. He was one of the foremost disciples of the Buddha and became the president of the First Great Council held shortly after the Buddha's Parinibbāna. See Helmuth Hecker, *Mahā Kassapa: Father of the Sangha* (BPS Wheel No. 345).

64. This Subhadda is a different person from the wanderer Subhadda who became the Buddha's last personal disciple.

29. Now at that time four Mallas of the foremost families, bathed from the crown of their heads and wearing new clothes, with the thought: "We will set alight the Blessed One's pyre," tried to do so but they could not. And the Mallas spoke to the Venerable Anuruddha, saying: "What is the cause, Venerable Anuruddha, what is the reason that these four Mallas of the foremost families, bathed from the crown of their heads and wearing new clothes, with the thought: 'We will set alight the Blessed One's pyre,' try to do so but cannot?"

"You, Vāseṭṭhas, have one purpose, the deities have another."

"Then what, venerable sir, is the purpose of the deities?"

"The purpose of the deities, Vāseṭṭhas, is this: 'The Venerable Mahā Kassapa is on his way from Pāvā to Kusinārā together with a large company of five hundred bhikkhus. Let not the Blessed One's pyre be set alight until the Venerable Mahā Kassapa has paid homage at the feet of the Blessed One.' "

"As the deities wish, venerable sir, so let it be."

30. And the Venerable Mahā Kassapa approached the pyre of the Blessed One, at the cetiya of the Mallas, Makuṭa-bandhana, in Kusinārā. And he arranged his upper robe on one shoulder, and with his clasped hands raised in salutation, he walked three times round the pyre, keeping his right side towards the Blessed One's body, and he paid homage at the feet of the Blessed One. And even so did the five hundred bhikkhus.

And when homage had been paid by the Venerable Mahā Kassapa and the five hundred bhikkhus, the pyre of the Blessed One burst into flame by itself.

31. And it came about that when the body of the Blessed One had been burned, no ashes or particles were to be seen of what had been skin, tissue, flesh, sinews, and fluid; only bones remained. Just as when ghee or oil is burned, it leaves no particles or ashes behind, even so when the body of the Blessed One had been burned, no ashes or particles were to be seen of what had been skin, tissue, flesh, sinews, and fluid; only bones remained. And of the five hundred linen wrappings, only two were not consumed, the innermost and the outermost.

32. And when the body of the Blessed One had been burned, water rained down from heaven and extinguished the pyre of the Blessed One, and from the sāla trees water came forth, and the

Mallas of Kusinārā brought water scented with many kinds of perfumes, and they too extinguished the pyre of the Blessed One.

And the Mallas of Kusinārā laid the relics of the Blessed One in their council hall, and surrounded them with a lattice-work of spears and encircled them with a fence of bows; and there for seven days they paid homage to the relics of the Blessed One with dance, song, music, flower-garlands, and perfume, and showed respect, honour, and veneration to the relics of the Blessed One.

Partition of the Relics

33. Then the king of Magadha, Ajātasattu, son of the Videhi queen, came to know that at Kusinārā the Blessed One had passed away. And he sent a message to the Mallas of Kusinārā, saying: "The Blessed One was of the warrior caste, and I am too. I am worthy to receive a portion of the relics of the Blessed One. I will erect a stūpa over the relics of the Blessed One and hold a festival in their honour."

34. And the Licchavis of Vesālī came to know that at Kusinārā the Blessed One had passed away. And they sent a message to the Mallas of Kusinārā, saying: "The Blessed One was of the warrior caste, and we are too. We are worthy to receive a portion of the relics of the Blessed One. We will erect a stūpa over the relics of the Blessed One and hold a festival in their honour."

35. And the Sakyas of Kapilavatthu came to know that at Kusinārā the Blessed One had passed away. And they sent a message to the Mallas of Kusinārā, saying: "The Blessed One was the greatest of our clan. We are worthy to receive a portion of the relics of the Blessed One. We will erect a stūpa over the relics of the Blessed One and hold a festival in their honour."

36. And the Bulis of Allakappa came to know that at Kusinārā the Blessed One had passed away. And they sent a message to the Mallas of Kusinārā, saying: "The Blessed One was of the warrior caste, and we are too. We are worthy to receive a portion of the relics of the Blessed One. We will erect a stūpa over the relics of the Blessed One and hold a festival in their honour."

37. And the Kolis of Rāmagāma came to know that at Kusinārā the Blessed One had passed away. And they sent a message to the Mallas of Kusinārā, saying: "The Blessed One was of the warrior

caste, and we are too. We are worthy to receive a portion of the relics of the Blessed One. We will erect a stūpa over the relics of the Blessed One and hold a festival in their honour."

38. And the Veṭhadīpa brahmin came to know that at Kusinārā the Blessed One had passed away. And he sent a message to the Mallas of Kusinārā, saying: "The Blessed One was of the warrior caste, and I am a brahmin. I am worthy to receive a portion of the relics of the Blessed One. I will erect a stūpa over the relics of the Blessed One and hold a festival in their honour."

39. And the Mallas of Pāvā came to know that at Kusinārā the Blessed One had passed away. And they sent a message to the Mallas of Kusinārā, saying: "The Blessed One was of the warrior caste, and we are too. We are worthy to receive a portion of the relics of the Blessed One. We will erect a stūpa over the relics of the Blessed One and hold a festival in their honour."

40. But when they heard these words, the Mallas of Kusinārā addressed the assembly, saying: "The Blessed One has passed away in our township. We shall not part with any portion of the relics of the Blessed One." Then the brahmin Doṇa spoke to the assembly, saying:

"One word from me, I beg you, sirs, to hear!
Our Buddha taught us ever to forbear;
Unseemly would it be should strife arise
And war and bloodshed, over the custody
Of his remains, who was the best of men!
Let us all, sirs, in friendliness agree
To share eight portions—so that far and wide
Stūpas may rise, and seeing them, mankind
Faith in the All-Enlightened One will find!"

"So be it, brahmin! Divide the relics into eight equal portions yourself."

And the brahmin Doṇa said to the assembly: "So be it, sirs." And he divided justly into eight equal portions the relics of the Blessed One, and having done so, he addressed the assembly, saying: "Let this urn, sirs, be given to me. Over this urn I will erect a stūpa, and in its honour I will hold a festival." And the urn was given to the brahmin Doṇa.

41. Then the Moriyas of Pipphalivana came to know that at Kusinārā the Blessed One had passed away. And they sent a

message to the Mallas of Kusinārā, saying: "The Blessed One was of the warrior caste, and we are too. We are worthy to receive a portion of the relics of the Blessed One. We will erect a stūpa over the relics of the Blessed One and hold a festival in their honour."

"There is no portion of the relics of the Blessed One remaining; the relics of the Blessed One have been divided. But take from here the ashes." And they took from there the ashes.

42. And the king of Magadha, Ajātasattu, son of the Videhi queen, erected a stūpa over the relics of the Blessed One at Rājagaha, and in their honour held a festival. The Licchavis of Vesālī erected a stūpa over the relics of the Blessed One at Vesālī, and in their honour held a festival. The Sakyas of Kapilavatthu erected a stūpa over the relics of the Blessed One at Kapilavatthu, and in their honour held a festival. The Bulis of Allakappa erected a stūpa over the relics of the Blessed One at Allakappa, and in their honour held a festival. The Kolis of Rāmagāma erected a stūpa over the relics of the Blessed One at Rāmagāma, and in their honour held a festival. The Veṭhadīpa brahmin erected a stūpa over the the relics of the Blessed One at Veṭhadīpa, and in their honour held a festival. The Mallas of Pāvā erected a stūpa over the relics of the Blessed One at Pāvā, and in their honour held a festival. The Mallas of Kusinārā erected a stūpa over the relics of the Blessed One at Kusinārā, and in their honour held a festival. The brahmin Doṇa erected a stūpa over the urn, and in its honour held a festival. And the Moriyas of Pipphalivana erected a stūpa over the ashes at Pipphalivana, and in their honour held a festival.

So it came about that there were eight stūpas for the relics, a ninth for the urn, and a tenth for the ashes.

And thus it was in the days of old.

43. Eight portions there were of the relics of him,
The All-Seeing One, the greatest of men.
Seven in Jambudīpa are honoured, and one
In Rāmagāma, by kings of the Nāga race.
One tooth is honoured in the Tāvatiṃsa heaven,
One in the realm of Kaliṅga, and one by the Nāga kings.
Through their brightness this bountiful earth
With its most excellent gifts is endowed;

For thus the relics of the All-Seeing One are best
honoured
By those who are worthy of honour—by gods and Nāgas
And lords of men, yea, by the highest of mankind.
Pay homage with clasped hands! For hard indeed it is
Through hundreds of ages to meet with an
All-Enlighten-ed One![65]

The Mahāparinibbāna Sutta is finished.

65. Comy. ascribes these verses to the "Elders of Tambapaṇṇi Island (Sri Lanka)."

Anāgārika Dharmapāla

A Biographical Sketch

by

Bhikkhu Sangharakshita

WHEEL PUBLICATION NO. 70/71/72

In Commemoration of the Birth Centenary (1864–1964) of the Late Venerable Bhikkhu Sri Devamitta Dhammapāla known in the annals of Buddhist History as the Anāgārika Dharmapāla. May his life be a source of inspiration to All!

Anāgārika Dharmapāla

The prospects of Ceylon Buddhism in the sixties of the 19th century were dark indeed. Successive waves of Portuguese, Dutch and British invasion had swept away much of the traditional culture of the country. Missionaries had descended upon the copper-coloured island like a cloud of locusts. Christian schools of every conceivable denomination had been opened, where Buddhist boys and girls were crammed with bible texts and taught to be ashamed of their religion, their culture, their language, their race and their colour. The attitude of the missionaries is expressed with unabashed directness in one of the verses of a famous hymn by the well-known Anglican Bishop Heber, a hymn which is still sung, though with less conviction than in the days when it first made its appearance, in churches all over England:

What through the spicy breezes
Blow soft o'er Ceylon's isle,
Where every prospect pleases,
And only man is vile;

In vain with lavish kindness
The gifts of God are strown,
The heathen in his blindness
Bows down to wood and stone.

Throughout the territories under Dutch occupation Buddhists had been compelled to declare themselves as Christians, and during the period of British rule this law was enforced for seventy years, being abrogated only in 1884, when, on behalf of the Buddhists of Ceylon, Col. Olcott made representations to the Secretary of State for the Colonies, in London. Children born of Buddhist parents had to be taken for registration to a church, where some biblical name would be bestowed on them, with the result that most Sinhalese bore either an English Christian name and a Portuguese surname, if they were Catholic 'converts,' or an English Christian name and a Sinhalese surname, if they were Anglicans. The majority of them were ashamed or afraid to declare themselves Buddhists, and only in the villages of the interior did the Dhamma of the Blessed One retain some vestige of its former power and popularity, though even here it was not free from the attacks of the thousands of catechists who, for twenty rupees a month, were prepared to go about slandering and insulting the religion of their fathers.

Members of the Sangha, with a few noble exceptions, were intellectually and spiritually moribund; monastic discipline was lax, the practice of meditation had been neglected and then forgotten; and even to those who truly loved the Buddha, the Dhamma and the Sangha, it must sometimes have seemed that, after reigning for more than twenty glorious centuries over the hearts and minds of the Sinhala race, they were doomed to be "cast as rubbish to the void," and swept into the blue waters of the Arabian Sea by the triumphant legions of militant Christianity. But this was not to be. Low though the fortunes of the Dhamma had sunk, the great beam of the national karma was beginning to right itself, and gigantic forces were being set in motion which in the future would lift them to a position even higher than their present one was low.

Beginnings of a great Sinhalese Patriot

Among the few well-to-do families which through all vicissitudes stood firmly and fearlessly on the side of their ancestral faith was the Hewavitarne family of Matara in South Ceylon. Hewavitarne Dingiri Appuhamy, the first member of this family with whom we are concerned, belonged to the large and respected '*goigama*' or cultivator class. He had two sons, both of whom exhibited the same devotion to the Dhamma as their father. One of them became a Bhikkhu known as Hittatiye Atthadassi Thera and occupied the incumbency of Hittatiya Raja Mahāvihāra. His teacher, Mirisse Revata Thera, was fourth in pupillary succession from the Sangharaja Saraṇaṅkara, the greatest name in eighteenth century Ceylon Buddhism. The other son, Don Carolis Hewavitarne, migrated to Colombo, established there a furniture-manufacturing business in the Pettah area, and married the daughter of a Colombo businessman, Andris Perera Dharmagunawardene, who had donated a piece of land at Maligakanda, erected on it the first Pirivena or Buddhist monastic college in Ceylon, and brought a monk from the remote village of Hikkaduwa to be its principal.

Since then the names of the Vidyodaya Pirivena and Hikkaduwa Siri Sumaṅgala Mahā Nāyaka Thera have passed, inseparably united, into the history of world Buddhism. Through the halls of this great institution of Buddhist learning, unrivalled throughout the length and breadth of Ceylon, have passed monks from Burma, Siam, India, Japan and China, and the memory of the great Buddhist scholar, mathematician and expert in comparative religion who for so many decades guided its destinies, is revered wherever the Dhamma taught in the Pali Scriptures is known. Both Don Carolis and his young wife Mallikā ardently desired a son, and when they knew that a child would be born to them their joy was great indeed. But although they both desired a son, the reasons for which they desired him were by no means the same: Mudaliyar Hewavitarne thought of a successor in the family business, while his wife dreamed of a bhikkhu who would guide the erring footsteps of the Sinhala people back to the Noble Eightfold Path from which they had so long been led astray.

Every morning before sunrise the young bride, who was not yet out of her teens, would gather a trayful of sweet-smelling five-petalled temple flowers and offer them, together with coconut-oil lamps and incense, at the feet of the Buddha-image in the family shrine, praying to the *devas* that she might bear a son who would rekindle the lamp of the Dhamma in a darkened land. Every evening, too, she would lie prostrate in supplication before the silent image, which was a wooden replica of one of the great stone Buddhas of Anurādhapura, the ancient city whose very name awakes in every Sinhala heart an unutterably deep nostalgia for the temporal and spiritual glories of long ago.

Who knows what subtle spiritual emanations from the liberated minds of old passed through that image and penetrated the receptive mind of the Sinhala maiden, steeping the lotus of her aspiration in the dews of kindliness and peace, and purifying her heart and mind until they were a fit receptacle for the Great Being who was to accomplish what even in her wildest dreams she had scarcely dared to hope for. As her time drew near, Bhikkhus were invited to the house, and on the full moon nights of three successive months the air was filled with the vibrations of the sacred Pali texts, as from dusk to dawn they chanted from the holy books. Then, on the night of September 17th, in the Pettah district of Colombo, where the national religion and culture had fallen to the lowest pitch of degeneration, there came, as though to strike the evil at its very heart, the birth of Dharmapāla like a vivid flash of lightning from a black and stormy sky.

Young David Hewavitarne, as he was named, grew up in an atmosphere of traditional Sinhala piety. Every day, morning and evening, he would kneel in the shrine with his father and mother, take refuge in the Buddha, the Dhamma and the Sangha, promise to observe the Five Precepts and chant the verses of worship with which millions of people have for five and twenty centuries expressed their gratitude to, and adoration of, Him who showed humanity for the first time the Way to Nirvāna. Nor was the practical application of the Dhamma forgotten, for sweetly and reasonably his mother would point out to him any infringement of the precepts, and gently chide him into the careful observance of them all.

It is a commonplace of educational psychology that the influences to which a child is subjected to during its earliest years more or less determine the whole course of its subsequent development, and the biography of Dharmapāla provides us with no exception to this rule. His deep and spontaneous devotion to the Buddha, his instinctive observance of the plain and simple rules of the Dhamma through the complexities and temptations of modern life, his ardent love of all that was pure and good, as well as his unsparing condemnation of whatever was unclean and evil, were undoubtedly the efflorescence of seeds which had been planted in the fertile soil of his young heart by his mother's loving advice and his father's austere example. The spectacle of a life such as his, so fruitful in good for the whole of humanity, should be sufficient to convince anyone who might doubt the advisability of bringing up Buddhist children in a traditional atmosphere, and imparting to them from their earliest years both instruction and training in the sublime Dharma. Without that early religious training young David Hewavitarne might have grown up to wear top hat and trousers, speaking English to his family and Sinhalese to the servants, like thousands of his contemporaries, and Dharmapāla, the Lion of Lanka, might never have been born, and the great difference which such a calamity would have made to India, Buddhism, and the world is now impossible for us to gauge.

It should never be forgotten that piety of the old Sinhala type was the plinth and foundation of Dharmapāla's whole character.

Though well versed in his religion, he was not a scholar. Though he wrote inexhaustibly, it is not as a writer that he will be remembered. For more than forty years he worked and organised and agitated unceasingly, but not even here is the secret of his character to be discovered. Fundamentally, he was a Sinhala passionately devoted to his religion as only a Sinhala, after centuries of civil oppression and religious persecution, could have been at that time. With him religion was not an intellectual conviction but an instinct. He lived and moved and had his being in Southern Buddhism, and after centuries of stagnation, it lived and moved and had its being again in him. Herein lies the secret of his appeal to the Sinhala people. He was not a detached scholar looking down at their simple but profound piety from the outside, as it were, but flesh of their flesh, spirit of their spirit, feeling as they felt and believing as they believed. In him all that was good in the national character was raised to a higher degree than they had dreamed was possible in modern times, and seeing him they saw and recognised themselves not only as they had been of old but as they yet might be again.

The child of Mallikā Hewavitarne's dreams was now five years old, and the time had come when the already ardently devout current of his temperament was to be impinged upon by influences which would give to it a definite direction, and obstacles which would serve only to increase its natural impetuosity and inherent momentum. His first contact with the world which lay outside the charmed circle of family life, where the influence of the Dhamma permeated everything like a sweet and subtle perfume, came when he was sent to a school where the majority of pupils were Burghers, that is to say, of mixed Dutch and Sinhala descent.

It is necessary to observe at this crucial point where, for the first time, the innate genius of David Hewavitarne came in contact with forces intrinsically hostile to all that he loved and believed in, that throughout the whole of his long life his character remained wonderfully integrated and harmonious. Whether confronted with a problem of personal conduct or business ethics, whether faced by the customs of his own beloved island or the bewilderingly unfamiliar civilisations of the West and the Far East, he stood firm and unshaken, seeing and judging all things in the clear light of the Dhamma, and doing straightforwardly and without fear or hesitation that which he knew was good and right. The suggestion that he might win a lawsuit by judicious bribery was scornfully rejected, with the characteristic comment that though the winning of the Buddha Gaya case was dearer to his heart than anything in the world he would rather lose it than resort to such detestable methods. When he saw the Niagara Falls, with their millions of tons of water thundering down every minute, he merely remarked that it was the most impressive illustration of the transitoriness of human personality that he had ever seen.

So long and deeply had he meditated upon the truths of the Dhamma that they had become part of his character, so that to think, speak and act in accordance with them was natural to him. But in spite of its inherent nobility, perhaps even because of it, such a character must sooner or later come into conflict with the cowardly conventions and mean hypocrisies of the world, so that it is perhaps inevitable that the life of a man like Dharmapāla should be one unceasing battle against injustice, untruth and unrighteousness in every conceivable form. Naturally, the conflict did not begin until several years after the period with which we are now concerned, but it is interesting to note that even at this time questions rose to his lips which his mother could not always answer, and which his father thought better repressed by the exercise of paternal authority.

Although he never experienced any diminution of his affection for the religious traditions of his family, he could not help becoming aware that those traditions were by no means universally accepted, nor refrain from trying to find some explanation for this difference. Gradually his childish mind came to understand that the world was divided into Buddhists like his mother and father who loved the Dhamma, and Christians like his school teachers who hated it and were seeking to destroy it; but already he knew on which side of the gulf which lay between the two parties he stood, and for whom it was his duty to do battle. But in these early years he gave no indication of the attitude he was insensibly adopting, and even when, at the age of six, he joined the Pettah Catholic School (later St, Mary's School), and was one day asked to kneel down and kiss the ring of the visiting Bishop Hilarion Sillani, he obediently did so, probably without fully understanding the significance of the act.

The next school which David Hewavitarne attended was a Sinhalese private school, where he remained for two years, leaving at the age of ten. "The first lesson was taught", writes Bhikkhu Devamitta Dhammapāla (*Reminiscences of my Early Life, Mahā Bodhi Journal* Vol. 41, Nos. 5 & 6, p. 152), "according to the old Sinhalese custom of offering betel to his teacher and making obeisance to him." He also writes of the teacher that be was a strict disciplinarian who impressed upon his pupil's tender mind the necessity of keeping everything clean and using plenty of water to keep the body physically pure. The lesson appears to have been well learned, for till the end of his life Dharmapāla was almost fanatically particular about the cleanliness and tidiness of the objects of his personal use and of his surroundings.

In the Sinhalese school he had to go through all the Sinhala books which were taught in the temples of Ceylon, with the result that he obtained a thorough grounding in the language and literature of his native land. On leaving the Sinhalese private school he was admitted to the lowest form of St. Benedict's Institute, where among his teachers were Brothers August, Daniel, Joshua and Cassion, several of whom he knew personally during the two years which he spent at the school. Every half hour the class had to repeat a short prayer in praise of the Virgin Mary, and on Thursdays the boy had to attend a special class conducted by a Brother as he was a Buddhist. On feast days he used to decorate the college chapel with sweet-smelling blossoms culled from the flowering trees of his father's garden, the family by this time having moved from Pettah to a new house in Kotahena, then a place of green paddy fields and graceful palms.

It was only to be expected that one day a reverend father should ask the lad why he should not become a Catholic, and in later years Dharmapāla himself commented that it was strange that, at a time when the power of Catholicism was so strong in Colombo, he did not become one. Moreover he made the illuminating remark that the influence of his parents and grandparents was largely responsible for keeping him within the Buddhist fold. This contains a reference not only to his participation in the ritual of daily worship, his regular visits to the Kotahena Temple in the company of his mother, or the Jātaka stories which he read aloud in the cool of the evening, for there was another religious experience which engraved upon his mind an impression perhaps deeper than that left by any of these.

In his ninth year he was initiated into the Brahmacharya vow by his father at the temple, and advised to be contented with whatever he got to eat, and to sleep but little. The impression left by this experience was permanent, and in later years the Anāgārika or 'homeless one', as he then called himself, was accustomed to satisfy his hunger with whatever food he received, and to sleep only two or three hours at night. It behoves us to remember, in this connection, that in spite of his devastatingly energetic career of practical activities and achievements, Dharmapāla's temperament had a pronouncedly ascetic side which was no less characteristic of the man as a whole. He loved solitude, meditation and study, and if these do not occupy a more prominent position in his biography the fact is due not to his own lack of inclination for them, but to the circumstances of the times in which he lived, when the task of rousing the Buddhist world from its centuries-long slumber was the one which made the most imperative demand upon the resources of his genius. In May 1876 he was asked by the school authorities to leave St. Benedict's, and although we are not informed of the circumstances which led to this request, it is not difficult, in view of the subsequent events of his career, to make a fairly accurate guess at what they were.

Even as a cub the Lion of Lanka had sharp claws. The next two years of young Hewavitarne's life were passed in the aggressively-missionary atmosphere of the Christian Boarding School, an Anglican (C. M. S.) institution situated at Kotte, a place six or seven miles from Colombo. Here he was daily forced to attend service at 6:30 a.m. in the Church, where the Rev. R. T, Dowbiggin would recite the prayers and read a text from the Bible. Religious instruction by no means ended here, however. In class he had to recite some verses from Genesis or Matthew, and lurid light is shed on the intensive missionary methods of the day by the fact that he had hardly entered his teens when he knew *by heart* Exodus, Numbers, Deuteronomy, Joshua, all four gospels, and the Acts of the Apostles.

The boarding master of the school was fond of liquor, and used to take delight in shooting the small birds which alighted on the trees. These revolting practices were against the teaching of mindfulness and compassion which he had learned in this own home and the boy, already beginning to think independently, could not reconcile himself with such barbarous behaviour. An incident which occurred at this period must have made his sensitive mind more keenly aware than ever of the gulf which lay between Christian missionary fanaticism on the one hand and Buddhist wisdom and tolerance on the other, and surely added fresh fuel to the already smouldering fires of revolt. One Sunday he was quietly reading a pamphlet on the Four Noble Truths when the same master came up to him and, true to missionary tradition, demanded the offending work from him and had it flung out of the room.

Another incident which happened at this time gives us a valuable glimpse of a trait strikingly characteristic of Dharmapāla during his whole life. A classmate died, and the teacher invited the students to gather round the dead body and join in the prayers which were to be offered. As David Hewavitarne looked first at the uneasy faces about him, and then at the corpse which lay so still on the bed, there came to him in a blinding flash of illumination the thought that prayer is born of fear, and at once his whole being revolted against the idea of being afraid of anything. In this dramatic manner he achieved that complete freedom from fear which was ever one of his most striking qualities, and entered into possession of that dauntless courage which is one of the surest signs of spiritual mastery.

Curiously enough, by continual reading of the Bible young Hewavitarne had acquired a fondness for the sonorous cadences of the *Authorised Version*, and even neglected his class studies in order to indulge his passion for the rhythmic beauty of its Jacobean diction. He did not read uncritically, however, and even at that early age his nimble wits were able to formulate questions which perplexed and irritated his teachers. The climax of his criticisms was reached when he drew a picture of a monkey and wrote underneath it 'Jesus Christ,' for which piece of juvenile impudence he was threatened with expulsion from the school. Of course, according to Buddhist teaching it was wrong of him to have offended Christian sentiment in this way; but we must remember that it was hardly possible for a boy of his age, intellectually undeveloped as he was, to express his opinions in any other manner.

Even in his later writings we find page after page of vigorous anti-Christian invective which appears strangely un-Buddhistic, until we remember how utterly unscrupulous, cunning and implacable the forces of missionary fanaticism then were, and how terrible was the ignorant hatred with which they assailed and sought to destroy the Dharma. When the young biblical critic eventually did leave the school it was not because the authorities found his presence embarrassing, but because the food he had to eat was, as he informs us himself, "horrible," so that his father had to remove him when he saw how lean the youth had become.

Then followed two months rest at home, after which, in September 1878, he attended St. Thomass Collegiate School, an Anglican institution in North Colombo. It was not long before his uncompromising championship of his ancestral Dhamma brought him into conflict with the rigid discipline of the school. Warden Miller, the head of the institution, was a pedagogue of the old type, firmly believing and unflinchingly practising the maxim "Spare the rod and spoil the child." The students of St. Thomass were certainly neither spared nor spoiled, and so great was the awe in which the stern disciplinarian was held that the sound of his step in the corridor was enough to send a shiver of terrified anticipation through a hundred youthful hearts. Great must have been the astonishment of this dreadful figure when, one fine May morning, a slim young Sinhala appeared before him in his study, and after explaining that the day was sacred to the Birth, Enlightenment and Death of the Buddha, whom he revered as the Founder of his religion, boldly asked for permission to spend the day at home in worship and other religious observances. Recovering from his astonishment, Warden Miller explained in his sternest tones that the day was not a school holiday, and that as the head of an Anglican public school he did not feel justified in granting a holiday merely for the observance of a Buddhist festival. Whereupon David Hewavitarne picked up his umbrella and his books, and without another word walked out of school for the day.

Next morning the young rebel received not only a wrathful reprimand for his insubordination but also a few of Warden Miller's best cane-strokes on the seat of his trousers. This painful and humiliating experience did not, however, prevent him from repeating the escapade on the two remaining Wesak Days which occurred during his career at St. Thomass and on both occasions the same punishment was meted out to him as before. His fellow students did not know whether to be amused at his impudence or to admire his courage, and Christian friends confided to him that they would not willingly have risked one of Warden Miller's thrashings for the doubtful privilege of observing Christmas Day.

But the mantle of destiny had already fallen upon his youthful shoulders, and even in his middle teens he must have been aware of the gulf of difference which lay between his own burning enthusiasm for the Dhamma and the dreamy adolescent indifference of his fellows. Not that this feeling of difference isolated him from his companions, or prevented him from making a number of friends. On the contrary, the circle of his friendship was always wide, and at a time when caste differences were keenly felt, even in Buddhist Lanka, it included boys of every class and community.

He loved to relate how the Buddha had admitted even a scavenger, that most despised member of orthodox Hindu society, into the noble brotherhood of the Sangha, and how in accordance with His Teaching even brahmin Buddhist converts had to bow their heads in worship at his feet. His friendships were not, however, of that sentimental kind so common in public schools. He made friends chiefly in order to have the pleasure of arguing with them, and he argued in order to taste the still sweeter pleasure of polemical victory. For the spirit of controversy was already rampant in him, and it is said that at this period he was unhappy if he could not disagree for the day. The favourite object of his attack were, of course, the dogmas of orthodox Christianity, and many were the occasions on which he gleefully confused and bewildered the minds of his opponents.

To a Kandyan Buddhist schoolfellow who, weakly succumbing to the persuasions of the missionaries, had said that he supposed there must be a First Cause, the budding debater posed the question, "Did God make a First Cause?" "God is the First Cause", glibly replied his friend. "Then who made God?" came the next question. The Kandyan, now thoroughly out of his depth, stammered that he supposed God must have made himself. This was the opportunity for which Dharmapāla had been eagerly waiting. "Then God must be a Buddhist," he retorted triumphantly. "Every Buddhist is a result of his past karma. Besides, every man makes himself. Every man is a potential God. But even man, who was his own first cause, did not create the world. Gods and men can create themselves, but they can't create others."

On the following Sunday the Kandyan went to Sunday School armed with a question from Dharmapāla. "If 'Thou shalt not kill' is a commandment, why did the Crusades ever take place, Sir?" The Sinhala padre, whose mind had probably not been troubled by such a question before, replied rather naively that they had been inspired from heaven. When the answer was carried back to Dharmapāla, who no longer attended Sunday School, he was ready with his usual unanswerable objection. "Every war is an inspiration for Christians. Why should God inspire people to break his own commandments ?"

The first rumblings of that great thunder of denunciation against sham religion and false philosophy which was to burst in later years from his lips were already beginning to make themselves heard, and it is an ironical fact that the biblical knowledge which he was to use with such deadly effect was fostered and developed by the missionaries themselves, who could never have imagined that they were thereby placing in the hands of their pupil the instruments of their own discomfiture. When the Sinhala padre who taught his religious class, attracted by the boy's intelligence and no doubt mindful of the desirability of inducing such a promising lad to become a convert, promised him a watch if he topped his class in religious knowledge, young Hewavitarne promptly studied hard and carried off the coveted prize. But if it was the Christian missionaries themselves who placed the weapons of debate in the hands of the youthful fighter it was a Buddhist monk who first taught him how to use them.

The Pānadura Controversy

Every day on his way to and from St. Thomas Dharmapāla used to pass the Kotahena Temple, the incumbent of which was Megettuvatte Guṇānanda, the greatest orator and debater of Ceylon in modern times. On Saturday evenings, during the seventies and early eighties of the 19th century, the place would be thronged with devotees, for on those days the great preacher, his forefinger raised as though to emphasise every word he uttered, his yellow robe flung back dramatically over his brown shoulder as if to leave his arms free for battle, and his black eyes flashing with the fire of denunciation, would launch one of those devastating attacks on Christianity the noise of which would echo, during the following week, from one end of the island to the other. Now it was the doctrine of creation on which he trained the batteries of Buddhist reason, now the belief in a permanent individual soul, until one by one the crumbling bastions of Christian dogmatic theology were reduced to a heap of smoking rubble. These lectures, which were the first visible sign of Buddhist reaction against centuries of Christian domination, aroused wild enthusiasm on the one hand and excited violent indignation on the other.

Determined to silence so formidable an antagonist once and for all, the Christians organised in 1873 a huge public meeting at Pānadura, a place near Colombo, and Guṇānanda was challenged to meet in open debate the most able among their controversialists. Alone but undaunted, he faced the united forces of Christian orthodoxy, and so impressive was his eloquence, so powerful his reasoning, that the Pānadura Controversy, which was intended to bring discredit to the Buddhists, sounded instead the death-knell of Christian influence in Ceylon, so that never again did Catholic or Protestant dogmatism venture to cross swords with Buddhist wisdom.

Colonel Olcott and Mme Blavatsky

The repercussions of this historic debate were felt more widely than even Guṇānanda could have thought possible, and great must have been his surprise and delight when, a few years later, he received a letter from an American colonel and a Russian lady of noble birth expressing satisfaction at his victory, and acquainting him with the formation of the Theosophical Society in New York in 1875. With the letter came two bulky volumes entitled *Isis Unveiled.* Guṇānanda immediately entered into regular correspondence with the two foreign sympathisers, and started translating their letters and extracts from *Isis Unveiled* into Sinhalese. These translations circulated all over the island, and before long the names of H. S. Olcott and H. P. Blavatsky were repeated with wonder and delight in every Buddhist home.

David Hewavitarne, who had become not only a frequent visitor to the temple but also a great favourite of its incumbent, was among those whose hearts leapt with joy to hear of this unexpected aid, and in 1879 he had the satisfaction of hearing from his master's lips the news that the Founders of the Theosophical

Society had arrived in Bombay and that they would shortly be coming to Ceylon to help in the revival of Buddhism.

He also saw the first number of *The Theosophist*, a copy of which had been sent to Migettuvatte, and he tells us himself that it was from this time, when he was fourteen years old, that his interest in Theosophy dated. His enthusiasm for the newly-founded movement was still further increased by the lectures which the great preacher had started giving on Col. Olcott, Mme. Blavatsky and the Theosophical Society, and when, in May 1880, the two Founders at last arrived in Ceylon from India, his excitement was shared by every Buddhist heart in the island, and the two visitors were received amidst scenes of religious fervour such as had not been witnessed within living memory.

After centuries of Christian persecution and oppression the Buddhists of Ceylon could hardly believe that this dignified American colonel, with his patriarchal grey beard, lofty forehead, aquiline nose, and shrewd blue eyes, and this unwieldy Russian woman, with her beringed fingers, puffy cheeks and dreamily hypnotic gaze—who were, to them, members of the ruling white race—had actually come to Ceylon not to attack the Dhamma, as thousands of Christian missionaries had done, but to defend and support it, that they had come neither as enemies nor conquerors, but simply as friends and brothers. However when, on that memorable May 21st, the Buddhist devotees flocked in their thousands from the surrounding villages to Galle, and saw the strange pair on their knees in front of the High Priest and actually heard them repeat the familiar words of the Three Refuges and Five Precepts, as no other Westerners had ever done before, all their suspicions were allayed, and it seemed as though their wildest dreams had come true. The tide had turned at last and Guṇānanda felt that all his labour had not been in vain.

This is not the place for an analysis of the characters of Col. Olcott and Mme. Blavatsky, nor for an examination of the motives with which they came to Ceylon, and space does not permit us to unravel the tangled skein of Theosophical history even prior to the events with which we are now concerned. To what extent the Founders were followers of the Dhamma as that term is understood in the monasteries of Ceylon, and with what mental reservations they publicly embraced Buddhism at Galle, are matters which, though in themselves interesting and important subjects of inquiry, could make no material difference to the course of the narrative now being unfolded. We are concerned not so much with psychology as with history, and it is not only a fact but also an extremely important fact that the conversion of Mme. Blavatsky and Col. Olcott to Buddhism marked the beginning of a new epoch in the annals of Ceylon Buddhism.

If at the Pānadura Controversy, Christian fanaticism suffered its first serious repulse, by the ceremony at Galle, Buddhism scored its first positive victory, and that this victory was won for Buddhism by the Founders of the Theosophical Society is impossible for any fair-minded person to deny. At any rate, boundless was the gratitude of the Sinhala Buddhists to the two converts through whose instrumentality the power of the Dhamma had been so abundantly demonstrated, and their triumphal tour from South Ceylon up to Colombo was the occasion for a series of outbreaks of popular enthusiasm. On their arrival at the capital in June, young Hewavitarne, his eyes bright with expectation and his heart thumping wildly at the prospect of seeing the idols whom he had until then been worshipping from afar, walked all the way from St. Thomas to the place where Col. Olcott was to deliver his first lecture.

At the close of the meeting, when everybody had left, his uncle and father remained behind, and with them the fourteen-year old boy. His uncle had already become a great favourite with Mme. Blavatsky, and more than half a century later, only a few months before his death, Dharmapāla wrote that he still remembered the delight he felt when along with them he shook hands with the Founders as they said goodbye. He adds that he was intuitively drawn to Mme. Blavatsky, though he never suspected that she would later carry him off to Adyar in the face of the protests of his whole family, together with those of the High Priest Sumaṅgala and Col. Olcott himself. However, that day was still four years ahead, and in the meantime the youthful enthusiast continued to attend St. Thomas. In spite of his strictness, Warden Miller liked the rebellious Sinhala boy for his truthfulness and one day told him, with rare candour, "We don't come to Ceylon to teach you English, but we come to Ceylon to convert you." Hewavitarne replied that he could not believe in the Old Testament although he liked the New.

In March 1863 the Catholic riots took place, when a Buddhist procession, which was passing by St. Lucia's Church in Kotahena to Migettuvatte Guṇānanda's temple, was brutally assaulted by a Catholic mob, and Dharmapāla's indignant father refused to allow him to study any longer in a Christian school, even though he had not yet matriculated. On his departure from the school Warden Miller gave him an excellent certificate. The next few months he spent eagerly devouring books in the Pettah Library, of which he was a member.

The range of his interests was always remarkably wide, and we are told that at this period of adolescent intellectual ferment his favourite subjects of study were ethics, philosophy, psychology, biography and history. Poetry he loved passionately, especially that of Keats and Shelley, whose *Queen Mab* had been his favourite poem ever since he had chanced to find it in a volume of poetry in his uncle's library. "I never ceased," he says, "to love its lyric indignation against the tyrannies and injustices that man heaps on himself and its passion for individual freedom." Shelley's poetry, the bulk of which was composed under the blue skies of sunny Italy, has a particularly exhilarating effect when read in the tropics on a starry night, when the palms sway to and fro in the moonlight, and the scent of the temple-flowers drifts intolerably sweet from the trees outside, particularly when the reader is in his late teens, and perhaps it would not be too fanciful to trace in the noble accomplishments of Dharmapāla's maturity the lingering influence of the poet of *Prometheus Unbound.* At any rate, he felt a strange sense of kinship with one who as a schoolboy had rebelled against the rigid dogmas of orthodox Christianity, and he wondered if Shelley and Keats had been reborn in the deva-world or on earth, and whether it would be possible to trace them in their present reincarnations and convert them to Buddhism.

Such are the dreams of youth, always aspiring after the impossible, ever enamoured of the unknown. Dharmapāla admits, in his *Reminiscences*, that from boyhood he was inclined towards the mystic, ascetic life, and that he was on the lookout for news about Arahants and the science of Abhiñña, or supernormal knowledge, even though, as he relates, the Bhikkhus of Ceylon were sceptical about the possibility of realising Arahantship, believing that the age of Arahants was past and that the realisation of Nirvāna by psychic training was no longer possible. But his thirst for direct spiritual experience, his craving for personal contact with beings of supernormal spiritual development, was by no means quenched by the worldly scepticism of the official custodians of the Dhamma, and it was with a thrill of joy that he read A. P. Sinnett's *The Occult World.*

The Theosophical Society

He decided to join the Himalayan School of Adepts, the necessary qualifications for which had been described in an article entitled "Chelas and Lay Chelas" which he had read in the pages of *The Theosophist* only a month before, and accordingly wrote to the "Unknown Brother" in November 1883 a letter intimating his desire to join the Order, and enclosed it in another letter to Mme. Blavatsky at her Adyar address. Three months later, in January 1884, Col. Olcott returned to Ceylon at the request of the Colombo Theosophists in order to institute legal proceedings against the Catholics for their murderous and unprovoked attack on a peaceful Buddhist procession, and Dharmapāla lost no time in meeting him and expressing his desire to join the Theosophical Society. The Colonel replied that the boy's letter had been received, and that he was prepared to admit him, even though he was under age.

The ceremony of initiation accordingly took place in the temporary headquarters of the Theosophical Society in Maliban Street, two other Sinhala Buddhists being initiated at the same time, and his grandfather, who was then President of the Society, paying the initiation fee of ten rupees. The young aspirant began to feel that his dreams of a higher life were beginning to come true; and as his thirst for occult knowledge increased it was inevitable that he should be drawn by the powerful magnetic influence of Mme. Blavatsky, who had accompanied Col. Olcott to Ceylon. Holding the boy spellbound with her hypnotic stare, she would speak to him in deep, guttural tones of the mysterious Brotherhood of Adepts who from their remote Himalayan fastnesses directed the destinies of the Theosophical Society of the Master K. H. and of the Master M., playing with a master hand upon his youthful sensibilities until Dharmapāla would feel himself being swept away on a current of uncontrollable enthusiasm.

Wholehearted devotion at the feet of the unseen Masters, whom he of course understood to be followers of the Lord Buddha, and a fervent aspiration to dedicate himself to their service, now became the ruling passion of his life, and when Mme. Blavatsky quoted to him the message that the Master K. H, had sent to A. P. Sinnett, "*the only refuge for him who aspires to true perfection is the Buddha alone*," it awoke in his heart reverberations which were to last from that day until the hour of his death. How deep was the impression made upon him by these pregnant words is best measured by the fact that nearly half a century later he was still writing them at the head of every alternate page in his diary, sometimes in a firm bold hand, sometimes in letters made shaky and almost illegible by acute physical suffering. At the time with which we are dealing Dharmapāla was completely under the influence of the Russian seeress, so that when she conveyed to aim a personal message from the same Master, asking him to accompany her to Adyar and continue to be her disciple there, he embraced with eagerness the opportunity of qualifying himself still further for direct contact with the members of the Adept Brotherhood.

Mudaliyar Hewavitarne agreed that he should go to Adyar in December, and all arrangements were made to leave Colombo. Col. Olcott and Dr. Franz Hartmann arrived from Madras to escort the party, which in addition to Mme. Blavatsky now included Mr. and Mrs. Oakley-Cooper and Rev. C. W. Leadbeater from London. On the morning of the day fixed for their departure, however, the boy's father told him that he had had an unlucky dream in the night and that he should therefore not go. Of course, the young disciple of the Masters protested vigorously against this unexpected frustration of his cherished desires, saying that as he was being taken to Adyar by Col. Olcott nothing would happen to him. His fears not set at rest by this reply, the Mudaliyar took his son to see his grandfather, who was also opposed to the Adyar journey. All three of them then entered a carriage and went to see the High Priest Sumaṅgala who, to Dharmapāla's dismay, also added his voice to the chorus of opposition. The boy gave vent to his grief, asking them why they should interfere with his karma, whereupon the High Priest deputed his assistant, Bhikkhu Amaramoli, to go with the party to Col. Olcott and finally settle the matter in consultation with him. They all went, and Col.

Olcott positively declined to take him against the wishes of his family and the advice of the High Priest. At this point, when Dharmapāla had sunk into the depths of despair, Mme. Blavatsky rushed upon the scene dramatically declaring that there was no cause for fear in going to Adyar, as she herself would be responsible for his safe return; but that if he was not allowed to go he would surely die. Frightened by this prediction, Mudaliyar Hewavitarne committed his son to Mme. Blavatsky's care, and exhorted him to lead the life of a Bodhisattva. The Mudaliyar's fears were of course the outcome of paternal love and solicitude for his first-born. Besides, he had given him an English education with the intention of qualifying him to carry on and develop the family business, so that it must have been a sore disappointment for him to see how decidedly his son's mind was turning away from material interests, how innocent he was of all worldly ambition. However, he was not only an affectionate, albeit stern, father, but also pious Buddhist, and reflecting that David's departure was in the interests of the Dhamma reconciled himself to the inevitable.

Adyar and Return to Ceylon

Dharmapāla had gone to Adyar with the intention of studying occultism, and there is no doubt that Mme. Blavatsky could have been of considerable assistance to him in pursuing his studies in that recondite field. But curiously enough, instead of encouraging his enthusiasm for the occult, she turned his interests in a quite different direction. Calling him to her room one day, she made him sit by her and told him that he need not take up the study of occultism, but that he should study Pali, where all that was needed could be found, and that he should work for the good of humanity, after which she gave him her blessings.

Years later Dharmapāla wrote in his "Reminiscences" that there and then he decided that henceforth his life should be devoted to the good of humanity, and the history of Buddhism during the last sixty years is the witness of how faithfully he observed his youthful vow. He also writes that "In those days the theosophic atmosphere was saturated with the aroma of the devotion of the Himalayan Masters to the Lord Buddha as is seen in the articles in the 'Theosophist' of the Adepts showing their devotion to the Buddha Gautama", and it could not have been without regret that after staying for only a short while at Adyar, he returned to Colombo, where he began faithfully carrying out his pledge. Meanwhile, the missionaries of Madras, rightly fearing that the presence of Col. Olcott and Mme. Blavatsky was prejudicial to the spread of Christianity in India, had been conducting a series of savage attacks on Mme. Blavatsky, impugning her character and alleging that her psychic powers were not genuine but fraudulent.

A couple called the Coulombs, whom she had discharged from her service, were bribed to furnish fabricated evidence, the husband (a carpenter) faking trap-doors, etc., in a cupboard to prove trickery, the wife forging letters purporting to come from Mme. Blavatsky herself. These letters the missionaries purchased and printed in their magazine. Shortly afterwards, the Society for Psychical Research published the report of an agent named Hodgson whom they had sent to India to investigate the phenomena which had been produced at A. P. Sinnett's Simla house in 1880, and who had based his findings on the evidence of the Coulombs, ignoring the fact that neither of them was present when the most important phenomena occurred, and deliberately suppressing the verdict of an expert graphologist, to whom he had submitted parts of letters attributed to a Master and some writing said to be by Mme. Blavatsky, that "Mme. Blavatsky was not the writer of the letters attributed to the Master."

These two blows, coming as they did in quick succession, created a panic in the Theosophical camp and fearing legal entanglements and difficulties with the Government neither Col. Olcott nor the Council would permit her to bring an action for libel, even though evidence against the Coulombs had been obtained, and in spite of the fact that the attacks were based on forged letters. Despite her protests Mme. Blavatsky was hurried away from Adyar, and once away from the headquarters excuses were easily found to prevent her from returning. The steamer which took her back to Europe called at Colombo and Dharmapāla went on board to say goodbye.

It was their last meeting, but so deep was the impression she had succeeded in making upon the youth's plastic mind that for the remainder of his life he cherished her memory with affection and gratitude, firmly believing her to have been the innocent victim of a foul conspiracy. In his eyes she was a Buddhist and the agent of

Masters, who were also Buddhists, and after her death it was with increasing concern and indignation that he saw the organisation she had founded, and which had, as she once wrote, her "magnetic fluid," turning under the leadership of Mrs. Besant away from Buddhism first to Brahmanism and thereafter to a succession of pseudo-religious mummeries each wilder, more extravagant, and further removed from Mme. Blavatsky's teachings than the last. It was the Anāgārika's suggestion that Alice Leighton Cleather wrote her well-known book *H. P. Blavatsky—Her Life and Work for Humanity,* which was published in book form in 1922 after appearing as a series of articles in the *Mahā Bodhi Journal,* and perhaps we shall not be guilty of serious error if we assume that Dharmapāla's mature views on the subject were in substantial agreement with those expressed in this work.

Leaving Home as Brahmacari

At the time of which we are writing, when he was in his twentieth year, he believed, with the majority of Sinhala Buddhists, that the interests of Buddhism and the interests of the Theosophical Society were identical. In these circumstances it was but natural that when, a few months after Mme. Blavatsky's departure, he wrote to his father a letter asking for permission to leave home and lead a brahmacari life as he wished to devote all his time to the welfare of the Sāsana, he should also request permission to stay at the Theosophical headquarters, on the grounds that the Society was working for the good of Buddhism. His father at first demurred, asking who would look after the younger members of the family if the eldest son left home.

Firm in his determination, Dharmapāla replied that each one had his own karma to protect him, and in the end the Mudaliyar had to agree to the arrangement. His mother, too, gave her blessings, saying that had it not been for his two younger brothers, who still required her care, she would have joined him in the new life he was about to adopt. The young man was now free to go forth from his home to the life of homelessness, free to dedicate his life to the service of humanity, and with characteristic enthusiasm he at once plunged into the work of the Theosophical Society. In a tribute which appeared shortly after his death an admirer has painted a vivid portrait of the Anāgārika's life at this period:

> "Nothing was too small or too big for him. He would clean his own room, make his own bed, attend to office work, write all the letters and take them to the post himself, not as a matter of virtue but as a part of his daily routine. He would interpret for one, he would prepare a programme for another, he would translate a lecture for some one else, he would write original articles for the newspaper, he would discuss the policy of the paper with the Editor and would correct proofs for him, and he would interview those who visited the office. He wrote to people all over Ceylon inviting them to visit the Head Office and to contribute their 'good will' towards the progress of the cause. All were alike to him, whether one was old or young or a school boy, learned or ignorant, rich or poor did not matter; he instinctively knew what each was able to contribute towards the common good. He spent well nigh fifteen to sixteen hours a day in intensive work. He had a pleasant manner, cheerful at all times; his written and spoken words were eloquent and their sincerity went to the hearts of all those who met him. This bundle of energy and goodwill continued his useful career at the Buddhist Headquarters for nearly five years. He helped in the foundation of schools, and in Buddhist propaganda. He attracted men to the new organisation till the Colombo Buddhist Theosophical Society became a power in the land."

This description might have been written at almost any time during the fifty subsequent years of Dharmapāla's career, for his tireless energy in doing good, his unflagging zeal for the propagation of the Dhamma, increased rather than diminished with the passing of years, so that we might fittingly apply to him the verse:

> Appamatto pamattesu suttesu bahujāgaro
> abalasaṃ' va sīghasso hitvā yāti sumedhaso.

> "Heedful among the heedless,
> wide awake among those who sleep,
> like a swift horse the wise man advances,
> leaving the feeble hack behind."

(Dhammapada, 29)

Touring Ceylon

In February 1886 Col. Olcott and C. W. Leadbeater arrived in Colombo to collect money for the Buddhist Educational Fund. Dharmapāla was then employed as a junior clerk in the Education Department, and his meals used to be sent daily from home to the Theosophical headquarters where he stayed. Col. Olcott had planned to tour the whole island, and for this purpose he needed the services of an interpreter. But when no one to accompany him could be found he declared that he would be merely wasting his time if no Buddhist was willing to go with him on his tour. Dharmapāla promptly offered his services, and applied to the Director of Education for three months leave.

Previous to this he had appeared in the Clerical Examination, pledging to himself, however, that if he passed he would not join Government service, but dedicate instead his whole life to the service of humanity. The trio set off from Colombo in the Colonel's two-storied travelling cart, Olcott and Leadbeater sleeping at night in the upper storey, while Dharmapāla occupied the lower berth. For two months they travelled up and down the country, thus inaugurating that long series of historic missionary drives which was eventually to make the bearded Colonel and his youthful companion familiar figures in the Sinhala countryside, and which was to surround them before the end of the decade with a halo of almost legendary fame.

The tour of 1886 occupies an important place in Dharmapāla's development. Besides bringing him in touch with the hopes and fears, the virtues and failings, of thousands of his fellow-countrymen, it also gave him a glimpse, through the commanding and active personality of Col. Olcott, of the practical efficiency of the western races. As interpreter he stood between two worlds, and it was not merely words but ideas which he had to translate. Circumstances made him the common denominator between ancient wisdom and modern knowledge, between the traditions of an old but decayed people and the innovating vitality of a people newly-born, and the constant need of passing rapidly from one pole of understanding to the other gave his mind an elasticity and nimbleness of movement of great value to the development of his character.

Before long he was not only functioning as the mouthpiece of Col. Olcott's or Mr. Leadbeater's ideas, but forcefully speaking out his own independent opinions on the various socio-religious problems of his day, many of which came under his clear-sighted scrutiny as he passed through the villages of the interior. He saw that many un-Buddhistic foreign customs had crept into the life of the people, and with youthful enthusiasm he extolled the glories of ancient and bewailed the degeneracy of modern Lanka. He fulminated against the habit of eating beef, railed against the use of foreign names and foreign dress, and to the huge delight of his listeners led them in smashing the head-combs which the Sinhalas had adopted from the Malays.

He saw how wide and deep was the influence of the Christian missions, how it had eaten into the vitals of the people and was corroding all that was noblest in the national character. He saw, too, how the villagers faith in and observance of the Dhamma were slowly crumbling before the attacks of the missionaries and their hirelings, and it was with all the eloquence of which he was capable that he interpreted Col. Olcott's magnificent vindications of Buddhism and his impassioned appeals for its revival throughout the length and breadth of the land. Contact with the people who ploughed the fields and planted the paddy not only gave him a first-hand knowledge of his country's problems, but also prevented him from developing any of the bookish humours of a scholar. The peasants that assembled to hear the white Buddhist speak were mostly illiterate, and in order to make Olcott's message intelligible to them his interpreter had to draw upon all his resources of wit and repartee, humour and homely illustration. Not that he ever made them feel he was talking down to them. He spoke as one of themselves, as a Buddhist and as a son of Sri Lanka and as such they accepted the young preacher and took him to their hearts. When Col. Olcott left Ceylon for Madras, Dharmapāla and Leadbeater carried on the lecturing tour alone.

They were still in the villages of the interior when a letter arrived from the Colonial Secretary informing Dharmapāla that he had passed the examination and had been appointed to a better post. Now completely absorbed in Buddhist work, the erstwhile junior clerk felt that the time had come to turn his back upon Government service for ever, so without delay he replied saying that he was going to work for his religion and requested the Colonial Secretary to accept his resignation. After their return to Colombo his father advised him to accept the post and hand over his earnings to the Theosophical Society for Buddhist work. He also took him to call on the Colonial Secretary, who asked him to withdraw his resignation; but despite their persuasions Dharmapāla was not to be shaken in his resolve, and in the end he was delighted to see that the last tie binding him to a worldly career had been broken. Henceforth he was free to devote himself single-mindedly to the work for which his own aspirations and the blessings of his teachers had already consecrated him.

'Sandaresa' and 'The Buddhist': He becomes 'The Anāgārika Dharmapāla'

From this time onwards it becomes more and more difficult to do even a semblance of justice to the many-sided activities of the greatest Buddhist missionary in modern times. During the years 1885-89 he devoted himself wholeheartedly to the affairs of the Buddhist Theosophical Society, and with the financial support of his grandfather and the co-operation of C. P. Goonewardana, Williams Abrew, Don Carolis and others the organisation prospered. At Col. Olcott's request, Leadbeater prepared a shorter version of his *Buddhist Catechism*, the first part being translated into Sinhalese by Dharmapāla with the help of Sumaṅgala Nāyaka Mahā Thera, the second by two teachers of the Buddhist English School, James Perera and Wimalasuriya. Both parts were published at the Buddhist Press which Col. Olcott and Dharmapāla had established with the money obtained by issuing debentures.

Resolving that this press should become the property of the Buddhist Theosophical Society, Dharmapāla requested his grandfather, who owned more shares than anybody else, to present them to the Society, and once he had agreed to do so it was not difficult to persuade the other shareholders to follow his generous example. After liquidating the debts of the *Sandaresa*, their Sinhalese weekly, and establishing it on a firm foundation, Dharmapāla decided that it was high time the Buddhists of Ceylon had an English weekly as well. Thirty friends contributed ten rupees each, and with the sum thus raised English type was obtained from Madras, and in December 1888 The Buddhist was issued under Leadbeater's editorship as a supplement to the *Sandaresa.* The Sinhalese organ gave publicity to the rural and urban branches of the Ceylon Theosophical Society, reported the progress of the educational fund, and appealed for the opening of more Buddhist schools to counteract Christian propaganda, while its English counterpart concentrated on more technical expositions of the Dhamma in relation to Western science and psychology. The latter not only enjoyed a wide circulation among the English educated upper classes of Ceylon but also circulated in Europe, America, India, Japan and Australia, thus encircling the earth with the Word of the Buddha, and preparing the way for its more famous successor, the *Mahā Bodhi Journal.*

Parallel to his journalistic ventures Dharmapāla carried on his preaching activities among the people, touring indefatigably from village to village in Col. Olcott's bullock cart, giving lectures, distributing Buddhist literature, and collecting funds for the educational work already inaugurated by the Theosophical Society. Meanwhile Leadbeater had started a number of Buddhist Sunday Schools in different parts of Colombo, besides establishing an English school (later Ananda College, one of the most celebrated schools in Ceylon) for the benefit of a few personal pupils, among whom was his young favourite Jinarajadasa, afterwards famous as the fourth President of the Theosophical Society at Adyar. It was during this period of intense activity that Don David Hewavitarne assumed the name of Dharmapāla, or Guardian of the Law, under which he was subsequently to win the admiration and homage of Buddhists all over the world.

In spite of his preoccupations in Ceylon Dharmapāla was able to find time for a number of trips to Adyar. Under Col. Olcott's active supervision the world headquarters of the Theosophical movement had expanded at an amazing rate, but with the advent of T. Subba Row the influence of Mme. Blavatsky had declined, the Buddha had lost ground to Sankara, and after seeing that the occult room had been dismantled Dharmapāla felt that the Masters had left the place.

Japan

In 1887 Dharmapāla read an article on Japan in an issue of the *Fortnightly Review*, and a desire to visit the Land of the Rising Sun at once took possession of his mind. Two years later, in 1889, it was fulfilled. The Buddhists of Japan, hearing of Col. Olcott's splendid services to the Dhamma in Ceylon, were eager that he should visit their country as well, and therefore sent him a cordial invitation. The emissary to whom was entrusted the responsibility of escorting the Colonel to Japan arrived in Colombo in December 1888, and after being entertained there by Dharmapāla was so pleased with the selfless young Buddhist worker that he extended the invitation to him also. Col. Olcott, seeing in the visit an opportunity of linking the Mahāyāna Buddhism of Japan with the Theravāda Buddhism of Ceylon, decided to accept the invitation, and urged his young friend, who had accompanied the emissary Noguchi to Adyar, to go with him.

Back went Dharmapāla to Colombo, and booked passages on the *S. S. Djeninah*, a French liner. Olcott arrived soon afterwards, and on January 17th 1889, the day before their departure, the Buddhists of Ceylon held a farewell function in their honour at the Theosophical Society Hall. After delivering a splendid discourse, in the course of which he invoked the blessings of the devas and the Triple Gem on the mission, Sumaṅgala Nāyaka Mahā Thera handed over to Col. Olcott a Sanskrit letter of good wishes addressed to the Chief High Priests of Japan. This historic letter, the first official communication which had passed for centuries between a Southern Buddhist dignitary and the heads of one of the most important branches of the Northern Buddhist Sangha, expressed the renewed hope that the Buddhists of Asia would unite for the good of the whole Eastern world. With the precious document in their charge, Olcott, Dharmapāla and the poet Noguchi left the shores of Ceylon, and after calling at Singapore, Saigon, Hong Kong and Shanghai (where Dharmapāla began to suffer from the intense cold, and saw snow for the first time in his life), the party arrived at Kobe, where the Chief High Priests of the seven leading sects of Japanese Buddhism had assembled on the jetty to receive them.

Col. Olcott had to respond alone to the warm welcome which they were accorded, as Dharmapāla was too ill to do more than sit on the deck and watch the proceedings. But to the young Sinhala's delight and gratification all seven high priests insisted on coming on to the deck and paying their respects to him as the representative of the Buddhists of Ceylon. The visitors were then conducted to the Tendai Sect temple in Kobe. Above the main gate the Buddhist flag fluttered in an icy wind, bearing huge Japanese characters which Noguchi translated as "Welcome to Dai Nippon." Inside the temple they found an enormous audience of Japanese youths waiting to hear a message from the West, which the imagination of Far Eastern Buddhists has always associated with the holy land of India.

After Col. Olcott had spoken in his usual impressive manner, Dharmapāla addressed them emphasising the cultural and religious unity of Japan and Ceylon, and pointing out that the present meeting was the first recorded contact in history between Sinhala and Japanese Buddhists. He concluded by saying that they were proud of Japan, eulogising her as "a sovereign star in a continent of servitude," words which not unnaturally drew loud and prolonged applause from his auditors.

Almost immediately after their reception at Kobe, Col. Olcott and Dharmapāla left for Kyoto, where they witnessed the celebrations which attended the promulgation of the New Japanese Constitution of 1889. Not long afterwards a convention of Chief High Priests was held in the Chiongin Temple, and Col. Olcott addressed them on his mission. Dharmapāla, who was now suffering from rheumatic fever, had to attend the convention in an invalid's chair, but in spite of physical suffering great was his elation when Col. Olcott read Sumaṅgala Nāyaka Thera's Sanskrit letter of goodwill to the Buddhists of Japan, a Japanese translation of which was presented to each High Priest.

The bearded American Theosophist and the slim, ascetic, young Sinhala Buddhist realised that they were playing the leading roles in one of the most important scenes in the great drama of modern Buddhist revival, marking as it did the first official contact which had taken place between the sundered branches of the Buddhist world for nearly a thousand years. But when the curtain had fallen on this historic scene Dharmapāla was forced to enter the Government Hospital at Kyoto for treatment, while Col. Olcott embarked upon his triumphal tour of Buddhist Japan. But if in the Colonel's case Mohammed went to meet the mountain, in Dharmapāla's the mountain came to meet Mohammed.

Doctors, priests, students, teachers, writers, philosophers and businessmen poured in an endless stream to his beside, so that by the time he was ready to leave the hospital Dharmapāla had not only added to his knowledge about Japan but also become an enthusiastic admirer of the Japanese. He was enthusiastic too about the ancient Buddhist city of Kyoto, where he saw the Daibutsu, the great image of Amitabha which is the biggest bronze statue in the world, and a temple which, when illuminated at night, glittered resplendently with five hundred golden figures of the Buddha. A few days before his departure from Japan, the officers and students of the Bungakurio, the Japanese Military Academy, several of whom had attended him during his illness with the utmost devotion, invited him to witness a huge military parade which was to be held in his honour.

Five hundred students participated in the parade, which was followed by athletic sports. The five-coloured Buddhist flag fluttered above the gathering, and the grounds were decorated with five hundred lanterns. The representative of the Chief High Priest, together with other officers of the Hongwanji Sect, attended the function, and deeply moved though he had been by the boundless hospitality accorded him Dharmapāla could not help feeling the incongruity of this union between Buddhism and militarism, even as he had previously been shocked by the way in which the majority of the Japanese clergy combined their religious duties with family life.

During the remainder of Dharmapāla's visit bouts of illness alternated with brief periods of lecturing and sightseeing, and eventually he was forced to leave the country sooner than he wished. A farewell address was given to the Chief High Priests of the Japanese Buddhist Sects, who handed over to Col. Olcott a reply to Sumaṅgala Nāyaka Thera's Sanskrit letter of goodwill. This letter reciprocated the High Priest's fraternal greetings, expressed the hope that in future the two great divisions of the Buddhist world might know each other more intimately, and described with satisfaction, the wonderful success which had attended the mission. All Kyoto was decorated for the occasion, and in the evening, at a meeting attended by the Governor and other high officials, Col. Olcott spoke on India and Ceylon, and Dharmapāla poured out his love and gratitude to Japan in a highly emotional speech which was wildly applauded.

After bidding the Colonel an affectionate and tearful farewell at Osaka Dharmapāla embarked for Ceylon, while Olcott, who had already delivered forty-five lectures all over the country, left for Kinsui Province to deliver ten more. The captain of the *Caledonia*, the ship for which Dharmapāla had exchanged the *Natal* at Shanghai, was a friend of Mme. Blavatsky, and it was therefore natural that he should soon be on friendly terms with his Sinhala passenger. He extolled Mme. Blavatsky to the skies, declaring that she was a "Miracle of nature," and Dharmapāla of course agreed enthusiastically with these eulogies of his beloved teacher. But when the captain confided that Olcott was jealous of her, and that he had engineered her departure from India, his young listener, ever faithful to his friends, hotly repudiated the suggestion, saying that if they had been jealous of each other the Masters would never have committed the destinies of the Theosophical Society to their joint care. After that they hardly spoke to each other again, and Dharmapāla made friends with an Italian with whom he played chess, and a Frenchman who prophesied war in Europe. His loyal, affectionate and grateful nature could never bear in silence an attack upon a friend, and at this period especially devotion to the Colonel was one of the major passions of his life.

A few years later, when serious charges were made against the Swami Vivekananda in Calcutta, it was Dharmapāla who spoke publicly in his defence with such vigour that he was at once restored to popular favour. To him a friend in need was a friend indeed, and great was his disappointment, therefore, when in the course of his career he discovered that people whom he had defended, helped and trusted were slandering him behind his back and secretly plotting to frustrate his plans. Ever frank, honest, open and outspoken himself, Dharmapāla heartily detested every form of trickery, subterfuge and intrigue.

Boldly and uncompromisingly he stated his objectives; fearlessly and wholeheartedly he strove to realise them. In a world where diplomacy in politics, cheating in business, misrepresentation of facts in journalism, and deceitfulness in all the relations of life, have become the order of the day, straightforwardness such as this does not always make for material success, but as a sign of absolute integrity of character it is one of the hallmarks of spiritual greatness, and as such must ever command our admiration and respect. Whatever Dharmapāla did was noble and upright, and it was therefore done, not in the obscurity of shadows, but in the full blaze of the all-revealing light of day.

Back in Ceylon

Colonel Olcott returned from his mission to Japan, where his activities had inaugurated a major revival of Buddhism, in the middle of June 1889, accompanied by three Japanese priests who intended to study Pali and the Theravāda traditions of Ceylon. A meeting of welcome was held in the Theosophical Society headquarters, which were gay with Buddhist flags and Japanese lanterns, and Col. Olcott told a crowded audience of the success of his mission and paid warm tribute to the work of his young Sinhala colleague. Receptions over, he and Dharmapāla plunged once more into the work of the Buddhist Theosophical Society, travelling together by train and bullock cart from one end of the country to the other, day after day for more than a year they collected funds, opened schools, and addressed meetings. Whenever Olcott was called on Theosophical business to India or Europe Dharmapāla carried on the work either single-handed or in co-operation with one or another of the European Theosophists who had started coming to Ceylon to help in the revival of Buddhism.

On one such occasion, when he was touring with Dr. Daly in the hill country near Kandy, he discovered at the Hanguranketa village temple a palm-leaf book on meditation, and requested the incumbent of the temple, Bhikkhu Ratnapala, to get it transcribed for him. Many years later the same work was published by the Pali Text Society, and translated by F. L Woodward as *The Manual of a Mystic*. In the course of his travels Dharmapāla came across a number of such books, but in spite of all his enquiries he never succeeded in finding even a single person, whether monk or layman, who could instruct him in the actual meditation practices which they described.

Being from boyhood of strongly mystical temperament, as we have already pointed out, it was impossible for him to rest satisfied with a merely theoretical knowledge of the subject, and in spite of all difficulties, after making a careful study of the *Satipaṭṭhāna Sutta* and the *Visuddhi Magga,* he embarked upon the regular practice of meditation, rising each day before dawn for the purpose. The personal diaries which he kept for more than forty years abound in references not only to the practice of yoga, but to his unremitting efforts to achieve absolute mental purity, his ceaseless cultivation of goodwill to all sentient beings and bear eloquent testimony to the fact that beneath the dynamic activity of the selfless worker for Buddhism there lay the serenity and mindfulness of the yogi.

At the Adyar Theosophical headquarters, whither he had gone to attend the Annual Convention of 1890, he joined the Esoteric Section of the Theosophical Society, and received some practical instructions on meditation from an old Burmese gentleman who had come with the deputation sent to Col. Olcott by the Buddhists of Rangoon, who had already collected a lakh of rupees for the propagation of Buddhism in foreign lands, inviting him to come to Burma and assist them in their work.

Pilgrimage in India

Col. Olcott left for Burma with the deputation while Dharmapāla, who had been spending most of his time in study and meditation, decided to visit the Buddhist holy places in Northern India, and invited the Japanese priest Kozen Guṇaratana, who had accompanied him to Adyar from Colombo, to go with him. He agreed, and they left on January 12th, arriving at Bombay, where they spent a couple of days sightseeing, on the 14th, and at Benares on the 18th. Hearing from his host of a yogini known as Maji (Reverend Mother) who lived in a cave on the banks of the Ganges, Dharmapāla at once went to see her, and after what he describes as a pleasant chat she presented him, at his request, with a rosary. The next day, January 26th, Babu Upendranath Basu drove them over to Sarnath, where the Lord Buddha had preached His First Sermon nearly five and twenty centuries before, and after describing the ruined appearance of the place Dharmapāla remarks in his diary for the day, "What a pity that no Buddhists are occupying the place to preserve them (the stupa and carvings) from the hand of vandals."

First Visit to Buddha Gaya: 1891

Yet it was not at Sarnath, but at Buddha Gaya, which they reached on January 22nd 1891, that Dharmapāla Hewavitarne, then in his twenty-ninth year, received the inspiration which was to change not only his own life but the whole course of modern Buddhist history. The crucial moment of his career had come. At last he stood face to face with his destiny. The happenings of that most decisive day in his whole life, when for a moment the fate of Buddhism in modern India, with all the incalculable consequences thereof, hung trembling in the balance, is best described in the words of his own diary:

> "Jan. 22. After taking breakfast we went in the company of Durga Babu and Dr. Chatterjee to Bodhgaya—the most sacred spot to the Buddhists. After driving 6 miles (from Gaya) we arrived at the holy spot. Within a mile you could see lying scattered here and there broken statues etc. of our blessed Lord. At the entrance to the Mahānt's temple on both sides of the portico there are statues of our Lord in the attitude of meditation and expounding the Law. How elevating! The sacred Vihāra—the Lord sitting on his throne and the great solemnity which pervades all round—makes the heart of the pious devotee weep. How delightful! As soon as I touched with my forehead the Vajrāsana a sudden impulse came to my mind. It prompted me to stop here and take care of this sacred spot—so sacred that nothing in the world is equal to this place where Prince Sakya Sinha gained Enlightenment under the Bodhi Tree ... When the sudden impulse came to me I asked Kozen priest whether he would join me, and he joyously assented and more than this he had been thinking the same thing. We both solemnly promised that we would stop here until some Buddhist priests came to take charge of the place."

It is characteristic of Dharmapāla that when he made this momentous decision the question of the ownership of the temple never even occurred to him. He saw that the most sacred spot in the Buddhist world was being shamefully neglected, its sculptures carted away, the image desecrated, and he assumed that as a Buddhist he had not only the duty but also the right to stay there and protect the holy place. Nor did the Government officials whom he met give him, as yet, any cause to think otherwise. The keys of the Burmese Rest House, built twenty years before by King Mindon of Burma, were given to him, and as soon as he had settled down there he started writing the first of those thousands of letters which he was afterwards to write in the interests of the Buddha Gaya Temple. He wrote to scores of people in Ceylon, Burma and India describing the appalling condition of the sacred spot, and pleading for the revival of Buddhism and the re-establishment of the Sangha there. He also wrote long articles in Sinhalese and English respectively to the *Sandaresa* and *The Buddhist.*

For some time he received no replies, and great was his agony of spirit when he began to think that his appeal had gone unheeded, and that the Buddhist world, still sunk in the torpor of centuries, was indifferent to the fate of the Mahā Bodhi Temple. Shortage of money began to add to his difficulties, for he had brought with him enough to provide the necessities of a few days only, but with his determination strengthened rather than weakened by the difficulties he was undergoing he resolved to die of starvation rather than quit the sacred place. In spite of mundane anxieties the atmosphere of the moonlit nights, when the imposing structure of the temple stood in bold relief against the starry sky, played upon his spiritual sensibilities to such an extent that one day he writes in his diary:

> "February 17. This night at 12 for the first time in my life I experienced that peace which passeth all understanding. How peaceful it was. The life of our Lord is a lofty and elevating subject for meditation. The Four Truths and the Noble Eightfold Path alone can make the devoted pupil of Nature happy."

At last the letters for which he had been waiting with such eagerness, and the money which he so badly needed, began to arrive and Dharmapāla no longer felt that he was alone with his enthusiasm in an indifferent world. Not until he met Mr. G. A. Grierson, the Collector of Gaya, did he begin to glimpse the enormous obstacles, the deeply-entrenched vested interests, which blocked his path. Hitherto he had been led to suppose by the minor officials with whom he had discussed the matter, that the Mahā Bodhi Temple was Government property, and that there would be no difficulty in transferring it from the management of the Hindu Mahānt to the custody of its legitimate proprietors, the Buddhists. But now, to his astonishment, Mr. Grierson informed him that the temple together with its revenues, belonged to the Mahānt, adding that with the help of the Government it might be possible for the Buddhists to buy it from him.

Having by this time spent more than six weeks in Buddha Gaya, Dharmapāla at once left for Calcutta, intending to raise funds in Burma for the purchase of the temple. In Calcutta, then not only the political but also the intellectual metropolis of India, he stayed at the house of a Bengali Theosophist, Babu Neel Comal Mookerjee, who became a lifelong friend of the Anāgārika and a loyal supporter of his mission. Together they visited various places of interest in the city, including the Indian Museum and the Royal Asiatic Society of Bengal where, to his great delight, Dharmapāla made the acquaintance of Sarat Chandra Das, famous for his travels in Tibet, and for his knowledge of the language and religious literature of that country. He also won the friendship of Narendra Nath Sen, the editor of the *Indian Mirror,* a Theosophist whose eloquent pen was for many years ready to plead for the revival of Buddhism in India.

From Calcutta Dharmapāla sailed for Rangoon, where he spent most of his stay with Moung Myhin, a Theosophist and a student of Buddhist yoga, who encouraged him in his plans for the restoration of Buddha Gaya to Buddhist hands, and promised to help financially. Other Burmans also became interested in the scheme, and although unable to raise the funds for which he had hoped, Dharmapāla was by no means disappointed with the success of his mission. He noted that the Burmese were better versed in the subtleties of their religion than were his own countrymen, and that in Burma the practice of meditation had not been allowed to die out as in Ceylon. He sailed for Colombo via Adyar with high hopes, determined to found a society for the reclamation of Buddha Gaya. On his arrival at Madras he heard of the unexpected death of Mme. Blavatsky. "The loss is irreparable", he wrote in his diary. "Humanity will feel the loss. The spiritual world lost its dearest well wisher, guide and Teacher in her. Who will take her place? I little expected that she would die so soon. The E. S. must be carried on if the T. S. is to live and do good; but who will be the agent between the world and the Masters?"

Establishment of the Mahā Bodhi Society: 1891

The Buddha Gaya Mahā Bodhi Society was founded in Colombo on May 31st 1891, The Ven. Hikkaduwe Sumaṅgala Nāyaka Mahā Thera presided over the inaugural meeting, at which Dharmapāla related how the impulse to restore the sacred shrine to Buddhist hands had come to him as he knelt beneath the ancient spreading branches of the Bodhi Tree. After the High Priest had spoken in support of the scheme the office-bearers of the newly-born Society were elected, with Ven. Sumaṅgala as President, Col. Olcott as Director, Weerasekera and Dharmapāla as Secretaries, W. de Abrew as Treasurer, and Pandit Batuwantudave and twelve others as members of the Committee. The formation of one more society did not attract much attention in those days of widespread Buddhist revival, and Dharmapāla not only experienced difficulties in rousing the interest of the laity, but also in finding monks willing to accompany him to Buddha Gaya.

But by this time he was used to difficulties. Determined that on the Full Moon Day of the month of Asalha, when the Buddha preached His First Sermon, members of the Sangha should once more be in residence in Buddha Gaya, he appealed first to the Siamese, then to the Burmese Sect, and in the end succeeded in obtaining four monks Dunuwila Chandajoti, Mātale Sumaṅgala, Anurādhapura Pemānanda, and Galle Sudassana. On July 10th the party set out on its historic mission, reaching Calcutta on the 15th and arriving at their destination a few days later. In the evening of the day following that of their arrival the full moon rose bright and glorious in the blue sky, and Dharmapāla notes with satisfaction in his diary that after seven centuries the Buddhist flag had been hoisted at Buddha Gaya:

"Ah, how beautifully it flutters in the moonlight breeze! May the mission be a success! I hope and sincerely trust that the priests may be a light to the people and they will lead a life of purity and show the people of India the intrinsic merits of our holy religion. On 22nd January last I pledged that I will work on to make this sacred spot to be cared for by our own Bhikkhus and I am glad that after seven months of hard work I have succeeded in establishing a Buddhist Mission."

Sanguine words! Having installed the four monks in the Burmese Rest House, Dharmapāla opened negotiations with the Mahānt for the purchase of a piece of land, and at this point begins the story of his unequal struggle with the second wealthiest landlord in the whole Province of Bihar, a struggle in which we hardly know whether to be more astonished at the invincible determination displayed on one side, or at the incredible baseness and brutality on the other. The intervention of Government, and the ambiguous nature of its policy in the matter, only served to "make confusion worse confounded," and it is impossible for us even to outline all the vicissitudes of Dharmapāla's single-handed struggle to secure for the Buddhists a foothold in their own most holy shrine. First the Mahānt promised a piece of land, then denied that he had promised, and in the end agreed to give a much smaller piece. Hereupon Mr. Grierson entered the scene, first ordering registration of the deed to be postponed, and then suggesting that a different plot of land should be selected.

Annoyed at Grierson's interference, the Mahānt told Dharmapāla to return to Ceylon and come back and discuss the matter later. After shuttling for some time between the two parties Dharmapāla succeeded in appeasing the Mahānt and persuading him to part with the plot indicated by the Collector. But this time the size of his original offer was reduced by half, and Dharmapāla had to interview his notary no less than seven times before the deed was considered to be in order. Weary of all these vacillations, which were only a foretaste of what was yet to come, Dharmapāla decided to organise an International Buddhist Conference, and after his return from a brief visit to Ceylon the conference had its memorable sitting at Buddha Gaya on October 31st 1891, on the eve of the Lt. Governor of Bengal's visit to the holy spot.

Representatives from Ceylon, China, Japan and Chittagong attended, and the Japanese delegates informed the conference that the Buddhists of their country would be willing to purchase the Temple from the Mahānt, in consequence of which it was resolved that a deputation should wait on him with a proposal to this effect. It was further resolved to call for subscriptions from all Buddhist countries for the construction of a Buddhist monastery, to establish Buddhist propaganda and to undertake the translation of Buddhist texts into the Indian vernaculars. Ever an enthusiastic admirer of Japan, Dharmapāla had hoisted the Japanese flag beneath the Bodhi Tree side-by-side with the Buddhist flag, and it is more than likely that when the Lt. Governor and his party visited the place the sight of it not only reminded him of the Russo-Japanese problem, but also suggested to his mind the possibility of the Japanese using Buddha Gaya as spearhead of their ambitions not only in India but throughout the whole of Asia. At any rate he refused to meet the Buddhist delegation, and sent Dharmapāla a message through Mr. Grierson to the effect that the Temple belonged to the Mahānt, and that the Government could not accede to the Buddhist request that it should intervene and restore Buddha Gaya to their control.

Mahā Bodhi Journal

On October 25th Dharmapāla gave his first public lecture in India, at the Albert Hall, Calcutta, under the presidency of Narendra Nath Sen, his subject being "Buddhism in Its Relation to Hinduism." At the beginning of 1892 the office of the Mahā Bodhi Society was shifted to Calcutta, where the Bengali intelligentsia looked with sympathy upon the object for which it had been founded, and in the month of May Dharmapāla started the *Mahā Bodhi Journal* in order to facilitate the interchange of news between Buddhist countries. The first issue of the magazine, which has now been published uninterruptedly for more than sixty years, consisted of eight closely-printed quarto pages, and bore as its motto the Buddha's great exhortation to His first sixty disciples, "Go ye, O Bhikkhus, and wander forth for the gain of the many, the welfare of the many, in compassion for the world, for the good, for the gain, for the welfare of gods and men. Proclaim, O Bhikkhus, the doctrine glorious. Preach ye a life of holiness, perfect and pure" (*Vinaya Piṭaka, Mahāvagga*).

The Journal was edited by Dharmapāla, and his two articles on "A United Buddhist World" and "The Mahāyāna School of Buddhism" were the first of the hundreds of articles which he was subsequently to write for its pages. It is interesting to find him controverting Sir Monier Williams' opinion that the Southern School of Buddhism belongs to the Hinayāna, maintaining instead that "the Buddhism of Ceylon belongs to the oldest school of the Mahāyāna", and asserting that only "The eighteen schismatic schools, off-shoots of the *Theravāda* school, because they taught the incomplete doctrines, were included in the Hinayāna." Besides an article by Col. Olcott entitled "The Sweet Spirit of Buddhism," the magazine contained historical notes by Dharmapāla, correspondence, news of Buddhist activities in Japan and Burma, and a reproduction of a significant article from the *Indian Mirror,* which contains the statement "India dates her misfortunes since the day of the disappearance of Buddhism," and indicates the extent to which educated Indian opinion was in agreement with Dharmapāla's views.

Translations from the Buddhist Scriptures, and papers on Buddhist philosophy, as well as articles on Buddhism by writers both oriental and occidental, were included in subsequent issues, and before many months had passed the Journal had attained a fairly wide circulation not only in Asia but in Europe and America as well. Progress was by no means either smooth or easy, however. Funds were often lacking, and frequently the Society's sole worker had to choose between buying stamps for posting the Journal and food for his evening meal. But the sacrifice was made joyfully, with the reflection that since there was no self there was no sacrifice either.

In those days Dharmapāla used to spend the night with the Mookerjee family at Baniapukur Road, rising at two or three o'clock in the morning for meditation. Then he would read the Buddhist Scriptures, together with the works of Max Muller, Sir Edwin Arnold and Sir William Hunter. During the day he would attend the office which the Mahā Bodhi Society and the Theosophical Society shared at 2, Creek Row, devoting himself to the editing and managing of the Journal, and engaging in a voluminous correspondence, frequently writing twenty or thirty letters with his own hand in the course of a single day. With unflagging zeal and tireless energy he worked for the cause to which he had dedicated his life, appealing for funds to Buddhists all over the world, arranging weekly public meetings, and labouring to interest every person he met in the redemption of Mahā Bodhi Temple from the sacrilegious hands of those to whom it was nothing but a source of income. In spite of his activities in Calcutta and at Buddha Gaya Dharmapāla found time to attend the Annual Conventions at Adyar, as well as to establish relations with the Himalayan Buddhists of Darjeeling, to whom he presented some Relics of the Buddha, a few leaves from the Bodhi Tree, and a Buddhist flag.

After the Relics had been taken in a colourful procession through the crowded streets of the town to the residence of Raja Tondub Pulger, where a number of Tibetan and Sikkimese dignitaries, both lay and ecclesiastical, had assembled, Dharmapāla gave a speech on the ancient decline and modern revival of Buddhism, and appealed to the Buddhists of Tibet to support the work of the Mahā Bodhi Society. Some months after this historic function, when Sinhala and Tibetan Buddhists met once again after centuries of separation, Col. Olcott arrived in Calcutta, and it was decided that he, Dharmapāla and Mr. Edge, a European Theosophist from Darjeeling, should visit Buddha Gaya.

On their arrival at Gaya Station on February 4th 1893 they were met by Ven. Chandajoti, who excitedly informed them that on the evening of the previous Friday the Mahānt's men had made a murderous assault on the two monks and their servants, at the Burmese Rest House, while they were peacefully engaged in reading the Vinaya and religious conversation. Bhikkhu Sumaṅgala, who is described as a particularly quiet and inoffensive monk, was so badly beaten about the head with sticks that he had to be removed to hospital, and when the horrified party visited the Rest House the bloodstains were still visible upon the floor. The news of this cowardly and unprovoked attack created a sensation, and meetings of protest were held not only in India but in several Buddhist countries as well. Col. Olcott at once interviewed the Mahānt, who stubbornly refused either to sell or lease the land on any terms, or to allow the Buddhists to erect a Rest House for pilgrims. Dharmapāla was insistent that the assailants should be detected and punished, and the well-known Gaya pleader Nanda Kishore Lall was therefore retained as counsel for the Mahā Bodhi Society.

In these circumstances began a connection which soon transcended the usual relation of lawyer and client, and developed into a strong mutual affection which was terminated only by death. The sole redeeming feature of the whole sordid business was the exemplary behaviour of the injured monk, who had not only made no attempt to defend himself from the vicious blows of his attackers, but who actually sent to the police, while still in hospital, an application stating that neither he nor his fellow monks could be witnesses to the case under issue and thus cause their assailants to be punished. It is said that the District Superintendent of Police roared with laughter when he read this, remarking "I always thought these Indian priests made a living out of religion. These Buddhist priests from Ceylon actually practise it." The Mahānt in his palace merely chuckled.

A few weeks later Dharmapāla was informed by Nanda Kishore Lall that the Mahānt's lease on the land had expired, and that he had renewed his application for a permanent lease. With his usual optimism, Dharmapāla was confident that it would now be easy for the Mahā Bodhi Society to acquire the place, and that the Buddhists of the world would willingly combine to subscribe the lakh of rupees which, he was informed, would be required to make the purchase.

He rushed back to Calcutta, and at once wrote appeals for help to every quarter. Chandajoti was despatched to Akyab, while Col. Olcott sailed on the same mission to Rangoon, where he found the city in the throes of a business depression and was compelled to return empty-handed. After a month devoted to office work, lectures on Buddhism in the public squares, Theosophical meetings, correspondence, study and meditation, conversations on yoga with his friend Nirodanath Mookerjee and exhortations to Nirodanath's son Naranath, a boy of sixteen or seventeen of whom he had become extremely fond, Dharmapāla left for Burma on May 13th, and on the 16th reached Rangoon, where he found his old friend Moung Hpo Mhyin and a number of other gentlemen waiting at the jetty to receive him.

Another month went by in a whirlwind round of visits to wealthy Buddhists in Rangoon, Mandalay and Moulmein, and although the required sum was not actually collected, the necessary promises were made, and Dharmapāla returned to Calcutta feeling that his mission had not been wholly unsuccessful. After extricating the Society's work from the confusion into which it had fallen during his absence, he entrained for Gaya, where he found that events were fast taking a new turn. Nanda Kishore told him that the Mahā Bodhi Temple was really situated in the village of Mahā Bodhi, and not in the village of Mastipur Taradi as the Mahānt's people claimed.

Again Dharmapāla's hopes rose high; but when they called upon the Collector, Mr. McPherson explained the situation to him, and mentioned Sir Edwin Arnold's recent article about Buddha Gaya in the London *Daily Telegraph,* he merely remarked that everything should be done as quietly as possible and that it would be better to postpone negotiations until after Dharmapāla's return from Chicago. The circle of the young Buddhist missionary's activities was becoming wider still, embracing not only India and Ceylon, not only Asia, but the whole world, and although the fate of the Mahā Bodhi Temple remained unsettled, the course of events was compelling Dharmapāla to direct his steps elsewhere, and the time had come for him to carry the Message of his Compassionate Master across the seas to races to whom it was as yet unknown.

'The World's Parliament of Religions' in Chicago

The World's Parliament of Religions which was held in Chicago in 1893 was one of the most important and characteristic events of the late nineteenth century. Fifty years earlier the influence of Christian dogma and popular ignorance even of the existence of the great oriental religions would have rendered such a gathering an impossibility. As it was, the organisers of the Parliament were accused by a missionary in China of "coquetting with false religions" and "planning treason against Christ." Fifty years later, political unrest and widespread indifference to religion would either have made the venture abortive or reduced it to little more than an anthropological curiosity. In the closing decade of the 19th century however, the time was ripe for the presentation of the diverse religions of the world from a common platform, not by scholars but by men who actually followed them, and when the special Committee appointed for the purpose by the President of the Columbian Exposition circulated their plans, the idea of a World's Parliament of Religions met with general acceptance.

The Chairman of the Committee, Dr. J. R. Burrows, who had received copies of the *Mahā Bodhi Journal*, entered into correspondence with Dharmapāla, and in the end invited him to Chicago as the representative of the Southern Buddhist Church. With his usual modesty, Dharmapāla doubted his ability to expound the Dhamma before such a distinguished gathering, but his friends were insistent that he should go, one of them declaring that far more important than any amount of scholarship was the living conviction of the truth of the Buddha's Word. Such a conviction was the breath of Dharmapāla's life. After much consideration he decided to accept the invitation, reflecting that it would enable him to visit Japan and China in the interests of the Society without putting any additional strain on its resources. Only Col. Olcott was against the trip, roundly declaring that with so much work to be done in India it was a waste of time.

However, Dharmapāla was by this time accustomed to deciding things for himself, and in the end the Colonel's opposition collapsed and he promised to write to Mrs. Besant, who was also attending the Parliament, asking her to keep an eye on his young colleague. After entrusting the Journal to Sarat Chandra Das, Dharmapāla left Calcutta at the beginning of July, and on the evening of the day of his arrival in Colombo was presented with a purse by the Ceylon Theosophical Society. Sumaṅgala Nāyaka Thera invoked the blessings of the devas on his mission, and on behalf of the Buddhists of Ceylon gave him a Mandate to Dr. Burrows.

On July 20th his parents, relatives and friends, together with a number of Buddhists and Theosophists, came on board the *Britannia* to bid the young adventurer farewell. His mother kissed him on the face, and his father, who had generously provided him with new clothes and money for the trip, kissed his hand. At last the ship weighed anchor, and as the sun set in red and golden splendour over the palm-fringed shores of Ceylon Dharmapāla was left alone with his Buddha-relic and image, and the twenty thousand copies of the Five Precepts which he had had printed for free distribution. The journey to England passed quietly enough in the usual round of study, meditation and voluminous correspondence, together with occasional sight-seeing at Aden, Port Said and Brindisi, and conversation with some of the passengers on board, to whom he distributed his leaflets. At Gibraltar he saw some fine silk handkerchiefs impressed with the picture of the Rock, and felt that he would like to see the Buddhist flag and the Five Precepts printed on silk handkerchiefs in the same way.

First visit to England

On August 11th he saw England for the first time, afterwards writing in his diary, "The first sight of English foliage made me think of England with a feeling of affection. I have seen beautiful scenery; but I was simply delighted at this first glimpse." A telegram arrived from Sir Edwin Arnold, author of *The Light of Asia* whom Dharmapāla reverenced as his "English Guru"; and his heart was warmed as he read the words, "Welcome to England, etc." Upon reaching Gravesend the following day Dharmapāla was delighted to find Sir Edwin himself waiting at the Albert Docks to receive him. With the poet were several Theosophists, including Leadbeater and his young favourite Jinarajadasa, whom he had kidnapped and carried off to England.

It was arranged that Dharmapāla should stay with Sir Edwin Arnold, with whom he called on the Secretary of State for India, Lord Kimberley, who promised that the letter Sir Edwin had already written him about the Mahā Bodhi Temple should be forwarded to the Viceroy. Leadbeater took him to see Mrs. Besant, introduced him to the leading British Theosophists, showed him the sights of London, took him out to lunch and dinner, and was in fact so unfailingly kind and lavishly hospitable that a mind less innocent of intrigue than Dharmapāla's would have immediately understood that the Theosophists, who had no doubt been warned by Col. Olcott that the young founder of the Mahā Bodhi Society had begun to be impatient of their control, were doing their best to entice him back into the fold. Leadbeater even told Dharmapāla that he had received money from the Master to be spent on his account.

Visits to the great Pali scholar Dr. Rhys Davids, the British Museum, and Theosophical groups filled the days until the time of their departure. With him on board the *City of Paris* were the Theosophists Chakravarti and Miss Muller, and of course Mrs. Besant, who had already told him in London that for the sake of the Masters and the Cause she must take care of him, and who now declared that before her death Mme. Blavatsky had actually said the same thing. Naturally, Dharmapāla was impressed by these statements, and wrote in his diary that Mrs. Besant was like a mother to him. On September 2nd the party arrived at New York, where more Theosophists were waiting to welcome them, and on the 6th they reached Chicago.

Chicago

Dharmapāla was one of the most popular speakers at the Parliament, and his addresses and lectures were considered to be important contributions to its proceedings. Apart from a sermon on "The Pure Life" which he delivered at the Unitarian Church, his first public appearance was at the close of the crowded first session of the Parliament when, surrounded by representatives of the world's religions, many of them attired in brilliant national costumes and gorgeous ecclesiastical vestments, he brought to the four thousand people who had assembled in the Hall of Columbus to hear him "the good wishes of four hundred and seventy-five millions of Buddhists, the blessings and peace of the religious founder of that system which has prevailed so many centuries in Asia, which has made Asia mild, and which is today, in its twenty-fourth century of existence, the prevailing religion of those countries."

The impression that he made on the assembly is preserved in a letter published at the time: "With his black, surly locks thrown back from his broad brow, his keen, clear eye fixed upon the audience, his long brown fingers emphasising the utterances of his vibrant voice, he looked the very image of a propagandist, and one trembled to know that such a figure stood at the head of the movement to consolidate all the disciples of Buddha and to spread 'the light of Asia' throughout the civilised world" (*St. Louis Observer*, September 21, 1893). During the week which followed Dharmapāla made the acquaintance of a number of the delegates, among whom were several Japanese Buddhists, spoke two or three times a day on Buddhism and Theosophy, and attended the protracted and crowded meetings of the Parliament, remarking with disgust after one long and tiring session, "All papers full of Theology and Anthropomorphism but pure life naught."

Needless to say, his own paper on "The World's Debt to Buddha" which he read on September 18th, with the centuries-old image of the Buddha on a table beside him, contained no trace of either Theology or Anthropomorphism, although quite a lot of it was devoted to the pure life. The paper was moreover innocent of oratorical effects, and showed none of the dazzling intellectual brilliance exhibited by other contributors, the modest young speaker doubtless feeling that after having endured for five and twenty centuries his venerable religion could make its way in the world without adventitious rhetoric. What he therefore laid before the Parliament was a plain statement of Buddhist principles supported by numerous citations from the Scriptures, without any plan or artistic arrangement, but simply classified under various subheadings.

Dharmapāla, "the servant of the Lord Buddha" as he loved to call himself, was not eager to make a splendid speech, being content if he could function as the humble mouthpiece of the voice of Truth. This very lack of artifice was not without its attractions, apparently, for Mr. C. T. Strauss, of New York, a lifelong student of philosophy and comparative religion, was so impressed by what he heard, that he expressed his desire to become a Buddhist, and at what the newspapers described as "a simple, yet impressive" ceremony held under the auspices of the Theosophical Society of Chicago he received the Five Precepts from Dharmapāla, becoming not only the first person to be admitted to the Buddhist fold on American soil, but also the devoted friend of his preceptor, and a staunch supporter of the Mahā Bodhi Society.

The closing days of the Parliament were for Dharmapāla full of strenuous activity. So striking was the impression made by the young preacher from Ceylon, that whereas his colleague Vivekananda was compared with the noble but passionate Othello, Dharmapāla was compared with no less a person than Jesus Christ. We are not told that any of the Christian delegates were paid this handsome compliment. So popular had he become, moreover, by his amiable disposition and evident spirituality that, in the words of a contemporary newspaper report, "The mere announcement that he would lecture in the Athenaeum building on Buddhism and Theosophy was sufficient to attract an audience too large for the hall."

By the time the final session of the Parliament had ended, and Dharmapāla had spoken his last words to the great gathering, the conviction had formed itself in his mind that he could disseminate the Dhamma in America, and he decided that after two years he would return and establish Buddhism. The concluding words of his farewell address are an apt summary of the message which he so earnestly sought to deliver to the peoples of the West, and of which he was himself the living embodiment. "Learn to think without prejudice, love all beings for love's sake, express your convictions fearlessly, lead a life of purity, and sunlight of truth will illuminate you. If theology and dogma stand in your way in the search of truth, put them aside. Be earnest and work out your salvation with diligence and the fruits of holiness will be yours."

Honolulu: Meeting with Mrs. Mary E. Foster

The Parliament of Religions closed on September 27th, and after delivering a number of lectures at Oakland and San Francisco, on October 10th Dharmapāla left the shores of America for India by way of Japan and China. At Honolulu Dr. Marques and two lady Theosophists came on board to see him, bringing with them gifts of brilliant South Sea flowers and fruits, all of which he distributed among the passengers. One of the visitors, a stout, middle-aged woman of about fifty, confessed that she suffered from violent outbursts of temper which were a source of misery to herself and her relations, and asked Dharmapāla how they could be controlled.

As a student of Buddhist yoga, Dharmapāla was able to give her the help for which she had sought in vain elsewhere, and by following his few simple words of advice she was eventually able to overcome her failing altogether. The name of the hot-tempered lady was Mrs. Mary E. Foster, a descendent on her mother's side of King Kamehameha the Great of Hawaii, and although their meeting lasted for only a few minutes so deep was the impression made by Dharmapāla's words upon her mind that she became in later years the most munificent of his supporters, her donations totalling in the end almost one million rupees. Temples, monasteries, schools, hospitals and numerous other institutions were through her generosity established in India and Ceylon, so that today her name is ranked with the names of Anathapindika and Visakha as one of the greatest benefactors of Buddhism that have ever lived, and will be remembered by millions of grateful Buddhists as long as that of Dharmapāla himself.

Japan, Siam, India

On the morning of the last day of October Dharmapāla disembarked at Yokohama, and by evening he was in Tokyo, where Noguchi, Horiuchi and about one hundred young priests had assembled at the station to receive him. During the four years which had passed since his first visit to Japan Dharmapāla had not only increased enormously in spiritual and intellectual stature, but he had also discovered the work he had been born to do, and it was of this great work, the deliverance of the Buddha Gaya Temple from the bondage of sacrilegious hands, that he spoke to the Japanese people, endeavouring through public lecture and private conversation to inflame their hearts with the burning enthusiasm of his own.

That they were capable of enthusiasm, devotion, and supreme self-sacrifice, he knew. Had not the old pilgrim-priest, who had visited Buddha Gaya on foot, out of excess of devotion fallen down senseless before the Buddha-image of the Gupta period which he had brought with him from Ceylon via Chicago? Yet in spite of the interest shown by high priests of various sects and the Japanese nobility his endeavours met with no tangible success, and when a meeting of priests at the Seishoji Temple informed him that after two years it might be possible to raise twenty thousand yen, which was a ridiculously small sum for such a huge country, Dharmapāla realised that he was wasting his time in Japan. Disputes between the priests over the custody of the Gupta image, and intrigues to monopolise the manufacture and sale of clay models of the sacred object had moreover embittered his stay, so feeling that his presence was more urgently required in India he left Japan on December 15th, having spent six weeks there, and at once began to think of calling on the Buddhist Kingdom of Siam for assistance.

At Shanghai Dharmapāla wrote a message to the Chinese Buddhists, and with the help of Dr. Timothi Richards, a Christian missionary who afterwards published an English translation of Aśvaghosha's *Awakening of Faith*, he addressed the priests of the temple at Mount Omei, and presented them with a Bodhi-tree leaf and some other relics. In Siam he was able to achieve no more concrete success than in Japan. Despite the interest and enthusiasm shown by several members of the Royal Family, and the sympathy of the Foreign Minister, Prince Devavongse, most people seemed apathetic in religious matters and indifferent to the propagation of the Dhamma, and he noted in his diary, "The true spirit of Buddhism has fled and only a lifeless corpse is to be seen in Buddhist countries of the Southern School."

After three busy weeks in Siam he left Bangkok for Singapore, arriving two weeks later in Colombo, having been not only the first native of Ceylon to travel round the world but, what was infinitely more important, the first Buddhist missionary of modern times to girdle the globe with the Message of the Master. A royal reception awaited him. The crowds that had assembled at the jetty rent the sir with thunderous shouts of "Sadhu!" as the long-absent hero again set foot on his native soil, and he was taken in a magnificent procession, with elephants, drummers, and yellow-robed monks, to the Vidyodaya Pirivena, Maligakanda, where his venerable preceptor, Sumaṅgala Nāyaka Mahā Thera, received him with blessing. But the time which be could spend in Ceylon was short, for the work in India called him, and after lecturing in Colombo, Kandy, Kalutara and other places on his Chicago experiences and the Buddha Gaya restoration scheme he left for Madras. At Adyar he met Col. Olcott, who told him that W. Q. Judge, the leader of the American Theosophists, was to be impeached by a committee for fabricating messages alleged to have come from the Masters.

Dharmapāla' hopes that harmony would prevail were doomed to disappointment, for the secession of Judge and his followers was the first of schisms which eventually broke up the Theosophical movement into a number of warring groups, and reduced the Adyar headquarters to a platform for the antics of Mrs. Besant and her followers. The last day of March saw the wanderer in the arms of his friends in Calcutta, where the Bengalis flocked to him for news of Swami Vivekananda, and his diary tersely records, "I told them of his heroic work and the great sensation he is creating in America." Unlike certain other religious leaders, Dharmapāla was free from petty feelings of competition and rivalry, and was ever ready not only to recognise but even to direct attention to the merits of other workers in the same field. On April 11th he arrived at Gaya, bringing with him for installation in the upper chamber of the Mahā Bodhi Temple a beautiful seven-hundred-year-old

Japanese image which was to be for many years the storm-centre of the battle for Buddha Gaya.

After Mr. McPherson, the Collector of Gaya, had advised him to win over Hindu opinion to his side, Dharmapāla visited Benares, the citadel of orthodoxy, and consulted the brahmin pandits there. But implacable as ever in their hatred of Buddhism, they were emphatic that since the Buddha was an incarnation of the Hindu god Vishnu the Buddha Gaya Temple was a Hindu shrine and that the Buddhists therefore had no right to it. The Mahānt was of course of the same opinion and objected to the installation of the Japanese image on the grounds that its presence would be a desecration. He moreover threatened that if Dharmapāla attempted to bring the image to Buddha Gaya five thousand men would be lying in wait to kill him and that he was prepared to spend one hundred thousand rupees for the purpose. It was not until a year later, however, after Dharmapāla had spent some months in Ceylon for the collection of funds, that the great clash between spiritual right and legal wrong finally came. Dharmapāla writes in his diary for February 25th, 1895:

> "At 2 in the morning I woke up and sat in meditation for a little time and then my mind suggested, as it did yesterday, under the Bodhi Tree, to take the Japanese image to the Mahā Bodhi Temple. I woke up the priests and then asked them to sit in contemplation for a time. Then it was decided that we should take the image early morning from Gaya to Buddha Gaya. In silence I vowed 7 times giving up my life for the Buddha's sake. Before dawn we packed the image and by 7 were off to Buddha Gaya. On our way we met two Mohammedan gentlemen driving towards Buddha Gaya. Soon after our arrival at Buddha Gaya the boxes containing the image were taken upstairs to the Mahā Bodhi Temple and by a strange coincidence these two gentlemen were present and were witnessing the placing of the image. My friend Bepin Babu was also present and when we were going to light candles the Mahānt's gosains and the Mohammedan Muktiar came up and threatening me asked me to remove the image. Oh, it was painful indeed. Buddhists are not allowed to worship in their own temple. Great excitement. The

Mahānt rushes off to Gaya and in the evening the Collector, Mr. D. J. McPherson, came to investigate the case. Several witnesses were examined and when he was leaving the place the Collector said a great desecration had been committed in the Temple. He ordered the Inspector to take care of our party. We stayed in the Burmese Rest House by the Temple."

Dharmapāla does not mention that the gosains (Hindu 'monks'), who were heavily armed with clubs and sticks, numbered forty or fifty, that he himself was grossly insulted, and that the ancient Japanese image was flung head foremost into the courtyard below. News of the outrage immediately flashed round the Buddhist world, and on all sides expressions of indignation were heard. Proceedings were instituted on the advice of Mr. McPherson, who in his capacity of Magistrate of Gaya, found the miscreants guilty and sentenced them to one month's simple imprisonment and a fine of one hundred rupees apiece, finding in his judgment that the temple had been continuously used by the Buddhists as a place of worship, whereas no Hindu, including the Mahānt and his disciples, ever worshipped there, and that there was nothing to show that the Mahānt was ever the Proprietor of the Temple.

This judgment was upheld by the District Court, to which the Mahānt's minions appealed, but set aside by the judges of the High Court, both of whom were distinctly hostile to Dharmapāla. They patronisingly conceded that although in the possession of the Mahānt the place had never been converted from a Buddhist into a Hindu Temple, and observed that there was no previous instance of any disturbance between the Buddhist worshippers and the Hindu Mahānts or their subordinates in regard to their respective rights. As though to add insult to injury, the Government of India ordered Dharmapāla to remove the Japanese image from the Burmese Rest house, but in view of the popular resentment roused in Burma and Ceylon by this high-handed action the order was eventually rescinded. In 1897 the Mahānt returned to the attack, making representations through the British Indian Association, a powerful organisation of big landowners, for the removal of the image on the grounds that its presence "near the Buddha Gaya Temple which had been held, it was stated to be a Hindu Temple by the High Court, was deemed objectionable by the Hindus."

The government did not accede to this request, however, stating that it could not admit any claim to treat the temple as a purely Hindu shrine, while at the same time it had no desire to interfere with the Mahānt's position. For the next few years the image remained in the Burmese Rest House, worshipped and cared for by the gentle Sumaṅgala, while Dharmapāla was scattering and broadcasting the seed of the Dhamma in foreign fields.

Second visit to America (1896/97)

With the advent of Dharmapāla in 1891, the founding of the Mahā Bodhi Journal in 1892, and the Buddha Gaya Temple Case of 1895-96, the cultured Bengali public was becoming more and more sympathetic towards Buddhism, with the result that on May 26th 1896 the Buddha's birthday was celebrated in Calcutta under the presidency of Narendra Nath Sen. It was the first organised celebration of its kind to be held in India for hundreds of years, and when, a few weeks later, Dharmapāla left for America at the invitation of Dr. Paul Carus, founder of the American Mahā Bodhi Society, he must have felt that although the Mahā Bodhi Temple was still in alien hands his work had not been wholly without fruit. In London he dined with Sir Edwin Arnold, renewed acquaintance with Prof. Rhys Davids, visited the venerable orientalist Max Muller at Oxford University, and lectured in the Theosophical Society and at Hyde Park.

During the year he spent in America he was no less busy, visiting among other places New York, Chicago, San Francisco, the Grand Rapids, Manistee, Freeport, Guelph in Canada, Cincinatti, Duluth, St. Cloud, Fargo, Minneapolis, Genesis, Davenport, Iowa City and Des Moines. Everywhere he went he proclaimed the unadulterated Dhamma of the Lord Buddha, popularised the Scriptures of Buddhism, expounded the subtleties of Buddhist psychology and yoga, and exposed the commercialised pseudo-Oriental mysticisms by which America was then deluged. Above all, he exhorted his listeners to lead "the life of holiness, perfect and pure." "Slaves of passion," he wrote in his diary, "controlled by the lower senses, wallowing in sensuality, these so-called Christians live in killing each other, hating each other, swindling each other, introducing liquor and vice where they hadn't existed.

Themselves slaves of passion they enslave others to themselves and their vices".

For Dharmapāla himself the trip to America was by no means without temptations. Several American women attempted to seduce the handsome young ascetic, but all their efforts to soil the radiant purity of his character failed, and instead of the words of endearment for which they had hoped they heard from his unsullied lips only the Word of the Buddha. The American Theosophists were at this time divided into two camps, one maintaining that, on the death of Mme. Blavatsky, W. Q. Judge had become the agent of the Masters, the other holding that Annie Besant had been to chosen, and both parties added to his vexations by trying to use him for their own ends. But shortly before his departure from India, Col. Olcott had resigned the office of Director and Chief Adviser of the Mahā Bodhi Society, so that Dharmapāla's link with official Theosophy was now weaker than it had ever been, and although for him "H. P. B." had no successor he refused to be drawn into the controversy.

He concentrated his energies instead on Buddhist work, and in May 1897 had the satisfaction of conducting the first Vaisakha celebration ever to be held in the United States. About four hundred people attended the service, which was held in a room that had been temporarily transformed into a Buddhist shrine. As thirty-seven candles, symbolising the thirty-seven principles of wisdom, blazed on the steps of the altar before the Buddha image, the Anāgārika gave an address on Buddhism and chanted the Mangala Sutta from an old palm-leaf book. In spite of his multifarious religious activities in America he did not forget the suffering masses of Bengal, and found time to collect funds for the Mahā Bodhi Famine Relief Work. His energy was in fact inexhaustible, and even after a year of strenuous missionary labours in America he could write:

> "I hope to leave the U. S. in November for London and via Paris, Berlin, Rome I shall go to Ceylon. Meet my dear mother and father, travel all round the island proclaiming the holy life and call upon all priests to practise *samādhi*, and then go to Darjeeling via Calcutta and Kapilavastu and then find the way to Tibet in search of the Holy Masters. There

make my way to Peking if possible, there to Japan and return to America. Death is nothing. I have died a million times and will die a million times. I will do this great work and save the world from the evils of ignorance, selfishness and passion."

Paris—London—Rome (1897)—Back in Ceylon (1898)—Touring India

In Paris, Dharmapāla attended the Congress of Orientalists, and on September 14th 1897 held a Buddhist Peace Celebration at the Musée Guimet. After a short sojourn in London where the Theosophists, finding that he was now completely free from their leading-strings, were unanimous in their opinion that he was "conceited," he proceeded via Zurich and Florence to Rome, "The centre of Roman Catholic superstition. Immense wealth," he remarks about St. Peter's in his diary. A cardinal who lived "in gorgeous and princely style" promised him an audience with the Pope, but when Dharmapāla, who could no more conceal his intentions than the sun its light, let it be known that he intended to speak to the Holy Father about the drunkenness which European civilisation had introduced into Ceylon, and that he wanted a letter asking the Catholics to live in peace and amity with the Buddhists, the horrified ecclesiastic not only cancelled the audience but refused to see Dharmapāla again.

Back in Ceylon, the solitary fighter found that a clique in the Theosophical Society was against the Mahā Bodhi Society, and feeling that Buddhism and Annie Besant's neo-Brahminism were incompatible he suggested to Col. Olcott that the word "Theosophical" should be dropped from the name of the Ceylon Buddhist Theosophical Society. Enraged at what he considered an impertinence, the Colonel did his best to check Dharmapāla's activities in Ceylon, and his erstwhile pupil regretfully came to the conclusion that the older man was jealous of his success, and that in his anxiety to remain in power at Adyar he was willing to allow Annie Besant and followers to drive the Buddha and His Dhamma from the place. Not until several years later, however, did he resign from the Society, and when, after Olcott's death, Annie Besant became President he was unsparing in his condemnation of the vagaries into which she and Leadbeater led the movement.

The whole of 1898 was spent working in Ceylon. Once again the Anāgārika, now a popular hero in the eyes of his countrymen, travelled by bullock cart from village to village until he had covered the whole island. Once again his ardent championship of the national religion and culture produced a wave of enthusiasm which swept from one end of the country to the other.

Feeling that in spite of all its advantages the Western university system of education was without ethical value, and that it failed to develop the mind's infinite potentialities, he persuaded his father to buy a plot of land near Colombo, and planned to start there the Ceylon Ethico-Psychological College. Worship, meditation, and study of comparative religion were to be included in the curriculum. Another institution known as the Sanghamitta Convent, for training Buddhist sisters in social work, was also started, and the Countess Canavarro, an American convert to Buddhism who had accompanied the Anāgārika to Ceylon, was placed in charge of the Convent and of the orphanages and schools attached to it.

Touring India

With so much to be done in his native land, Dharmapāla did not return to India until the beginning of 1899, and after spending two months in Calcutta he went on an extended tour of North India. Bankipore, Buddha Gaya, Gaya, Benares, Cawnpore, Meerut, Aligarh, Delhi, Agra, Saharanpur, Amritsar, Lubhiana, Amballa City, Amballa, Muttra, Brindavan, Thaneswar, Lahore, Rawalpindi, Peshawar, Nowshera, Abbotabad, Hassan Abdul, Mardan and the Yusufsai Valley were the places included in his itinerary. A contemporary account of the tour, which lasted for four months, and in the course of which he travelled more than fifteen hundred miles, says:

> "He travelled as a pilgrim, not caring at all for comforts, mixing with the sanyasins, ascetics, Hindu pilgrims, and with passengers of the third and intermediate classes, eating at times the poorest food, sleeping at times in places where the poor sleep and gaining an insight into the characteristics of the poor classes, who are suffering from intense ignorance, superstition and poverty."

How keenly his compassionate heart felt the suffering of the masses with whom he mixed may be judged by the following extract from an open letter which he wrote from Saharanpur:

> "Open your eyes and see, listen to the cries of distress of the 141 millions of people, and let their tears cool your dry hearts. Don't imagine that 'Providence' will take care of you; for the 'Almighty' does not calculate time by your watches. 'A thousand years is *one hour*' for him, and it is foolish for you to wait with folded hands. Wake up, my brothers, for life in this world is short. Give up your dreamy philosophies and sensualising ceremonies. Millions are daily suffering the pangs of hunger; drinking the water that animals in the forest would not drink, sleeping and living in houses, inhaling poison day after day. There is wealth in India enough to feed all. But the abominations of caste, creed and sect are making the millions suffer."

His missionary labours for the year were by no means ended, however, for on his return to Calcutta from the Punjab he received an invitation to South India, where he not only lectured on Buddhism but also emphasised the need of educating the masses and removing the disabilities of the untouchable community. With the founding of a branch of the Mahā Bodhi Society in Madras, the Banner of the Dhamma was firmly planted in the South, where differences of caste and sect were perhaps more strongly felt than in any other part of the country. The early months of 1900 saw the indefatigable missionary in Siam and Ceylon, after which he again visited Burma, this time to raise funds for the erection of a Rest House at Buddha Gaya, the District Board having undertaken to do the work provided the Buddhists would meet the cost.

Third Visit to America (1902–1904)

From 1902 till early 1904 he was again in the United States, where the campaign inaugurated during his second visit to that country was continued with unabated vigour. As before, he was eager not only to teach but also to learn, and visits to laboratories and technical institutes alternated with lectures on the Dhamma and exhortations to lead a life of purity. In Boston he wished to attend one of the classes which Prof. William James, the celebrated psychologist, was holding at Harvard University. The yellow dress that he had adopted after his return from the Parliament of Religions made him a conspicuous figure in the hall, and as soon as Prof. James saw him he motioned him to the front. "Take my chair," he said, "and I shall sit with my students. You are better equipped to lecture on psychology than I am." After Dharmapāla had given a short account of Buddhist doctrines the great psychologist turned to his pupils and remarked, "This is the psychology everybody will be studying twenty-five years from now." Time may not have fulfilled the Professor's prediction to the letter, but it is beyond dispute that to Anāgārika Dharmapāla belongs much of the credit for making the existence of Buddhist psychology more widely known in Western countries.

Mrs. Foster's help–England–Industrial School in Sarnath

Numerous visits to leading educational institutions had convinced him that the East needed the technology of the West no less than the West needed the psychology of the East, and he therefore wrote to Mrs. Foster asking her to help in the establishment of an Industrial School at Sarnath. She promptly sent him a cheque for five hundred dollars, following it up a year later with another for three thousand. Thanks to these generous contributions he was able to engage the services of an American expert, and to despatch, before his departure from the country, the necessary agricultural implements from Chicago to Calcutta.

Arriving in Liverpool after a rough passage across the Atlantic, this preacher who took the world for his parish proceeded to London, where he met not only old friends like Sir Edwin Arnold, now totally blind, but also made new ones like Prince Peter Kropotkin, the famous anarchist, by whom he was introduced to Lady Welby, Mr. Thyndman, Mrs. Cobden Unwin, Professor Patrick Geddes, and a number of other socialist and radical intellectuals. As though his energy and curiosity were still unexhausted, he took boat from Harwich to Holland, where he visited elementary schools and industries in Bussum, Copenhagen, Askov Vigin, and Amsterdam, thence returning to London. Another excursion took him to Genoa via Paris and Turin, after which he at last boarded the steamer for Colombo.

Once again his native land saw him for a few weeks only. Hurrying back to India, he at once began to put into operation his long-cherished plans for industrial, agricultural and manual education, The Industrial School at Saranath was opened, and Mr. Veggars, the American expert, installed as director. But the Theosophists of Benares displayed open hostility to the scheme, and upon the Commissioner desiring the removal of Mr. Veggars the project upon which the Anāgārika had lavished so much time and energy, and which would have been a source of manifold blessings to the local people, had to be abandoned. Arrangements for instruction in the vernacular were continued, however, and some years later took shape first as a High School and then as a College.

Back in Ceylon 'Sinhala Bauddhaya'

In November 1904 the Anāgārika went to Ceylon at the request of the Lanka Mahā Bodhi Society to conduct a campaign in the general interest of the Buddhists of the island. Once again he travelled by bullock cart from village to village, lecturing, this time not only on religion but on the various projects for technical education which then engrossed his attention as well. Impressed by the astonishingly rapid industrial progress made by the Japanese, he persuaded his father to organise a fund of sixty thousand rupees for sending Sinhala students to Japan in order to learn weaving and other arts and crafts. The first Weaving School was established in Ceylon in 1906 and soon developed into a large and flourishing institution.

In the same year the Anāgārika sustained a heavy blow in the loss of his father, the good Mudaliyar, who since 1891 had given unstinted financial support to his son's efforts to resuscitate the Dharma. When the sad news was communicated to Mrs. Foster the warm-hearted lady wrote to Dharmapāla asking him to regard her as his 'foster-mother,' and at once embarked upon that series of benefactions without which the Anāgārika's work could hardly have achieved such ample proportions. For six years she sent an annual donation of three thousand rupees, most of which was spent by Dharmapāla on the establishment of Buddhist Schools, a printing press, and a vernacular weekly called the *Sinhala*

Bauddhaya which he started to counteract the un-Buddhistic tendencies of the Theosophical Society.

Loss of Buddha Gaya law case (1906)

In 1905 the great legal battle between the Anāgārika Dharmapāla and the Mahānt entered its final phase, and for four years the whole Buddhist world watched the sordid proceedings drag on to a conclusion as shameful to the Government of India and orthodox Hinduism as it was bitter, humiliating and outrageous to the feelings of the Buddhists. The offensive was of course taken by the Mahānt, who at the instigation of the Commissioner of Patna filed a suit against Sumaṅgala Thera, who all these years had been taking care of the image, and Dharmapāla, for a declaration that he was the sole owner of the Burmese Rest House, and for the ejection of the defendants and the removal of the image. The Government of India was also made a party to the suit inasmuch as it had refused to order the removal of the image in 1896.

"The sub-judge who decided the suit," says a Mahā Bodhi publication, "in the first instance held that the Rest House had been built by the Mahānt for convenience of the Burmese Buddhists who had been allowed to stop in it, that the defendants were not entitled to make it their permanent abode and to place the image in it and ordered their ejection with the image." Dharmapāla not unnaturally appealed against this infamous decision to the High Court, which varied the decree of the sub-judge, holding that inasmuch as the building had been intended for the use of Buddhists in general, the defendants were not entitled to make it their permanent abode or to install any image there. They found that the Rest House had been erected with money at least part of which had been donated by the Burmese. The Mahānt's position was found to be that he held possession of the building and had the control and superintendence of it subject to the right to use it in the customary manner, if any such right be shown to have existed; but no decision was given on this question of right as in this suit it did not arise.

Two decades of struggle to regain the lost rights of the Buddhists thus ended in total failure, and the sinister collaboration between political and religions imperialism at last succeeded in depriving the followers of the Buddha of any foothold in their own most sacred shrine. One stands aghast at the enormity of the wrong done by a powerful Government to the largest religious community on earth; one beholds with amazement the brazen impudence with which a mercenary Hindu Mahānt is permitted to pollute and desecrate the holy of holies of the Buddhist world. Nor is the position at present very much better, even though nearly fifty years have passed since Dharmapāla was ejected from the Rest House, and even though an independent government has meanwhile arisen bearing on its enfranchised brow the symbols of Buddhist India. Buddha Gaya languishes in the hands of a predominantly Hindu Managing Committee, and the Buddhists continue to be deprived of all effective control over their own most sacred shrine.

Work for national revival in Ceylon

With the Mahā Bodhi Rest House as the sole concrete result of twenty years of selfless labour for the holy spot, Dharmapāla left Buddha Gaya for Ceylon, where he spent the greater part of 1911 and 1912 striving to infuse some of his own boundless vitality into the sluggish veins of his countrymen. He was now at the height of his powers, and as though unable to exhaust himself by incessant travel and lecturing, he poured out his ideas for the regeneration of the nation in a series of articles entitled "Things That Should Be Known" which he contributed to the *Sinhala Bauddhaya.* Of these articles it has been said, "They became the basis of a propaganda which was confined to no single question. They scintillated with wit and wisdom and called men and women to a more truthful and courageous life. These articles led to a reawakening of the national spirit among the Sinhalese."

With characteristic bluntness he attacked the shortcomings of the clergy, the majority of whom were corrupt and indolent, and soon the fires of controversy were ablaze. The class of unworthy Bhikkhus found a champion in a member of the Buddhist Theosophical Society, who criticised the Anāgārika personally in the *Sandaresa,* the journal for whose improvement the great Buddhist missionary had as a young man done so much. Religion was in Dharmapāla's eyes not separate from life but most intimately connected with every part of it. To his comprehensive vision, religious revival, moral uplift and economic development were aspects of one great progressive movement which should include in its scope every department of individual and social life. He therefore inveighed against the Sinhala people not only for surrendering their religious and cultural individuality to the Christians, but also for giving up their economic independence to the Hambayas, a class of immigrant Indian Muslim traders who had practically monopolised the retail business of the coast and the interior. The revival which he inaugurated therefore had not only religious, but also political and economic, consequences, for the Muslims, dismayed by the reawakened commercial spirit of the Buddhists, began resorting to methods of intimidation and coercion which eventually led to disaster.

Visit to Mrs. Foster (1913)—World war (1914) and Ceylon Riots (1915)

Having once again galvanised his fellow-countrymen into activity, in 1913 Anāgārika Dharmapāla left Ceylon for Honolulu in order to thank Mrs. Foster personally for the magnificent support which for so many years she had given the Mahā Bodhi Society, due to which it had been possible to purchase a building in Calcutta and to increase the usefulness of the Society in numerous other ways. The good lady, now well stricken with years, was so pleased to see the Anāgārika that before his departure she gave him sixty thousand rupees with which to found in Colombo a charitable hospital in memory of her father. The Foster Robinson Hospital, open to all in need of medical treatment, was started immediately after Dharmapāla's return in a large house which he had inherited from his father. At public request the treatment given in the hospital was in accordance with indigenous Sinhala medical science.

On the way back to Ceylon the Anāgārika called at Japan, and, although shadowed by two detectives, boldly criticised the shortcomings of British administration in India at a number of meetings. In Seoul, the capital of Korea, he addressed a distinguished gathering which included the ex-Empress, and presented to the Korean Sangha a Relic of the Buddha. After travelling in Manchuria and

China, the Anāgārika visited Shanghai and Singapore, and having seen the ruins of Borobodur in Java returned to Ceylon at the end of the year. In 1914 war broke out in Europe, and in the middle of the following year the increasing arrogance of the Hambayas, whose aggressions culminated in an attack on a Buddhist procession in Gampola near Kandy, and the murder of a Sinhala youth under the indifferent eyes of the police, precipitated the Muslim-Buddhist riots. Excited crowds streamed from the surrounding villages into Kandy to protect the Temple of the Sacred Tooth from violence, and immediately the disturbances spread to other parts of the island.

Alarmed by what they interpreted as a revolt against British rule, the authorities proclaimed Martial Law on June 2nd, and for three months the innocent Sinhala Buddhists were ground beneath an iron heel as ruthless as any which marched to the battlefields of distant Europe. Influential persons were arrested without a scrap of evidence against them, public servants were dismissed, and civilians tried by Courts Martial after the cessation of the riots, while the ordinary Courts of Justice were sitting uninterruptedly. Had Dharmapāla not had the good fortune to be in India at the time he would certainly have been arrested and shot, as his frequent visits to Japan and his efforts to regain the Buddha Gaya Temple had already made him an object of suspicion. Determined to wreak vengeance on the Hewavitarne family, the authorities arrested the Anāgārika's younger brother Edmund, tried him by Court Martial for treason, found him guilty and sentenced him to penal servitude for life. He contracted enteric fever owing to the unsanitary condition of the jail in which he was confined, and before the end of the year he was dead.

Internment in Calcutta—Dharmarajika Vihāra (1920)

Dharmapāla himself was not allowed to escape punishment altogether, being interned for five years in Calcutta at the request of the Government of Ceylon. This long period of confinement within the limits of a city was naturally irksome to one who all his life had been accustomed to the freedom of three continents, and the volcanic energy which continued to explode in the pages of the *Mahā Bodhi Journal* must have found such a narrowing of its activities almost unendurable. These years were by no means devoid of solid achievement, however, and with the erection of the Sri Dharmarajika Chaitya Vihāra, which had been made possible chiefly by donations from Mrs. Foster and the Anāgārika himself, his long-cherished ambition of building a Vihāra in Calcutta was at last fulfilled.

At an impressive and colourful ceremony at Government House towards the end of 1920, Lord Ronaldshay presented a Sacred Body-Relic of the Buddha, which had been discovered in a rock crystal casket during excavations at Bhattiprolu Stupa in Madras Presidency, for enshrinement in the Vihāra, and it was with deep emotion that the now ageing Anāgārika descended the carpeted grand staircase bearing in his hands the golden casket which contained the sacred object, and bore it through the reverential crowds to the open phaeton in which it was to be drawn in procession by six horses through the streets of Calcutta. Lord Ronaldshay also presided over the consecration ceremony of the Vihāra, which was witnessed by a large and distinguished gathering, and in the course of an eloquent speech paid splendid tribute to the Buddha and His Teaching concluding with the hope that "this ceremony in which we have taken part today may prove symbolic? of a return once more to that peace which is the most treasured offspring of the gentle and lofty teaching which Gautama Buddha bequeathed to men two thousand five hundred years ago."

Illness

In spite of these triumphs, Anāgārika Dharmapāla was not permitted to return to Ceylon until 1922, by which time his health had completely broken down, the combined effects of the privations he had endured as a young man and the lack of sufficient exercise from which he had recently suffered being responsible for attacks of sciatica, beriberi, palpitation of the heart and anaemia which troubled him for the rest of his life. Physical suffering was not able, however, to prevent him from reviving the *Sinhala Bauddhaya*, which had been suppressed during the riots of 1915, nor from attempting to increase the usefulness of the various institutions which he had organised some years before. In 1919 and 1923 Mrs. Foster had continued her apparently inexhaustible benefactions with donations of fifty thousand and one hundred thousand dollars respectively, the major portion of which was carefully invested by the Anāgārika so as to ensure a regular income out of which to maintain in perpetuity the various institutions and activities of the Mahā Bodhi Society.

By 1925 the condition of his health had become a matter for serious concern, and at the beginning of the year he had to go for treatment to a sanatorium near Zurich in Switzerland, where an operation for sciatica in both legs was successfully performed. Even while his body was lying on the sickbed his mind was busy formulating plans for what was to be his last great missionary venture—the founding of the British Mahā Bodhi Society and the establishment of a Vihāra in London. Though he had suffered much at the hands of the British Government in Ceylon and India, he had no hatred for the English people. Knowing that hatred ceases not by hatred but only by love, and that force could be overcome only by patience, in return for the injuries which he had received at their hands he wished to give the people of England the most precious gift he had, the Gift of the Dharma. Such a gesture is typical of Dharmapāla. Frequently deceived and swindled by those whom he had trusted, betrayed by those whom he had helped, he entertained no desire for retaliation, but like the great broad earth patiently endured and suffered all.

Mission work in London

Arriving in London in August 1925, the Anāgārika commenced activities by giving lectures and talks under the auspices of the Buddhist Lodge of the Theosophical Society (now the Buddhist Society, London), the first of these meetings being attended by the three existing English Buddhist organisations, as well as by members of the United Lodge of Theosophists and the Blavatsky Association. Convinced that the association he planned to start should function in its own premises, he sailed for San Francisco to appeal for help to Mrs. Foster, who agreed to give not only a substantial initial contribution but also a regular monthly grant.

Returning to England at the beginning of 1926 after a severe illness, he took up residence at 52, Lancaster Gate, where he was interviewed by Francis Yeats-Brown, well known as the author of

The Lives of a Bengal Lancer, who a few weeks before had heard him lecture in the New York Town Hall on "The Message of Buddha". Yeats-Brown incorporated his impressions of the transatlantic lecture and a report on the proposed Buddhist Mission in London into an article which he published in the *Spectator* of January 30th entitled "A Buddhist in Bayswater". This article gives a good picture of the Anāgārika at this period of his life, when he was more than sixty years of age. "Certainly he looked delicate", wrote the *Bengal Lancer,* "but he seemed to hold an inner light within him, a latent fire of purpose".

After summarising the New York lecture he describes its effect upon those who heard it:

> "Not a move or cough from the audience. Not a tremble in those lips that thundered the denunciations of Isaiah against our spiritual sloth nor any hint of exhaustion in that frail frame. Here was a man with a message. He delivered it erect, composed, master of himself and his hearers, with the art of an orator and the dignity of a priest to whom the world is nothing. When he sat down there was a dead silence, followed by a burst of applause."

A report of his interview with the Anāgārika follows, after which Yeats-Brown concludes:

> "The Anāgārika Dharmapāla will create few eddies in the spiritual life of this country for his teaching is too alien to our mental habits. But he should be heard by those interested in Eastern faiths for as a teacher he is as authentic as he is eloquent."

In May the Anāgārika spoke at the Vaisakha Meeting held by the London Buddhist organisations at the Holborn Town Hall, and in July he purchased a house in Ealing which he called Foster House, in honour of his patroness. Meetings were held on Sunday afternoons and evenings, and a number of distinguished speakers were always ready to address the audience.

At the end of the year Dharmapāla left England to raise funds in Ceylon for the London Mission, and to visit India in connection with the great temple, afterwards known as the Mulagandhakuti Vihāra, that he was building in Sarnath for the enshrinement of a Sacred Relic of the Lord Buddha which had been offered by the Government of India. Before leaving England he had started a monthly journal, *The British Buddhist*, the first number of which was written entirely by himself. His expectations of aid from Ceylon and Burma were as usual disappointed, but he returned to London before the middle of 1927 with funds sufficient for the purchase of a house in Gloucester Road, Regent's Park, which was to be used for the mission work prior to the construction of the stately Vihāra of his dreams.

In November of the same year he succumbed to an attack of bronchitis, and years of overwork began to take their final toll of his frail body. Leaving the London Mission in the hands of his nephew, Dayananda Hewavitarne, he returned to Ceylon with his health irreparably broken. The physical suffering which he now had to endure did not cause him to forget the work for which he could no longer labour personally, and in June be despatched three Sinhala Bhikkhus, Pandits Parawahera Vajiranana, Hegoda Nandasara and Dehigaspe Pannasara to keep burning in England the Lamp of the Sublime Law.

They were accompanied by the Anāgārika's personal disciple Devapriya Valisinha, a young student from Ceylon who since 1917 had been gradually taking over from his master the heavy responsibility of maintaining the Society's institutions and activities in India. During the two years in which the party propagated the Dhamma in England Mr. Valisinha attended to the management of the mission, helped the Bhikkhus to form classes for the study of Pali, Buddhism and meditation, and by his amiable disposition endeared himself to all with whom he came in contact. On his return to India in 1930 he resumed his secretarial duties, after the ordination of the Anāgārika succeeding him as General Secretary of the Society, and becoming, on his death, the inheritor of his unfulfilled ambitions and the chief instrument for the perpetuation of the work and ideals to which he had dedicated his life.

Back in Ceylon 1927

After his return to Ceylon Anāgārika Dharmapāla began the painful entry upon the last stages of his heroic career. For three years he was confined to bed with stomach trouble and heart disease, and his sufferings were acute. In June and August 1929, and in February 1930, his life was despaired of, and when the heart disease finally left him, Dr. Frank Gunasekera, his physician, was astonished at the seeming miracle and declared that it was not so much the effect of medical treatment as of the Anāgārika's will power, of his strong determination to see the consummation of the last of his prodigious labours, the opening of the Mulagandhakuti Vihāra at Sarnath. But life had still a few more blows in store for the aged warrior before she would permit him to quit the field.

In 1929 his only surviving brother, Dr. C. A. Hewavitarne, who had for many years been of inestimable help to him in all his undertakings, met a tragic death in a railway accident, and Dharmapāla felt as though his right hand had been cut off. Then in January 1931 he received belated news of Mrs. Foster's death in Honolulu on December 22nd 1930 at the advanced age of eighty-six years and three months, and although he must have known that her days would soon be numbered, so sudden was the shock that it almost brought about a relapse of his heart disease. In great agony of spirit he recalled her unparalleled benefactions to the Buddhist cause, and wondered who would support the London mission now that she was gone. The future seemed dark. There was still so much to be done, and those who would carry on his life-work were still few in number, and young in years and experience.

Even while he had been lying on his sickbed, when more than once it had seemed that the messengers of death had drawn near and warned him to make ready for the journey, certain of his fellow countrymen had not suffered him to lie in peace, but had launched shafts of spiteful criticism against the stricken giant whom they had never before dared to face, finding fault with the life which they were too selfish to follow, and picking holes in the work with which they had never lifted a finger to help. Only the sympathy of the poor and oppressed, who when he was nigh to death prayed in their thousands that the devas might restore him to health, comforted him in the midst of his afflictions. The teachers, friends and colleagues of his youth and maturity had all departed, and he knew that he must soon follow whither they had gone. Of all he had loved only his aged mother now remained, having outlived three sons and two daughters, and having now to behold her firstborn, who had so wonderfully fulfilled the pious dreams of her youth, stricken down by mortal sickness in the midst of his gigantic labours.

Sarnath—Lower Ordination (1931)

By March 1931 the Anāgārika had recovered sufficiently to be borne in a chair onto the steamer which would take him to Calcutta. With a last great gesture of renunciation he had disencumbered himself of worldly goods, creating from the Mary Foster Fund and his own handsome patrimony the Anāgārika Dharmapāla Trust, which was to be administered by five Trustees for the furtherance of the objects to which he had dedicated his life. As a free man, therefore, he watched for the last time the palm-fringed shores of his native land disappear over the horizon, and steadfastly set his face towards the holy land wherein for so many years he had laboured, and the sacred site at which was to be enacted the closing scene of his career.

He arrived in Holy Isipatana, Sarnath, from Calcutta at the end of the month, and although his doctors had ordered him to take a complete rest he at once began to take an active interest in the Society's affairs. His body was infirm, but his thought flashed out with all its old brilliance and grandeur, and his voice could still thunder denunciation or ring out in reproof. He paid special attention to the training of the ten young samaneras whom he had sent from the Foster Seminary in Kandy to Santiniketan, Rabindranath Tagore's beautiful rural academy, and who were now completing their studies in Sarnath. Knowing that the future of Buddhism in India depended to a great extent on their endeavours, he was continually exhorting them to lead lives of purity and self-sacrifice. One of the samaneras was particularly attentive to the Anāgārika's needs, and with unflagging devotion was ready to serve him at any hour of the day or night.

This zealous attendant is now known as Ven. M. Sangharatna Thera, who has for many years occupied the responsible position of Secretary at Sarnath. Himself unwearied in his efforts to diffuse the Light of the Dhamma among the Indian masses, he is never tired of talking about the Anāgārika's wonderful energy and exhorting people to follow his glorious example. Another project which occupied Dharmapāla's thoughts at this time was the creation of an International Buddhist Institute, whereto he saw in his mind's eye students flocking in their thousands from every corner of the Buddhist world. Busy as he was with mundane schemes of this kind, his eagle mind soared often upon the trackless paths of higher spiritual experience, and on July 13th he took the Pabbajjā or lower ordination from Ven. Boruggamuwe Revata Thera, receiving the monastic name of Sri Devamitta Dhammapāla.

In August he was strong enough to spend a month in Calcutta and deliver there a public lecture, and at the end of the year he had the satisfaction of seeing the opening ceremony of the Mulagandhakuti Vihāra set as it were as a crown upon his labours. The celebrations lasted for three days, during which there were accommodated in Sarnath nearly one thousand visitors, more than half of whom had arrived from overseas. In the afternoon of November 11th, when the sun shone from a clear blue winter sky on the yellow robes of the Bhikkhus and the brilliant silks of the assembled devotees, a golden casket containing Sacred Relics of the Lord Buddha was presented by the Director General of Archaeology to the Mahā Bodhi Society on behalf of the Government of India.

Amidst great jubilation the Sacred Relics were placed on the back of an elephant, and taken in a colourful procession which circumambulated the Vihāra thrice. In his address at the opening ceremony of the Vihāra Ven. Dharmapāla recalled his first visit to Sarnath in January 1891 when, he said, it was "in the occupation of low-class hog breeders." The vast audience was silent as he recounted some of the difficulties he had faced, and it was with a thrill of triumph in his voice that the old warrior, who had been wheeled to the pandal in an invalid-chair, declared, "After an exile of eight hundred years the Buddhists have returned to their own dear Holy Isipatana. It is the wish of the Mahā Bodhi Society," he said in conclusion, "to give to the people of India without distinction of caste and creed the compassionate doctrine of the Samma Sambuddha. I trust that you would come forward to disseminate the Arya Dhamma of the Tathāgata throughout India."

Higher Ordination (1933)

He knew that his days were numbered, and that the work which he had so nobly begun would have to be continued by younger and stronger hands. In April and December of 1932 he was again seriously ill, and wishing to die as a full member of the Holy Order he received the Upasampada or higher ordination on January 16th 1933. More than a dozen leading monks arrived from Ceylon to perform the historic ceremony, which took place in a Sima specially consecrated for the occasion. Though he had been suffering from a variety of complaints, particularly from heart disease, he appeared so active and energetic, so radiantly happy, that none could have suspected that he was in reality a chronic invalid. After his initiation he spoke as though he had shed for ever all worries, cares and anxieties, writing in his diary that he felt like one of the Abhassara gods, that live only on joy. His spiritual happiness seemed to inspire him with fresh energy for the sacred cause which he had for so many years espoused, and he not only published the first number of the *Sarnath Bulletin* but even spoke of setting up his headquarters at Gaya and conducting a final campaign for the recovery of the Mahā Bodhi Temple.

Last illness and death

It was the last flaring up of the candle of his life before its extinction. In the middle of April he caught a chill, and fever developed. As his condition became more and more serious his disciple Devapriya Valisinha was summoned from Calcutta, and his physician Dr. Nandy arrived soon after. A few days later his nephew Raja Hewavitarne came from Ceylon, and the six samaneras who had been despatched to Buddha Gaya returned to the bedside of their beloved leader. Ven. Dharmapāla, now in the grip of excruciating pain, had no wish to live any longer. Many times he refused to take medicine, saying that it was a useless expenditure on his decrepit body. "Leave the money for Buddhist work", he would tell Mr. Valisinha, pouring the mixture into the spittoon.

As his sufferings increased he again and again repeated, "Let me die soon; let me be born again: I can no longer prolong my agony. I would like to be reborn twenty-five times to spread Lord

Buddha's Dharma." This was not the cry of a coward, but of a warrior whose weapons have been broken in battle and who calls for a new suit of armour so that he may carry on the fight. Towards the end of his life, when the vigorous mind felt keenly the body's decrepitude he made a solemn asseveration that he would take birth in a brahmin family of Benares and in a new body continue the battle for Buddha Gaya. With all the strength at his command he willed that it should so come to pass, and today his intimate followers believe that before long he will return to direct the movement to which he had vowed to dedicate himself life after life.

Even while he was lying on his deathbed, however, his enemies did not scruple to direct a blow at his defenceless head. The leader of a certain Buddhist group in Ceylon eager for notoriety, concluded a secret agreement with the Mahānt which would have ruined Ven. Dharmapāla's labours. Subsequent protests from the Ceylon Buddhist public prevented this agreement from being put into operation, but when he heard of the treachery his grief and indignation were terrible to behold. "It was the greatest shock of his life," writes Devapriya Valisinha, "and I can vividly recollect his pain and anguish ... Alas! He never recovered from the shock. How could he forget such treachery even on his sickbed?" He exhorted those about him to carry on the great work of his life, and never rest until Buddha Gaya was restored to Buddhist hands.

There after, he showed no desire for food, which had to be injected into him against his will. On the 27th he suddenly demanded pen and paper, and despite his semi-conscious condition with great difficulty scribbled something. One line was illegible, but the others read, "Doctor Nandy, I am tired of injections: I may pass away." His eyes were now closed.

The following morning he was almost unconscious, and made no sound except to mutter "Devapriya" once. At twelve o'clock his temperature began to rise, and in spite of the physician's efforts by two o'clock it had risen to 104.6. With anguish in their hearts, those who stood round his bedside realised that the hour which was to release him from his sufferings had come. The Bhikkhus and sāmaṇeras were summoned and requested to chant *paritta*, and as they recited the age-old verses of the sacred texts, the Great

Being's consciousness, radiant with a lifetime of wisdom, energy and love, relaxed its hold on the worn-out body and flashed into new realms of service, leaving upon the face of the corpse it had forsaken a serene smile of happiness and contentment.

The Blessings of Piṇḍapāta

by

Bhikkhu Khantipālo

WHEEL PUBLICATION NO. 73

The Bodhisatta's Piṇḍapāta

... Then our Lord,

After the manner of a Rishi, hailed
The rising orb, and went—ablutions made—
Down by the winding path unto the town;
And in the fashion of a Rishi passed
From street to street, with begging-bowl in hand,
Gathering the little pittance of his needs.
Soon was it filled, for all the townsmen cried,
"Take of our store, great sir!" and "Take of ours!"
Marking his godlike face and eyes enwrapt;
And mothers, when they saw our Lord go by,
Would bid their children fall and kiss his feet,
And lift his robe's hem to their brows, or run
To fill his jar, and fetch him milk and cakes.

... But he

Passed onward with the bowl and yellow robe,
By mild speech paying all those gifts of hearts,
Wending his way back to the solitudes
To sit upon his hill with holy men,
And hear and ask of wisdom and its roads.

Lord Buddha's Piṇḍapāta

One slow approaching with his head close shorn,
A yellow cloth over his shoulder cast,
Girt as the hermits are, and in his hand
An earthen bowl, shaped melonwise, the which
Meekly at each hut-door he held aspace,
Taking the granted dole with gentle thanks
And all as gently passing where none gave.
Two followed him wearing the yellow robe,

But he who bore the bowl so lordly seemed,
So reverend, and with such a passage moved,
With so commanding presence filled the air.
With such sweet eyes of holiness smote all,
That, as they reached him alms the givers gazed
Awestruck upon his face, and some bent down
In worship, and some ran to fetch fresh gifts,
Grieved to be poor; till slowly group by group,
Children and men and women drew behind
Into his steps, whispering with covered lips,
Who is he? who? when looked a Rishi thus?"

Edwin Arnold
Light of Asia

The Blessings of Piṇḍapāta

To those who live in lands where the teachings of the Lord Buddha have been long established, the sight of a *bhikkhu* (Buddhist monk) collecting food in the early morning, is a common one. But where the teachings are newly arrived, or where bhikkhus are few, the practice of giving food to wandering monks is known only by pictures or from written accounts.

Neither of these convey the real atmosphere of this giving and receiving to those interested in the Buddhist Way and yet live in countries where the Teaching is not the traditional form of religion. Even many Buddhists living in Northern Buddhist lands may know little of *piṇḍapāta*;[1] for the practice of alms-gathering by bhikkhus there has, for various reasons which we need not here investigate, been largely discontinued and the traditional practice now survives only in Southeast Asian countries practicing the Theravāda Buddhist tradition.

Though this too is also a written account of alms-giving and collecting, it is written from experience and will try to be as evocative of the atmosphere of the *piṇḍapāta* as possible, and as many factors basic to the Buddhist way of life are involved in this simple act, it is hoped that this may prove useful to all those Buddhists who are far separated from these Buddhist lands.

Apart from his three robes, a bhikkhu's most prized possession (and he only possesses eight articles)[2] is his bowl (*patta*). He takes great care of it so that it may last long: after eating he wipes it carefully each day to prevent it rusting; always places it on a stand so that it may not fall and break, and often carries it in a sling for it is heavy when full of food and may be dropped by tired hands. In doing so he carries out the Lord Buddha's injunction to practice mindfulness with regard to his bowl, which has been given him by others and without which he may not collect food.

1. The Pāli word *piṇḍapāta*, the common term for the Buddhist monk's alms-food gathering, means literally "the food-morsel's fall (into the alms-bowl)."

2. They are: upper robe, under-garment, double robe, girdle, alms-bowl, razor, needle, water strainer.

Practice varies in different countries and *vihāras* (monasteries). In those *vihāras* where meditation is practiced, the bhikkhus will have arisen early, sitting long in the cool darkness of the meditation hall. In the country, the only sounds at this time are the night insects, a frog or two, perhaps a forward cockerel long anticipating the dawn and a cool wind in the trees which may blow away the ever-present mosquitoes. The quietness is at last ended as the assembled monks prostrate themselves before the Buddha-image and clear rings out the homage to the Enlightened One:

Namo tassa bhagavato arahato sammā sambuddhassa...

Two hours or so will have passed in this way before it is light enough to gather food. Not only must the bhikkhus allow the laywomen (*upāsikā*) time to cook food, they also have to consider the dangers of going out while it is yet dark. In counties where snakes, centipedes and scorpions abound, it is wise to be able to see the ground under one's feet; and apart from this quite important fact there are the fears and suspicions of others to consider, as one rather amusing incident in the Majjhima Nikāya shows. A bhikkhu wandering for food while it was still dark frightened a woman who saw him in the lightning flash. She mistook him for a demon and cried out "How terrible! A demon is after me!" (see *Middle Length Sayings* No. 66).

Only after having robed himself correctly does the bhikkhu start upon his food-collecting round. Both shoulders are covered at this time for he is going "among the houses" and must have his body covered from the neck down to below the knees. He may go with a senior bhikkhu, in which case the latter walks in front and he follows, or a novice (*sāmaṇera*) may accompany him. Sometimes the sāmaṇera or a young boy following him may collect the liquid curries, soups, etc., in a tiffin-carrier.

So he sets out, observing good conduct in many ways. Perhaps he remembers at this time the earnest injunction of the Dhammapada:

Better it were to swallow an iron-ball,
Red-hot as the blaze of a fire,
Than to eat the alms of the people
As an immoral and uncontrolled man. Dhp 308[3]

Sometimes one sees bhikkhus following gently and quietly after an elder monk (*thera*), perhaps carrying his bowl for him until the first house is reached upon the alms-round. The monk does not speak unless spoken to, silence being considered a part of the training during one's round. Nor does he look here and there but keeps his eyes directed to the ground in front of him; by so doing he practices restraint of the eye (*cakkhu-saṃvara*). Lastly, whether his round takes ten minutes or two hours, he does not rush along as though anxious to get over it and be done with it. The well-trained bhikkhu walks with mindfulness, steadily and dignified. We remember that it was the noble bearing and restraint of the Venerable Assaji, one of Lord Buddha's first five disciples, that deeply impressed Upatissa, who shortly after become known as Venerable Sāriputta, the foremost among Lord Buddha's disciples.

If a bhikkhu practices meditation, he will strive to keep his subject of meditation in mind while both going and coming. It is related that the Venerable Sāriputta developed access concentration in the practice of loving-kindness (*mettā-bhāvanā*) while walking for food-collection. As some bhikkhus are engaged in the practice of the study (*gantha-dhura*), rather than meditation, they frequently take with them a passage of the Pāli scriptures written upon a small piece of paper and mentally recite this while walking.

* * *

Now that we have gathered so many facts, what is the picture of *piṇḍapāta* like?

Imagine the time about six in the morning. It is still cool but there is light and bhikkhus are robing themselves in the *sālā* (a hall, often without walls). If they practice the Vinaya strictly they will go out wearing all three of their robes—none should be left behind

3. All quotations from the Dhammapada in this essay are from the translation by Buddharakkhitta Thera (Maha Bodhi Society, Bangalore, India).

in the monastery lest they be stolen, so precious are the robes. At this same time monastery boys are scuttling about on last-minute preparations which ought to have been made on the previous day. Then when everyone is ready, they set out, in groups or singly. If the *vihāra* is in the country the little groups of monks can be seen like an orange ripple spreading out into the green country-side. Soon they are lost to sight as the roads or paths they walk upon, wind between trees, over canals, through fields, around hills or among villages.

On the morning which we describe, the sun shines brightly, at first a great red ball glowing upon the horizon and all is easy going under foot. Other days may be different, with bhikkhus slithering over muddy tracks, sinking deeply into black ooze, and huddling beneath umbrellas which sometimes keep off some of the torrential monsoon rains.

As, however, this day is bright, let us follow one of these bhikkhus and observe what happens upon his round. He walks as we have described, holding his bowl in its sling drawn under one hem of his upper robe, and he walks until it is apparent to him that in some house which he is approaching a lay-supporter wishes to offer some food. How does he know this? Outside that house there may be a little table on which food (and perhaps little bunches of flowers, incense sticks, and candles as additional offerings), is placed; or lay-supporters may have invited him to take food from their house every day. Or perhaps he just perceives a lay-person coming out of the house with a tray of offerings. If he passes such a house, he may hear (in Thailand) the word "*nimon*" called out to invite him to stop there (Pāli: *nimantana* = invitation).

Any of these things we may observe. We shall also see that he stops to take food from *everyone* who wishes to give[4]. A very poor

4. This is a continuation of Lord Buddha's practice; for he accepted out of compassion for the donors any food that they wished to give — apart from the flesh of forbidden animals (including man, dog, tiger, and bear) and apart from meat or fish which is seen, heard, or suspected to have been killed specially for monks. There is considerable disagreement between the different Buddhist traditions as to whether the Buddha was or was not a vegetarian and whether bhikkhus were to be so or not, but what is evident is that they were allowed to *accept* any sorts of food apart from those mentioned above.

person may invite him and reverently spoon out some coarse rice into his bowl; at a wealthy house the donor may serve perhaps fifty or more monks every morning and they may receive the finest rice, curries in little plastic bags, and sweets wrapped in banana leaves—it is all the same to him and, without discriminating, it all goes into the same bowl.

Lord Buddha out of his great compassion once accepted from a poor child, who had nothing else to offer, a handful of dust; from this one learns that it is not *what* is given that is important but rather what is *at the heart of the giving.*

But before we proceed, we shall notice a very curious thing. Here is man, without any other means of getting food (for a good bhikkhu has no money), and yet he makes no effort to attract the attention of anyone. Quite the contrary, he undertakes to train himself in a rule of conduct which forbids him to make any sound while he goes "among the houses." If he comes to a house where a regular supporter of his lives or where he knows that food is to be offered, he just stands in silence, neither does he cough, nor stamp his feet, and unlike many other ascetic orders originating in India, he may not carry any musical instrument or sing as they do, to attract attention. This is a time for cultivating patience (*khanti*), a virtue which in the Buddhist training finds its highest expression in the perfection of patience (*khanti-pāramitā*). He may wait for many minutes before anyone sees him, or he may decide that no one is giving him anything that day and go his way. It happens sometimes that a bhikkhu, who patiently waits, gets nothing at all. It even happened at least once, to Lord Buddha and a little story from modern times will emphasize this.

There was a young bhikkhu newly come to Bangkok some years ago. He knew no one, he had no supporters on the first morning. He went out from the monastery where he was staying and walked through the streets to gather food—with hundreds of other bhikkhus from the monasteries around. He received nothing. He went back to his *kuti* (dwelling) and practiced meditation. The

---

Lord Buddha himself ignored the artificial barriers of caste distinction when he walked for *piṇḍapāta.* He took — and his monks still take — food from all, regardless of their social status. All men have the right to practice giving (*dāna*) if they wish to do so and to reap the merits deriving therefrom.

second morning he went out again received nothing and again spent the day in meditation perhaps consoling himself with the words of the Buddha:

> Hunger is the worst disease,
> Compounded existence is the worst distress,
> Knowing this as it really is
> The wise realize Nibbāna, the highest bliss.
>
> Dhp 203

The third day, feeling a little weak, he passed silently through the streets and at one house he was given a banana. And that was all. He came back to his monastery and saw there a starving dog. Opening his bowl he gave half the banana to the dog. But bananas are not fare for dogs—even starving ones—and having sniffed it, it limped disdainfully away. The young bhikkhu reached out his hand to take that rejected half back into his bowl. Then he paused remembering that when a bhikkhu has given something to someone, it must be returned into his hands by a layman—and there was no layman in sight. The bhikkhu closed his bowl and went into his *kuti* where he ate his half of the banana washing it down with a good draught of water. The next day his patience and compassion were rewarded and thereafter someone offered him food every day.

When Māra closed peoples' hearts against giving food to him, Lord Buddha spoke the following famous verse from the Dhammapada showing his power to obtain spiritual food from meditation:

> Happy, indeed, we live,
> We who possess nothing,
> Feeders on joy shall we be,
> Even as gods of the radiant realm.
>
> Dhp 200

The bhikkhu of whom we have spoken also practiced meditation, and later become a famous teacher and a founder of a new school of meditation in Bangkok. He has but recently passed away.

To come back, after this little digression, to our bhikkhu on *piṇḍapāta*. We shall notice perhaps with surprise that he is treated with great respect by the lay-people. Perhaps only yesterday he was a layman himself, yet today, shorn, barefoot, in orange robes, and bowl in hand, he is reverenced by those who serve him. People passing him may stop, crouch down, and raise their hands to their foreheads in reverence, others may walk past him the hands reverentially raised, while laymen and laywomen who wish to give him food squat down, raise their hands in worship before offering to him whatever they have prepared.

Seeing this, one might ask why they did it and why do they regard him so highly? The skeptical man of this materialistic age might indeed ask what all this fuss is about. He might say, "Here is this beggar, who does no work, contributes no material gain to society and yet people treat him as though he was a god walking in their midst." In saying this, he would be right, for Buddhist monks in these countries are beggars in the sense that they depend for their sustenance on others; moreover, the word by which they are known (*bhikkhu*) is derived from the root "*bhik*" whence "*bhikkhati*" = to beg for food. They would also be correct in their *limited* assessment of his worth to society as he does not indeed increase the society's material wealth.

Against such a materialistic approach born of conceit, an ancient verse might be quoted and then two relevant considerations regarding this charge:

> For one ever eager to honor and respect elders,
> These four blessings accrue:
> Long life, beauty, happiness, and power.
>
> Dhp 109

("Elders" here means not only elder relations but refers to *theras*—i.e., senior Buddhist monks).

The first consideration must be to stress again that a bhikkhu does not beg as do ordinary beggars but passes on silently *collecting offered food*; and secondly, it is a narrow system of thought indeed that assesses a man's worth by material gain alone. The Bhikkhu is treated with reverence simply because he offers to others an example by his own pure conduct. He shows the way to deliverance, and if all cannot follow his example completely and lay off the cares of the world, then there can be many who may profit from seeing his life and listening to his advice. He is thus highly regarded as one who is striving for deliverance from suffering, for that supreme bliss which is Nibbāna (*nibbānaṃ paramaṃ sukhaṃ*). To attain this, it is emphasized all through the Buddhist tradition that renunciation (*nekkhamma*) is essential. Thus he is worshipped as an example of renunciation: one who has given up worldly pleasures and comforts, given up family attachments, and one who tries to make the greatest renunciation—that of the craving-and-ignorance complex. Indeed Lord Buddha's words in the Dhammapada have a deep truth in them:

Not therefore is he a bhikkhu
Merely because he begs from others.
Not by adopting the outward form
Does one truly become a bhikkhu.
He who wholly subdues evil,
Both small and great,
Is called a monk (bhikkhu)
Because he has overcome all evil.

Dhp 266, 267

Such are some of the paths which thought might take as we witness a householder give food to him. Following the scene before us we see that the lay-supporter has raised the bowl of food to be given, to her forehead and remains thus for half-a-minute or so. While doing this, she is making some fervent wish or vow that the good merit (*puñña*) which accrues to her by this beneficent act shall result in some particular blessing—health, wealth, family, or those who think further, the attainment of heavenly states, or higher still, the end of rebirth—the unsurpassed peace of Nibbāna.

The food is placed in the bowl by the supporter and while this is taking place, the bhikkhu does not look to see *who* is giving him food. We notice that, with senses well-controlled, he keeps his eyed fixed upon the open bowl and is not inclined to speak to lay people unless they ask him something. In this way his mind is not disturbed by the sight of the members of the opposite sex or any other desire-arousing object. The same applies to Buddhist nuns (*chee*, in Thailand) when they go out for the collection, though very few of them do so. The writer observed in Bangkok a few nuns who, wearing the dark cloth indicating a meditative life, walk on *piṇḍapāta* with great dignity and evident sincerity.

They, of course, are concerned to avoid the sight of men. This is one practical application of the step of Buddhist training called restraint of senses (*indriya-saṃvara*).

The food having being placed in his bowl, the lay-supporter may, as the monk is turning to go on his way, reverence him again (as the symbol of renunciation of which he is an example). On his part the bhikkhu feels no elation at reverence, nor distress if such salutation is not performed, for in the Buddhist teaching reverence is a skillful act (*kusala kamma*) and profits him who performs it.

Further, as we are within earshot, we may be surprised by another fact: the bhikkhu utters no thanks for his food.[5] He goes as silently as he arrives and from what we see it appears indeed as though the lay-supporters feel more disposed to thank him for having taken the food from their hands.

As we follow our bhikkhu, this matter may give us further food for thought—until he reaches another house where we can again observe what takes place. Why then does the bhikkhu offer no thanks for what he has received? The answer to this lies in an understanding of the Buddhist teaching regarding merit (*puñña*). Merit is acquired by the performance of skillful action (*kusala kamma*). An example of such an action which is easy for all to practice is "giving" (*dāna*). Indeed, this too is not only a perfection in the highest ranges of Buddhist practice but is the first among all the ten perfections: the perfection of giving (*dāna-pāramitā*). So deeply is giving felt to be an essential for the beginning of the holy life, that it stands first also in the triad of practices so often recommended for the Buddhist laity (giving, *dāna*; morality, *sīla*; meditation, *bhāvanā*), and the bhikkhu practices it by giving to other bhikkhus and to lay-people the gift of Teaching (*dhammadāna*), which is the highest (Dhp 354).

"To give" opens the heart and is manifestly opposed to the worldly way "to get." The latter is linked to attachment, while the former is generosity and close to renunciation. Thus thanks for giving lie in the very act itself and the householder is happy that the bhikkhu has given him the opportunity to give.

5. In Ceylon, sometimes, the words *sukhi hotu* – "May you be happy" – are spoken in a low voice.

The merit which one "gets" from giving is really not a "possession" which ensures a good birth in the future, etc., but a change in heart, a raising in the level of skillful consciousness so that one performs and rejoices in performing skillful acts. This, of course, does have its effect (but of this more below, as our bhikkhu has now arrived at another house).

A little family group stands outside the house: an old lady, a young lady, perhaps her daughter, and two small boys, one of whom is only just old enough to toddle. They cry out joyfully and loud enough for all the neighborhood to hear, "The bhikkhu has come." The mother of the house balances a tray on her knees as she crouches down, her daughter reverences likewise, while the small boys each have to be restrained from running towards the bhikkhu in order to give him something—so great is their desire to do so. The bhikkhu opens his bowl, and bends down so that the elder of the little boys can give a little bowl of rice. This having been successfully engineered into the bowl, the bhikkhu smiles. Now the smaller boy reaches up to place curry in a plastic bag into the bowl, even this is successful and he manages this without falling over which indeed he came close to doing. Then without prompting he raises two podgy hands in the direction of his forehead and toddles unsteadily back to the girl. The elder one, however, is rather boisterous and has forgotten this bit of training. Then that monk says to him for his good, "*Wai phra*"—"Salute the bhikkhu"—and the boy laughingly, gently, dutifully raises his hands. The people of the house, who have invited him to take food from them every day, then inquire from him when there will be a preaching (*desanā*) at the *vihāra* and where the teacher (*ācariya*) is now. Having learned such-like matters, which take but a minute for the bhikkhu to relate, they invite him, as he goes on his way, to come again on the morrow—and the little boys call out again and again, "Come again! Come again!"

The bhikkhu goes on his way, the sun rises higher and it begins to be a little warm. His next donor (*dāyaka*) is nearby and he walks slowly to give her time to come from her little house. We see him suddenly step rather wide and not until we are up to that place do we see why he did so. Across the road there march in milling millions, an army of ants and, quite apart from the undesirability of being bitten by this species, the bhikkhus must go barefoot for *piṇḍapāta*—their way of training instructs them to practice harmlessness (*ahiṃsā*). That is, never to take life intentionally and to be as careful (= mindfulness, *sati*) as possible so as not to kill, even without intention. In the Dhammapada we read one of Lord Buddha's beautiful verses:

> Just as a bee gathers honey from a flower
> Without injuring its color or fragrance,
> Even so let the sage move in the world
> (To collect alms).
>
> Dhp 49

An old, old woman, bent with age and hard work totters out from her little cabin to invite him to receive. It is true that she need not exert herself in this way for she has a younger woman living with her, but she desires, as her life grows shorter and death comes nearer, to give to a bhikkhu every day and so pile up as much merit as she may in the short time left to her. She lives by the side of a little canal and makes a perilous living by rotting down fish in water and salt and so producing the ubiquitous "fish-water," which is used as sauce and source of salt, by many Thais. Leaning on a stick she brings her thin, toil-worn hands shakily upwards while her face, bronzed by the sun and wrinkled in a thousand places, reflects a serene devotion. She carries an old and rusty tin out of which she ladles some of her fish-water. As silently as he opened his bowl to receive her offering so silently, he closes it, as she turns, now happy, towards her door. Lord Buddha has said:

> If a bhikkhu does not despise
> What he has received,
> Even though it be little,
> Him who is pure in livelihood
> And unremitting in effort,
> Even the gods praise.
>
> Dhp 366

We follow again as he goes on his way to the right of the road. There is at this point, a low area of marshy swamp in which grow tall sedges. It is rather surprising therefore to see the bhikkhu apparently step into this swamp and yet go forward freely. The mystery is soon resolved as we see a single-plank gangway in front of us which will carry the wary walker some two hundred yards across to further side. The bhikkhu has already gone far along the planks, carefully picking his way, and so there is nothing else to do but to follow him. Gingerly we set out, the six-inch wide plank swaying and bending with our weight; it seems very likely that at any moment we may be precipitated into the ooze beneath. Here is indeed, a time for mindfulness! We manage the hazard well-enough—it is perhaps more a matter of good luck than judgment—and when at last we raise our eyes from the gangway, the bhikkhu is almost out of sight. However, we manage to catch up with him just in time to see that he entered the courtyard gate of a big house. Evidently he is invited to take food here each day; indeed, he has already been invited to sit down for a few minutes. We watch the monk and his supporters through the open gate.

The compound lying inside this gate seems to be a very large one and at least three good sized houses are visible interspersed by lawns, trees, courtyards and such decorative features as some hundreds of orchids growing hung up in little pots, or great glazed blue-and-white Chinese water jars and in them water lilies flowering. The bhikkhu sits in a little summer house and before him is placed a table upon which are three trays with little bowls of rice and various fruits, with unknown foods done up in banana leaves.

Meanwhile a crowd of bhikkhus has gathered. We did not notice them come but now they stand silently, waiting. A young man carries a stout table and places it outside the gate where the other bhikkhus are standing and comes back shortly afterwards staggering under the weight of a huge bowl of steaming rice. An elderly lady in the traditional dress follows him carrying a large tray stacked high with oranges and banana-leaf packets.

A bhikkhu is standing near us and so we ask him quietly whose house this is. "Oh," he says, "this house belongs to one of the noble families closely related to the king. Every day they give food to about eighty monks."

We watch this general almsgiving in progress. Each bhikkhu approaches the table when the one before has already left. Everything is very orderly and each bhikkhu is obviously very careful to avoid jumping his turn. Young bhikkhus and sāmaṇeras are seen to invite elder monks to take their food first; courtesy and care are observed by all. The rice, spooned out into bowl after bowl, grows less and the numbers of waiting monks dwindle; but the lady householder seems happier and happier with every spoonful she gives. The monks silently go—old *theras* (elder monks) of many years standing go slowly, while little sāmaṇeras, scarcely four feet high or twelve years old, make off at a good speed.

Our attention now reverts to "our" bhikkhu. He has been seated the while and offered a glass of coffee. A lady sits at a respectful distance upon the summer-house floor while her small daughter wanders about. She has been asking him some problem regarding the teaching and he has briefly replied. She gets up and invites him saying "*nimon*". As it is her daughter's birthday, the lady holds the tray of offerings while the little girl places the rice and various foods into his bowl. Thus the small girl has earned great merit upon this day. Indeed, it is common in Buddhist lands to give on the day of one's birth; and whatever the giving may be, the birthday is thought an excellent occasion for merit-making. Those who cannot afford, or somehow just do not give on other days, usually make a point of offering to a monk or monks *piṇḍapāta* on the day of their own or their children's birth.

The elder lady having finished her giving at the gate, now comes and salutes the bhikkhu. She provides him with food from another tray. The young man, her gardener, offers yet another, while just as the bhikkhu is preparing to depart, a cry of "*nimon*" halts him as another member of this many-branched family comes up with his offering.

With a bowl now become heavy but we hope a little refreshed by the coffee, the bhikkhu goes on his way, the elder lady of the house inviting him to come again on the morrow.

The last house on his round obviously also belongs to an affluent family. He waits, as they have promised food. Locked gate and wide lawns separate the family from the roadside and they do not see him as easily as his other patrons. At last someone spots him and sings out, "the monk has come." The householders here do not come to the door but send who are possibly their son and daughter with food. They are both near to grown-up and perhaps with less understanding of their teaching than they ought to have. At any rate, they are rather careless: the boy while opening their big gates drops a banana or two on the ground, which they wipe before offering, while the girl, tipping rice into the bowl in a lackadaisical fashion manages to empty half of it on the ground. They chatter while doing this and then prance off. It seems that they do this as though it was all rather a drudge.

The bhikkhu carefully removes the rice grains from his robes and from his bowl-sling, so that they do not become soiled, and starts back on his long walk to the monastery. He passes down the whole road of rich men's houses but there is nothing. He does not care, for he has more than enough to keep him going, enough "medicine" to allay the disease of hunger for another day. Still we note that those who give most (and if we went with him every day, we should note those that give most often) are, if not poor people, at least those in the middle ranges of income. Riches, alas, do not usually lead to great generosity! It is the poor and those moderately well-off who give generously. Too many of the rich are too much sunk into the supposed comforts of this world to think overmuch of giving. Lord Buddha has taught them with the following word of warning:

> Riches ruin the fool,
> But not if one is in the quest of the beyond
> By craving for riches
> The witless man ruins himself and ruins others.
>
> Dhp 355

But those who know the sting of poverty, know also a way to rid themselves of this sting. By *giving* however little it is, they may attain to greater wealth in future than they possess now—and greater happiness, too. One of the factors which governs the lack or possession of wealth is what one had done with money, when one had it. If one misuses it for others' pain, squanders it all upon fleeting pleasures, or only amasses a great collection of status symbols about oneself—then in a future life one is very liable to meet with poverty and misery which this entails. The results (*vipāka*) of action (*kamma*) are, so Buddhism teaches, very just indeed.

Those who give, however, are assured of receiving, so that all that must be decided is how and what should one give. Besides occasional giving (such as the construction of a rest-house, bridge, school or if one is rich, a new wing to the hospital and so forth), there are gifts made to the Sangha (order of Buddhist monks). According to a well-known passage in the Pāli scriptures, the bhikkhus (especially if they are emancipated sages—*ariya*) are "*anuttaraṃ puññākkhettaṃ lokassā'tī*"—"The supreme field (in which to sow the seed) of merit in the world." All this is summed up as follows:

> In this world it is good to serve mother,
> Good is it to server father,
> Good is to serve the monks,
> And good is it to serve the ariyan sages.
>
> Dhp 332

Now again *occasionally* bhikkhus require robes, dwellings or medicines, but *every day* they walk out for food-collecting. Therefore, this is a great opportunity to gain merit which should not be missed; for all, whether poor or rich, can do with more merit! There is indeed nothing like merits made in this way for ensuring a happy life, a peaceful death, and a blissful life hereafter. Lord Buddha has said:

> When a man after a long absence,
> Returns home safe from afar,
> His relatives, friends and well-wishers,
> Welcome him on his arrival.
> Likewise his own good deeds
> Will welcome the doer of the good,
> Who had gone from this world to the next,
> As kinsmen welcome a dear one's arrival.
>
> Dhp 219–20

This is obviously one reason why people give to the bhikkhu who passes their doors—and it is a very important reason. The skeptic might butt in, objecting that the motive for that giving is very selfish—to make oneself happy in future. But then he must be told that it is possible in Buddhism (where *kamma-vipāka* is not a rigid personal cause-and-effect), by means of goodwill (*mettā*) and compassion (*karuṇā*), to make over one's merits for the good of others. Thus a mother might make merit by giving food, etc., for her children's happiness, or recovery from sickness. Or a king may make merit, turning this over to the welfare of his people. And expressions of utterly selfless—indeed universal—benevolence are by no means rare among the merit-dedications of quite ordinary folk, while the unlimited compassion of the wisdom beings (*bodhisatta*—those who work towards becoming a Buddha) is expressed in many sublime engravings and writings. With the merit which such a one piles up, he vows to lighten beings innumerable and to deliver all from the woes of continued existence.

However, few aspire so high; their reasons for giving are correspondingly less exalted, though nevertheless they may be deeply religious. For instance, many laypeople give out of great devotion (*saddhā*) to their religion. Sometimes, too, a particularly esteemed bhikkhu may be the object of this great devotion. Then there are gifts to relatives who are now bhikkhus, for in the country, a bhikkhu may live in his own village temple and pass his former house and relatives often. Naturally, they give to him. Then there are those who give out of habit or from convention. One sometimes comes across cases of this; such giving being no longer accompanied by the warmth of devotion tends to become mechanical. It is quite easy to understand that in this case the merit from giving is decidedly less. Lastly comes a category of giving which hardly applies to our present subject: grudged giving. From this and from giving for commercial advantage—purely selfish, this—come the least amount of merit.

The attitude of "Why should I give something?"—which really means "What do I get out of it?"—is hardly found in Buddhist lands. Where the Buddhist Teaching has distinctly taught that deliberate actions are liable to give rise to results, even those who have little knowledge of the heights of Buddhist philosophy, will readily understand that the results of giving is happiness.

The writer was once asked if people who give much and often, but nevertheless came across disasters and grief in their lives, would lose faith and thereafter cease to give. But the Buddhist reaction is not thus. Disasters and grief do not arise causelessly, nor yet from one cause (the "wrath of god" for instance), but they are often attributed more soundly, it would seem, to misdeeds committed in the past—if not in this life then in the individual's past existences. Hence a Buddhist thinks that such misdeeds can only come to fruition if conditions are suitable, which is more likely to be when one has but little a storehouse of merit. Therefore, to cure this lamentable circumstance, the answer is to give more and give more often, rather than neglecting to give. This connection between knowledge and generosity is illumined by a verse in the Dhammapada:

> Verily misers fare not to heavenly realms,
> Nor, indeed, do fools ever praise liberality;
> But the wise man rejoices in giving,
> And by that alone does he become happy hereafter.
>
> Dhp 177

And again on this subject, we find:

> Should a person do good,
> Let him do it again and again;
> Let him find pleasure therein,
> For, blissful is the accumulation of good.
>
> Dhp 118

* * *

And so we have now followed the bhikkhu back to his monastery. He is, perhaps, a little footsore and, if his bowl is full (and it easily fills up, for generally people are marvelously generous), his shoulder may ache; and his hands and arms also if he uses no sling for the bowl.

Memories arise at this point of having seen in some book a writer complaining of the size of a bhikkhus' bowl—as though to imply that they were greedy! This is far from the truth. Firstly a bhikkhu's bowl has to be reasonably large to accommodate all the food that people wish to give him. We should not forget that lay-supporters wish to make their merit each day and that a very small bowl would mean that he would have to refuse their offerings. Secondly, a bowl may be really large if the bhikkhu to whom it belongs goes wandering on foot staying in caves, mountain fastness or forest. His bowl is then his suitcase and in it must be packed the very few items which he can easily take along with him.

Back to the monastery, the food that all have collected is shared by all, and the bhikkhu himself makes a little merit by offering something choice from his bowl to his teacher, usually an elder monk (*thera*), and also by seeing that those who have collected little food that day—and such is the fate of many sāmaṇeras (novices)—have sufficient fare. He practices thus one method of promoting loving-kindness (*mettā*) among his fellow-monks—that is, "the sharing of the contents of even an alms bowl."

In the monasteries where meditation is practiced it is common (in Thailand) to undertake also the ascetic practices (*dhutaṅgas*). In such monasteries, therefore, the monks take only one meal, at about eight in the morning, immediately after returning from *piṇḍapāta*. Their alms-food is shared with the monastery-boys and anyone else who cares to eat. No one need starve, or be without a meal in a Buddhist country—one has only to go to a monastery (before midday), and some sort of food will be available.

As for the monks—bhikkhus or sāmaṇera—if they have undertaken the *dhutaṅgas* they mix all their food together, determining just how much will be suitable for them, and then apply the meditation on the loathsomeness of food, which prevents the arising of greed. (See *The Path of Purification*, Chapter XI, p. 372.)

It is eaten in silence so as to maintain this concentration. And when fingers have scooped enough of this medicine into the mouth, monastery-boys will be happy with remaining delicacies, while the mixture still unconsumed will feed the animals which have taken refuge in the vihāra grounds away from the harshness of worldlings. Thus none of this precious food is wasted. In all ways there are benefits to be seen for all—for the donors who give there is merit, for the bhikkhus who take there is support, and for many other beings there is good food.

This little description of *piṇḍapāta* and its virtues may be fittingly brought to an end with another verse expressing wherein lies the taste of truth:

Having tasted the sweetness,
Of solitude and peace (Nibbāna),
Woeless and stainless he becomes,
Imbibing the flavour of dhamma's bliss.

Dhp 205

May all beings, wheresoever they be, taste of this truth.

German Buddhist Writers

An Anthology

WHEEL PUBLICATION NO. 74/75

Introduction

Next to the English, it was in the German language, that outstanding writers have made large contributions to the spreading of Buddhism in the West. German philosophers and orientalists were early attracted to the message of the Buddha. And the German mind, so well adapted for painstaking research, delved deeply into the texts of the ancient Pali Canon producing translations of exemplary clarity. Again there were others who pondered over the teachings, interpreted them, lectured on them, wrote essays and books, published periodicals, organized societies, all for the sole purpose of disseminating knowledge and acquainting German speaking people with the Buddha's Doctrine. In this short anthology of German Buddhist writers it was not possible to do justice to all of them. Notable writers have been mentioned only by name without the inclusion of articles of theirs. This does not signify that their writings are of lesser importance and value. These omissions are caused primarily by limitations of space; in some cases suitable essays were not available, or because other exterior reasons prevented inclusion. Hence this anthology does not claim completeness or even a fully representative collection. It is hoped, however, that, in spite of these shortcomings, this book will succeed in giving a fairly comprehensive idea of the depth and insight matched equally with their love for the Buddha's Teaching of which German Buddhist writers give so convincing evidence. It is the aim of this anthology to present a roster of prominent names of active workers, scholars and writers in this field, with short biographical notes on the major ones and translations of some typical examples of their work. The scope of this book is not confined to German nationals alone but includes writers from countries where German is spoken, such as Austria and Switzerland. We begin with one great German philosopher, Arthur Schopenhauer, whose work has been a major influence in the growth of German Buddhism. Then we shall follow with the names of early scholars and writers on Buddhism in approximately chronological order.

Arthur Schopenhauer (1788–1860) had access only to the very earliest and scanty publications on Buddhism based chiefly on

Mahāyāna sources. But his genius enabled him to understand the essentials of the Doctrine and he was well pleased to find that they corresponded fundamentally with his own ideas. While Schopenhauer is not in a strict sense a "Buddhist" writer, his many laudatory references in *The World as Will and Idea* to the person and the Doctrine of the Buddha encouraged many a young student and admirer to the further study of Buddhism. It was in this way that he did—and still does—help the spread of the Buddha's Teaching in the Western world.

Friedrich Spiegel (1820–1905) was among the first editors and translators of Pali texts. His *Anecdota Palica* were printed in 1845. It contained in Devanāgari script the Pali text of the Uraga Sutta with extracts from the Commentary, and also an extract from the *Rasavāhinī*, a collection of stories written in Ceylon.

Albrecht Weber (1825–1901) made the first translation of the Dhammapada in a living Western tongue. It was printed in German in the *Zeitschrift der Morgenländischen Gesellschaft*, Leipzig 1860. He published numerous papers, books and translations in the field of Indology.

Hermann Oldenberg (1854–1920) was an outstanding figure among the Indologists of the last century. He edited the entire *Vinaya Piṭaka of* which his learned introduction brought the Rule and Discipline of the Sangha to the forefront and thus opened up a new field for the study of Buddhist monasticism. His chief work: *Buddha, sein Leben und seine Gemeinde* (1881), was the first comprehensive exposition of Buddhism in Europe based on first-hand Pali sources. The book was translated into English by Hoeg in 1882: *The Buddha, his Life and his Order of Monks.*

Wilhelm Geiger (1856–1953) was the great German pioneer of Sinhalese philology. One of his chief works was the complete and scientific edition of the *Mahāvaṃsa*, an ancient chronicle of Ceylon written in Pali, which he also translated into English. He translated into German the first two volumes of the Saṃyutta Nikāya (1925–1930) and edited from 1921–1926 the scholarly German periodical *Zeitschrift fur Buddhismus.*

Karl Eugen Neumann (1865–1915) was one of the foremost translators of Buddhist Pali texts. His work had been facilitated by the establishment of the Pali Text Society (London), although some of his translations were based on oriental texts. In 1892 appeared his first book, *Buddhistische Anthologie,* followed by a long list of German translations of important Pali texts. The beauty of his language through which he tried to reproduce the rhythm and force of the Pali original, his wide reading in the field of world-literature and mysticism, embodied in his notes, attracted many of the prominent personalities of his day to the Buddha's Teaching. Of all the printed texts already existing in Germany, Neumann's rendition had the widest public appeal for his erudition and mastery of the German tongue. George Bernard Shaw, who admired him greatly, declared that only Martin Luther whose genius gave the Germans their Bible can compare with him. Neumann translated the Majjhima Nikāya in its entirety, further Dīgha Nikāya, Thera and Therīgāthā, Suttanipāta and Dhammapada. With the Majjhima Nikāya he opened up the heart of Buddhist Canonical Literature. For this reason alone German Buddhism owes him a debt of undying gratitude. Neumann has sometimes sacrificed literalness to beauty of language, yet his translations will continue to be treasured and remain a masterwork of German literature.

Friedrich Zimmermann (1852–1917), another great pioneer of the Dhamma in Germany, died in 1917, two years after Dr. Neumann's passing. He became known throughout Europe as the author of a *Buddhist Catechism* which he published under the pseudonym of "Subhadra Bhikshu." This *Catechism*, a masterpiece of doctrinal precision and clarity of style, saw nine editions in Germany alone and was translated into more than ten languages, including Japanese.

Paul Dahlke (1865–1928) is another name of distinction in the German Buddhist movement. Early in his life he was attracted to the Buddha's Teaching and later travelled in the East. He was a Doctor of Medicine and a herbalist of note. In Ceylon he received Pali lessons from scholarly monks and translated parts of the Sutta Piṭaka. This he followed up with the publication of several books on Buddhism and from 1918 onward with two periodicals, the *Neubuddhistische Zeitschrift,* "New-Buddhist Journal," and later *Die Brockensammlung,* "Odds and Ends," for which he wrote many erudite articles. Returning from his travels in the East, he conceived the idea to establish a Buddhist Community Centre in the environs of Berlin. "We Buddhists have no churches, do not want them, do not need them, but we need places where, after the burden of daily life, one can rest the spirit in tranquillity. Particularly must we try and establish such places in large cities." At the time he was already in poor health yet he proceeded with his project in 1924. The Centre was built in Berlin-Frohnau on a 75 acre estate and included, among others, a large main building with a temple-like auditorium. The grounds were beautifully terraced and landscaped. This place, which is a showplace in all Europe, was acquired in the 1950s by a Buddhist Society of Ceylon, the German Dhammaduta Society of Colombo. It is now inhabited by Sri Lankan monks and open for those who come to inquire, to meditate and to receive instruction in the Buddha's Teaching. Some of his books were translated into English and became quite popular under the titles "Buddhist Essays" and "Buddhism and Science." Also his last and philosophically most mature book appeared in English under the title "Buddhism in the Intellectual Life of Mankind."

Georg Grimm (1868–1945) became widely known in Germany and abroad through his main work, *The Doctrine of the Buddha, The Religion of Reason and Meditation,* the 14th impression of which was translated into English by Bhikkhu Sīlācāra. Destined to become a Catholic priest, he completed his theological studies; however, he left the seminary before receiving holy orders, on grounds of conscience, chose jurisprudence and became a judge. Amongst his colleagues on the bench he was known as "the most benevolent judge in Bavaria." His deep interest in philosophical problems soon induced him to bestow his intensive attention upon the study of Arthur Schopenhauer's scriptures. It was the influence of Schopenhauer that led him to Indological studies, particularly to the study of the Pali language. Therewith he came more and more into the attractive force of the Buddha's Teaching. In the year 1923 he caused himself to be pensioned as a Counsel of Provincial Court of Appeal in Munich. Georg Grimm wrote his books from an attitude acquired by his own practical realization of the Dhamma. He was writing them, as he often said, for himself. The last twelve years of his life he spent in the rural stillness on the shore of Lake Ammer in Southern Bavaria. With the well-known Indologist and philosopher Paul Deussen (1845–1919)—the early friend of Nietzsche—he was connected by a lasting friendship until death. It was together with the Indologist Dr. Karl Seidenstücker that Georg Grimm founded the "Old Buddhist Community" in Utting am Ammersee. This community which is headed now by Frau Maya Keller-Grimm, the daughter of the founder, with the able assistance of Max Hoppe, issues a monthly magazine, *Yāna*.

Dr. Karl Seidenstücker (1876–1936), a prominent Indologist and a pupil of Professor Windisch, is to be credited with being the founder of the first Buddhist Society in Germany (1903) dedicated to the establishment of a Buddhist Mission. In 1905 he published the first Buddhist magazine in Germany, *Der Buddhist*, which lasted up to the first World War. In 1919 he joined George Grimm as publisher and co-editor of the magazine *Buddhistischer Weltspiegel*, "Buddhist World-Mirror." Dr. Karl Seidenstücker was a prolific writer and translator of Pali texts. He published a number of books; among them the first German translation of the *Udāna* (1920) and *Itivuttaka* (1922), and also an elementary grammar of the Pali language.

Nyanatiloka Mahāthera (1878–1957) had the honour of being the first ordained Bhikkhu of German origin and also the first from continental Europe. Early he became attracted to Buddhist philosophy and this moved him to come to Ceylon in 1903. He was ordained in Burma in 1904, and soon after returned to Ceylon. From there on practically his entire life was spent in the East. He became a thorough student and renowned scholar of Pali and the Dhamma and wrote many books both in English and German. In 1911 he established the "Island Hermitage" near Dodanduwa in Ceylon, which became famous all over the Buddhist world. During the first and second World War his activities were interrupted, as both times he was interned by the British on account of his German citizenship. During these periods the Mahāthera's life was rather difficult, but in spite of the handicaps his literary output is impressively large. His first publication in German as well as in English was the *Word of the Buddha* (1906) which still is today a classic in Buddhist literature; other English publications were the *Guide through the Abhidhamma Piṭaka* and the *Buddhist Dictionary*. However the larger part of his work was done in the German language. Among many publications were the translation of the *Milinda-pañhā* and his most voluminous work, the complete translation of the *Aṅguttara Nikāya* (5 vols. of 2000 pages). In *1950* his German translation of the *Visuddhimagga* was printed. This work alone would be enough to place the Mahāthera in the first ranks of Buddhist scholarship.

The worldwide fame and his noble example drew many Western Buddhists into the ranks of the Sangha. Among his German pupils were: Ven. Sumano Sāmaṇera (ordained 1905; died 1910 in Ceylon), a saintly character whose posthumous essay "*Pabbajjā*" (Wheel, No. 27/28) had inspired many German Buddhists. Ven. Vappo Mahāthera (1874–1960), ordained in 1911 (see *Bodhi Leaves* 3); Ven. Nyanaponika Mahāthera (1901–1993), ordained 1936, Editor, Buddhist Publication Society. German publications: *Kompendium der Dingwelt* (German translation of *Dhammasaṅgaṇī*), *Satipaṭṭhāna*, 1950; *Suttanipāta* (trans.), 1955; *Der Einzige Weg* (*Sati: Anthology*) 1956; *Geistestraining durch Achtsamkeit*, 1970.

Kurt Schmidt (1879–1975), graduated as Doctor of Law in 1901 from the University of Rostock. He went first into journalism and became a newspaper editor. Hereafter he engaged in Buddhist studies, learned Pali, Sanskrit and Chinese. Apart from numerous essays, he published several books on Buddhism, among them introductions to the Doctrine, biographies of Buddhist Saints, two anthologies from the Pali scriptures, a short popular Pali Grammar, and a condensed translation of the *Majjhima Nikāya.*

Helmuth von Glasnapp (1891–1963). Professor of Indology in Königsberg and Tübingen. Some of his numerous publications on Buddhism: *Der Buddhismus in Indien und im Fernen Osten* ("Buddhism in India and the Far East"), 1936; *Die Weisheit des Buddha* (The Wisdom of the Buddha), 1946; *Vedanta und Buddhismus,* 1950 (English trans. *Wheel* No. 2); *Buddhismus und Christentum,* 1949 (Engl. trans. *Wheel* No. 16); *Der Buddhismus und Die Gottesidee,* ("Buddhism and the God-idea"), 1954; *Der Pfad zur Erleuchtung, Grundtexte der Buddhistischen Heilslehre* ("The Path to Enlightenment, Basic texts of Buddhism"), 1956.

Martin Steinke—Tao Chuen (1882–1966). Founded in 1922 the "Gemeinde um Buddha" ("Fellowship around Buddha") which issued a periodical up to 1932. Extensive activity in public lecturing, doctrinal courses, etc. In 1933, he received Mahāyāna Ordination in China. Among his published works is his latest: *Das Lebensgesetz* ("The Law of Life"), 1962.

Kurt Fischer (1892–1942). Friend and secretary of Dr. Paul Dahlke. After the latter's death he continued lecturing and teaching and conducting the Uposatha celebrations. He edited a Buddhist quarterly, *Buddhistisches Leben und Denken* ("Buddhist Life and Thought") (1930–1942).

Max Ladner (1890–1963). He was the editor of *Die Einsicht* which became the leading Theravada monthly for all German-speaking countries. He wrote two important books: *Wirklichkeit und Erlösung*, "Reality and Deliverance," and *Gotama Buddha.* Max Ladner was a writer of great literary charm combined with profound philosophical acumen.

Lionel Stützer (1901–1991) joined the *"Fellowship around Buddha"* in 1922. After the prohibition of all Buddhist Societies in 1942 by the Nazi regime, and after the end of the second World War, he founded in 1946 the *Buddhistische Gemeinde* (Buddhist Community) in Berlin. which continues up to this day. In 1952 he was initiated into the Western Branch of the Order Ariya-Maitreya Mandala. He lectured extensively to both groups.

Dr. Anton Kropatsch, Wien (1897–1971), Dermatologist. Retired Chief Physician of the Leprosy Hospital, Vienna. Apart from medical writings, he wrote numerous Buddhist essays in *Indische Welt*, (The Mahā Bodhi). He published books in German; *Die Letzte Freiheit des Menschen* ("Man's Last Freedom", on Anattā), 1957. *Wiedergeburt und Erlösung in der Lehre des Buddha* ("Rebirth and Deliverance in the Buddha's Doctrine"), 1903.

Paul Debes (1906–2004) was a widely known lecturer and writer in the northwestern parts of Germany. He wrote: *Meisterung der Existenz durch die Lehre des Buddha* ("Mastery of Human Existence through the Doctrine of the Buddha"), 1982. Paul Debes has been conducting Seminars for beginners and advanced students of the Buddha's Teaching. He is the founder of Buddhistisches Seminar für Seinskunde, situated near Hamburg, which issues a monthly magazine, *Wissen und Wandel* ("Knowledge and Conduct").

Dr. Hellmuth Hecker (born 1923) is an international jurist and Buddhist scholar. He wrote numerous scholarly articles for the magazine *Die Einsicht*, and published *Die Ethik des Buddha* ("Buddhist Ethics"), 1976.

* * *

Finally, mention must be made that Buddhism in Germany of today has become a living force and is fast outgrowing the narrow academic circles of merely scholarly interests. A recent survey, done in 1963, reveals that an intensive activity is carried on in eighteen Buddhist Societies and study groups, to which have to be added three Buddhist shrines and teaching centres.

In preparing this *Wheel* issue for printing, the Buddhist Publication Society wishes to acknowledge with thanks its appreciation of Mr. W. A. Koster's share in the work. He not only gladly accepted the request of the Society to assist in the issue of the present anthology, but in addition carried the heavy burden of numerous draft translations and furnished biographical data about the authors, which proved very helpful in the preparation of the final revision. The Buddhist Publication Society plans, in the future to issue more essays and articles by noted German Buddhist writers which will supplement the present anthology.

Ven. Nyanaponika Thera,
BPS Editor

Schopenhauer and Buddhism

by Max Ladner

There can be hardly any doubt that it was Schopenhauer's philosophy which paved the way for Buddhism in Europe. For in its basic propositions there exists a complete agreement with the first of the Four Noble Truths, i.e. that Life is not only subject to, but inherently, *suffering*. One may be inclined to brand such a worldview as the blackest pessimism, but a closer look reveals that it has nothing in common with sentimental *Weltschmerz* (world-weariness) nor with pessimism as commonly understood. It is simply a statement of fact and quite obvious to anyone who realises the impermanence and transitoriness of all existence and in this transitoriness recognises the root cause of ever recurring suffering. This need not plunge us into a state of despondency; on the contrary, it can lead to an even loftier concept of life, culminating in an equanimity of heart and mind in which peace and harmony reign, in comparison with which all the running and rushing after an imagined "happiness" looks like the wasted labours of Sisyphus.

About 150 years ago, when Schopenhauer wrote his book *The World as Will and Idea,* he had already gained a wide knowledge of the Buddha's teachings. He obtained this knowledge from the meagre sources extant at that time, such as Upham's *Doctrine of Buddhism,* Spence Hardy's *Manual of Buddhism*, Köppen's *Religion des Buddha*, as well as Burnouf's *Introduction à L'histoire du Bouddhisme*, and the *Dhammapada* edited by Fausböll. Schopenhauer's profound grasp of the essentials of the Dhamma is truly astounding. Thus, for instance, in the 41st chapter of vol. 2 of his main work, which deals with death in relation to the indestructibility of our being in-it-self, Schopenhauer states clearly that the Buddha's teachings on rebirth are unquestionably based on palingenesis and not on metamorphosis. Furthermore, he states that Buddhism keeps itself free of all exaggerated forms of asceticism, and if Nirvāna is defined as "nothing" this only means the absence of a single element in saṃsāra, which could serve as a definition of Nirvāna. It was a great satisfaction for him to have found that his own philosophy was essentially in accord with the Doctrine of the Buddha reached already 500 years before the beginning of the Christian era. And this explains the readiness and open-mindedness on the part of Schopenhauer's as mirrors for Buddhist thought, which was not strange to the German mind but in principle familiar. To which must be added that generations of scholars up to this day have progressed far beyond Schopenhauer in the interpretation and *practical application of the Buddha's Teaching.*

Excerpt from an article "Buddhistische Mission in Europa"
by Max Ladner, 1960/1.

Character

by Paul Dahlke

Someone confessed to me recently: "I would not mind becoming a better man if I only knew how to go about it." To which I replied: all of us have the same difficulty and for all of us there is only one way out of it—by simply making a start. We must make that start, and if failures and shortcomings seem to overwhelm us, don't give up, just start all over again. There is no other way and we must all tread this path with patience and humility. Every evening, when going to bed and every morning when awaking, one should examine one's conscience:

"There, now I have done this and that again! This bad habit of mine, again I have lost control over it!" If we have to admit this our heart should not be heavy, we just keep trying again and again to do better next time. This is the secret of the good, that in the attempt itself there lies the remedy and blessing. Here even the attempt itself is already a step forward. There is no proof, no logical method by which I can make myself better or lift myself from a lower to a higher state and thus become a better man. A person who waits for such a method by which he could guide himself is like a man, reading on a sign-post which says: "To ... in 1 hour," but he remains standing there. When the hour has lapsed he complains: "This sign-post is worthless. The hour has passed and I am still here!" There is no proof, no logic that can take him to his destination but only his actually starting to walk to that place.

The same applies to us who groan under the weight of passions and ignorance: there is no other way than to start immediately to overcome our weaknesses and improve our character. The only question that arises is whether one should strive in solitude or in company with others similarly inclined. It appears to me that sometimes, and for some, moral effort undertaken along with others, may bring better results. It creates an atmosphere of the good by which everyone will be benefited; and in the race for the goal the individual will bring out his best, in noble competition.

However, for some to strive alone may be better. It may be that for one and the same person striving alone and, at other times, in company is preferable.

The present writer owes to solitude all his knowledge (*vijjā*) but very little for his progress in conduct (*caraṇa*). This was the main reason that prompted him to undertake the venture of the *Buddhist House.*

None among us should be discouraged, not even he who is most dissatisfied with himself. The most precious gift of the Word of the Buddha consists in the fact that it does not make the improvement of character dependent on laws and institutions, violence and coercion, or on divine grace. The Buddha's message teaches us that individual existence is not rooted in any metaphysical entity, and accordingly, it is not the result of divine decree or predestination. Nor is man's existence a purely physical process, and, consequently, it cannot be explained as being merely the result of other, external physical processes (such as those of the parents). Buddhism teaches that the so-called individuality is entirely "*Kamma*" (action) and, at any given moment, it is the outcome of its own "*Kamma.*" Furthermore, the individual is neither unconditioned (faith) nor conditioned (science) but is conditioning itself in every new mental and physical "conception," i.e. acts of grasping physically and mentally. Thus concepts, ideas, consciousness in general are not the handles with which I "handle" the Cup of Life, nor the means of playing with Life by way of proof through logical inference. Neither are they the springboard from which I try to get a hold on Life, but consciousness, a conceiving (grasping) and conceptualizing force is Life in the act of ever anew experiencing (conceiving) itself, in the process of living. And in this the secret of reality stands revealed: Life is the pathway which opens up by going on it and it is the going itself. Through this very fact it may be possible that I can become thoroughly susceptible, amenable, and malleable. Thereby it further happens that the very attempt to do good is already a form of good, and every move to become better constitutes the first step on the path. "Therefore, Cunda, should you think thus: though others be violent we shall instead be gentle," etc. and, "even as there is, Cunda, a rough way and another smooth way to circumvent the rough way, so also for the violent man there is gentleness to circumvent violence. Just as all bad actions lead downwards, so all good actions lead upwards. So also for the violent man there is gentleness to reach higher states of being." (MN 8)

Our only action is to give up, to loosen the grip. This is so and is also the other secret of reality. It was this kind of action that moved the future Buddha Gotama, when, as a Bodhisatta, in his birth as King Sudassana, he resolved: "Be gone, thou impulse of lust! Be gone, thou impulse of ill-will! Be gone, thou impulse of violence!" (DN 17)! When the clouds retreat, the blue sky appears. This is the secret of reality: if we let go of violence, gentleness appears; if we let go of ill-will, then good-will appears; if we let go of sensuality, chastity appears. Every step toward the goal is a form of the goal. And the path opens up by going on it and is the going itself. Therefore the violent man should not despair of becoming gentle, nor the liar of becoming truthful, nor the sensuous of becoming chaste, nor the glutton of becoming moderate. If he sets his mind and heart to the task and makes a start, all this will eventually be his.

Let therefore no one counter this by saying: "That's just what I am unable to do: to make a start!" Life itself is a continuous beginning and in life only does potentiality become potency. In other words: Life is growth. One does not go from violence to gentleness, from sensuality to chastity, from fear to fearlessness with the help of logic or the jugglery of proofs. By logic and proof no coward ever turned into a brave man, no sensuous person chaste; no timid soul self-confident. But one grows out of these weaknesses. And one day, upon him who has done evil deeds before, the realisation dawns he would never commit them again; neither logic nor proof forced him into it: he simply grew above them; he is unable to do evil deeds any more. This was brought about through real thinking, i.e. about reality and its ability to cease, to be given up, and by the ever renewed attempt to give up, i.e. by trying over and over again to bring thought and action into harmony.

Therefore the Buddha said of Himself: "As he says so he does, as he does so he says." Hence we should earnestly strive to gain right understanding. If a person follows this path then he will experience it by himself that the only worthwhile action is that of "giving up," and he will always strive to achieve it.

To overcome a beginningless habit is difficult indeed. But there is also the possibility of ceasing, of giving up and letting go. I experience this myself when thoughts of lust, violence and ill-will that have entered my mind vanish like a drop of water on a red-hot plate, like the morning mist before the rising sun. And surely, the start will not be fruitless nor the energy spent on it.

This is the glad news that awaits us, this is the last hope that smiles upon us all: this last possibility resulting from this mind-form which is god and creature in one. What is God and what would he be if he were not omnipotent? And what is omnipotence? What should it be if not a power that can master itself? Helpless is God as pure mind! All-powerful is man as mind-form, because this mind-form is capable of self-mastery and thus of attaining its complete end.

Homage, to Him, the Teacher
Written 1923.
(Source Unknown.)

What is Interesting?

by Paul Dahlke

It is well known how we were overfed with interesting news in the last war (1914–1918), and even to this day there is no end to new news. Recently, while crossing the street Unter den Linden, a newspaper vendor at the corner was calling out the news about Tuthankamon and how his tomb was discovered. At other times, I hear the news of some great man's assassination, about an earthquake somewhere, of a certain crowned head losing his throne, of the sudden death of the richest man on earth, caused most probably by calling too many doctors to his bedside.

Thus on every corner, over and over again, news flashes up and keeps us worried about everything, except those things we ought to worry about. We are drawn to the "news" like moths to the light.

What, after all, is it we ought to worry about? About the interesting, of course. Only "interesting" is something other than people think. The word *interesting* is derived from the Latin word *interesse* which means "to be in the midst of it." That of which I am a part of is interesting. And whereof am I a part? If any urge to violence, sensuality or ill-will arises within me, like unto a flame shooting forth by the friction of two sticks of wood; and then insight rushes in to extinguish the fire with the all-quenching water-jet of the thought of *anattā* (not-self), now with success and now with less success, some other time without any success—that is interesting, there I am in the midst of it, and that ought to be above all our concern, as the most important item in the whole business.

But worldly wisdom is not easily confounded. Such a wise one interjects: "Whatever happens at the other end of the earth is of vital concern for me too. Not only, as in the poem of Horace, when the neighbour's wall is on fire is the *mea res agitur* ("this is business of mine") valid, but in the last analysis, for everything that goes on in the world. Our economic and political organism, today, has become so highly sensitive that I am affected in some way or another when there is a change of President in the United States, or there is a wheat crop failure in Canada, or Ireland gets Home-Rule, or the franc is devaluated, or in India the Swaraj-movement spreads, or new coal deposits are discovered in Spitzbergen, or the Dalai Lama dies in Tibet, etc."

To which I reply: "Indeed, I am affected by all this. And what's more, the radius of my being affected reaches not only to the Ganges and the North Pole and into the heart of Inner Asia, but up to Sirius and to the farthest nebular constellation in the starry heavens. Astrology, which teaches our "interest" in the stars, is not at all entire foolishness. Besides, I should like to know what on earth constitutes pure foolishness? Even nonsense is—after some fashion—a form of sense. The pure wise man does exist, that is, as a Tathāgata, the Perfect One; whereas the pure fool does not exist, except in myth and legend, just as pure chaos does not exist."

To live implies the capacity for keeping alive which means to be related to all and everything. It simmers down to feeding, be it physically or mentally. We all eat out of one large trough, called Universe. A Buddhist would be the last person to deny possibilities here present; the essence of Buddhism in its *Kamma* Doctrine is basically a view of the Universe as interplay of ever-ready potentiality versus potency (*Kamma*), in which time and space are seen neither as rigidly existing in themselves, according to the Biblical view and accepted even by Newton, nor as mere relations to which science, in a relentless melting-down process, had reduced them (as in Einstein's theory). In Buddhism time and space become moral destiny in which, as the case may be, weal or woe turn the balance. *Viññāṇa* (consciousness) from the moment of its clinging to the new womb defies time, defies space: For it experiences itself as both time and space.

The Time-Space-Doctrine of Buddhism, i.e. of reality, is yet to be written. As Buddhism takes its stand over and above faith and science, so stands its Time-Space-Doctrine over the doctrine of absolute time and absolute space, on the one hand (faith), and above relative time and relative space (science) on the other. These allusions may suffice.

Certainly, I am not only interested in objects and events of this earth alone, but in the ongoings of the whole universe. But I am interested in it like unto one's interest in his fodder-trough out of which he gets his food. This fodder-trough is inexhaustible, and so is interest, as long as the insatiable feeding urge prevails. What really counts is not my presence in all this, but whether or not I actively participate and permit myself to be a participant; and that again depends on where I stand and the clarity of my insight. There is a standpoint from which all this is seen as a whole, i.e. the standpoint of "feeder and fodder-trough"; may this standpoint be elaborated after the fashion of faith or after the fashion of science; in the first case the whole will be seen as the incomprehensibility of divine creation, in the latter it is to become comprehensibility, without residue, in the form of scientific law.

Yet there exists another standpoint from whence this whole, called universe, is recognised in its total incompleteness and inadequacy; whereupon cognition, leaving behind both the beginningless incomprehensibility of faith and the endless comprehensibility of science, focuses itself on this whole, which alone is real, comprehending itself over and again in experience, just as the flame comprehends itself over and again in the very act of burning.

> "The whole, Bhikkhus, I will teach you. Listen! Be intent! I shall speak. What then is the whole? The eye and the forms, the ear and the sounds, the nose and the smells, the tongue and the savours, the body and the touch, thinking and the things. All these are called the whole." (SN 35:23)

This is the truly "interesting" at which each single person is not only an interested bystander and more or less a participant, but exactly that of which each single individual consists. This is the most soul-shaking news because it leads to an ego-shattering renewal of the personality itself. Whosoever in this new insight comprehends that which is most interesting, for him this super-fodder-trough, the world, ceases to be of interest; nor will he be afraid of the ensuing consequences: that of having to abstain from the big meal. After all, what is there to be afraid of for one who is always ready to suffer?

The Buddhist's Attitude Towards Christians

by Georg Grimm

The outstanding character of modern civilisation is materialism in the realm of thought and ruthless egotism in all walks of practical every day life. It seems that humanity as a whole is totally immersed in materialism. None but a relative few are left that are still deeply religious in their outlook and conscious of the fact that there is more to existence than just this short lifespan between the cradle and the grave; and who feel concerned about a future life for which they prepare themselves through moral conduct. Among these few are members of various Christian churches which they have come to regard as the only guardians of religion. These people are still capable of believing wholeheartedly in the tenets of their respective faiths. May they continue to find shelter under the protective wings of their churches! No man in his right conscience, let alone a Buddhist, could wish to take away from them the moral support they have found in their beliefs.

However, aside from these, there are some deeply religious individuals who have completely lost faith in dogmatic religion but who would rather follow the dictates of their conscience as the only authority to guide them. This type of people can be counted upon as prospective hearers of the Buddha Word to which they feel attracted, and to them primarily the Doctrine of Deliverance should be presented. These people are ready for it. The faithful Christian believers should be left strictly alone and undisturbed. Should it not be possible, one might ask, to enlist the sympathy of even the leaders of the different Christian churches to this form of Buddhist propaganda? To whom, after all, would this "propaganda" be directed if not to those who are lost to the faith, anyhow, who have become unbelievers? Should it not rather be an occasion for rejoicing in the heart of every religious person to see how people, unbelievers, though not irreligious, are still kept and nourished in a religious atmosphere? And more important still: that all religious people, inside or outside the churches, are joining hands in fighting the enemy of all religion: materialism?

This is how at least a Buddhist views the situation: He respects and honours every sincerely religious person no matter what religion he confesses or church he belongs to. He sees in him a fellow pilgrim, a brother on the road, voyaging towards the same home, although the other may find in the resthouse on the way already the abode he thinks he is looking for.

From: *Buddhistischer Weltspiegel,*
1919, Vol. 1, p. 94.

The Buddha's Code of Conduct
A Consideration of the Sīlas for Buddhists

by Georg Grimm

I

It is of prime importance to ask oneself the question: how does the Buddha justify the promulgation of his code of conduct known as the five precepts or *sīlas*? Are they merely "commandments" resting completely on the will of the Buddha, somewhat similar to the Christian commandments, which are really nothing more than the manifestation of the will of a personal God? In this case the sīlas would be seen as not binding at all, without any sanction whatsoever. There are no threats of punishment uttered for disobeying, nor any tangible rewards offered for obeying them. In fact, the sīlas are no decrees of the Buddha's will but rather the expression of the Buddha's transcendental insight into the nature of reality itself. In other words, the sīlas represent the practical application of the Buddha's fully enlightened consciousness with regard to those cosmic laws, which govern the results of every individual act. Were we to verbalize these cosmic laws they would communicate to us as follows: "If you behave according to us, you may expect a greatly desirable, delightful harvest. If, however, you do not act according to us, placing yourself in contradiction with "reality," then the outcome will be a definitely undesired, undesirable and unhappy harvest."

II

But how does reality present itself to the supreme cognition of the All-Enlightened-One so that the sīlas follow therefrom? Whatever we may be, however we may choose to doubt, *one principle* is irrefutable, for this principle is absolutely established and experienced by each and every one of us, namely: "We are creatures who desire well-being and abhor pain." This "we" includes everything that "lives and breathes," every animal, indeed every plant. All of these are living beings which desire well-being and abhor pain.

This is the very first and the last principle at which cognition arrives in its striving to find out what makes "the world go round." In the same way, the "world" itself, being nothing but the sum total of all individual lives, desires in each of them well-being and abhorrence in them of pain. Therefore this urge for well-being and the abhorrence of pain is equally justified in every living being, from the microbe to the noblest Brahmin. For they are all parts of the "world," of the one reality, which wells up in them. From this follows the right of everything alive to well-being and immunity from pain. It stands to reason then that the promotion of well-being in its widest sense must be the mainspring of every human act.

We call behaviour in accordance with this principle: Kindness. This is the highest ethical imperative, to be kind towards everything that lives and breathes. It is the guiding star from which all human behaviour takes its direction, and from which all morality takes its ultimate justification. Every act in accordance with it we call ethical. And conversely, any act in conflict with this highest imperative, we call immoral. Whenever collisions arise between the highest imperative and any particular ethical rule, the conflict ought to be resolved in favour of kindness. Kindness is, as it were, the Queen on the Throne of Morality, and the particular rules are her executive agencies. All this is likewise true of the five precepts (*sīlas*) of the Buddha. Even they are only the messengers of kindness, and are supposed to support their ruler.

III

Yet the penetrating insight of the Buddha-eye brings forth another all-inclusive truth: in the phenomenal world, the satisfaction of our desire for well-being and avoidance of pain is absolutely impossible. For everything in the world is transitory. No well-being perseveres: it is always suffering that triumphs in the end, the very suffering of transitoriness. And not only that. Each form of life in this world can maintain itself only at the expense of other forms of life.

Obviously, these life-forms can only exist by incorporating matter into their own constitution. And every speck of matter is already owned, as it were, by others, similarly constituted. There is a continuous snatching going on, an appropriation and destruction of lives, which brings in its wake concomitant suffering: Thus every form of existence transgresses the highest law of morality, kindness. From this state of affairs the Buddha could draw only one conclusion: everything which militates against the highest moral imperative, namely kindness, ought not to exist, ought to be done away with. As we have seen, every form of existence transgresses against kindness. Consequently the entire phenomenal world is something which ought not to be. In practice this great and universal law of kindness assumes this imperative: *"You shall not desire!"* And this explains why all true morality presents itself in negative form, enjoining omissions. Thus *we* find that all specific commandments prescribe omissions. The five precepts (*sīla*) of he Buddha do exactly the same. This notwithstanding, positive actions can also be commanded for the realization of kindness, but even these lead back, in final analysis, to the negative, to omission, to endurance, to universal renunciation.

IV

To this highest position we are led by the liberating insight of the Buddha. And because it was the Buddha's supreme insight, which led to the discovery of kindness as a cosmic principle, carrying it over into the sīlas, the latter are on this account the most perfect expression of kindness. They are neither in need nor capable of further improvement. They are valid even for one who has fully realized them, who has become kindness himself, who has become completely holy. Indeed, for such a holy person the question whether the sīlas could be abrogated in any specific case is simply utter nonsense. The Holy One has become kindness itself, and is on this very account, the embodiment of the sīlas. He is therefore absolutely incapable of "sinning" against them. He can no longer conceive the very thoughts which lead to transgression. No conflict can arise for him with regard to any situation confronting him. By way of illustration let us suppose the following case. Amongst peoples in which revenge for homicide is still practiced, a shepherd by the name of Essa is falsely accused of the sex murder of a woman. He flees from the revenge of the husband and comes to a hermit who is known as a holy man.

The latter gives him temporary shelter in his hut. Presently the husband of the murdered woman, who had followed Essa's trail, comes to the hut and asks the hermit whether Essa is inside it. The hermit knows with certainty that if he tells the truth, and even if he says nothing, the man will without further ado force his way into the hut and kill Essa there, without listening to any advice. In addition let us suppose the circumstances to be such, that if Essa's life can be spared for just one more day, his innocence will be revealed. How then would the Holy Man answer the husband's question as to whether Essa is in the hut? As already shown, even this dilemma can present no problem to the Holy Man. It is inconceivable of him to resolve it by means of a lie. Such attitude is as foreign to him as in a man deprived of both his arms the gesture would be of helping some one fallen up to his feet again. Just as the armless man, in spite of overflowing kindness, lacks the possibility of helping the fallen friend, so the hermit in the case of Essa has no other way out than to say nothing. In doing this he has done what was possible for him to do. As water cannot burn, a Holy Man cannot lie. Indeed, a Holy Man, in the Buddhist sense, has finally become incapable of all karma-producing volitions. He cannot engage in competitive-strife for a livelihood. Consequently he becomes dependent for his sustenance on alms given by his faithful supporters. Although in the world, he has ceased to be of the world (as it says in the Suttanipāta); and it is exactly for these reasons that he withdraws completely from it. In the Aṅguttara Nikāya (AN 9:7), the Buddha speaks thus:

> "Previously, Sutava, I maintained as I do now: A monk imbued with holiness, a conqueror over desire, who has run the path, has thrown away his burden, worked out his own deliverance, freed himself from the fetters of becoming, is anchored in true wisdom, is incapable of doing the following nine things: He is incapable of taking the life of any living being; incapable of taking anything which is not given to him; incapable of performing sexual acts; incapable of speaking knowingly untruth; incapable of hoarding and enjoying treasures; incapable of walking in the path of greed; incapable of walking in the path of hate; incapable of walking in the path of delusion; incapable of walking in the path of fear."

V

Thus, for one who has attained to the highest spiritual understanding, a conflict between kindness, of which he is the embodiment, and the sīlas is no longer possible. Wherever such a conflict does arise, it is an infallible proof that one is still capable of stealing, of killing, of practising forbidden sexual intercourse, of lying. In other words, he is potentially able to do all this. However, in so far as one is still capable of doing all this, and therefore a conflict becomes a possibility, the conflict must always be resolved in favour of kindness. One may even have to kill, to take what is not one's own, or may have to tell a lie. But let it be understood that the aforesaid acts are (humanly speaking) excusable only, if one in observance of a sīla would be unkind, unloving or even cruel to his neighbour. The sīlas have, let this be said again, no independent status but derive their justification exclusively as expressions of kindness.

Let us explain this seeming paradox further. Every person, even the kindest, would probably save a child by killing the vermin with which this child is infested. Or let me introduce a personal experience that happened during our stay in Spain. A miserable, mutilated kitten ran up to us—my daughter and me—its body covered with lice and ants burrowed deeply in its tongue. My daughter freed the kitten from its attackers, although she was forced to squeeze the ants, one by one, from its tongue. The kitten itself lived a long time and displayed a touching tenderness and gratitude. Naturally my daughter did the right thing. She acted out of kindness toward the kitten, preventing much greater suffering by means of a lesser one. Likewise in the case of the shepherd Essa, a person would have to deny that Essa is in the hut. Out of kindness he would have to lie or else he would be excessively cruel and unkind. It would be ignorance in the sense of spiritual blindness if a person, who is still able to violate the sīlas, tries to observe them tenaciously to the point of being actually cruel. He is blind because he does not know that even ethical observances have no spiritual value in themselves. His error consists in holding the sīlas to be the unconditional decrees of a personal God, instead of recognizing them to be merely the means of expressing kindness. This Teaching is difficult to grasp and open to misunderstanding. As an example let us quote one famous passage from the *Dhammapada:*

> "Even for the sake of the greatest happiness of another, do not ever give up your own salvation."

If this isolated passage is taken up literally, and out of context, an ignorant person would not only be doing harm to the well-being of another, but also to his own, just because of being unkind. For in the last analysis his own salvation is dependent upon the cultivation of kindness, which under no circumstances can ever be harmful.

That the Enlightened One denounced lying, particularly because it causes suffering to others, follows from Verse 408 of the Dhammapada:

> "He who utters gentle, instructive and true words, not insulting anyone—him do I call Brāhmaṇa."

Moreover, if the sīlas are violated solely out of kindness, then the urge and the craving for the "world" will in no way be encouraged. Whosoever takes his nourishment without attachment, just for his sustenance, has, according to the Buddha, prevailed over the nourishment, although he did take it. And whosoever transgresses one of the sīlas only so that he may not be unkind has overcome the desire to transgress them. Although he is still doing it in a particular case, such a transgression does not at all prevent him from becoming ever more perfect as time goes on. Until in the end he reaches a state of complete inability to violate them, and therewith to be removed from every possibility of an ethical conflict.

Because a transgression of the sīlas can be indicated only out of kindness, every violation of them from selfish motives is immoral. It goes without saying that selfishness begets injustice, an infringement of our neighbour's rights, and therewith acts of unkindness.

Fortunately, the cases in which one is compelled to violate one of the sīlas are generally rare. If they occur at all it is if the well-being of another person is at stake, never in the case of one's own. In the great majority of cases one will, if the well-being of another is in question, be able to promote it, without violating the sīlas. This can be done only if the basic requirement of all action is carefully observed, namely *mindfulness.* The case in which one must lie out of pure kindness can almost always be avoided. Yes, even in the most difficult situation, where one dare not say the truth for fear of being unkind, a question can be met with silence or an evasion. Such an evasion, provided it is not patently untrue, is not formally a lie, and therefore, is no transgression of the fourth sīla. And for this reason alone can the above outlined practice be placed in closest proximity to the Buddha's silence.

In the light of the foregoing exposition the conflict between duty and observance of the sīlas can be resolved without difficulty. Either the concrete behaviour, as being called for by duty, is in conformity with the demands of loving-kindness and then no problem exists. If, however, the call of duty is not mitigated by loving-kindness, and, what would be even worse, implies at the same time a violation of the sīlas, then only one answer can be given: abandon any such activity as being unwholesome and not leading to liberation.

The Path for the Buddhist Lay Follower

by Georg Grimm

The Buddha realised that most people are incapable of understanding the nature of Nibbāna. But as He was "filled with kindness and compassion towards all living beings," He showed a path and furnished a guide for lay followers, so that they too can pass through the numberless existences of Life with maximum happiness and minimum suffering. This guide consists of the five sīlas: Not to kill or injure any living being; not to take what is not given; not to indulge in illicit lusts; not to tell an untruth; not to partake of intoxicants and narcotics.

A life in harmony with the sīlas brings happiness and peace; transgression of the sīlas results in suffering and misfortune. The truth of this can readily be observed during one's lifetime, but the effect on one's afterlife is less easily seen. To gain a better understanding, the lay follower should be well acquainted with the fundamentals of the Buddha's teachings. He should be familiar with the working of the Law of *Kamma* and the process of rebirth. He should develop sufficient insight to have confidence in the teaching and know in his innermost heart that it represents the truth.

What progress one makes along these lines depends entirely on the effort one expends on the study of the teaching. A sincere lay follower *should* spend at least one hour daily, either in the morning before going to work, or after work in the evening, on the study of Buddhist texts of a kind that will benefit his progress. This also provides an excellent opportunity for the practice of concentration. The knowledge acquired in this manner should be applied in daily life and should permeate all of one's activities. Eventually a refinement of mind takes place that renders one incapable of inflicting harm to any living being.

Whenever one violates the sīlas one can be sure that at that moment the teaching has been forgotten and has slipped from one's mind. To strengthen its hold on the mind, it is advisable to acquire the habit of reciting mornings and evenings some verses of Buddhist thought. In the morning one may begin with the Tisaraṇa like this:

> "*Namo Tassa Bhagavato Arahato Sammāsambuddhassa.*
> *Buddhaṃ saraṇaṃ gacchāmi*
> *Dhammaṃ saraṇaṃ gacchāmī*
> *Saṅghaṃ saraṇaṃ gacchāmi.*"

> "Another day calls for my new endeavour, on this my journey through the world; I will follow the Buddha's teaching for mine and other's best welfare. Through me no being pain shall suffer; kindness will I show to all, who breathe as man, as beast or plant; blessed be all that lives on earth. So will I use this day of living to gain in peace and happiness, and as the Master recommended, build up good deeds for future life."

"I observe the precept to abstain from destruction of life and injury.

I observe the precept to abstain from taking what is not given.

I observe the precept to abstain from illicit lusts.

I observe the precept to abstain from lies and deceit.

I observe the precept to abstain from intoxicants and narcotics.

Namo Buddhāya.

In the evening one may recite the Tisaraṇa again and then follow up with the verse:

> "Another day has come to end, and again I am nearer to my death.
> What good or bad I have performed on that my future life depends.
> May thou Jewel, Holy Teaching, of the Greatest ever born,
> Whom I honour as the Buddha give me confidence and strength.
> Tomorrow I shall try again to make more progress on the path,
> and in the course of time to come I shall attain the highest goal."

To the *Namo Buddhāya* morning and evening recital one may also add the extended Tisaraṇa which is the creed formula for every Buddhist:

In the Buddha I will put my trust: He is the Exalted One, the Arahat, Fully Awakened, perfect in Knowledge and Conduct, who reached the end of the Path, who knows all the worlds, the Highest, the Teacher of Gods and Men, the Awakened, the Exalted One.

In the Dhamma I will put my trust: Well taught by the Exalted One, crystal clear, not tied to any age, it means "come and see for yourself," it leads to Liberation, the wise recognise it in their inner self.

In the Sangha I will put my trust: in correct and straight conduct live the disciples, worthy of the gifts, worthy of the alms, worthy of lifting one's hands before them in reverence. The best seedbed for happiness-producing charity.

Furthermore, a devout lay follower will not forget to recite before each meal a suitable text to create the proper atmosphere for the partaking of food. Too often this occasion only stimulates the lower appetites. For this purpose he may quote the example of the Exalted One from the Brahmāyu Sutta, MN 91:

> "Offering the rice bowl, he does not turn it upward nor downward, nor sidewards. He accepts the right amount, not too little, not too much. Any sauce or relish he accepts only as such and dips each morsel only as much as necessary. He chews each bite thoroughly, two to three times before swallowing, so that no unchewed food remains in his mouth. Only then does he take the next bite. He feels the sensation of tasting the food but derives no pleasure from it. By eight ways is marked the food eaten by the Exalted One: He eats not for pleasure, nor for comfort, nor to become handsome, nor to become stout, but to maintain his body, to keep it alive, to prevent damage to his system and to be able to lead a pure life. Thereby he thinks: thus the results of my previous life will be worn away and no new results will arise. My life will be kept pure, and I shall feel well."

Namo Buddhāya.

After the meal one may occupy one's mind with the thought :

"Concluding the meal, the Exalted One remains seated in

silence for a while. But not for long. He is satisfied with what He has eaten. He does not complain about the food nor ask for any other kind, rather He cheers His table companions with instructive and encouraging talk which they accept with gratitude and joy."

Namo Buddhāya.

In addition to those regular periods of devotion, a good Buddhist will, during working hours, when the occasion lends itself, turn his mind inward and concentrate on the Three Characteristics of Existence: *anicca, dukkha, anattā* or any other beneficial thought from which he can draw new strength for daily life. Also from time to time he should search his conscience and take inventory of any weaknesses and cravings still in existence.

Who can doubt that even a lay follower living in this manner will gradually be pervaded by the spirit of the Buddha's teaching? His mind will be purified, he shuns crude pleasures and enjoys the spotless serenity and joyfulness arising from a clear conscience and from profound loving-kindness. And even this is not the full path that a lay follower can pursue. He who wants to be very devout should, if his living conditions permit, also observe the Buddhist Sabbath or Uposatha. This is done by being particularly careful on this day to keep the sīlas. Further, one should wear no jewellery, nor flowers and use no cosmetics; should not indulge in amusements like visiting shows, etc.* No solid food should be taken after the noon meal until next morning. The night should be spent on bedding spread on the ground.* On that day the third sīla enjoins complete chastity.

If he leads such a life, then he is a true and perfect, worthy lay follower of the Buddha. After death he will join the world of the "shining Gods."

(From: *The Buddha-Way for you*)*
Additions by the editor.

Three Kinds of People

by Dr. Karl Seidenstücker

There are three kinds of people. Who are these three? Those who enjoy the world, those who abhor the world, and those who overcome the world.

Those who enjoy the world's pleasures are the ones who with imperturbable optimism gorge themselves. They may be compared with the ox before the filled manger, disregarding the approaching butcher and persisting in full enjoyment of the food, until suddenly the butcher's hand descends on his neck.

Those who abhor the world are the inveterate pessimists. They can be likened unto a man who sits down to the table hungry, filled with eagerness and appetite for the dainty food he expects. But when he uncovers the dish he sees carrion in it, ordure and loathsome vermin. His appetite changes into aversion, repugnance and disgust. Those who overcome the world are the ones who dwell in serene equanimity, those who have recognized that:

> "The profane exists and the exalted exists. And there is a refuge beyond the world of the senses."

They are like the soaring eagle, leaving behind the dreary plains, flying up into the endless sky, toward the stillness of its fathomless immensity.

Relatively speaking, aversion to the world ranges higher than worldly pleasure, but far higher stands the overcoming of the world in Holy Wisdom, Holy Conduct, Holy Equanimity.

Aversion to the world running counter against worldly pleasure can be good and wholesome if exercised in a period of transition and of short duration. As a permanent state of mind it is undesirable, leading nowhere.

The one who indulges in worldly pleasures sees reality through rose-coloured glasses. He who *overcomes* the world sees reality for what it is.

Pleasure and desire are *Rati* and *Rāga*, the enchanting daughters of Māra, the king of death. He has a third, whose name is *Arati*, i.e. aversion or disgust. Beware against all three of them!

The so-called pessimists imagine that they have overcome the world. But the very loathing of the world, which fills them, proves that this is not true. For aversion, which is desire turned into its opposite, indicates that the one ridden with it expected to find something else, something better than he did find. Therefore the craving is still there, only hidden and suppressed. The former positive attraction has now become negative repulsion, but as passion it is by no means extinguished. The renunciation of such a person is not an *overcoming;* it does not lead to liberation, it is only the painfully and frustratingly felt necessity to abstain.

Now we come to those who say: "The world is a garden of delight. It must be fully enjoyed, there is nothing wrong in sensual pleasures." They fall into one extreme, while those who declare the world to be loathsome fall into the other extreme. Here the Buddha proclaims the *Middle Way*, avoiding both these extremes and from which, in keeping with reality, the disciple visualizes:

> "All the factors of existence, be they our own, or those of others, near or far away, of coarse or fine nature, are transitory, and what is transitory is a womb of pain. What is painful is *anattā*, what is *anattā* is not mine, this am I not, this is not my self."

Penetrating to the depth of this realization, the high-minded disciple will become weary of the six senses and their objects, which is the World. In becoming weary of them, he detaches himself from passion and in doing so, he becomes free. Having thus become free, he is fully awakened and exclaims: "the painful round of birth and death is exhausted, the Holy Life is lived, this world is no longer for me."

This is the Middle Way, which avoids both the extremes of worldly pleasure and world-disgust. This is the overcoming of the world as taught by the Buddha. This is Holy Equanimity, a state of mind that keeps itself free from blinding passion, be it attractive or repulsive, positive or negative. Again, the disciple who is calm, collected and mindful can proclaim: "I neither desire World and Life nor do I abhor World and Life. However, I do know one thing with certainty: this whole world together with my organism, and this manyfold panorama called Life,—*I am not this; this does not belong to me; this is not my self.* Just as little as the dry leaves swept away by the scavenger belong to me and might be called myself."

This is the state of the Enlightened Man; the world does not touch him any more; its weight does not crush him any more, because he has seen through it and found it empty.

Three kinds of people there are, it has been told: those who enjoy the world, those who abhor the world, and those who overcome the world. Would that every earnest seeker put this question to himself: "To which of these three classes of people do I belong?"

Sotāpatti and Sotāpanna

by Dr. Karl Seidenstücker
(English translation by A. A. G. Bennett)

The following comprises the bulk of the third chapter of *Die Vier Gruppen des Heilspfades* ("The Four Stages of the Path of Deliverance"), an unpublished work by Dr. Karl Seidenstücker. The two previous chapters are entitled: *Massenmensch und Ariya* ("The ordinary man and the Ariya"), and *Die Gemeinde der Ariya* ("The Community of the Noble Ones").

Sotāpatti means "entry into the stream," and *sotāpanna* "one who has entered the stream." "Stream" in this context is a designation of the Noble Eightfold Path (SN 55:55), so that the meaning of sotāpanna comes to be "one who has entered upon the Noble Path." Thus *sotāpanna* is even defined in one place as "one who is equipped with the Noble Eightfold Path," that is, one in whom the eight constituents of the Path (right view, right aspiration, etc.) have become active factors (SN 55:55). Right and firm confidence in the Buddha as the teacher of the minds and guide of the stubborn hearts of men; firm confidence in the Teaching, comprehensible, in no long time, to the wise, each for himself, that invites one to come and see, and leads to the goal; confidence in the Noble Community of Monks (that community which walks uprightly according to vows taken upon), and faithful adherence to the rules of moral conduct, cherished by the Noble Ones, these are the four characteristic signs that indicate the one who has entered the Stream. They are, at the same time, the "mirror of truth," in possession and with the help of which a noble monk may know himself and proclaim of himself: "Exhausted for me is the state of torment, the animal state, the region of ghosts, the abyss and evil wanderings, the world of pain; I have entered the Stream; to the states of suffering I am no more liable; I am certain of attaining to the full Awakening." (DN 16.2.9; 33.1.11; AN 4:52; 5:179; 9:12; SN 12:41. In AN 5:15, the four signs quoted bear the name of *sotāpattiyaṅgāni*, constituents of the Stream-Entry.)

Of the *sotāpannas* who after death are reborn as devas in one of the six lesser heavens of the sensual world-spheres, only those who possess this fourfold "mirror of truth" know that they have no more bad rebirths to expect; the others do not know this (AN 6:34). Still, independently of that statement, the certainty of one who has entered the Stream, that he is no more liable to rebirth in miserable states, and that he will finally attain to Enlightenment, is also brought into prominence as a special characteristic of the *sotāpanna*. (DN 16.2.7; MN 22, 34, 68; AN 4:88; Ud 5.3).

One must at some time become earnestly absorbed in the meaning of this statement, or promise, or whatever one likes to call it, in order to understand what good tidings—in the true sense of the words—it must have been for the age. In the Buddha's lifetime, the belief in the ripening of deeds (*kamma*) and the course of rebirths (saṃsāra) had already become common property, and with it the belief in rebirth in worlds or conditions of gruesome torture. Considered in this light, the full significance of verse 178 of the Dhammapada becomes clear, a passage that may be called a triumphal song on the fruit of the entry into the Stream: "Better than supremacy over the earth, or entry into a heaven, (even) than dominion over all the worlds, is the goal of entry into the Stream."

In order to realise this definite aim of entering the Stream, and as far as possible to accelerate it, four means of help are recommended: (1) association with good people, (2) the hearing of the teachings, (3) wise attention, and (4) a way of living that is in conformity with the Teaching. The first point coincides with the frequently mentioned "salutary friendship" (or friendship with people morally good, *kalyāṇamittatā*). How this, particularly, was considered as promoting the spiritual life is evident in many places in the Canon. (See especially: Ud 4.1; AN 9:3; It 17.) It is a valuable exterior aid for the religious, whilst its internal and equally precious concomitant is "wise attention" (It 16, 17). The hearing of the teachings cannot be too highly valued, for, particularly in olden times, it constituted the chief means of impressing the most important discourses and maxims on the memory. As regards the way of life, which should conform in every respect to the teachings, this is only a shorter rendering of the demand made in the pattern of the Noble Way:

> "He is pure in morals, and lives restrained within the restrictions which are binding for a monk (*pātimokkha*); in conduct and deportment he is dignified, sees danger in the smallest things he should avoid, and exercises himself in the rules which he has taken upon himself to observe" (DN 11, 42; MN 53; 107; 125; Ud 4.1; AN 9:3).

This holds for the case in which the *sotāpanna* is a monk; if he is a lay-follower (*upāsaka*), in place of the above demands he is required to show his mastery and self-control by means of faithful and exact observance of the five general precepts: not to take life, not to take what is not given, not to pursue immorality, not to speak falsehood, and not to indulge in intoxicating drinks and narcotics (AN 5:179). Naturally, there is also required of the lay *sotāpanna* unshakable confidence in the Buddha, the Dhamma and the Sangha in addition to holding firmly to the main principles of a moral life.

After what has been said, it follows as a matter of course that the actual entry into the Stream must itself have a beneficial effect for the follower of the Path, and this is brought into particular prominence in the Canon. The stream-entrant has to expect what are called the six benefits: "He becomes firm and sure in the Dhamma; he is not liable to backsliding; if he presses on perseveringly to the end of his way, he is free from suffering (in so far as he is no more exposed to any bad rebirth); he becomes possessed of a knowledge beyond the ordinary; he penetrates into the causal connexion of all things" (AN 6:37).

It was said repeatedly that the *sotāpanna*, as all *sekhas*[1], is no longer liable to a bad rebirth in one of the realms of misery. How do the Canonical texts pronounce on future rebirths of those who have entered the Stream? "Those who understand the Four Noble Truths set forth with profound wisdom by the Teacher, however negligent they may be, they do not reach, an eighth existence" (Sn 230; Khp 11.9). "Insofar as that person understands the Noble Truths in right wisdom, after having been reborn at most seven times, through the destruction of all the fetters (as Arahat) he

1. *Sekha*, a learner not yet perfected; so are called the three persons who have attained the stages prior to Sainthood, namely that of the Stream Entrant, the Once-returner and the Non-returner.

makes an end to suffering" (It 24). These statements, if taken in conjunction with other texts, point necessarily to the "stream-entrant." Thus the *sotāpanna* will be reborn at most seven times, until he has entirely forced his way out of the entanglement; this is, by the way, a good example of the extension of the Path which reaches far beyond the short span of a single lifetime. Where do the prospective rebirths take place? The texts say that they do so in the lowest of the three world-spheres, i.e. in the *kāma-loka*. Since the person who has entered the Stream can no more be reborn in the realms of misery (hell, the animal states, and the realm of ghosts), there are available for him the world of men and the six lesser heavens of the *kāma-loka*, the so-called *deva-loka*. And the texts state expressly "consequent upon full destruction of the three fetters he becomes "one who is reborn at most seven times, wandering through seven rebirths amongst gods and men, he will make an end to suffering"(AN 3:86; 87; 9, 12; 10:63. Concerning the rebirth of a *sotāpanna* in a deva-heaven, compare the story contained in Udāna 5.3).

The texts emphasize that the *sotāpanna* will be reborn at most seven times, whence follows that, in certain circumstances, even less than seven embodiments may await him. And for this there is ample corroboration in the texts. He can be reborn two or three times exclusively in the human world under favourable circumstances, before attaining the final goal; he is then "one who goes from one noble clan to another" (*kolaṅkola*). Indeed, it is even possible that a stream-entrant as "one who germinates only once more" (*ekabījin*), has only one more rebirth to expect, and that in the human world (AN 3:86; 87; 9:12; 10:63). But it is very questionable whether this threefold division was known in the early days of Buddhism. Older in comparison with it is the teaching that the *sotāpanna*, after he has laid aside the three fetters and has won a deep insight into the Four Noble Truths, has escaped from the worlds of suffering and will enter the worlds of becoming at most seven times (MN 6; 22; 34; 68. Sn 230. It 24).

In general, the *sotāpanna* ranks as a religious aspirant who, although firm in moral discipline (*sīla*), has not yet fully but only partially reached perfection in the two other sections of the teaching of the path: mind-development and higher wisdom (A III 85, 86; 9, 12). To this mastery in the moral discipline (*sīla*) corresponds then rebirth in a lesser deva-heaven or in the human world under favourable circumstances. And in so far as moral discipline (*sīla*) forms the essential preliminary condition for the right unfolding of *samādhi* and of the higher wisdom (DN 16:1; 2.4; 2.20; 4.2–4. AN 5:22), *sotāpanna*hood is, in fact, the first step, the first stage, on the road to Arahantship.

The first "three fetters" which are brought to dissolution on the way to entry into the Stream, particularly through deep meditation on the Fourfold Truth of Suffering (MN 2) are: 1. the belief in personality, i.e. in a persisting ego-entity, 2. sceptical doubt, 3. belief in the efficacy of customs and ritual acts. The disciple who achieves the dissolution of these three fetters is characterised by the stereotyped formula: "As a result of having burst the three fetters, as one who has entered the stream, is exempt from rebirth in states of woe; he is assured of attaining to full enlightenment" (DN 16: 16.2.7. MN 6; 22; 34; 68; 118. Ud V 3).

The first of the three fetters is the belief in personality, *sakkāya-diṭṭhi.* It concerns a *diṭṭhi,* a view, a belief, which today is still the overruling view of the mass of mankind. The Pali word translated here as "personality" is a compound formed from *sat* and *kāya* (*sakkāya* = *satkāya*). *Sakkāya* comprises the "five groups of clinging to existence" (*upādānakkhandha*). "These five groups of clinging the Exalted One has called personality (*sakkāya*), i.e., the group of corporeality, of feeling, of perception, of mental formations (*saṅkhāra*) and consciousness" (MN 44). It is this personality in which the worldly-minded person fancies himself to consist, in that he regards the transitory fivefold clinging-complex as *sat,* that is as the essential and ultimately real. *Sakkāyadiṭṭhi* is, then, the view (*diṭṭhi*) that the fivefold clinging-complex is the truly existing, the true nature or essence. This erroneous view, taking the transitory and evanescent organic processes for the permanent and unchangeable core of a living being is therefore that belief in personality, which the Suttas describe in this way: "An ordinary, untaught man regards the corporeal form as the self, or the self as with form, or he sees the corporeal form in the self, or the self in the corporeal form; he regards feeling as the self, or the self as endowed with feeling, or he sees feeling in the self or the self in feeling; ... perception; ... the mental functions; ... or the self in consciousness. So arises the belief in personality " (M 44; 109). To state the matter in another way, the belief in personality—known in this aspect as the *attavāda* (positive) teaching of the self—is described as follows: "An ordinary man, untaught, considers the corporeal form, feeling, perception, mental formations, and what there is seen, heard, thought, recognised, attained, and weighed in, the mind (i.e. consciousness) in this way: that is mine, that am I that is my self" (MN 22.8). This erroneous notion of consisting essentially in these five khandhas—aggregates—the *sotāpanna* must overcome, working himself out of it, incorporating himself, as it were, in the Buddha's standpoint. The point of view taken by the Buddha, diametrically opposed to this personality-belief, is that the experienced noble disciple no longer regards any of the five groups of clinging as the self, or the self as equipped with them (as essential qualities), that he does not see in them the self, nor the five khandhas, individually or collectively, as dwelling in the self (MN 44; 109). Rather, "Whatever there is of corporeal form, feeling, perception, mental formations, consciousness, past, future or present, as belonging to one's self or as foreign to the self, coarse or fine, ugly or beautiful, far or near, all this he must regard with right insight, according to reality: 'That is not mine, I am not that, that is not myself'" (MN 22, 8; especially MV 2.6; 38 ff.). All that he is capable of laying hold of with his mind and senses, presents itself to him as a sum of changing, transitory processes external to himself which are experienced as *dukkha* (suffering), as a condition of misfortune and as bondage. And it is a matter of importance in Buddhism, for just this step by step progress of alienation from the personality and the world of appearances constitutes already a considerable measure of deliverance. It is thus entirely logical that under the ten fetters to be broken *sakkāyadiṭṭhi* is named in the first place.

As the second fetter appears sceptical doubt (*vicikicchā*). Its opposite is the belief, the strong confidence (*saddhā*), in the Buddha, in the Dharma he declared, and in the community of the Sangha. Engaging in a matter with insufficient confidence, or with no confidence at all, will not lead to the desired goal. Shortly before his *parinibbāna*, the Buddha drew special attention to the fact that no one of the monks present would again be disturbed by any doubt or wavering whatever with regard to the Buddha, the Dhamma, the Sangha, the Way, and progression along the Way. Even the straggler would enter the Stream, exhaust the states of woe, and surely attain to full Enlightenment (DN 16.6.6).

The third and last fetter which will be torn away on the path of *sotāpatti* bears the name *sīlabbata-parāmāsa.* This term is to be understood as "to depend on external and ceremonial acts, prepossessed with ritual,"[2] in the belief that the practice of certain prescribed moral customs and ceremonies are conducive and necessary to salvation (see Dhp 271). The Pali Canon gives us an abundance of examples of what the Buddhists call *sīlabbata* and of what they reject for themselves.

By the widespread ascetic endeavours of the Buddha's time, we are led to recognise how strong in the India of that day was the interest in religious questions, how deep the longing induced throughout the general population for deliverance from rebirths

---

2. This translation, and the explanation that follows, is too narrow. Sīla refers to moral, virtuous practices, or precepts. For example, it is said of the stream-enterer that "he keeps the five precepts (*sīla*) unbroken, ... without grasping them, (but as a means) conducive to concentration." (SN 40.1: *sīlehi samannāgato hoti akhaṇḍehi ... aparāmaṭṭhehi samādhisaṃvattanikehi.*) This indicates that sīla includes the Buddhist precepts itself. The sotāpanna keeps the precepts strictly, but does not see them as the essence of the path, only as means (*upanisā*) to attain the concentration necessary to attain Nibbāna. The word *vata* literally means "duty" or "vow" and the term includes practices such as the "dog-vow" (MN 57).

The Mahāniddesa (Nid I 66–67, on Sn 782) gives a useful description of *sīlabbata*: "'Precepts and vows': There is *sīla* (precept) and there is *vata* (vow), and there is *vata* but not *sīla*. How is there *sīla* and *vata*? 'Here, a bhikkhu is virtuous: he dwells restrained with the restraint of the Disciplinary Code (*Pātimokkha*), ... he trains undertaking the training-rules (MN 6)'—the self-control, restraint, non-transgression: this is *sīla*. Whatever is undertaken (*samādāna*) is *vata*. How is there *vata* but not *sīla*? '(There are) eight factors of removing [defilements] (*dhutaṅga*): the factor of forest-dwelling, ... (Nid I 66).' This is called *vata* but not *sīla*. The undertaking of effort is *vata*. 'May only skin, tendons, and bones remain, may the flesh and blood in the body dry up: until having attained whatever (i.e., Nibbāna) can be attained by personal strength and power, there shall be no abating of effort (MN 70),' (thus) he exerts and exercises his mind. Such undertaking of effort: this is called *vata* but not *sīla*."

See also the note on *sīlabbata* in *Connected Discourses of the Buddha*, p. 726. (BPS editor)

and successive deaths. In spite of this, we encounter continuously inflexible holding to certain customs and ritual actions within and without the ascetic and Brahmanical groups. We find in the Pali Canon long lists of such "moral customs" (*sīlāni*) and ritual acts (*vattāni*) that were observed and practised by numerous ascetics. The basic position of the Buddha on the question of asceticism and religious practices generally is shown in the Canonical formula to be as follows: All kinds of asceticism and devout works during the practice of which bad qualities increase and good qualities diminish are not only worthless but are definitely harmful. Conversely, any kind of religious activity by the practice of which bad qualities vanish and good qualities grow and increase is valuable and salutary (AN 3:78; 10:94; compare also DN 8:15 ff., where it is shown that the rigorous and painstaking asceticism of a cultivated man, in the case that he is not schooled in moral discipline, is alienated from true asceticism, but that if he surrenders himself entirely to inner purification he deserves rightfully the name of "ascetic"). In the appraisal of ascetic practices, Buddhism at all times lays the main stress on the motive and sentiment on which the asceticism is practised.

In addition to the ascetic extravagances rejected by the Buddha, there is also a whole range of usages, ritual or ceremonial, which, in wide circles, were considered as very important, partly even as necessary, to purification. In the first place stands sacrifice, particularly the blood sacrifice of animals, which played such a great part in Brahmanism and which the Buddha opposed with the greatest resolution in the first sīla (not to destroy life). In the Canon this sacrifice is often mentioned with allusion to its useless and pernicious nature. He who offers a fire sacrifice and erects the sacrificial pile already draws, even before the sacrifice is carried out, three evil swords to create suffering and pain: a sword of the thought, a sword of speech, and a sword of deed; for thereby he contemplates how many animal sacrifices shall be offered; he gives the order to the slaughter, and then he himself lays his hands to complete the bloody work (AN 8:44). Once when a Brahman asked the Buddha whether he approved of sacrifice, the Buddha answered that he did not approve of every sacrifice but that he also did not disapprove of every sacrifice. He approved of a sacrifice not of the sort in which many kind animals were destroyed but of that which is untiring giving; the latter is truly productive of merit. Such a sacrifice finds full approval by the Venerable Ones and by those who have trodden the way to deliverance (AN 4:39–40). For the monk who in fulfilment of his renunciation of the world has disposed of all earthly possessions, the sacrifice of giving consists in the offering and spreading of the Dhamma. And this gift of the Dhamma, it is stated, is greater than all other gifts (Dhp 354).

Besides the sacramental sacrifice in its manifold gradations, there were in India of the olden days many customs, ritual in character, which likewise come within the Buddhist conception of *sīlabbata.* There existed a kind of baptismal ceremony, a ritualistic bathing and cleansing, especially in certain waters considered to be holy. The subject of *sīlabbata* deserves our full attention and consideration because it informs us of the position taken by the Buddha concerning religious activities in general. We see here his basic rejection of rigid ritual insofar as one understands that expression to mean a holding to the belief that the practice of certain customs, rites and ceremonies further one's true deliverance. We see, further, his unconditional rejection of every matter of cult which stands in opposition to the law of morality as taught by him, especially in animal sacrifice, and many ascetic practices which are not conductive to corporeal well-being. But we also become aware of the tendency springing up in Buddhism to spiritualise certain ritual and ceremonial actions, to fill their form with new purport, to give them a deeper significance, as though to raise them to a higher sphere. The sacrifice of animals is replaced by the sacrifice of giving, sharing and charity; in place of the ritual washings in waters we have the inner cleansing of the Dhamma, and so on. If we add to this the fact that the Buddha's teaching opened the doors to persons of all castes, races, classes, and standing, we have indeed a great reforming movement which in its cultural aspect can hardly be overestimated.

But the first stage of the Path consists in the accomplishment and exact observance of moral discipline. Yet when moral discipline is earnestly practised, whether by monks or in lay circles, the individual man becomes more refined, nobler, more reflective; from such men is built a noble community, a highly moral family, a spiritually healthy population in village, town, and nation. A strongly moral man is more mature, thinks more clearly, sees more keenly; of that which he formerly sought he will recognise much as worthless or harmful and will lay it aside. That Buddhism in India was defeated by Brahman reaction has for its basic reason not a weakness of the system as contrasted with its older rival, but its complete degeneration, its falling away from the original ideal.

Thoughts on the Buddha's "Fire-Discourse"

by Dr. Anton Kropatsch

Translated from the German text by A. A. G. Bennett. All quotations are translated as from the German text provided.

In his celebrated "Fire-Discourse," the Buddha says:

> "Everything, O monks, burns. And what, O monks, is this "everything" that burns? The eye burns, the corporeal forms burn, the sight-consciousness burns, the sight-contact of the eye with the objects burns, the sensation released through contact, whether of pleasure, displeasure, neither-pleasure nor-displeasure, this also burns. The ear and the sounds, the nose and the scents, the tongue and the tastes, the body and the things of touch, thought and the objects of thought burn; the ear-consciousness, the smell-consciousness, the taste-consciousness, the touch-consciousness, the thought-consciousness burn; the contact of the ear, nose, tongue, body, thought and their objects burn; the sensations released by contact, whether pleasant, unpleasant or neutral, these also burn. And why do they burn? I say: They burn because of the fire of greed, because of the fire of hatred, because of the fire of delusion; they burn because of birth, old age and death, tribulation, sorrow and pain, through grief and despair."

For the Buddha, all being and happening in the world, universally, without differentiating between subject and object, dissolves into an uninterrupted and persisting activity. For this unceasing, ever-enduring operation he chooses the apt description: It burns, it goes on burning. But does this not set the animate in relation to the inanimate in an unreal manner—in a manner not in agreement with practical reality? Can one, then, equate the living expressions of the organism with the inorganic process of burning; indeed, can one compare them with each other at all? Can the gulf which stretches between animate and inanimate material be so easily closed; are we not, in this attempt, subject to a deception which results from a similarity existing only in our own minds?

Opinions against this, as well as those in favour of it, seem to have their justification. Against the Buddha's comparison—assuming that behind his words there lay no more than a comparison—experience tells that, in the domain of the animate, laws pertain which are quite different from those in the realm of the inanimate. The processes of nutrition, change of matter, and growth, the most important biological processes, obey not only physical laws, as for example those of gravitation, but they belong to a domain of laws peculiar to themselves which seems to remove them sharply from the realm of inorganic material. Not only biologists, but also philosophers, like Nicolai Hartmann, will have nothing to do with a setting aside of the enclosing boundaries.

Yet on the opposite side, such a distinguished modern research scientist as C. F. von Weizsäcker says: "In the characterization of the animate, the concept of the individual complies with a specific form of the totality. Thus a crystal can grow without limit and a part of it is still a crystal; the butterfly has neither attribute. In this connection, one recalls processes like growth, assimilation, and propagation by which constantly new material develops to bearers of the same form with the same associated function. Yet, one can also point to every single phenomenon of this kind in physical types. By way of example, a "simple" candle-flame has the aforementioned characteristics of individuality such as assimilation and the possibility of propagation." With these words von Weizsäcker really goes further than the Buddha; he not only compares, but he equates—a proceeding which cannot follow absolutely from the Buddha's Discourse. In modern materialism, which can, perhaps, best be described by the term "Dynamic Materialism," and which the Russian biologist Oparin advocates, life does not originate fortuitously from inorganic material, as seemed to the materialism of past centuries the most probable case, but the simplest living organisms are to be apprehended as a "definite stage of the universal historical development of the material." Thereby interior and exterior factors have been responsible for the origin of life on the earth. The principal effective interior factor is to be found in the activity of catalysators, identical with ferments. These ferments alter, especially accelerating, the chemico-physical relations peculiar to the inorganic material, in such a way that they become "life-processes." The transitions are demonstrated in the colloidal reactions of the albumen. The decisive external factor is Darwin's "Natural Selection," probably in conjunction with mutations: "The fastest reaction wins the race."

But of this there can be no doubt: however much one exerts oneself to bring together macrophysics and macrobiology, to induce the latter from the former and to show it as the natural continuation, the forging of the chain of evidence has always something artificial; it is due more to the spasmodic effort of a single investigator with a biased conception of the world than to a natural penetration of Reality. This took a new turn when Microphysics and Microbiology, to an ever-increasing extent, came into the purview of research. One recognises now, or at least one thinks one recognises, that the connecting band between inanimate material and living organisms must be sought in strata of reality which formerly, in the days of classical Physics and Biology, were closed to the investigator's eye. Thus has modern Physics, as the first, led over from the static world-picture of classical times with its material particles and energies motivating them, to a dynamical picture in which Plank's "Quanta of Action" play the decisive role. From now on, the emphasis of physical knowledge is shifted from macrophysics to the microphysical events of the "physical underworld," as Pascual Jordan names the realm of microphysics. Modern Biology follows the new trend; for this new Biology the mutations, the sudden transitions within the heritage-content of the embryo, gain an ever-increasing significance. In the case of the important mutations arising from exterior influence, particularly the "ray-induced" mutations, only one quantum of action is already able to influence a gene, the elementary unit of the reproductive event, so that, as a result of its alteration, macrobiological effects make their appearance. The aforementioned physicist Pascual Jordan, who has become famous by his studies dedicated to the borderline territory between microphysics and microbiology, says :

"The rooting in the microphysical and the emerging into the macrophysical may be characteristic and essential to life in equal measure." For Jean Gebser, "the teaching of the mutations follows the Planck theory, by which is established that the development is not continuous (constant and in a straight line) but occurs by means of "quanta" (with interruptions)." Physics and Biology obey similar laws. For here, as there, according to Heisenberg the "quantum of action" is the "intrinsic and final elementary particle of nature" which is split into an organic and an inorganic realm for our minds only. Jordan says: "The aspect of the Quantum Physics laws of reaction forces on us, in a distinction hardly to be avoided, the impression of certain traces of the living-state"; and: "The unity and totality of an organism, that is, its individuality, in which form alone all life in this world always occurs, must in the last instance signify nothing other than the centralised steering of its reactions." But according to the same investigator this steering proceeds on microphysical lines.

The more knowledge of microphysics and microbiology progresses, the more that which in macrophysics and macrobiology is still hypothesis and debatable theory advances to a passage by verified experiment, between living and dead material for which Planck's "quanta," as the final elementary particles, are common basic and building material, in so far as one may apply to an essentially dynamical event, the concepts end descriptions of substantiality such as these. Does not the Buddha avoid just such an error in description when He speaks of a "burning," when for Him the dynamic basic structure of reality, which Whitehead calls a "network of events," is an activity without an activator? But can we carry over the imagery of the flame and the burning, which we employ for the characterizing of the physical processes of the living organism, to the mental processes also? Are these not separated from the physiological processes of the material body by a greater distance than is the material body from the inanimate material? Not for the Buddha, and not for modern psychology. A dualistic opinion is foreign to both; for both, physical and psychical processes stand in close connection. They have one and the same dynamic basic character, which reduces the more or less artificial boundaries between Physiology and Psychology to vanishing point; their common ground of origin, the "*saṅkhāras*" of Buddhist terminology, engages the latest research of Rhine in the territory of the Body-Soul problem.

In the Buddha's teaching, at the centre of all psychical events stands "*taṇhā*," thirst, will. It is the intrinsic motive agency of life which, from the first moment of our being onwards, fills us with rudimentary power and lies at the base of all psychical phenomena. The Buddha says: "It is thirst that creates man"; the biologist Driesch: "We know that there is at least an elementary basic factor, our own will"; the psychologist Rohracher: "The will to live is the strongest and most direct psychical fact"; and finally, most clearly, the religious philosopher Drews: "In the analysis of the content of our consciousness, the final principle we strike is the will. It lies at the base of all the content of consciousness as its essential foundation and bearer.—In the content of our consciousness there is no activity of a mental nature, no movement, no change which is not introduced through will and which would not be consummated through its agency.—Accordingly, the will is indeed the principle of mental activity, the basic attribute of all the life of our consciousness, so far as this is really a life. Every individual is, in point of fact, a being of will or impulse, a bundle of impulse, wishes and strivings, which are held together in him by a concealed power, but a power which we have to understand again as a will." The Buddhist Dahlke says similarly when he comments on the Buddhist "thirst" as follows: "Thirst is the power through which a living being constantly arises new." Thus one can say: "I am thirst, in the sense that nothing remains of me but this thirst, this burning." If then the thirst ceases, there remains no being deprived of thirst, but the whole play of being ceases, is extinguished, as the flame is extinguished when it ceases to burn. It is throughout nothing more than this burning. Even so is 'I' nothing more than this thirst.

With these words of Dahlke we come again to the utterance of the Buddha's "Fire Discourse." The world around us, we ourselves in our physical and psychical expressions of life, are no other than an activity, an event without a nucleus, without the quiescent pole of a self in the flux of phenomena. Everything is an activity, an operation, a burning. Indeed this latter description forces itself on us directly, if we are led by the Buddha and by modern Natural Science to a new consideration of Reality.

Professor Paley's Famous Clock-Argument

by Max Ladner

About 150 years ago, W. Paley, Professor of Theology at Cambridge, presented in one of his books the famous "clock" argument, which he intended to be irrefutable proof of the existence of a Creator—God. It runs as follows:

> "Wherever we find orderliness and meaningful arrangement, made to serve definite purpose, we can be reasonably certain that these owe their origin to the workings of an intelligent being. Supposing we look at a clock. From its ingenious mechanism we are led to the conclusion that it must have been put together by a master of his craft, who knew its purpose and constructed the mechanism accordingly. The different parts of the clock could not have come into being by themselves nor could they have assembled themselves. And if we assume that the clock has been so ingeniously constructed that it could even reproduce its own kind, our admiration for the craftsman's skill would be boundless. The world we live in is far more ingeniously constructed than a mere clock. It stands to reason, therefore, it must have had a creator."[3]

What is to be said of this argument? Does it actually present cogent proof for the existence of a creator? We shall see.

A clock may be of excellent workmanship and run accurately, or it may be poorly constructed and not at all dependable. The clockmaker who produces a timepiece of the highest order deserves praise for his handiwork, whereas the less skilled mechanic lays himself open to criticism and ridicule; it would have been better had he kept his hands off his work altogether.

This world of ours is certainly wonderfully constructed and it seems—at first sight, at least—that every part in it manifests order and purpose. But to call this world *perfect* is open to serious doubt.

---

3. Translated from the German Version.

When we look at MAN, the apex and crown of creation, on every side we see him exposed to ruin and destruction. Of this there is further an abundance of horrible examples in nature: plants and trees in their struggle for air and light are choked to death by parasitical growths. Animals feed on animals, stalking and devouring each other. Human beings are suffering from incurable diseases, insanity, pain, misery, famine and inescapable death. There is enmity, hatred, bloodshed and war. There are epidemics, earthquakes, and volcanic eruptions. To speak of a "perfect" world in the face of this catalogue of horrors betrays only lack of insight and an immature mind.

And how are we to explain the riddle of an all-knowing Creator whose very essence is said to be Love, to have brought forth so much suffering and cruelty, such palpable imperfections, incongruities and shortcomings? To which only one answer can be given: either he could not do it any other way or he did not want to. In the first case he is powerless, in the second he must be held responsible for the untold miseries his own creatures have to endure. As the creator of such a world he must be condemned; as the originator of human and animal suffering he bears the distinctive mark of an evil demon.

Paley's argument, in fact, is a classical example of false reasoning. To build a clock a clockmaker needs a great variety of materials. He cannot make the clock out of nothing. Therefore a world-creator could not have fashioned the universe without pre-existing matter. The material elements, called solids, liquids, fiery and gaseous, how were they created? Out of nothing? Or by magic? And who created primeval matter? Another creator?—and from what?

A second theory of creation has been proposed, which appears in a philosophical garb and has been called the Doctrine of Emanation. The exponents of this theory consider the universe as having issued from the essence of God whereby the unfathomable essence of God remained unchanged. Aside from the fact that such an assumption is quite gratuitous and arbitrary, the question of the purpose and the meaning of such an emanation remains unanswered. Still more, what were the reasons or motives behind such an out-flowing? Of this we cannot have any knowledge. Any argument advanced to support the emanation theory lacks a sound foundation in fact and is not verifiable.

Can we imagine the same clockmaker who—as in a dream—conjures up the steel for the spindles, the silver or gold for the casing—out of nothing? Such an incredible feat of magic not even Professor Paley could have been able to conceive. And what he never would credit a clockmaker with, *that* he expects of a being he does not even know and of which he cannot have the slightest conception. By way of analogy, taking his and the clockmaker's existence as a starting point, he draws from it the inference that, like the clock, man and the world, too, must have a maker.

It goes without saying that to construct a perfect clock requires above all—apart from technical skill—a clear mind and consciousness. Consciousness, however, does not function without a bodily organism; a free-floating consciousness, without some kind of physical substratum, is unthinkable. Furthermore, consciousness implies purposive thinking or planning. Consequently, the assumed world-creator must be endowed with a consciousness to plan and to execute his ideas. In other words, he would have to be thought of as being equipped with a kind of bodily organism through which alone his consciousness could function.

This leads again to the question about the nature and origin of the physical substance through which the creator's consciousness functions, and further to the question who the creator of the creator is, and so on *ad infinitum.* Whence it follows how poorly Professor Paley's argument has been thought-out, which was demonstrated by following it through to its absurd consequences.

There is a tendency in human beings to interpret each and everything according to one's own needs; it is no easy task to disabuse oneself of the mistaken idea that every single event must have a "meaning" and a "purpose." In human life situations arise sometimes that create the impression of a higher power at work, or of an intelligence superior to our own. This leads to the mistaken idea of a superhuman agency, or some mysterious, divine guiding power behind the scene, leading everything to its preordained destination. Hereby one fundamental fact is almost always overlooked, that man finds himself, like any other living being, in a set of circumstances to which he adapts himself. And likewise, in accordance to which his behaviour patterns develop. The decisive factor here is anything but the wisdom and understanding of a world-creator. This is a specific human situation with its problems and challenges; and it remains the noble task of serious research to find order in the tangled web of human volitions.

Man instinctively rebels against the idea that life has no meaning or purpose whatsoever. But as so often, here too, man overlooks the obvious, i.e. that it is only man's prerogative to endow his acts with meaning and purpose. In this respect man always undervalues himself when, instead of facing the inevitable, he tries to find comfort in a divine intelligence. There is no single fact in nature to support such a belief. Besides, nature cares nothing about man's happiness or misery. Thus the endless quest for the why's and wherefore's of existence continues. This is a far cry from Prof. Paley's way of thinking. The solution has been found: it can be gained from the teaching of the Exalted One, from the Doctrine of the Buddha, who, two and one half thousand years ago, found Enlightenment under the Bodhi-tree.

Einsicht, Vol. 7 No. 9.

Void is the World
The Buddhist Doctrine of Cognition

by Kurt Schmidt

Thus spoke the Exalted One:

> "Regard the world as void, Mogharāja, and be always mindful: thus will you be able to overcome death! Who regards the world thus, the King of Death sees him not." (Sn 1119).

This also was said by the Blessed One:

> "In this body of six foot height with its perceiving and its consciousness, is contained the world, the arising of the world, the end of the world, and the way that leads to the end of the world." (AN 4:45)

And again the Exalted One has spoken thus:

> "When, O Monk, for some reason or other, various perceptions of world-expansion enter into a man's awareness (*papañca-saññā-saṅkhā*) and he takes neither delight nor gratification in them, nor clings to them—this is the end of both lusting and anger-propensities; the end of opinionative, doubting, and conceit-propensities; the end of craving-propensities toward renewed existence; the end of nescience-propensities; this is the end of fights and wars, of contentions, strife, discord, slander and lies. It is here that those unwholesome things cease."

After these words the Exalted One rose from his seat and went to his room inside the monastery. Thereupon, the Bhikkhus who were present, requested the venerable Mahā-Kaccāna to explain the Buddha's utterance. Kaccāna first advised them to address the Buddha himself, but when the Bhikkhus insisted that he should give them his explanation, the venerable Mahā-Kaccāna spoke thus:

> "When eyes and visual objects are present, visual-consciousness arises; from the conjunction of the three, contact (sense-

impression). Through contact sensation (feeling) arises. What one senses (feels) that is perceived. What one perceives is worked upon by the mind into concepts. Whereof the mind has formed concepts that is expanded as the external world (*papañceti*). What one expands as the external world is nothing but those manifold perceptions of the external world that enter into a man's awareness by way of visible forms, be they past, future, or present.

"When ears and sounds are present, consciousness of hearing arises ... when nose and odours are present, consciousness of smelling ... when tongue and flavours are present, consciousness of taste arises ... when body and tangible objects are present, body-consciousness (touch) arises ... when mind (the organ of thought) and ideas are present mind-consciousness arises; from the conjunction of the three a contact (impression) arises. Contact (impression) being present sensation (feeling) arises. What one senses (feels) that is perceived. What one perceives is worked upon by the mind into concepts. The concepts so formed are expanded into the external world; what is thus expanded as the external world is nothing but these manifold perceptions of the external world that enter into man's awareness in the form of ideas, be they past, future or present."

And the venerable Kaccāna said further: "When the eyes are present, visual objects are present, and visual consciousness is present, then it is possible that what is called contact (sense impression) will occur. When contact (impression) is present, then it is possible that what is called sensation will occur. When sensation is present, then it is possible that what is called perception will occur. When perception is present, it is possible that what is called the forming of concepts will occur. When forming of concepts is present, that what is called the affecting of the mind by perceptions of the outside world of plurality will occur."

In the same words the occurrence of the other five perceptions is explained. Then follows the negative statement:

"When eyes, visual objects and visual consciousness are absent, there is no possibility that what is called impression (contact) will occur. When contact (impression) is absent, there is no possibility that what is called sensation will occur. When sensation is absent, there is no possibility that what is called perception will occur. When perception is absent, there is no possibility that what is called forming of concepts will occur. When concepts are absent, that what is called the manifold perceptions of the external world have no possibility of entering the mind."

And again, the same is said about the other five senses. Then the venerable Mahā-Kaccāna continues:

"This, friends, as I understand it, is the meaning in full of the Blessed One's brief utterance, but if the venerable Bhikkhus so wish, they may go and inquire from the Exalted One himself, and as he answers, thus you may bear it in mind." (Majjhima Nikāya 18)

The Bhikkhus did so and the Exalted One replied: "Capable and wise is Mahā-Kaccāna, O Bhikkhus. If you had questioned me about this matter, I would have explained it to you in the same way. This is the very meaning of it and thus you may preserve it."

This utterance of the Buddha as explained by Mahā-Kaccāna is a genuine sutta (Sanskrit: sūtra), that is a basic "thread" of thought, a concise maxim, a collection of keywords to be memorized, elaborated and explained orally. It was in the form of such pithy sayings that in ancient India the doctrines of the sages were committed to memory and passed on from teacher to pupil. Along with these suttas or concise sayings, a more or less free commentary to them was handed down at the same time, as in the case of many passages of the Pali Canon; moreover the venerable Kaccāna added even a second commentary which we have quoted above beginning with the words: "And the venerable Kaccāna said further ..." The wording of these two commentaries is as firmly established as that of the Master's own words found in that Sutta. Within the community of monks these commentaries themselves will have been further expounded, and this, in some case, doubtlessly also in free speech. Also for us, in present times, such further explanation is necessary.

If one contemplates the Buddha's utterance by itself, the emphasis seems to be on the ethical aspect. If one frees oneself from attachment to worldly things, one will overcome all evil states of mind and attain to final peace. The Buddha doubtlessly felt the necessity to hold forth to his disciples in an especially impressive way on this essential doctrine so frequently expounded by him. But trained Bhikkhus, though familiar with that doctrine, noticed immediately that this time the Buddha wanted to convey something special and new which they had not yet heard from him. This special viewpoint was rightly traced by them to the word *papañca* which obviously is here the key word requiring attention and explanation.

This word was rarely used and, in addition, it carried several meanings; therefore the Bhikkhus asked the venerable Mahā-Kaccāna, known to be learned and wise, for an elucidation. Also Kaccāna noticed immediately that everything hinged on the word *papañca* and he also knew the significance hidden "behind" the term. He therefore ignored the ethical content of the Buddha-word as being well known and engaged exclusively in a detailed explanation of the word *papañca*.

According to the Pali dictionaries, this word means: diffuseness, copiousness; delay, procrastination, obstacle and, in the religious sense, any evil state that hinders the spiritual progress of man. The Sanskrit equivalent *prapañca* means also the visible universe. Obviously it is in this philosophical meaning that the Buddha had used the word. This was unusual and the disciples desired an explanation. Kaccāna told them that it had that philosophical meaning and the Buddha confirmed it afterward.

But that brief saying of the Buddha has still further implications. "When for some reason or another various perceptions of '*papañca*,' the external world, enter into a man's awareness ..." he said, and an explanation was required of its meaning. How do in fact the various perceptions of the *papañca* enter the human mind? In philosophical language this means: "How does cognition of the world come about in man?" Or, as Kant expressed it: How is cognition possible? This is the basic problem of the Theory of Knowledge, that Kant, as the first philosopher in the West solved in his *Critique of Pure Reason*. But from the 18th Sutta of the Majjhima-Nikāya, we learn that, long before Kant, the Buddha had seen the problem and solved it, and that Kaccāna knew the solution and was able to explain it in accordance with the Buddha's insight. Although the wording of that solution as expressed by these two great thinkers differs—quite understandably, since they lived more than 2000 years apart—yet the meaning is the same. And necessarily so, inasmuch as to the problem there can be only one correct solution. Kaccāna starts his exposition, first of all, with the activity of the six senses. These are the five external senses, familiar to all of us, and as the sixth, the inner sense, the receptivity for external mental phenomena. As to the eye, the organ of vision, correspond visible things (*rūpa*), so to the organ of the inner sense, *manas*, correspond non-corporeal mental things (*dhamma*). Hence *manas* is to be understood as an organ having the capacity to receive impressions from the outside which are not conveyed by the five external senses. In other words: *manas* is either the organ for perceiving the ideas and concepts formed in the subconscious by the *saṅkhāras*, or the organ of telepathy, spatial clairvoyance, thought-reading and similar phenomena. Which of the two meanings the word *manas* may have in this context has to be left undecided. At any rate, it must signify the organ that receives nonmaterial stimuli affecting man's psyche from outside, otherwise *manas* would not be analogous to eye, ear, nose, tongue and body-sensitivity.

Included in the fifth sense, the body-sensitivity (*kāya*), are several receptivity-types: apart from the tactile sense, proper, which distinguishes hard and soft, solid and liquid, also the muscular sensations belong to it, which provide the basis for such concepts as motion and rest, long, broad, high, etc., i.e. extension in space, and also the sense for temperature and other qualitative sensations.

The receptivity of the senses, i.e. the capacity to register impressions or, according to Kant, "to be affected by objects," constitutes what Kant calls "sensibility" (*Sinnlichkeit*). Let us now compare the first part of Kaccāna's exposition with the beginning of Kant's *Critique of Pure Reason*, chapter 1 :

> "In whatever manner and by whatever means a mode of knowledge may relate to objects, sense perception is that through which all thought as a means is directed. This again

is only possible to man at least, in so far as the mind is affected in a certain way. The capacity (receptivity) for receiving representations through the mode in which we are affected by objects is called sensibility."

Objects are given to us by means of sensibility, and it alone yields us perceptions; they are thought through the intellect and from the intellect arise concepts. But all thought must, directly or indirectly, by way of certain characters, relate ultimately to sense perception and therefore with us to sensibility, because in no other way can an object be given to us. "The effect of an object upon the faculty of representation so far as we are affected by it, is sensation. By means of an outer sense, a property of our mind, we represent to ourselves objects as outside us, and all without exception in space. In space their shape, magnitude, and relation to one another are determined or determinable." So for Kant is not the meaning exactly, almost sentence after sentence, the same as that expounded by Kaccāna? Let us summarize it once more: If there is sense receptivity (Kant's "Sensibility"), contact with the sense objects can take place; we can be "affected" by them. Through contact a sensation can arise. Sensation is something non-material, psychical. It is non-spatial and does not contain anything spatial. But at least for the fivefold sense perception, sensation has also no duration but is strictly tied to the present moment. The present moment is nothing more than a point between past and future. Just as a spatial point has no extension, a point or instant in time has no duration either.

But here we must make a reservation: the statement that a point has no extension holds good only for pure mathematics, which deals with thought-constructs. In nature there are no mathematical points, hence there are also no mathematical time-instants in reality whose duration would equal zero; and the present, being the time between past and future, is not zero but is only of unnoticeably and immeasurably brief duration. If the present were equal to zero, so would also be sensation; hence never could any perception originate from a sensation, whatever number of sensations may be added to each other. The duration of a single sensation is so brief that, for our ordinary perception, it almost equals zero. In the very moment of a sensation's arising it has already vanished. The sensation is not perceived, it is not yet a perception; but it must be there as the basis of all perceptions. It is not a single sensation that can be perceived but only the synthesis of a sequence of sensations; and this synthesizing is performed by the mind (or intellect: *Verstand*).

This was also known to Dharmakirti, a great Buddhist philosopher of the 7th century CE, who wrote about this as follows:

> "The single moments are united in our consciousness into a series; the unity represented by that series exists only by virtue of our consciousness that unites the single moments to a series. Only the serial processes of united moments are clearly cognized by our consciousness. The single moment is entirely inaccessible to consciousness." (According to T. Stcherbatsky, *Buddhist Logic*)

While sensation is instantaneous and does not register in consciousness, perception takes place within time; it requires a definite, though very brief, duration and always combines in itself many single moments which already belong to the past. What we perceive is never what is actually present, but only that what has been, what has already vanished.

In ordinary life we do not notice this fact, because the interval between contact (first impression), sensation and perception is very brief.[4] But we can easily see that there is actually a difference in time between the state of the object that is to be perceived and the act of perceiving; if we think of the velocity of light and the time it needs to reach us from the sun or a star which are no longer at the position in which we see them. In the case of sound it is still easier to observe the time difference: when we hear the fall of a bomb, it has already exploded and done its damage. In these examples, however, the major part of the time-difference lies between the occurrence of the object and the sensation, and not between sensation and perception. But there is surely also a brief time interval between sensation and perception; and perception

4. According to the Buddhist psychology of Abhidhamma, the three phases here named, do not occur as isolated functions but within complete moments of consciousness in which the respective function is dominant. (Editor)

itself, unlike sensation, has a measurable duration in time, for which reason it can only relate to something past and gone.

Kaccāna says: "What one perceives of that one forms concepts"; Kant says the same in these words:

"If we give the name of "sensibility" to the receptivity of our mind to receive representations (percepts) when affected in some way, then the faculty to produce by itself representations or the spontaneity of cognition, is the "Intellect" (*Verstand*). It is inherent in our nature that sense perception (*Anschauung*) can never be anything else than sensuous, i.e. in exactly the same mode by which objects affect us. Whereas the faculty of turning the object over in one's mind is the intellect. None of these properties is preferable to the other. Without sensibility no object can be perceived, and without intellect no thinking about it can take place. Concepts without percepts are empty; percepts without concepts are blind. The intellect cannot perceive and the senses cannot conceive. From their union only can knowledge be produced." (Kant, *Elementar-lehre*, II.1)

Kaccāna continues: "Of what one has formed concepts that is expanded as the external world." Kant expresses the same idea as follows: "In order that certain sensations can he related to something outside myself, and likewise to be able to conceive them as extraneous to each other, and in juxtaposition, hence not only as different, but also as being at different places, antecedent to all that, the idea of space must be innate in us. Consequently the idea of space is not something abstracted from perceptual data, but, rather in and contributed by our minds, without which spatial conception would be impossible." (*Critique of Pure Reason*, I.2.)

The solution of the problem is thus the same: the expanse of the external world or the knowledge of the spatial world is produced by two factors of which both must be present. One factor is the receptivity of the senses, the "sensibility," due to which the senses come into contact with, or are affected by, anything outside the cognizing subject. The other factor is the mental activity of the same subject, the intellect, due to which the sensory data are summarized and integrated into the space-concept so that concepts of bodies can arise. The cooperation of the two factors is an unconscious one, and only the result of that cooperation comes into consciousness as the spreading-out, the expansion, of the external world. The nature of that "something" that comes into contact with the senses or affects the senses—Kant calls it the "thing-in-itself"—can never be known because it lies beyond the cognitive process. What we know as external world, is only the product of the impressions received from the senses and of the intellect. One example may illustrate this. The following is being perceived: with the eye something red in various shades and something green; with the nose. It's peculiar, lovely scent; with the touching finger a painful prick. These perceptions do not occur separately or by chance, but always in the same combination when attention is directed thereto. Then one will say: There is a thing that has the qualities perceived: it is red, below and close-by it is green, it smells lovely and pricks if touched. Such a thing is called a rose with stalk, leaves and thorns. The concepts "thing" and "rose" are formed by the intellect, and when it has formed them, it attributes to them as qualities the perceptions produced by the senses. What it is that causes the sensations from which the perceptions arise, we can never know. But this we can know that "thing" and "rose" are concepts formed by the intellect. The intellect is induced, and even compelled to do so by the regular concourse of the various perceptions, but nevertheless it creates these concepts by its own activity. As with all things, also the rose is a product of the mind, a thought construction; and so are our body, our personality, the whole world nothing but thought constructions. Hence that what we call the "world" is comprised in this body of six foot height, with its perceiving and its consciousness, as well as the arising of the world, the end of the world and the way leading to its end. And if we understand that the expansion, or diffuseness of the world comes to be in such a manner, then we shall regard the world as void. But if, on account of this knowledge, we regard the world as void, then all attachment to the world ceases and Death has lost its terror for us; he can no longer touch us: "The King of Death sees us not."

(Source unknown.)

The Root of Intuitive Perceptions

by Lionel Stützer

The human personality, according to the Buddha's teaching, is a combination of five "khandhas" or, better, the result of an interplay of five "aggregates of grasping": corporeality, feeling, perception, (mental) formations, and consciousness. This is a fact of existence and applies to every human being without exception. A being becomes human in contrast to other forms of existence, due to this interplay of his personality-components. In this essay an attempt will be made to show how the human personality experiences itself in relation to the external world, in other words, how he arrives at a Weltanschauung or a philosophical worldview. The worldview of a materialistic philosopher postulates that life in general, including mental phenomena, takes its rise from matter, i.e. through physical-chemical causes and processes, which again depend on antecedent causes of the same nature, and so on *ad infinitum*. Or, some of them assume a hypothetical beginning to which they attach quite gratuitously the labels of "primordial slime" and "primeval cosmic dust". All possible events are based on materiality; mental and psychological phenomena are reduced to cerebral processes, and the latter derive from metabolism. "As the liver secrets bile so the brain exudes thoughts." Consequently, the individual, defining himself in experience as a unit of material processes, will point to his body and exclaim: "This is I—my body!"

The Buddha teaches: "The body is not the self."

In contrast to the materialistic outlook based on the physical only, the religions of faith exhibit a distinctly emotional bias, centred mainly on feeling and sensation. The believer has no material proof for the existence of his "soul" but he "feels" it. He "senses" the presence of God, in his "soul." He "feels" himself as a child of God, as a wretched sinner, as one who is saved. The firm believer will never be convinced—the most flawless logical propositions notwithstanding—that only matter constitutes ultimate reality; for an "inner voice" is louder and drowns out all mere denials of the soul's existence. Whosoever identifies his personality with his feelings is a believing person, not yet imbued with knowledge, still dreaming.

The Buddha teaches: "Feeling and sensation are not the self."

There is another human type who is athirst for "knowledge." This one says: "Seeing is believing. " He is not satisfied with hypotheses nor with naive assumptions. He strains his perceptive faculties to the utmost and strives relentlessly towards a deeper understanding of events and their causal nexus. The scientist wants to substantiate, to prove, to demonstrate. Cause and effect in the world of form is being explored by chemical analysis and experiments in physics. Through the use of the microscope the invisible becomes visible; through the use of the telescope the farthest cosmic bodies are brought within the range of vision. Physics investigates the intangible world of energy, tracing its impact on the more tangible realms of experience. Science is neither materialistic nor spiritualistic, it can furnish "evidential proof" to both. To exalt perception and to define the essence of human personality by it, constitutes the scientific worldview.

The Buddha teaches: "Perception is not the self."

Again other people say: "Neither materialism which explains the phenomena of mind as an adventitious by-product of material events, nor religious faith, unable to prove its dogmas, nor science dissecting everything, yet incapable of finding the life-giving element, can satisfy the thinking mind. Only philosophy, the love of wisdom, that derives its power and reason for its existence from the faculties of the mind, is able to provide the seeker after truth with substantial nourishment." To erect one's own thought structures, to tear down those of others, to assemble and rend asunder word-images and concepts, to search for cognitive meanings through the organon of thought—that is how philosophy is understood by the great schools. He who builds his personality image on the basis of pure thought and identifies himself with his power of reasoning, synthetically or analytically, works on a philosophical world view which is as shifting and fluctuating as are the very thoughts themselves.

The Buddha teaches: "Mind is not the self."

But there are some who recognize: "The material world is one mode of nutrition, the world of feeling is another, and both are interwoven in the same fashion as perception, which digests material seized upon by sensation. Thinking, too, is a mode of nutrition, is grasping, digesting and eliminating of concepts. All food—intake, all grasping, takes its rise from craving, hunger, desire and volition. And desire, craving, spring from the roots of nescience, i.e. lack of insight into the three characteristics of all phenomena: impermanence, suffering and insubstantiality. It is through *consciousness* that these truths are revealed.

He who in clear consciousness realizes the true nature of things, has outgrown hypotheses and beliefs, speculations and vain imaginings. He intuits the interrelatedness of the psycho-somatic process and discovers the conditioned co-production of all phenomena. One who seeks in consciousness a clear insight into the nature of things as they are—is a Buddhist.

The Buddha teaches: "Consciousness is not the self."

These five aggregates of clinging constitute the transitory personality that enters the world at birth and passes away at death. This personality is the result of previous actions, just as one's present actions develop those tendencies which go into the making of a new personality in the next birth. This is not mere belief nor can it be objectively demonstrated. It is rather a conscious, immediately felt awareness of reality—not of the intellect, but the result of profound meditative absorption. This state can be achieved only by purifying the mind of all defilements. The Eightfold Noble Path leads to this purification by cultivating right views, right resolve, and through moral conduct. Evil tendencies should not be repressed but gradually weakened. Thus cleansed and prepared, the mind is freed of obstacles and ready for meditation. In meditation, *anattā* (non-ego) becomes fully realized; it ceases to be a debatable item in Buddhist theory with its pros and cons. *Anattā* (non-ego) is now the at-one-ment with the principle of Buddhahood, the state of being fully illuminated where the fetter of personality-belief has been done away with once and for all.

The Doctrine and the Norm of the Buddha is clear and well defined, its framework not difficult to comprehend. But behind its basic principles profound insights are hidden offering rich rewards for the true seeker only. "This is the Doctrine of the Exalted-One, well defined, timeless, stimulating, inviting, self-explanatory; the wise ones discover it in their innermost selves."

Die Einsicht, xi, 3/4

Of Cats and Monkeys

by Paul Debes

Animal behaviour is amongst the most fascinating sights to watch. We call the world of animals dumb because of their lack of speech, but they make up for this deficiency by the extraordinary care they take of their small and helpless young. Take the mother-cat for an example: at the slightest warning of danger, either from a hawk in the sky or a vicious dog on the ground, she will grab her kitten by the nape of its neck and swiftly carry it to a place of safety. It is an amusing spectacle to behold the helpless kitten, limp and fluffy like a powder-puff, hanging from the mouth of its mother. A mother-monkey and her young behaves quite differently. When danger threatens she does not take it in her mouth, it is the baby-monkey who clings to the mother's belly, and holding tightly on to her body, is carried by its mother up to the highest branches of a tree and out of danger.

From the habits of cats and monkeys the beginner on the Path to Enlightenment has much to learn. Although the Buddha himself did not use the term explicitly, the whole trend of His Noble Doctrine shows clearly that the "Way of the Monkey" is to be preferred to the "Way of the Cat." For the Exalted One teaches that a person aiming at Enlightenment cannot attain the goal without exerting his own willpower and vigorous effort. Which calls to mind the baby-monkey's holding on firmly to his mother's belly. And to carry the analogy a little further: just as it is the mother-monkey alone who senses the danger and not her baby—so the great Buddhas of all times have intuited the misery of all existence while untold generations of humans were totally blind of the fact of their being chained to the endless cycle of necessity with its ever-recurring rounds of birth and death. This blindness is the inevitable result of a mode of thinking enmeshed in worldly cares and weakened by the lures of sense gratification. Again we watch the baby-monkey who thoroughly frightened and by sheer animal instinct clings to his mother's belly where there is safety and security from danger. In the same way is the beginner on the Path shaken out of his false sense of security and becomes aware of the Misery that chains him to existence. Seriously he studies the Word of the Buddha and realises that only by clinging to His message a way to safety and complete security can be found. And just as the mother-monkey with her experience and strength leads all those young ones who trustingly cling to her, from danger to safety, so Right Views as expounded by the Buddha help those who hold on to them over obstacles, from present danger to perfect liberation.

And just as the baby-monkey, now clinging to his mother, will grow up in time and become alert to danger and the ways of escape, so will the disciple of the Buddha by practising Right Views gain more and more with every advancing step. He will gain in freedom from fear and misery; his life will be enriched; he will acquire peace and well-being. His mere belief in the efficacy and wholesomeness of Right Views will grow into knowledge and firm conviction.

Among some dedicated followers of the Buddha the thought may arise that confident clinging to Right Views alone might not be enough, that the disciple ought to strive with greater force, forging ahead in relentless battle until final victory is won. Those, however, who have progressed on the Path know from experience that every inch of advance depends on nothing else so much as to the steadfast clinging to Right Views. With these in mind and heart it is well-nigh impossible to give in to evil in thought, word or action. And yet, in spite of the fact that—as a residue from old habits—evil tendencies do still exist, if the disciple clings tenaciously to Right Views, he will in time free himself from unwholesome inclinations and move towards full Enlightenment.

Let therefore no one deceive himself that the Path can be travelled in the manner of cats. The very thought of it arises from weakness, begets more weakness, and leads nowhere. Rather let the Path be travelled in the manner of monkeys but with sufficient self-exertion and mindfulness.

Wissen und Wandel, 1962, No. 1.

The Way to Peace and Harmony

by Hellmuth Hecker

This is a Way, helpful and agreeable, which leads to Peace and Harmony. What is this Way? It is fourfold and consists of: Giving, Kind Words, Helpfulness, and Self-forgetfulness.

What is the Way of Giving?

Here a person is fond of sharing: he gives, makes presents, is generous, hospitable, magnanimous. Wherever he meets need and suffering he is ready to help. Wherever he can bring joy with a gift to someone, he gives it. His motive for giving is to alleviate want and to bring happiness. Giving makes him glad, makes him happy, fills his heart with joy. He is free from envy, ill-temper and avarice. People like him, enjoy his company. He is of good repute, his bearing invites confidence, his mind is serene and calm. He earns for himself merit and strength—even for a future life. He manages his affairs wisely, never becoming a burden unto others. He does not give blindly, he always considers time and circumstances when help is called for. The more his mind is filled with the spirit of giving, the more unselfish he becomes. Thus by caring for his fellow men he reaps the benefits of his own welfare. But soon he notices that this is not yet the perfect way to Peace and Harmony. And why is this? Because he discovers that, by giving alone, it is not always possible to make people happy. Strange to say, he finds himself at times with full hands—empty-handed and with all his ardent endeavour to help—standing helpless. And what seems to be more disconcerting, he realizes that in a less generous mood, with a single harsh word he destroys the atmosphere of Peace and Harmony, which his gifts have helped to build up.

Thus the Way of Giving stimulates him to strive for deeper understanding of the plight of others, to be watchful over himself, to correct his own shortcomings.

What is the Way of Kind Words ?

Here a person speaks kind words, is mild-mannered, gentle and sincere. What comes from the bottom of his heart touches other hearts. He will never hurt the feelings of anybody but rather try to remove misunderstandings and tensions among people. Kind words gladden him; harshness, cynicism and sarcasm he abhors. He knows that to relieve mental strain, kind words may prove more effective than gifts. An indifferent donor, even if not motivated by kindness, can be of great material help, but sweet words spoken without genuine feeling are nothing but empty sounds. And why is this? Because words spoken with true kindness reach beyond and go deeper than the ordinary range of words; they awaken response and understanding. To place oneself in the other's position one must discard anger, irritation, and arrogance. The more the heart is filled with the spirit of kindness the more unselfish one becomes. Thus with a heart reaching out for the benefit of others he benefits his own welfare.

But soon he notices that this too is not the perfect way which leads to Peace and Harmony. And why is this? Because he finds that it is not always possible to make others happy by merely saying words of kindness and understanding. Or that any gain they bring is only of short duration. Furthermore he discovers that, in a less favourable mood, he destroys the Peace and Harmony of others by his impetuosity and thoughtlessness. Thus, the Way of Kind Words arouses an earnest longing in him to strive for deeper understanding of the plight of others and to correct his own shortcomings.

What is the Way of Helpfulness?

Here one helps others by giving good advice and counsel, well thought out, wise and useful, to the advantage and well-being of one's fellow man. Whatever he speaks about is well considered. He warns others of paths leading to destruction and guides them to paths leading to happiness. He advises others how to avoid strife, idle gossip, vain arguments and noisy quarrels. He helps them to become self-reliant and less dependent on someone else's assistance. The more he knows of things which lead to trouble and sorrow, the more he avoids them and the more convincingly he can talk to others. Thus he benefits his own welfare and the welfare of others. But soon he realizes that this is not yet the perfect way to Peace and Harmony. And why is this ? Because he discovers that not even the best advice is followed and that one can only help in a limited way. Furthermore, he finds himself at times listless and cold, indifferent to the welfare of others. His manner becomes condescending and thus hurts the pride and self-esteem of others. As a result even his good counsel is not heeded, Peace and Harmony are shattered. Thus the Way of Helpfulness stimulates him to strive for deeper understanding of the afflictions of others and correct his own shortcomings.

What is the Way of Self-forgetfulness?

Here a person gives up all his thoughts about: "This is I, there are the others." More and more he gives up pride, conceit and self-esteem. He does not think of himself as better than others but considers himself their equal. In thought, speech and action he serves in a kindly manner; open-minded, without reservation. He is ever ready to listen to the problems of others, is at their disposal, has time for them. He is not self-centred, he does not insist having his own way. In all his actions he manifests inner strength, modesty and humility. A better way, more helpful and agreeable, which leads to Peace and Harmony does not exist.

Wissen und Wandel, 8, No. 7

ABOUT PARIYATTI

Pariyatti is dedicated to providing affordable access to authentic teachings of the Buddha about the Dhamma theory (*pariyatti*) and practice (*paṭipatti*) of Vipassana meditation. A 501(c)(3) nonprofit charitable organization since 2002, Pariyatti is sustained by contributions from individuals who appreciate and want to share the incalculable value of the Dhamma teachings. We invite you to visit www.pariyatti.org to learn about our programs, services, and ways to support publishing and other undertakings.

Pariyatti Publishing Imprints

Vipassana Research Publications (focus on Vipassana as taught by S.N. Goenka in the tradition of Sayagyi U Ba Khin)

BPS Pariyatti Editions (selected titles from the Buddhist Publication Society, copublished by Pariyatti)

MPA Pariyatti Editions (selected titles from the Myanmar Pitaka Association, copublished by Pariyatti)

Pariyatti Digital Editions (audio and video titles, including discourses)

Pariyatti Press (classic titles returned to print and inspirational writing by contemporary authors)

Pariyatti enriches the world by

- disseminating the words of the Buddha,
- providing sustenance for the seeker's journey,
- illuminating the meditator's path.

www.ingramcontent.com/pod-product-compliance
Lightning Source LLC
Chambersburg PA
CBHW021921180426
43200CB00027B/85
* 9 7 8 1 6 8 1 7 2 1 4 0 8 *